LANDMARK CASES IN LAND LAW

Landmark Cases in Land Law is the sixth volume in the Landmark Cases series of collected essays on leading cases (previous volumes in the series having covered Restitution, Contract, Tort, Equity and Family Law). The eleven cases in this volume cover the period 1834 to 2011, although, interestingly, no fewer than six of the cases were decided or reported in the 1980s. The names of the selected cases will be familiar to property lawyers. However, individually, the essays provide a reappraisal of the cases from a wide range of perspectives—focusing on their historical, social or theoretical context, highlighting previously neglected aspects and even questioning their perceived importance. Collectively, the essays explore several common themes that pervade the law of property—the *numerus clausus* principle, the conclusiveness of registration, the desirability of certainty in the law and the central question of the enforceability of interests through changes in ownership of land. This volume provides a collection of essays that will be of interest to academics, students and practitioners.

Landmark Cases in Land Law

Edited by

Nigel Gravells

·HART·
PUBLISHING
OXFORD AND PORTLAND, OREGON
2016

Published in the United Kingdom by Hart Publishing Ltd
16C Worcester Place, Oxford, OX1 2JW
Telephone: +44 (0)1865 517530
Fax: +44 (0)1865 510710
E-mail: mail@hartpub.co.uk
Website: http://www.hartpub.co.uk

Published in North America (US and Canada) by
Hart Publishing
c/o International Specialized Book Services
920 NE 58th Avenue, Suite 300
Portland, OR 97213-3786
USA
Tel: +1 503 287 3093 or toll-free: (1) 800 944 6190
Fax: +1 503 280 8832
E-mail: orders@isbs.com
Website: http://www.isbs.com

British Library Cataloguing in Publication Data
Data Available

ISBN: 978-1-50990-509-6

Typeset by Compuscript Ltd, Shannon
Printed and bound in Great Britain by
TJ International Ltd, Padstow, Cornwall

Preface

Landmark Cases in Land Law continues the series of collected essays on leading cases originally conceived by Charles Mitchell and Paul Mitchell. Previous volumes in the series have covered Restitution, Contract, Tort, Equity and Family Law. I am grateful to them for their permission and encouragement to extend the series to Land Law.

The present volume adopts the same *modus operandi* as the previous volumes. Each author was given a free choice of case and method of approach and treatment. Interestingly, the final selection of eleven cases includes no fewer than six that were decided or reported in the 1980s.

The names of the selected cases will be familiar to property lawyers. However, individually, the essays provide a reappraisal of the cases from a wide range of perspectives—focusing on their historical, social or theoretical context, highlighting previously neglected aspects and even questioning the perceived their importance. Collectively, the essays explore several common themes that pervade the law of property—the *numerus clausus* principle, the conclusiveness of registration, the desirability of certainty in the law and the central question of the enforceability of interests through changes in ownership of land. Many of the essays demonstrate that landmark case status is confirmed and enhanced by the refinement provided in subsequent cases. Indeed, as a reflection of this, three chapters each identify two landmark cases.

Most of the chapters were presented in draft form and discussed at a workshop held at the University of Reading in May 2012 and subsequently revised in the light of that discussion. I am grateful to all the workshop participants for their constructive contributions; to the University of Reading Law School for its hospitality; and to Hart Publishing for its generous contribution to funding the workshop.

Nigel P Gravells
March 2013

Contents

Notes on Contributors

Stuart Bridge is one of Her Majesty's Circuit Judges. He lectured in property law at the University of Cambridge Law Faculty from 1990 until 2012 and served as a Law Commissioner for England and Wales from 2001 until 2008 with particular responsibility for property, trusts and family law. He is a Life Fellow of Queens' College, Cambridge, and a Bencher of the Middle Temple. He is one of the editors of Megarry & Wade, *The Law of Real Property* (8th edn, 2012) and a member of the Editorial Board of *The Conveyancer and Property Lawyer*.

Susan Bright is Professor of Land Law and McGregor Fellow at New College, Oxford. She has a particular research interest in how the law relates to the way in which homes are owned, occupied and used, and in the legal protections available when owners seek repossession of homes. She is the author of *Landlord and Tenant Law in Context* (2007).

Peter Butt is Emeritus Professor of Law at the University of Sydney. He is the author of *Land Law* (6th edn, 2010) and of *The Standard Contract for Sale of Land in New South Wales* (two editions). He has also written books on the rule against perpetuities, on native title, a student casebook on real property, and a co-authored loose-leaf service on the Torrens system. He writes the monthly 'Property and Conveyancing' column in the *Australian Law Journal*. He has also written a book on legal drafting (*Modern Legal Drafting*) and edited a book on the same subject (*Piesse's Elements of Drafting*). He is a co-editor of *The Australian Legal Dictionary* and *The Concise Australian Legal Dictionary*.

Elizabeth Cooke is Professor of Law at the University of Reading and she is currently serving as a Law Commissioner for England and Wales with responsibility for family law and property law projects. Her research interests include land law, land registration and family property. She is the author of *Land Law* (2nd edn, 2012), *The New Law of Land Registration* (2002) and *The Modern Law of Estoppel* (2000). She edited the first four volumes of *Modern Studies in Property Law* (2001, 2003, 2005, 2007); and she is the Consultant Editor of the new 'Real Property' volume in *Halsbury's Laws* and a member of the Editorial Board of *The Conveyancer and Property Lawyer*.

Martin Dixon is Reader in the Law of Real Property and Fellow of Queens' College, Cambridge and Visiting Professor of Law at City University, London. He is the author of *Modern Land Law* (8th edn, 2012) and one of the editors of Megarry & Wade, *The Law of Real Property* (8th edn, 2012). He is the General Editor of *The Conveyancer and Property Lawyer*.

Nigel Gravells is Professor of English Law at the University of Nottingham and Adjunct Professor of Law at the University of Canterbury, New Zealand. He is the author of *Land Law: Text and Materials* (4th edn, 2010). He has published numerous articles on many aspects of property law.

Andrew Hayward is Lecturer in Law at Durham Law School, Durham University. His publications are in the areas of family law, land law and trusts. His research concentrates on family property, in particular, the issues generated within the trusts of the family home framework predominantly used by cohabitants and home-sharers. Recent publications include 'The "Context" of Home: Cohabitation and Ownership Disputes in England and Wales' in M Diamond and T Turnipseed, *Community, Home and Identity* (2012) and 'Family Property and the Process of Familialisation of Property Law' in the *Child and Family Law Quarterly* (2012).

Nicholas Hopkins is Professor of Law at the University of Southampton. His research interests lie in land law and equity and with the intersection of these subjects with other areas of law, including unjust enrichment and housing law and policy. He has a particular interest in the legal regulation of the home. He is the author of *The Informal Acquisition of Rights in Land* (2000) and co-author of *Land Law: Text, Cases and Materials* (2nd edn, 2012), in addition to publishing widely in law journals. He is case notes editor of *The Conveyancer and Property Lawyer*.

Ben McFarlane is Professor of Law at University College, London. He is the author of *The Structure of Property Law* (2008) and is one of the authors of *Land Law: Text, Cases and Materials* (2nd edn, 2012). Part of his recent work has focused on the justifications of the *numerus clausus* principle and its operation in common law systems.

Roger Smith has been Fellow and Tutor in Law at Magdalen College, Oxford, since 1974, having previously taught at Birmingham University and Fitzwilliam College, Cambridge. He is currently Vice-Chair of the Law Faculty Board, Oxford University. He is the author of *Property Law* (7th edn, 2011), *Property Law: Cases and Materials* (5th edn, 2012) and *Introduction to Land Law* (all published by Longman), as well as *Plural Ownership* (2005).

Mark Thompson is Professor of Law and Senior Pro-Vice-Chancellor at the University of Leicester. In addition to numerous articles and commentaries, he is the author of eleven books on land law and conveyancing, including *Modern Land Law* (5th edn, 2012) He has also acted as a consultant to the Law Commission in respect of their reports on the Rule in *Bain v Fothergill* and the Passing of the Risk from Vendor to Purchaser. He was case notes editor of *The Conveyancer and Property Lawyer* between 1994 and 2004 and continues to be a member of the Editorial Board of that journal.

1

Keppell v Bailey *(1834)*; Hill v Tupper *(1863)*

The Numerus Clausus *and the Common Law*

BEN McFARLANE*

OVERVIEW

IN EACH OF *Keppell v Bailey*[1] and *Hill v Tupper*,[2] nothing happened. In the former case, shareholders of the Trevil Railroad, including Keppell, failed in their attempt to obtain an injunction preventing the Baileys, the new owners of the Beaufort Ironworks, from using a different railroad to carry limestone to those works. In the latter case, Hill, who was in the business of hiring out pleasure boats on the Basingstoke Canal, failed to establish a cause of action against Tupper, whose operation of boats on the same canal was said to interfere with Hill's business. In neither case, then, did the court recognise a new form of property right, or create a new form of liability for interference with land. Given this, it may seem strange to regard either case as a landmark. The original purpose of a landmark, however, was to establish a boundary. As a result, cases that clarify or set limits are just as worthy of landmark status as those decisions that blur or remove pre-existing boundaries. Indeed, it will be argued here that the continuing significance of each of *Keppell* and *Hill* lies not in the location of the specific boundary drawn in each case, but rather in the approach adopted to the general question of how the courts should police the most important boundary in land law: that between personal rights, on one side of the line, and estates and interests in land on the other.

* I am grateful to the Leverhulme Trust for the support provided by a Philip Leverhulme Prize, and to Christopher Knowles and Toby Boncey for their helpful research assistance.

[1] *Keppell v Bailey* (1834) 2 My & K 517, 47 ER 106.

[2] *Hill v Tupper* (1863) 2 H & C 121, 159 ER 51.

The specific boundaries drawn in *Keppell* and *Hill* are of course important to our understanding of the law of covenants and of easements. This chapter, however, is concerned with the significance of the courts' approach to a wider question: where A, an owner of land, confers a right on B, will B be able to assert that right against a third party? Crucially, each of the decisions recognised that, whatever sound economic or private reasons A and B may have had for giving B a particular right in relation to A's land, a wider public interest is at stake in deciding if that right is to be capable of binding third parties. This is true both in a case such as *Keppell*, where the third party in question is a successor in title to A, and in a case such as *Hill*, where the third party is a stranger, who has acquired no rights from A. The doctrinal concept giving force to this wider public interest is the *numerus clausus* principle: first, if B's right is to have a particular form of third party effect, it has to be a legal or equitable property right; secondly, B's right can count as such a right only if its content matches that of the limited number of rights currently recognised as legal or equitable property rights. While the operation of the *numerus clausus* principle is perhaps most familiar in cases such as *Keppell*, where B attempts to assert a right against C, a successor in title of A, *Hill* provides a valuable reminder that it is also relevant where B brings a claim against X, a stranger, who has acquired no rights from A. Indeed, cases such as *Hill*, in which B brings a claim to recover compensation for a financial loss caused by X's conduct, demonstrate that the principle has an important effect not only in property law, but also in the law of tort. The distinction between the form of liability at issue in *Keppell* (enforcement against a successor in title to A) and in *Hill* (enforcement against a stranger) also raises two important questions, each of which will be considered here: first, is it possible for B to have a right which is capable of binding A's successor in title but cannot bind a stranger? Secondly, and conversely, can B's right be capable of binding a stranger but not a successor?

In a common law system, general concepts such as the *numerus clausus* principle cannot be established in a definitive code but have to be deduced from decisions given on specific facts.[3] One of the dangers of such a system is that, if the true significance of previous decisions is overlooked, future judgments may inadvertently or unjustifiably depart from general concepts. Indeed, as certain more recent cases seem to have overlooked the lessons

---

[3] In relation to land, ss 1 and 4 of the Law of Property Act 1925 do seem to give legislative force to the second aspect of the *numerus clausus* principle, by fixing the list of possible legal estates or interests in land (s 1) and of possible equitable interests in land (s 4(1)). Nonetheless, these provisions have not prevented the courts (even in cases relating to land as opposed to personal property) from giving new third party effects to particular rights: see n 4 below.

of *Keppell* and *Hill*,[4] it is now particularly important to draw attention to the two cases. Moreover, as legislative reform of the law of covenants is contemplated,[5] it is also timely to consider the basis of the judicial desire to maintain a relatively small list of legal and equitable property rights. In other words, recognising *Keppell* and *Hill* as landmarks will assist both the courts and the legislature in their crucial task of maintaining and policing the boundary between personal rights and property rights: a boundary on which the whole map of property law depends.

THE FACTUAL CONTEXTS

Keppell v Bailey

The story of *Keppell* begins in 1792, with the establishment, under the Monmouthshire Canal Act of that year, of the Company of Proprietors of the Monmouthshire Canal Navigation. The chief purpose of the Act was to give the company the powers necessary to establish, with or without the consent of the relevant landowners, a canal of approximately 12 miles in length, linking Pontnewynydd to the River Usk near Newport. The canal, opened in 1796, is credited as having kick-started the industrial revolution in that part of the Welsh valleys.[6] Further legislation allowed the company to establish ancillary canals, and the company also had a statutory power, under the 'eight-mile clause'[7] to build railways linking the canal to iron-works, quarries and coal mines located within that distance of any part of the canals or railways built under the Act. The clause also gave that power to any 'owners of any lands containing mines, minerals or quarries, or the proprietors, lessees or occupiers of any iron furnaces' within the eight-mile zone, if they 'should find it necessary that any railways or roads should be made over the lands of any other persons for the purpose of conveying the produce of their mines or quarries to the canals or railways of the company', provided that the company had first failed, within three months from the interested parties' application, to build that railway or road itself.

---

[4] See, eg, the discussion of *Manchester Airport plc v Dutton* [2000] QB 133 (CA) and *Shell UK Ltd v Total UK Ltd* [2010] EWCA Civ 180, [2011] QB 86, pp 24–26 and 30–31 below. See also *Iran v Barakat Galleries* [2007] EWCA Civ 1374, [2009] QB 22; *Mayor of London v Hall* [2010] EWCA Civ 817, [2011] 1 WLR 504 and *Vehicle Control Services Ltd v HM Revenue & Customs* [2013] EWCA Civ 186.

[5] See Law Commission Report No 327, *Making Land Work: Easements, Covenants and Profits à Prendre* (2011) Pts 5 and 6.

[6] By the Monmouthshire, Brecon and Abergavenny Canals Trust: see www.mon-brec-canal-trust.org.uk.

[7] Monmouthshire Canal Act 1792, s 128.

These powers to build over others' land without their consent were of course subject to statutory limits. For example, if a railway or road was built under the eight-mile clause, it had to be open to the public; and the company, or anyone building under the eight-mile clause, was limited in the charges it could levy for taking material over the canals, railways or roads: the maximum price permitted for the conveyance of (inter alia) ironstone, iron ore, coal and limestone was 2.5 pence per ton per mile. The company was however allowed to charge at twice that rate for the carriage of such goods on any railway or road built at the request of those who wished to have a railway or road built from their land to the company's canal or railways.

In 1795, those in charge of three local operations (the Sirhowy Furnace, the Ebbw Vale Ironworks and the Beaufort Ironworks) decided to take advantage of the 'eight-mile clause' by constructing the Trevil Railroad. Along with other investors, they formed a joint stock company, and executed an indenture setting out their mutual rights and duties. The indenture recited that the railroad was intended to allow for the more convenient carriage of limestone from the Trevil Quarry to the furnaces of the three local ironworks, and that the proprietors of each agreed to: (i) procure all the limestone they might want for their works from that quarry; (ii) convey it along the new railroad; (iii) to use such part of the railroad as would lie between their mines and furnaces to convey all the ironstone carried to their furnaces; and (iv) to pay 5 pence per ton per mile for the conveyance of all material on the railroad, other than stone for building, which was to cost 1.5 pence per ton per mile. As a result, this four-part promise was made by Edward and Jonathan Kendall as a joint and several covenant 'for themselves, their heirs, executors, administrators, and assigns' with all the other subscribers 'and their executors, administrators, and assigns'. The same covenants were of course also made by the owners of the Sirhowy Furnace and the Ebbw Vale Ironworks. The Trevil Railroad opened in 1796 and, along with the Rassau Railroad opened in the same year, linked the quarry to the Sirhowy and Beaufort works.[8]

The Beaufort Ironworks had been opened in 1780, following the Duke of Beaufort's grant to the Kendalls of a long lease.[9] The Kendalls came to be literally synonymous with the area (known in Welsh as Cendl) situated roughly half way between Abergavenny and Merthyr Tydfil, just south of the edge of what is now the Brecon Beacons National Park. The Beaufort Ironworks, however, was not a local business. The British iron industry in the eighteenth and nineteenth centuries—like televisual depictions of the

---

[8] The link to the more distant Ebbw Vale Ironworks was not completed until 1813.

[9] *Keppell v Bailey* is not the only significant land law case involving the Duke of Beaufort's land: see *Duke of Beaufort v Patrick* (1853) 17 Beav 60, 51 ER 954, relied on in *Crabb v Arun DC* [1976] Ch 179 (CA) as authority for the court's approach to satisfying an equity arising through proprietary estoppel.

Texas oil industry in the late twentieth century—was dominated by (often interconnected) families.[10] In 1710, an earlier Edward Kendall had become joint manager of the Staffordshire ironworks, and he consolidated his place in the industry by marrying Anna Cotton, whose father was a force in Yorkshire iron. In the first half of the eighteenth century, the family operated in Shropshire and Cheshire as well as Staffordshire and Yorkshire. The opening of the Beaufort Ironworks, in which the younger Edward was the driving force, was a new venture for the family, involving not only a change of location, but a switch from charcoal smelting to smelting with coke. Edward died suddenly in 1807 and his own son, while sharing his father's name, did not share his passion for iron. When, in 1833, the Beaufort works were sold to Joseph and Crawshay Bailey, owners of the nearby Nantyglo ironworks, the Kendalls' iron dynasty ended and the problem that led to *Keppell v Bailey* began.

It is, in fact, still possible to walk over the cause of the litigation. Blaenau Gwent County Borough Council provides a guide to the 'Kendall Trail' (fifth in its series of 'In the Footsteps of the Iron-Makers' walks) a gentle three-and-a-half mile walk which starts at Furnace Street in Beaufort, takes in the site of Beaufort House, the Kendalls' former mansion, and includes an uphill stretch of footpath known locally as 'The Incline'. This was once part of the Beaufort to Nantyglo Tramroad, built in 1833 by the Baileys to link the Beaufort works with their existing operation. When the Baileys began to build, the shareholders of the Trevil Railroad, including Keppell, sought an injunction to prevent the Baileys and their agents from acting contrary to the terms of the 1795 indenture by using the new tramroad, or any road other than the Trevil Railroad. An ex parte injunction was swiftly obtained in August 1833, but in January 1834 Lord Brougham LC, heard, and granted, the Baileys' motion to dissolve that injunction.

Hill v Tupper

The factual context of *Hill* shares some features with that of *Keppell*. The story also begins with canal legislation: in this case, the Basingstoke Canal Act of 1778. The canal was built in 1794 and ran for 37 miles, its purpose being to assist in the transport of agricultural goods from Hampshire to London. The scene of the action is also visible on a walk, in this case a two-mile trail centred on the village of Ash Vale, located roughly half way between Farnborough and Aldershot. The trail passes The Swan, now inevitably owned by a pub chain, but retaining the name of the original public house, opened beside the canal around 1857. In the second half of

---

[10] See, eg, A Raistrick, *Dynasty of Iron Founders: The Darbys and Coalbrookdale*, 2nd edn (Sessions Book Trust/Ironbridge Gorge Museum Trust, 1989).

the nineteenth century, the pub was more commonly known as Tupper's Tavern and was thus literally synonymous with John Tupper, who moved from London to found the pub and died there, still its landlord, in 1902, having claimed to be the longest continuous holder of a licence in England. He had a keen interest in boxing, and combat more generally, and the pub, popular with cadets from the local Royal Military College, was well known for its cock fights and rat pit.

It was, however, Tupper's interest in less bloody activities that attracted the attention, and writ, of Hill. For, taking advantage of the pub's location, Tupper kept some pleasure boats, admitting that he used them for himself and his family (he left 10 sons and daughters on his death) and from time to time allowed visitors to his inn to use the boats for fishing and bathing. Hill claimed that Tupper had in fact also been hiring out his boats in return for direct payment, and this activity interfered with the sole and exclusive right, granted to Hill by the Company of Proprietors of the Basingstoke Canal Navigation, to hire out pleasure boats on the canal. Hill had been granted this right by the company in 1860, as part of a seven-year lease, at an annual rent of £25, of a small piece of land (including a boathouse) adjoining Aldershot Wharf. The company, in fact, was to go into liquidation before the end of that seven-year period, as businesses made less use of the canal, preferring to have their goods carried by rail. It may be that the grant of the lease to Hill was part of an attempt to encourage non-trade use of the canal, and certainly pleasure boating grew in popularity in the second half of the nineteenth century.[11] Indeed, Hill claimed that Tupper's actions had caused him to lose 'great gains and profits'. It seems that Hill sought damages only, and no injunction; at the trial of the action the jury did find in his favour, but awarded damages of only one farthing. Tupper challenged the result by obtaining a rule nisi to enter a nonsuit or verdict for the defendant; and the Exchequer Chamber, without even needing to call on Tupper's counsel, decreed that the rule should be made absolute, on the basis that Hill had no cause of action against Tupper.

THE DECISIONS

Keppell v Bailey

As stated in Mylne and Keen's report, *Keppell* was 'very elaborately argued on both sides'.[12] Each side, in fact, was represented by a future Lord Chancellor, with Charles Pepys (later Lord Cottenham) the most senior

---

[11] See G Crocker, *The History of the Basingstoke Canal*, 2nd edn (The Surrey & Hampshire Canal Society Ltd, 1977) ch 5.
[12] (1834) 2 My & K 517, 524.

of three barristers appearing for the Baileys, and Sir Edward Sugden (the future Lord St Leonards) fulfilling the same role for the shareholders. The issues at stake certainly merited such thorough treatment. The Third Report of the Commissioners on the Law of Real Property, published less than two years earlier,[13] had considered that the law relating to the effect of covenants on third parties was 'defective, or imperfectly settled'[14] and that 'there is considerable difficulty in determining the extent to which the assigns of the covenantor can be charged with the obligation'.[15] There were two fundamental questions, and uncertainty as to each. First, in what circumstances could the burden of a covenant 'run at law': that is to say, when would the covenant made by a predecessor in title impose a legal duty on a successor in title to the covenantor? Secondly, if a covenant did not run at law when, if at all, could equity intervene to enforce the covenant against the successor?

It should immediately be noted that, strictly speaking, there was no need for the court in *Keppell* to have embarked on an examination of the law relating to covenants. As Lord Brougham pointed out, judgment could have been given for the Baileys simply on the ground that the 1795 agreement was inconsistent with the scheme of the 1792 Act. That Act placed certain limits on the railroad company's right to build: in particular, the charges to be levied by anyone other than the Monmouthshire Canal Company for the carriage of (inter alia) ironstone, iron ore, coal and limestone on a railroad built under the eight-mile clause could not exceed 2.5 pence per ton per mile. The Act gave the canal company—if it chose to build the road at the shareholders' request—the power to charge twice that rate; but that power did not extend to any other party exercising the statutory right to build. As a result, in the words of Lord Brougham, the 1795 agreement violated the scheme of the 1792 Act in two ways:

> It deprives the company of its prior right to make the road subject to the higher rate of charge, and it deprives the neighbouring owners of the security intended to be given to them that their property should not be invaded unless a traffic of a certain amount was to be expected.[16]

Despite recognising that this incompatibility with the statutory scheme provided 'a sufficient ground for dissolving the injunction',[17] Lord Brougham went on to discuss the important general question of the circumstances in which a covenant entered into by A and B might bind C. Sugden had

---

[13] *Third Report of the Commissioners on the Law of Real Property (1832), Parliamentary Papers 1832* (484) XXIII (Third Report).

[14] Ibid, 45. A similar complaint has recently been made by the Law Commission of England and Wales: see Law Com No 327, *Making Land Work*, above (n 5) paras 5.4–5.20.

[15] Third Report, above (n 13) 46.

[16] *Keppell v Bailey* (1834) 2 My & K 517, 532. See further pp 26–27 below.

[17] Ibid, 533.

submitted that, first, the covenant ran with the land at law, so as to bind the current proprietors; and, secondly and separately:

> [T]he notice which, prior to their purchase, the defendants had received of the existence and nature of the covenant, imposed an obligation which bound them in conscience, and which a Court of Equity would not suffer them to violate.[18]

On this view, the basis for equitable intervention is provided by the successor in title's notice, *prior* to their acquisition of the land, of the covenant.

Lord Brougham's rejection of Sugden's first argument remains the most eloquent judicial defence of the *numerus clausus* principle in the common law world and includes the justly famous statement that

> great detriment would arise and much confusion of rights if parties were allowed to invent new modes of holding and enjoying real property, and to impress upon their lands and tenements a peculiar character, which should follow them into all hands, however remote.[19]

It is perhaps worth noting that while Sugden's legal learning, not least in this area, greatly exceeded that of Lord Brougham, the latter's judgment testifies to its author's eloquence, and a writing style that had been honed not in treatises on the law of vendor and purchaser[20] but rather in such varied contributions as an excoriating review of Byron,[21] articles on the scientific properties of light[22] and a notorious denunciation of aristocratic government[23] (and all these completed before Henry Brougham had reached the age of 30).[24] Lord Brougham distinguished the covenant entered into by the Kendalls from recognised burdens on land, such as 'rights of way or of common', which are 'of a public as well as of a simple nature' and easily discoverable by those potentially bound. He distinguished the rules relating to covenants in a lease, as applying only in cases of privity of estate, while also noting that, even where such privity exists, there is a limit to the

---

[18] Ibid, 526.

[19] Ibid, 536.

[20] Sugden's *A Practical Treatise of the Law of Vendors and Purchasers of Estates* was in its ninth edition by 1834.

[21] *Edinburgh Review* (1808). It prompted Byron's 'English Bards and Scottish Reviewers'. Brougham, who read humanity and philosophy, as well as law, at Edinburgh University was one of the founders of the *Edinburgh Review*.

[22] Brougham, when aged only 18, published these two articles in the Transactions of the Royal Society. He was made a Fellow of the Royal Society on 3 March 1803 at the age of 24.

[23] The 'Don Cevallos' article, published in October 1808 in the *Edinburgh Review*, caused quite a stir, and led Sir Walter Scott immediately to cancel his subscription.

[24] Brougham went on to give his name to both a style of trouser (black and white check) and a small horse carriage and was also instrumental in the growth of Cannes as a tourist destination, building a chateau there and remaining in the town to this day, in the form of a statute in a square formerly also named for him, but renamed Square Frédéric Mistral in 1963. He was also president of University College, London, from its birth in 1826 to his death in 1868.

content of those covenants that are allowed to run with the land, and that a covenant to use a particular railroad would not fall within that limit.

As to the second submission, Lord Brougham's analysis of the position in equity was clearly informed by the need not to undermine the limits thus imposed on 'real burdens'. In his view, a covenant which does not impose such a burden

> cannot bind such assignee by affecting his conscience. If it did, then the illegality would be of no consequence; and however wild the attempt might be to create new kinds of holding and new species of estate, and however repugnant such devices might be to the rules of law, they would prove perfectly successful in the result, because equity would enable their authors to prevail.[25]

In particular, his Lordship noted, if notice alone sufficed, this would subvert the limits on the content of leasehold covenants capable of running at law, as every assignee of a lease has notice of the lessor's covenants. It should be emphasised that Lord Brougham did not suggest that there could *never* be an independent equitable basis on which an obligation could bind a third party: he recognised, for example, that equity could intervene where a party receives an estate in land with knowledge of a prior contract for the sale of that estate. That case could, however, be distinguished from *Keppell*, as

> [s]uch a purchaser has done an unconscientious act, or at least made himself accessory to the unconscientious act of his vendor in selling another man's property ... but that of which he had notice was the legal and valid act of the vendor; whereas that of which the assignees here had notice was their assignor's covenant affecting to bind the land, on which, by law it could not operate.[26]

Hill v Tupper

As in *Keppell v Bailey*, there was, in the words of Chief Baron Pollock, 'very full argument', but this took the form of a debate between Hill's counsel and the three members of the court of the Exchequer Chamber, as Tupper's counsel was not called on. The essence of the argument for Hill was that, as his exclusive right to put pleasure boats on the canal had been infringed, 'an action lies for the infringement'. An analogy was drawn between Hill's right and a profit à prendre. Martin B interjected that, in fact, Hill's right was 'of a perfectly novel character' and cited Lord Brougham's judgment in *Keppell*.[27] The implied point was spelled out later in the argument by

[25] *Keppell v Bailey* (1834) 2 My & K 517, 547.
[26] Ibid.
[27] *Hill v Tupper* (1863) 2 H & C 121, 125.

Pollock CB, who stated that 'The whole question depends on whether a new species of property can be created, or whether the alleged right merely exists in covenant'.[28] In other words, while Hill and the canal company were free, as between themselves, to create personal rights and obligations, this freedom did not extend to the creation of rights capable of binding strangers to the transaction. In response, Hill's counsel sought to distinguish *Keppell* by pointing out that Hill, in his current action, was not seeking to burden the canal with an obligation that would bind future owners; he was, instead, simply trying to maintain an action against a wrongdoer. This line of argument raises one of the questions highlighted above:[29] is it possible for B to have a right which cannot bind a successor in title to A, but which can bind a stranger?

This possible distinction was not, however, considered in the short judgments of Pollock CB, Martin B or Bramwell B. The first of these, with which the latter two judges agreed, viewed *Ackroyd v Smith*[30] as determinative, as it 'expressly decided that it is not competent to create rights unconnected with the use and enjoyment of land, and annex them to it so as to constitute a property in the grantee'.[31] This reliance on *Ackroyd*, although shared by Martin B, is difficult to justify. That case focused on the different question of the passing of the *benefit* of a claimed right over A's land from B1 to B2. It was held that B1's right to use a road on A's land, if the use of the road was not limited to uses connected with the enjoyment of B1's land, did not pass automatically on an assignment of B1's land to B2. In *Ackroyd*, Cresswell J in turn relied on *Keppell*, in particular on Lord Brougham's examination of the circumstances in which a landlord can enforce a covenant against a successor in title to the original tenant: this was the source of the requirement in *Ackroyd* that, if it is to pass automatically on an assignment of the land to B2, the content of B1's right must inhere in, or be connected with the use of, that land.[32] Cresswell J thus also failed to distinguish the question of the passing of the benefit of a right from the different question of the enforcement of a burden of a right. So, just as the analysis in *Hill* rested on a misreading of *Ackroyd*, so did the analysis in that case rest on a misreading of *Keppell*. Ironically enough, these two errors effectively cancelled each other out: Pollock CB's reference to 'property in the grantee' seems to refer to the question of whether the burden of B's right can pass to a party other than A and, while the facts of *Ackroyd* did not raise that question, the judgment in that case did rely on *Keppell*, in which the question *was* squarely

---

[28] Ibid, 126.
[29] See p 2.
[30] *Ackroyd v Smith* (1850) 10 CB 164, 138 ER 68.
[31] *Hill v Tupper* (1863) 2 H & C 121, 127.
[32] *Ackroyd v Smith* (1850) 10 CB 164, 187.

raised. Certainly, the influence of Lord Brougham's judgment is very clear in Pollock CB's statement:

> A new species of incorporeal hereditament cannot be created at the will and pleasure of the owner of property; but he must be content to accept the estate and the right to dispose of it subject to the law as settled by decisions or controlled by act of parliament.[33]

The decision in *Keppell* is also reflected in Martin B's judgment:

> None of the cases cited are at all analogous to this, and some authority must be produced before we can hold that such a right can be created. To admit the right would lead to the creation of an infinite variety of interests in land, and an indefinite increase of possible estates.[34]

It is significant that none of the judgments specifically addressed the attempt of counsel to distinguish the *Keppell* question of whether B's right is capable of binding C (a successor in title of A) from the *Hill* question of whether B's right is capable of binding X (a stranger). This may be interpreted in (at least) two ways. First, it could be said that the distinction was simply overlooked. Certainly, as shown by the court's treatment of *Ackroyd v Smith* (and also by that decision's own treatment of *Keppell v Bailey*) there is a risk of a number of distinct questions being lost in a general discussion of whether a right is, to use Pollock CB's term, 'property'. For example, that term can be used to refer to (at least)[35] the four following questions: (i) the *Keppell* question of whether a right given by A to B can also bind C, A's successor in title; (ii) the question discussed in *Keppell* of whether a right given by A (a landlord/tenant) to B (the corresponding tenant/landlord) as part of a lease can also bind A2 (A's privy in estate) or B2 (B's privy in estate); (iii) the *Ackroyd* question of whether a right held by B1 passes automatically to B2 on an assignment of B1's estate in land to B2; and (iv) the *Hill* question of whether a right given by A to B can also bind X, a stranger.

Indeed, the confusion that can be caused by using the term 'property' as a shibboleth to answer a broad range of not necessarily connected questions is still evident today. For example, in *OBG Ltd v Allan*,[36] one of the questions for the House of Lords was whether the tort of conversion can be committed by X's action in interfering with or taking over B's contractual

---

[33] *Hill v Tupper* (1863) 2 H & C 121, 127–28.
[34] Ibid, 128.
[35] One further question is considered below (n 38). Still further questions can concern, eg, the application of insolvency legislation (see, eg, *Bristol Airport v Powdrill* [1990] Ch 744 (CA)) or the ambit of constitutional protection (see, eg, *ICM Agriculture Pty Ltd v The Commonwealth of Australia* [2009] HCA 51, considering the meaning of 'property' in s 51(xxxi) of the Commonwealth's Constitution).
[36] *OBG Ltd v Allan* [2008] 1 AC 1 (HL).

right to payment from A. The majority of their Lordships confirmed that the answer was 'no', but Lord Nicholls and Baroness Hale dissented. Those dissents were based in part on the fact that B's purely contractual right to payment from X can be termed 'property': if so, why should it not attract the protection of the tort of conversion, which remedies particular interferences with property rights?[37] Yet such contractual rights are viewed as 'property' because they are assignable by B: if B chooses, he or she can pass the benefit of the right to payment to B2.[38] There is no necessary reason why this quality of assignability should also entail that B's right can be asserted against a stranger. Confusion is therefore caused by the continued use of the term 'property' to capture each of these two distinct qualities that a right may possess.

There is also a second, more positive interpretation of the approach of the court in *Hill*. The judgments could be said to depend not on a blurring of different questions, but on an implied claim that there is a link between the answers to a particular pair of those questions. That claim would be that if a right is not capable of binding the successor in title of A (ie, if it fails the *Keppell* test) then, a fortiori, it is not capable of binding strangers. If this claim is justified, then the attempted distinction made by Hill's counsel is invalid, and the *Keppell* approach can be used to defeat Hill's claim. On this interpretation, the decision in *Hill* is important because it not only adopts the reasoning in *Keppell*, it also expands it. After all, a particular motivation for Lord Brougham was the need to prevent land being impressed with a 'particular character, which should follow them into all hands, however remote'.[39] On this interpretation of *Hill*, the limitation placed on A and B extends further, and also regulates their power to impose obligations on strangers who do not acquire any land from A. It will be argued here that this second interpretation provides the best way to read *Hill*. Further, while it would not be logically impossible for a different stance to have been adopted, it is true that in English law if a right is not capable of binding successor in title of A, then it is not capable of binding strangers.[40] As will be seen in the next section, however, this position did not go unchallenged.

---

[37] See, eg, *OBG Ltd v Allan* [2008] 1 AC 1, [311] (Baroness Hale): '[o]nce the law recognises something as property, the law should extend a proprietary remedy to protect it'.

[38] Note that this is a further, fifth, question that can be at stake in a general discussion of whether a right is 'property': it is separate from the *Ackroyd* question set out above, as it concerns B's general power to assign the right expressly, not the distinct question of whether the right is assigned automatically on an assignment of B's estate in land.

[39] *Keppell v Bailey* (1834) 2 My & K 517, 536.

[40] See further pp 29–31 below.

THE INITIAL IMPACT OF THE DECISIONS

Keppell v Bailey[41]

The eloquence of its expression notwithstanding, the specific reasoning of *Keppell* was soon challenged. Certainly, the lapidary nature of Lord Brougham's judgment did not daunt the losing counsel in the case. In his *Vendors and Purchasers*,[42] Sugden provided by far the most sophisticated contemporary account of the controversy surrounding the effect of covenants on successors in title, and did not hesitate to set out his objections to Lord Brougham's analysis. It would perhaps be dangerous to follow a commentator in the *Harvard Law Review* of 1891, and to use Sugden's work as evidence that *Keppell v Bailey* was 'unfavourably received by the profession'[43]—it rather shows that, perhaps unsurprisingly, the decision was not welcomed by losing counsel in the case.[44] Nonetheless, there was some force in Sugden's rejoinder.

The first point made by Sugden seems incontrovertible: Lord Brougham went too far in describing as an 'illegality' a covenant that, at law, does not bind C, A's successor in title.[45] After all, the covenant is not null and void—it does operate to impose a duty on A, and that duty is one which, in a suitable case, equity may enforce by an injunction. This leads to Sugden's second, less convincing assertion. It is that the protection provided by equity to B's initial right against A may also take the form of an injunction against C: as the purpose of such an injunction would be simply to protect B's (perfectly valid) right against A, equity would not thereby undermine the common law's refusal to allow B's right to run with A's land. In making this second point, Sugden placed particular reliance on an analogy with the case where B's right arises under a contract for the sale of an estate in land. As we have seen,[46] Lord Brougham rejected the soundness of that comparison when Sugden the barrister relied on it in *Keppell*,[47] but Sugden the author

[41] The discussion in this section is based in part on B McFarlane, '*Tulk v Moxhay* (1848)' in C Mitchell and P Mitchell (eds), *Landmark Cases in Equity* (Oxford, Hart Publishing, 2012) 203, 212–14.

[42] E Sugden, *A Practical Treatise on the Law of Vendors & Purchasers of Estates*, 11th edn (London, Butterworths, 1839) 496–507.

[43] C Giddings, 'Restrictions upon the Use of Land' (1891) 5 *Harvard Law Review* 274, 274.

[44] Sugden and Lord Brougham crossed swords on other occasions, with the latter's wit apparently giving him the upper hand in the House of Commons—see WS Holdsworth, *A History of English Law* vol 15 (London, Methuen, 1972 edn) 646.

[45] It may be that Lord Brougham's use of the term 'illegality' was influenced by the statutory context discussed at p 7 above, but it nonetheless seems that he intended the term to refer more broadly so as to include any covenant that does not run with A's land at law.

[46] See the text to n 26 above.

[47] *Keppell v Bailey* (1834) 2 My & K 517, 547: 'A case like this bears no analogy to the ordinary case of a purchase with notice of a prior agreement by the vendor to sell the premises to another'.

thought that '[i]t is remarkable that the strict analogy should not have presented itself to the mind of the learned judge'.[48]

The problem with Sugden's second point was identified by another future Lord Chancellor, Roundell Palmer (later Lord Selborne),[49] in his submissions in *Tulk v Moxhay*.[50] Acting—ultimately unsuccessfully of course—for Moxhay, Palmer pointed out that in the case of the vendor–purchaser constructive trust, a promised act by A (the vendor) remains unperformed, as no conveyance has been made. In recognising an equitable property right, a court of equity can therefore latch on to (or anticipate) this duty to transfer a common law property right. In contrast, in a case such as *Keppell* or *Tulk*, B's argument is that A's promise to B immediately gives rise to a right capable of binding C, even though there is no further conveyance to anticipate. Building on this point, it can further be argued that, in the vendor–purchaser constructive trust, the vendor does not come under a contractual duty to transfer land to the purchaser; he comes under a duty to transfer his *right to the land*. The subject-matter of the trust is therefore the vendor's right to the land, rather than the land itself. A similar analysis applies in all trusts: the essence of the trust is that a trustee is under a duty in relation to a specific right.[51] It may further be argued that this need for the initial duty to relate to a specific right may be used as a general, conceptual test for the existence of an equitable property right:[52] on that view, there is a gulf between a case where A is under a duty to transfer a right in A's land and one where A simply promises to perform (or not to perform) a particular act in relation to A's land.

This flaw in Sugden's reasoning notwithstanding, support for his attack on *Keppell* was soon provided by *Whatman v Gibson*[53] and *Mann v Stephens*:[54] in each case, an injunction was granted against a holder of a fee simple in order to prevent action contrary to a covenant entered into by his predecessor in title. The report of Shadwell V-C's judgment in *Whatman* contains no reference to authority; instead, there is a recognition of the practical benefits to all local proprietors in allowing the enforcement against

---

[48] Sugden, above (n 42) 505.

[49] Like Lord Brougham, Palmer was also elected as a Fellow of the Royal Society (on 7 June 1860), although at the riper age of 47.

[50] *Tulk v Moxhay* (1848) 2 Ph 774, 41 ER 1143.

[51] W Swadling, 'Property' in AS Burrows (ed), *English Private Law*, 2nd edn (Oxford, OUP, 2007) 4–140; B McFarlane and R Stevens, 'The Nature of Equitable Property' (2010) 4 *Journal of Equity* 1.

[52] For further detail, and refinements of this test, see McFarlane and Stevens, above (n 51); and B McFarlane, *The Structure of Property Law* (Oxford, Hart Publishing, 2008) Pt D2. For the difficulties of applying it to the particular context of restrictive covenants, see B McFarlane, 'The *Numerus Clausus* Principle and Covenants Relating to Land' in S Bright (ed), *Modern Studies in Property Law, Volume 6* (Oxford, Hart Publishing, 2011) 311, 321–25.

[53] *Whatman v Gibson* (1838) 9 Sim 196, 59 ER 333.

[54] *Mann v Stephens* (1846) 15 Sim 377, 60 ER 665.

successors in title of a covenant which, by preventing houses being converted into shops or taverns, preserved the 'general uniformity and respectability' of a row of houses in Ramsgate.[55] Interestingly Shadwell V-C also relied on the defendant's notice of the original covenant,[56] thereby rejecting (without consideration) Lord Brougham's view in *Keppell* that notice alone cannot justify the enforcement of a covenant against a successor in title. In *Mann*, counsel for the defendants did refer to *Keppell*, but Shadwell V-C relied on his judgment in *Whatman* to grant an injunction against the erection of a beer-shop and a brewery. The defendant later appealed against a committal order granted on his breach of the injunction, and Lord Cottenham LC allowed the appeal, on the basis that Shadwell V-C's initial injunction had been too broadly phrased. Having tightened up its wording, however, Lord Cottenham confirmed that the injunction had been properly granted.

These cases were simply the first of a flow of decisions seemingly contrary to the spirit, and often the express reasoning, of *Keppell*. In *Tulk v Moxhay*, as noted above, counsel for Moxhay relied heavily on *Keppell* but, in the judgment as it appears in the available reports at least, Lord Cottenham LC brushed those concerns away:

> With respect to the observations of Lord Brougham in Keppell v Bailey, he never could have meant to lay down that this Court would not enforce an equity attached to land by the owner, unless under such circumstances as would maintain an action at law. If that be the result of his observations, I can only say that I cannot coincide with it.[57]

In the Hall and Twell report—which gives a longer, but less coherent version of the decision—Lord Cottenham expands on this point by asking rhetorically: 'If a man has, in law, a fee-simple, cannot he in equity contract with it in a way which may be beneficial, or not injurious to his neighbour?'[58] *Tulk* also forms one of a number of decisions that directly rejected Lord Brougham's view that a successor's notice of a pre-existing covenant could not, by itself, make that covenant binding on the successor.[59] Indeed, by 1877, Fry J felt able to conclude that, as *Keppell* had been decided at a time when 'the equitable doctrine of notice had not received the development which it has since received',[60] Lord Brougham's view was no longer binding.

---

[55] *Whatman v Gibson* (1838) 9 Sim 196, 207, 59 ER 333, 338.

[56] Ibid: 'I see no reason why such an agreement should not be binding in equity on the parties so coming in with notice'.

[57] *Tulk v Moxhay* (1848) 2 Ph 774, 779.

[58] *Tulk v Moxhay* (1848) 1 H & Tw 105, 116.

[59] See also *de Mattos v Gibson* (1849) 4 De G & J 276, 70 ER 669 and *Catt v Tourle* (1869) LR 4 Ch App 654 (CA).

[60] *Luker v Dennis* (1877) 7 Ch D 227, 235.

Hill v Tupper

The decision in *Hill*, like that in *Keppell*, soon faced challenges. For example, despite having been both the trial judge and a member of the Exchequer Chamber in *Hill*, Bramwell B less than a year later gave a significant dissenting judgment in *Stockport Waterworks Co v Potter*.[61] The claimant company (B) had, in 1850, taken over the supply of water to Stockport. In 1853, A, a riparian owner, granted B all A's rights in its waterworks, including the right to take water from the adjacent River Mersey. A had, however, retained its ownership of the riparian land. The defendant calico printers (X), who used arsenic and other noxious substances in their operations, had discharged waste into upstream water and so had polluted the water used by B. B's claim against X failed. In giving the majority judgment, Pollock CB found that it is not possible for A, a riparian owner, to keep his riparian land and deal separately with the concomitant property rights with respect to the water, noting that:

> The case of *Hill v Tupper*, recently decided in this Court, is an authority for the proposition that a person cannot create by grant new rights of property so as to give the grantee a right of suing in his own name for an interruption of the right by a third party.[62]

In his dissent, Bramwell B argued that as X had clearly committed a wrong against A, and other riparian owners, by polluting the river, he could not object to paying compensation to B, who had acquired rights from A and had suffered loss as a result of X's wrongful action. His Lordship asserted that:

> There can be no doubt that the grant as between the riparian grantor and the grantee is good. And there is this to be said in favour of supporting the present claim, that we must suppose that the grantor and grantee have found the arrangement to be to their mutual advantage, that the stream can be more beneficially used this way than otherwise. Consequently that such an arrangement is for the public good. Why, then, should it not be effectual against a person, who as against the riparian proprietor is a wrongdoer?[63]

Significantly, Bramwell B did not regard this view as being contrary to either *Keppell* or *Hill*. His Lordship's method for distinguishing *Keppell*, however, makes his analysis very hard to reconcile with *Hill*. For that method consisted of reliance on the very same distinction that counsel for Hill had unsuccessfully sought to draw: between, on the one hand, cases where B attempts to impose a burden on A's successor in title and, on the other, cases such as *Hill* or *Stockport Waterworks*, where B instead makes a

---

[61] *Stockport Waterworks Co v Potter* (1864) 3 H & C 300, 159 ER 545.
[62] Ibid, 327.
[63] Ibid, 319.

claim against a stranger. To support the distinction, Bramwell B noted that permitting a claim by B did not impose any additional duties on X who is, in any case, a wrongdoer against A. Of course, if that view were correct, the result should have been different in *Hill*. Bramwell B attempted to deal with this difficulty by describing *Hill* as a case in which B's right was 'merely a right of action', in contrast with the quasi-possessory nature of the Stockport Waterworks' right to take water from the Mersey.[64] It is hard to see, however, that this is a convincing difference between a right to put boats on a canal and a right to take water from a river.

In *Nuttall v Bracewell*,[65] Bramwell B made another attempt to distinguish and limit *Hill*. The new analysis was that:

> It was competent for the grantors in [Hill] to grant to [B] a right of rowing boats on the canal; and had any one interfered with that right, [B] might have maintained an action against him. But [B] there did not sue for any such cause of action. He sued, not because his rowing was interfered with, but because the defendant used a boat on the water.[66]

On this view Hill's claim failed because Tupper had not been interfering with the positive exercise of Hill's right. In contrast, in *Nuttall*, the defendant, by taking upstream water, had prevented B positively exercising his right to take that same water from further down the stream.[67] This distinction is an important one. If it accommodates a dominant tenement of B, and is sufficiently well-defined,[68] a right of B to put pleasure boats on A's canal, it is submitted, should be capable of counting as an easement. On this view if, for example, Tupper had poisoned the water in the canal and thus prevented Hill exercising his liberty to put boats on the canal, then it would have been possible for Hill (had he been able to show a dominant tenement)[69] to bring a nuisance action against Tupper, based on Tupper's having interfered with the canal in such a way as to interfere with Hill's permitted use of it. For example, in *Fitzgerald v Firbank*,[70] the defendant, by discharging water

---

[64] Ibid, 322.

[65] *Nuttall v Bracewell* (1866–67) LR 2 Ex 1.

[66] Ibid, 11–12.

[67] Bramwell B's comments in *Nuttall*, ibid, were not made in dissent as B's right, to the flow of water through a goit, was, as noted by Martin B at 10, a 'well-known easement'. Bramwell B, at 11–12, however, based his judgment on the far wider ground that it was not for B to show that his right counted as an easement, but it was rather for the defendant to show why B's right should not count as a property right.

[68] For the need for certainty in the content of an easement, see eg *Burrows v Lang* [1901] 2 Ch 502.

[69] In *Nuttall*, (n 65) 7, Martin B noted in argument that *Hill* was distinguishable as a case in which 'it was attempted to create a right in gross.' Hill had however been given, along with the exclusive right to put boats on the canal, a demise of land at Aldershot on the bank of the canal. The question would therefore be whether a right to put pleasure boats on the canal could properly be seen as accommodating such land.

[70] *Fitzgerald v Firbank* [1897] 2 Ch 96 (CA).

loaded with sediment into a stream, interfered with an 'exclusive right of fishing' that A, the riparian owner, had granted to B. The Court of Appeal upheld B's claim on the grounds that B's right, by virtue of its content, qualified as a profit à prendre.[71] The purported exclusivity of B's right was irrelevant to B's claim, as the defendant had interfered with the land in such a way as to interfere with B's personal use of the land. Hill's claim, however, necessarily depended on the exclusivity of his right, as it asserted that Tupper was under a simple duty not to put boats on the canal. Such action of Tupper, in itself, might reduce the value of Hill's right, but it would not, as matter of fact, interfere in its exercise. The right to exclude which Hill claimed can only properly arise, it is submitted, as part of a legal estate, and it was clear that Hill had no right to exclusive possession of the canal.

THE LASTING SIGNIFICANCE OF THE DECISIONS

Each of *Keppell* and *Hill* withstood the immediate challenges made to it and came to be a significant landmark in land law. The durability of the decisions depends on the robustness of their reasoning. The following part will consider four key aspects of that reasoning.

Notice and Information Costs

As was noted above, decisions following *Keppell* soon departed from the position that C is not bound by mere knowledge or notice of a pre-existing covenant between A and B.[72] Lord Brougham's stance, however, won out in the end and was vindicated in important later decisions such as *London & South Western Rwy Co v Gomm*,[73] *Barker v Stickney*,[74] *Port Line Ltd v Ben Line Steamers Ltd*[75] and *Swiss Bank Corp v Lloyds Bank Ltd*.[76] The eventual success of Lord Brougham's position is justified by the very reason

---

[71] Compare the first instance judgment of Kekewich J, ibid, in which B's right was said to have been worthy of protection against the defendant even if it were a mere licence. That view rests on a fundamental misunderstanding of the nature of a licence.

[72] See, eg, *de Mattos v Gibson* (1849) 4 De G & J 276, 45 ER 108; *Tulk v Moxhay* (1848) 2 Ph 774, 41 ER 1143; *Catt v Tourle* (1869) LR 4 Ch App 654 (CA); *Luker v Dennis* (1877) 7 Ch D 227.

[73] *London & South Western Rwy Co v Gomm* (1881) 20 Ch D 562 (CA). It seems the defendant may well have been related to the defendant in *Whatman v Gibson* (1838) 9 Sim 196, 59 ER 333.

[74] *Barker v Stickney* [1919] 1 KB 121 (CA).

[75] *Port Line Ltd v Ben Line Steamers Ltd* [1958] 2 QB 146 (QB).

[76] *Swiss Bank Corp v Lloyds Bank Ltd* [1979] 1 Ch 548 (note that Browne-Wilkinson J's decision in this case was reversed on other grounds by the Court of Appeal ([1980] 3 WLR 457 (CA)) and a further appeal to the House of Lords was dismissed: [1982] AC 584 (HL).

provided in *Keppell* itself: if there is to be a restriction on the content of proprietary rights, the usefulness of that limit in protecting successors in title would be imperilled by allowing C to be bound by mere knowledge or notice of a pre-existing personal right of B.[77] Similarly, as emphasised by the Law Commission work leading to the Land Registration Act 2002,[78] and as noted recently by the Court of Appeal in *Chaudhary v Yavuz*,[79] if C's protection against B's pre-existing right instead comes from registration provisions (such provisions not denying the proprietary nature of B's right, but rather providing C with priority to such a right) then, again, C's mere knowledge or notice of B's right cannot be allowed to give B a right against C.

This victory of Lord Brougham's view of notice would not have been possible without a re-analysis of the decisions in cases such as *Tulk*. Rather than resting on C's notice of B's pre-existing right against A, those decisions were seen as depending on that pre-existing right's counting as an equitable property right.[80] As a result, attention was focused on the content of that pre-existing right and limits developed so as to ensure that only particular forms of such right were capable of binding C. In *Tulk* itself, for example, Lord Cottenham LC gave no attention to the question of whether the covenant between A and B was positive or negative; such questions are irrelevant if C's notice, rather than the content of B's right, provides the reason for C's being bound.[81] In contrast, when the principle applied in *Tulk* is seen to depend on the content of B's right, it becomes possible to distinguish between negative and positive covenants.[82] The Court of Appeal's decision in *Haywood v Brunswick Permanent Building Society*,[83] confirmed of course in *Austerberry v Corporation of Oldham*,[84] attached great weight to this distinction. In doing so, it provided further support to the decision in *Keppell*, by confirming that A's positive duty to B to use a particular railroad does not give rise to an equitable proprietary right capable of binding C.

---

[77] *Keppell v Bailey* (1834) 2 My & K 517, 548.

[78] See Law Commission Report No 254, *Land Registration for the Twenty-First Century: A Consultative Document* (1998) paras 3.44–3.50; Law Commission Report No 271, *Land Registration for the Twenty-First Century: A Conveyancing Revolution* (2001) paras 5.16–5.21; Land Registration Act 2002, s 28.

[79] *Chaudhary v Yavuz* [2011] EWCA Civ 1314, [2012] 2 All ER 418, [57]–[70].

[80] For a particularly influential example of this re-analysis, see *London & South Western Rwy Co v Gomm* (1881) 20 Ch D 562 (CA), where Jessel MR at 583 described the doctrine in *Tulk* as an equitable extension of either common law rules as to leasehold covenants, or of common law rules as to negative easements.

[81] See, eg, *Cooke v Chilcott* (1876) 3 Ch D 694, in which *Tulk* was relied on in allowing a positive covenant to bind C, who acquired his land with notice of the covenant.

[82] It is also possible to distinguish between those covenants that benefit some retained land of B and those that do not: see, eg, *London County Council v Allen* [1914] 3 KB 642 (CA). Note that Jessel MR's suggestion that the *Tulk* doctrine (above, n 80) consists of an equitable extension of the common law rules as to negative easements of course depends on the limitation of that doctrine to negative covenants that benefit or accommodate some retained land of B.

[83] *Haywood v Brunswick Permanent Building Society* (1881) 8 QBD 403 (CA).

[84] *Austerberry v Corporation of Oldham* (1885) 29 Ch D 750 (CA).

Simpson, noting that the limits imposed on *Tulk* were not demanded by the decision itself, concluded that '[i]n the typical manner of lawyers a new history was invented to give plausibility to these restrictions'.[85] This reinterpretation of *Tulk*, however, can be seen as giving force to one of the key ideas behind each of *Keppell* and *Hill*: the choice as to whether a right has proprietary effect is made not by A and B, but by the courts and legislature and, if a right is allowed to have such an effect, its content must be carefully controlled.

Lord Brougham's position that knowledge or notice of a pre-existing personal right does not suffice to bind a third party is also important when considering more recent economic arguments in favour of liberalising A's and B's ability to create new forms of property right. For example, one of the supposed arguments in favour of the *numerus clausus* principle, also made by Lord Brougham in *Keppell*,[86] consists of the need to prevent A's land being burdened by duties that will bind not only A, but A's successors in title. Epstein has argued that the real problem arises only if successors are bound by *undiscoverable* burdens: if C knows of a particular burden, it can be taken into account when negotiating the price paid for A's land.[87] On this view, a robust registration system is sufficient to protect successors in title, and there is no need to limit A and B's ability to create proprietary rights. The argument, however, is flatly inconsistent with the courts' rejection of the view that, if C has knowledge or notice of B's pre-existing right, then that right, no matter what its content, can bind C. The courts' current position, foreshadowed by *Keppell*, thus suggests that the importance of the *numerus clausus* principle extends beyond limiting information costs to A's successors in title.

Allocating Rights and the 'Bundle of Sticks'

As was noted above,[88] Bramwell B, while formally attempting to reconcile his reasoning with the decision in *Hill*, developed a quite different view of the circumstances in which B's right is capable of binding X, a stranger who interferes with B's use of A's land. His arguments, in the short term, were not successful: for example, in 1875, when given an opportunity to re-examine the law relating to the rights of riparian owners, the House of Lords, in

---

[85] A Simpson, *A History of the Land Law*, 2nd edn (Oxford, Clarendon Press, 1986) 259.
[86] *Keppell v Bailey* (1834) 2 My & K 517, 535–36.
[87] See R Epstein, 'Notice and Freedom of Contract in the Law of Servitudes' (1981–82) 55 *Southern California Law Review* 1353. See also B Edgeworth, 'The *Numerus Clausus* Principle in Contemporary Australian Property Law' (2006) 32 *Monash University Law Review* 387.
[88] pp 16–17.

Swindon Waterworks Co Ltd v Wilts and Berks Canal Navigation Co,[89] recognised limits on the powers of such owners to deal with abstracted water, rather than allowing them the freedoms advocated by Bramwell B.[90] On a longer view, however, his arguments can be seen as extraordinarily prophetic: his thinking (not only in this area, but in relation to freedom of contract and industrial tort liability)[91] is very close to that advocated in much of the economic analysis that now has such prominence in American legal scholarship. It is no surprise that Epstein has said that Bramwell B 'deserves his place with the greatest English judges of his own time, which is to say with the greatest common law judges of all time'.[92] More significantly, Bramwell B's reluctance to embrace the *numerus clausus* reasoning behind *Hill* foreshadows the difficulties that scholars have faced in attempting to reconcile that principle with economic analysis.[93]

It is particularly worth noting Bramwell B's point, made in *Nuttall v Bracewell*,[94] that it should, prima facie at least, be possible for A to separate out a particular proprietary right he or she enjoys as an owner of land and to grant that right to B. This view reflects another staple of American legal analysis, again inimical to the *numerus clausus* principle: the 'bundle of sticks' picture of property.[95] On this view, the property right held by an owner of land can be seen as made up of a bundle of distinct (also proprietary) rights including, for example, rights to make particular uses of the land. So, in *Hill*, one of the rights held by A was the exclusive right to put pleasure boats on the canal, and a good reason must be provided if the law is to prevent A simply separating that right from A's bundle and conferring it on B.

The lack of fit between the 'bundle of sticks' view and the decision in *Hill* provides an insight into both the durability of the decision and the

---

[89] *Swindon Waterworks Co Ltd v Wilts and Berks Canal Navigation Co* (1874–75) LR 7 HL 697.

[90] For discussion of the House of Lords' decision, see J Getzler, *A History of Water Rights at Common Law* (Oxford, OUP, 2004) 320–24.

[91] See further, R Epstein, 'For a Bramwell Revival' (1994) 38 *American Journal of Legal History* 246.

[92] Ibid, 248. Equally, it is no surprise that Atiyah referred to Bramwell B as 'something of a fanatic' P Atiyah, *The Rise and Fall of Freedom of Contract* (Oxford, Clarendon Press, 1979) 377.

[93] See especially B Rudden, 'Economic Theory v Property Law: The *Numerus Clausus* Problem' in J Eekelaar and J Bell (eds), *Oxford Essays in Jurisprudence, Third Series* (Oxford, OUP, 1987). For more recent attempts to find an economic basis for the principle, see, eg, T Merrill and H Smith, 'Optimal Standardization in the Law of Property: The *Numerus Clausus* Principle' (2000–01) 110 *Yale Law Journal* 3 and H Hansman and R Kraakman, 'Property, Contract, and Verification: The *Numerus Clausus* Problem and the Divisibility of Rights' (2002) 31 *Journal of Legal Studies* S373.

[94] *Nuttall v Bracewell* (1866–67) LR 2 Ex 1, 11.

[95] See, eg, S Munzer, 'A Bundle Theorist Holds on to His Collection of Sticks' (2011) *Economic Journal Watch* 265. For a general review of the hold of the bundle of sticks view, and challenges made to it, see E Claeys, 'Property 101: Is Property a Thing or a Bundle?' (2009) 32 *Seattle University Law Review* 617.

weaknesses of the bundle view. The court did not view A's dealings with B
as amounting to the transfer of a proprietary 'right to put pleasure boats on
the canal'. A Hohfeldian analysis can provide support for this conclusion.[96]
After all, the Basingstoke Canal Co (A) itself had no claim-right against
Tupper (X) to put boats on the canal. As Finnis has noted, a claim-right 'can
never be to do or omit something: it always is a claim that somebody else
do or omit something'.[97] This flows from the correlativity of the Hohfeldian
scheme: what content could X's duty have if A were to have a claim-right
against X to act (or not act) in a specific way? This is why it is possible for
X to interfere with a particular use of A's property without incurring any
liability to A. For example, in *Spartan Steel & Alloys Ltd v Martin & Co Ltd*[98]
the defendant (X), while carrying out road maintenance, carelessly damaged
a power cable and thus cut off power to the factory of the claimant (A). The
power loss prevented A from processing a number of its metal ingots and
offering them for sale. X, therefore, had interfered with a particular use of
A's land and chattels. Nonetheless, it was held that X was not liable for the
profits lost through A's inability to use his land and chattels in that way:
by merely preventing electricity from coming into the factory, X had not
physically interfered with A's land, or with those ingots.[99]

On a Hohfeldian analysis then, any right of an owner to make use of his
or her land is not a claim-right: it is a liberty. This is not to say that the law
has no interest in the uses that A may make of his or her land; rather, those
uses are protected indirectly, through X's duty not to interfere physically
with A's land. In *Hill*, of course, B had a liberty against X to put boats on
the canal; but to succeed in his action, B also needed a claim-right against
X. Such a claim-right cannot be found by simply relying on a transfer of
one of A's proprietary bundle of sticks. This is because A had no such
claim-right against X. This analysis shows the problem with Bramwell B's
suggestion[100] that Hill would have been able to sue X if X had interfered
with B's positive action in putting boats on the canal. The fact that A or B
has a liberty as against X to use the canal in this way does not mean that

---

[96] It may seem surprising to use Hohfeldian analysis to point out problems in the 'bundle
of sticks' theory, as Hohfeld's insistence on disaggregating rights into component legal rela-
tions was an important part of the intellectual background to the bundle view, as pointed
out by, eg, J Penner 'The "Bundle of Rights" Picture of Property' (1996) *UCLA Law Review*
711, 724–31. Nonetheless, a rigorously Hohfeldian analysis can reveal defects in the bundle
theory: this point is explored in detail in S Douglas and B McFarlane, 'Defining Property
Rights' in J Penner and H Smith (eds), *Philosophical Foundations of Property Law* (Oxford,
OUP, 2013).

[97] J Finnis, 'Some Professorial Fallacies About Rights' (1972) 4 *Adelaide Law Review* 377, 380.

[98] *Spartan Steel & Alloys Ltd v Martin & Co Ltd* [1973] QB 27 (CA).

[99] In contrast, A was able to recover for the profits lost on ingots that had been in the
course of processing at the time of the power cut, as the sudden lack of power caused physical
damage to those ingots.

[100] *Nuttall v Bracewell* (1866–67) LR 2 Ex 1, 11–12. See text above (n 69).

X is necessarily under a duty not to interfere with the exercise of that liberty. For example, consider the more recent decision of Flaux J in *Club Cruise Entertainment and Travelling Services Europe BV v Department for Transport (The Van Gogh)*.[101] The claimant was an owner of a ship that was scheduled to cruise from Harwich to Norway but, owing to an outbreak of norovirus on the ship the defendant issued a detention notice to the claimant under section 95 of the Merchant Shipping Act 1995. It later transpired that this had been done improperly, there being no statutory basis for the detention notice, and the claimant sued in conversion. The court held that the defendant's conduct—which consisted of no more than handing a sheet of paper to the claimant with the details of the detention notice on it—did not amount to a tort. In a telling passage Flaux J said that 'if there had been actual physical restraint of the ship by chaining it to the quayside, that would have constituted the tort of trespass to goods'.[102] In other words, while the defendant was under a duty not to interfere physically with the ship, it was not under a further duty not to interfere with the claimant's liberty to make a particular use of the ship.[103]

Bramwell B's analysis could be interpreted in a different way. It could be said to depend on giving B a claim-right against X that does not go beyond the content of A's claim-right against X: on this view, X's disruption of B's planned use of A's land can give rise to liability only if X's acts also involve physical interference with A's land. If B were allowed to sue X in those circumstances then, to adopt a term of Rudden,[104] X's duty to A would be 'cloned': whereas X previously had a duty to A not to interfere physically, deliberately or carelessly, with A's land, X would now owe a similar (albeit not identical)[105] duty to B. In his dissent in *Stockport Waterworks*, Bramwell B supported such 'cloning' on the basis that looked at globally, 'no additional burden' is imposed on X, as X in any case already owes a duty to A not to interfere with A's land.[106] A Hohfeldian analysis, however, shows this reasoning to be disingenuous. If we say that X has a duty not to

---

[101] *Club Cruise Entertainment and Travelling Services Europe BV v Department for Transport (The Van Gogh)* [2008] EWHC 2794 (Comm). See also *Mogul Steamship Co Ltd v McGregor, Gow & Co* [1892] AC 25 (HL) and *Perre v Apand Pty Ltd* [1999] HCA 36.

[102] [2008] EWHC 2794 (Comm), [50].

[103] See also *D Pride & Partners (A Firm) v Institute for Animal Health* [2009] EWHC 685 (QB): the defendant carelessly caused an outbreak of foot and mouth disease close to the claimant's land. As a result, a quarantine order prevented the claimant from sending his pigs to the abattoir and thus realising their commercial value. Tugendhat J held that, in the absence of any physical damage to the pigs, there was no claim. The defendant had clearly interfered with a particular liberty of the claimant, but that did not suffice for liability.

[104] Rudden, above (n 93).

[105] Not identical because more limited: X's interference with A's land would only count as a wrong against B if it also interfered with B's particular use of A's land.

[106] *Stockport Waterworks v Potter* (1864) 3 H & C 300, 319.

do something, we need to ask *to whom* X owes that duty: in other words, who has the claim-right correlating to that duty?

If each of A and B (rather than A alone) has a claim-right against X, then this carries significant practical implications for X. First, the power to enforce (or waive) X's duty is no longer in the sole control of A. The importance of this point may have been overlooked by the majority of the Court of Appeal in *Manchester Airport plc v Dutton*.[107] The National Trust (A) held freehold land entered by a trespasser (X). X had entered as part of a protest against the construction of a second runway by Manchester Airport plc (B). A's land was situated close to the airport, and A had granted B a licence to enter the land so as to reduce the height of obstacles within the flight paths to and from the second runway (ie, to cut down trees). However, at the time of X's trespass, B had not yet entered into possession of A's land. The majority of the Court of Appeal held that as B's licence gave it a right to go into possession of the land, B was also able to institute possession proceedings against X. Chadwick LJ, in a powerful dissent,[108] pointed out that there was no previous authority acknowledging that strangers owed any duty to a licensee who did not have possession of land. The reasoning of the majority shares Bramwell B's lack of concern with the 'cloning' of claims: Laws LJ, for example, stated that 'the court today has ample power to grant a remedy to a licensee which will protect but not exceed his legal rights granted by the licence'.[109] It is true that the remedy sought by B was possession of the land, and A's contract with B gave B a right to go into possession, but Laws LJ's analysis overlooks the vital difference between a right *against A* that A permit B to take possession, and a right *against X* to take possession. Giving B a right not only against A, but against the rest of the world does involve increasing B's rights beyond those granted by a licence as it is well-established that a licence gives A only a personal right against B.[110] Certainly, B's practical position is changed. In *Manchester Airport*, for example, it may have been the case that the National Trust, mindful perhaps of adverse publicity, would have been much less willing than Manchester Airport to use its power to bring possession proceedings.[111]

---

[107] *Manchester Airport plc v Dutton* [2000] QB 133 (CA).

[108] For support of that dissent, see W Swadling, 'Opening the *Numerus Clausus*' (2000) 116 *LQR* 358.

[109] *Manchester Airport plc v Dutton* [2000] QB 133, 150.

[110] See, eg, *King v David Allen & Sons, Billposting Ltd* [1936] 3 All ER 483 (HL); *National Provincial Bank Ltd v Ainsworth* [1965] AC 1175 (HL).

[111] In *Mayor of London v Hall* [2010] EWCA Civ 817, [2011] 1 WLR 504, counsel for Hall submitted that the decision in *Dutton* was inconsistent with authorities such as *Hill*. Lord Neuberger MR (at [26]) acknowledged that this argument 'seems very powerful' if it is assumed that 'the law governing the right to claim possession is governed by the same principles as those that governed the right to maintain a claim in ejectment'. His Lordship also noted (at [27]) the opposing point of view, that 'there is obvious force in the point that the modern law relating to possession claims should not be shackled by the arcane and archaic rules

A second practical consequence of extending X's duty to B is the exposure of X—should he interfere with A's land—to a liability to pay damages as compensation for consequential loss suffered not only by A, but by B. The importance of this point may have been overlooked by the Court of Appeal in *Shell UK Ltd v Total UK Ltd*,[112] when holding that, where X breached its duty not carelessly to interfere with A's land, and A's property right in the land was held on trust for B, X was liable for consequential economic loss suffered by B, at least if A was joined in any action brought by B against X. The decision has been widely criticised[113] and is contrary to previous case law establishing that if A holds A's right to a physical thing on trust for B, X is under no duty to B not to interfere with that physical thing.[114] The practical problem for X is the prospect of open-ended liability for an interference with a physical thing, if it turns out that title to that physical thing is held on trust for a large number of parties, each of whom suffers consequential loss as a result of X's action.[115]

It should also be noted that, even on its own terms, the reasoning of the Court of Appeal in *Shell UK Ltd v Total UK Ltd*[116] is confused. Crucially, the Court regards the claimants as having suffered a form of pure economic loss, but goes on to see the case as outside the scope of the 'exclusionary rule' barring recovery for such loss, because of 'the special relationship' between the claimant and the damaged property.[117] Two points can be made. First, if the Court did indeed view the beneficiaries of the trust as the 'real owners'[118] of the property, then it would be wrong to categorise their loss as purely economic, as that loss would instead flow from interference with a proprietary right. Secondly, the Court cited *Clerk & Lindsell on Torts* for the proposition that recovery in a pure economic loss case is possible if there is a 'special relationship between the defendant and the

---

relating to ejectment, and, in particular, that it should develop and adapt to accommodate a claim by anyone entitled to use and control, effectively amounting to possession, of the land in question'. See too *Vehicle Control Services Ltd v HM Revenue & Customs* [2013] EWCA Civ 186 at [35].

[112] *Shell UK Ltd v Total UK Ltd* [2010] EWCA Civ 180, [2011] QB 86.

[113] See, eg, A Scott and A Rushworth '*Shell UK Ltd v Total UK Ltd*: Total Chaos' [2010] *LMCLQ* 536; P Turner, 'Consequential Economic Loss and the Trust Beneficiary' [2010] *CLJ* 445; K Low, 'Equitable Title and Economic Loss' (2010) 126 *LQR* 507.

[114] See, eg, *Earl of Worcester v Finch* (1600) 2 And 162, 123 ER 600; *Lord Compton's Case* (1580) 2 Leon 211, 74 ER 485; *Leigh & Sillavan Ltd v Aliakmon Shipping Co Ltd (The Aliakmon)* [1986] AC 785 (HL); *MCC Proceeds Inc v Lehman Bros* [1998] 4 All ER 675 (CA). See also S Douglas, *Liability for Wrongful Interferences with Chattels* (Oxford, Hart Publishing, 2011) 39–47.

[115] This point is raised by Scott and Rushworth, above (n 113).

[116] *Shell UK Ltd v Total UK Ltd* [2010] EWCA Civ 180, [2011] QB 86.

[117] Ibid, [132]–[36].

[118] Ibid, [132].

person suffering relational economic loss'.[119] That is an accurate statement of the relevant English case law, which generally depends on an assumption of responsibility by the defendant to the claimant, such assumption establishing a special relationship between the parties.[120] The Court of Appeal, however, pointed to a quite different special relationship: that between the claimant and the damaged property. Of course, if the claimant has a legal property right in that property, recovery is allowed, as the loss suffered is not purely economic. Yet it is odd—and contrary to authority—for the Court to view the loss as economic, and then to impose liability even in the absence of any special relationship between the claimant and defendant.

Restricting Property Rights and Preserving Liberties

In each of *Keppell* and *Hill*, the Court preserved the defendant's liberty, as against the claimant, to act in a particular way. In *Keppell*, this meant that the Baileys were not compelled to carry on paying a set price for use of the Trevil Railroad: they were free to explore more efficient methods of carrying limestone to their ironworks. The initial construction of the Trevil Railroad, which may well have conferred a great benefit not only on its shareholders but on its other users, may have been economically possible only because of the willingness of the owners of the local ironworks to make a contractual commitment to use the road and to pay a particular price for doing so. This compact provided a guaranteed source of future income and so lessened the risks entailed in the building of the railroad. Nonetheless, it equally gave rise to a significant problem: a duty on future owners of the ironworks to use the railroad and to do so at a fixed price, could artificially prop up the railroad even after it had become inefficient. This was particularly problematic given the limits placed on the statutory powers that had been invoked to acquire land over which the railroad was built. For example, as noted above,[121] statute provided that the railroad had to be open to the public, and that the charges made were to be restricted (to a level below that agreed in the ironworks' compact). Lord Brougham identified the purpose of this second restriction:

> [T]he public, that is, the proprietors of adjoining closes, are not to be subject to the strong powers of the Act (powers which it has in common with all such Acts, but which are always to be most strictly pursued), unless there is the reasonable

---

[119] M Jones et al (eds), *Clerk & Lindsell on Torts*, 20th edn (London, Sweet & Maxwell, 2010) 8–116, cited in *Shell UK Ltd v Total UK Ltd* [2010] EWCA Civ 180, [2011] QB 86, [135].

[120] See, eg, *Hedley Byrne & Co v Heller & Partners* [1964] AC 465 (HL); *Williams v Natural Life Health Foods* [1998] 1 WLR 830 (HL).

[121] p 7.

certainty that there will be a considerable traffic on the road—a traffic sufficient to maintain it at the limited rate of charge.[122]

Given that, as noted above, the *numerus clausus* principle has been subjected to criticism on economic grounds, it is interesting to note that on the facts of *Keppell*, there were sound economic reasons for preventing the Baileys from being locked in to an arrangement which might no longer provide the most efficient way of supplying their ironworks. Moreover, while Lord Brougham did refer to the need not to burden titles to *land* with particular duties, the liberty of the Baileys, preserved by the decision in *Keppell*, was in fact unconnected with any particular title to land: it was their liberty to choose not to use the Trevil Railroad.

This analysis shows that although *Keppell* concerned the position of a successor in title, and *Hill* the position of a stranger, each case preserved liberties unconnected with the use of the defendant's land. Certainly, it is hard to see that the decisions would have been any different if either of the defendants had not been owners of land. The same point can be made of another important nineteenth century case, preserving a liberty of X: *Bradford Corporation v Pickles*.[123] That case is often discussed as part of a broader examination of the abuse of property rights.[124] As in *Keppell* and *Hill*, however, there is nothing to suggest that the absence of liability depended on the fact that the defendant was an owner of land. The reasoning of the House of Lords is premised on the fact that the claimant corporation did not have a general claim-right to receive water percolating under the defendant's land.[125] This means that *everyone* had a liberty, as against the claimant, to interfere with the flow of that water to the claimant.[126]

Indeed, the broader point at stake in each of *Keppell*, *Hill* and *Bradford* could be seen to relate to X's liberty to cause A economic loss: if X is not under a general duty to A not to perform a particular act, then X has a liberty against A to act in that way, even if X thereby causes an economic loss to B. The cases can thus be linked with other important nineteenth century

---

[122] *Keppell v Bailey* (1834) 2 My & K 517, 532.

[123] *Bradford Corporation v Pickles* [1895] AC 587 (HL).

[124] See, eg, L Katz, 'A Principle of Abuse of Property Right' *Yale Law Journal*, (forthcoming). Available at SSRN: http://ssrn.com/abstract=1417955 or http://dx.doi.org/10.2139/ssrn.1417955 (accessed 13 February 2013).

[125] See, eg, Lord Halsbury LC in *Bradford Corporation v Pickles* [1895] AC 587, 592: 'although [the defendant's action] deprives [the claimant corporation] of water which they would otherwise get, it is necessary for the plaintiffs to establish that they have a right to the flow of water, and that the defendant has no right to do what he is doing'.

[126] In *Allen v Flood* [1898] AC 1, 124, Lord Herschell described the decision in *Bradford* as establishing that 'acts done by the defendant upon his own land were not actionable when they were within his legal rights, even though his motive were to prejudice his neighbour'. The fact that the defendant acted on his own land is best seen as part of a description of the facts of the case, rather than a requirement of the principle applied.

decisions, such as *Cattle v Stockton Waterworks Co*[127] and *Allen v Flood*.[128] In *Cattle*, for example, Blackburn J emphasised the point—given little weight in Bramwell B's dissenting judgment in *Stockport Waterworks*—that even if the defendant's action is in any case a breach of duty to A, a court must think carefully before allowing other parties (such as B) to sue for economic loss caused as a result of the defendant's action. In the case where the defendant's act floods A's mine, for example, the result of allowing such further claims would be that

> the defendant would be liable, not only to an action by the owner of the drowned mine, and by such workmen as had their tools or clothes destroyed, but also to an action by every workman and person employed in the mine, who in consequence of its stoppage made less wages than he would otherwise have done.[129]

It is important to note that the presence of a property right separates those cases where recovery is allowed (where X has physically interfered with the claimant's land, tools or clothes) from those where it is not (where X's actions cause only pure economic loss to the claimant). This approach to attributing liability in tort necessarily rests on the *numerus clausus* principle, and thus on decisions such as *Keppell* and *Hill*. For the existence of a property right serves as a useful demarcation only if the content of property rights is also controlled.

It was suggested above[130] that the significance of the *numerus clausus* principle extends beyond the protection it provides to A's successors in title. It can be argued that the preservation of general liberties provides an additional and more compelling justification for the principle, and explains why it is at stake not only in cases such as *Keppell*, dealing with the position of successors, but those such at *Hill*, concerning the liability of strangers. First, it can be argued that the *numerus clausus* principle recognises that A and B have no general power to impose a new duty on X.[131] The fact that A is an owner of property, and is thus owed particular duties by X, does not provide a reason why A should also be free, at his or her choice, to impose on X new duties to B. The law admits, of course, that A can impose such duties if the right given by A to B counts as a recognised legal property right, such as a lease or easement. The content of such rights, however, is strictly controlled, so that the goal of preserving X's liberties gives way only in compelling cases. Secondly, it can be argued that the preservation of X's liberties also has important economic consequences. The strong beliefs of Bramwell B in A's and B's freedom to create new forms of property rights, like his conviction in freedom of contract, arose in the particular nineteenth century

---

[127] *Cattle v Stockton Waterworks Co* (1875) LR 10 QB 453 (QB).
[128] *Allen v Flood* [1898] AC 1 (HL).
[129] *Cattle v Stockton Waterworks Co* (1875) LR 10 QB 453, 457.
[130] p 2.
[131] See B McFarlane, 'The *Numerus Clausus* Principle', above (n 52) 311.

context of rapid commercial growth and increased trade. The networks created as a result led to increased economic interconnectedness: as a result, as noted in *Cattle v Stockton Waterworks*, a single action by a defendant could cause economic loss to a wide number of possible claimants. In such a world, robust control mechanisms are needed if the defendant's liberties (such liberties, of course, often being used for the pursuit of the defendant's economic goals) are not to be unduly restricted. One such mechanism is provided by the *numerus clausus* principle, coupled with a prima facie bar on liability for causing pure economic loss.

The Structure of Property Law

As noted above,[132] one of the key questions raised by *Hill* is whether there is a valid distinction between cases such as *Keppell*, which concern the position of C (A's successor in title) and cases such as *Hill* itself, which instead concern the position of X (a stranger, who acquires no right from A). Hill's counsel attempted to distinguish *Keppell* on that basis, and there is certainly some plausibility in the view that in the former class of case, the protection given to C may rest on the need to permit an owner of land to be free to make the best use of his or her land; whereas in the latter class of case, the action of X is less worthy of protection, as it may well be, in any case, a wrong against A.

The first problem with this argument is shown by the point, discussed above,[133] that the Baileys' liberty against Keppell, protected by the court's decision, was not a liberty that the Baileys held in their capacity as owners of land. On the contrary, *everyone* had a general liberty against Keppell not to make use of the Trevil Railroad. The liberty of which Keppell sought to deprive the Baileys was thus not a liberty derived from the Baileys' ownership of any land. This point may underlie Lord Templeman's explanation, in *Rhone v Stephens*,[134] of why positive covenants do not count as equitable proprietary rights: 'Enforcement of a positive covenant lies in contract; a positive covenant compels an owner to exercise his rights. Enforcement of a negative covenant lies in property; a negative covenant deprives the owner of a right over property'.[135] As has been pointed out,[136] this statement contains more than a hint of circularity. Nonetheless, it may be based on the idea that the type of freedom that a positive covenant seeks to deny (a freedom not to act) is a general freedom, whereas the type of freedom removed by

---

[132] pp 10–12.
[133] p 27.
[134] *Rhone v Stephens* [1994] 2 AC 310 (HL).
[135] Ibid, 318.
[136] See, eg, S Gardner, 'Two Maxims of Equity' [1995] *CLJ* 60, pp 67–68.

a restrictive covenant (a freedom to make a particular use of land) depends specifically on the defendant's position as an owner of land.[137]

This leads to a second—and perhaps surprising—difficulty with the distinction drawn by Hill's counsel. It might seem perfectly logical for a property law system to have one list of rights that can bind successors in title and a different, longer list of rights that can bind strangers. Nonetheless, it seems that English law does not operate in this way. To the extent that there is a need to give special protection to successors in title, it is met through giving such parties a greater chance (as compared with strangers) of establishing a defence to a pre-existing proprietary right. For example, the basic lack of registration defence, which forms an important part of the scheme of the Land Registration Act 2002, is available to C only if C has acquired a right from A and thus gives special protection to a successor in title.[138]

Moreover, and more importantly, it seems that English law in fact recognises a group of rights that *can* bind A's successors in title, but do not bind X. Where B has such a right, C's acquisition of a right from A does not protect C from liability to B but is, on the contrary, a necessary condition of C's being bound. For example, consider a case in which B is a beneficiary of a trust. It is of course well established that if A holds a right on trust for B and then transfers that right to C, B may be able to make a claim against C. If C does not acquire A's right for value, then B can make such a claim even if C, at the time of acquiring A's right, had no notice of B's right. At the same time, there is no direct claim that B can make against X, a stranger whose interference reduces the value of the right held on trust for B.[139] This is clear in the case where the right held on trust for B is intangible, such as a chose in action. At least until the Court of Appeal's decision in *Shell UK Ltd v Total UK Ltd* [140] it was also clear in cases where the right held on trust for B relates to a physical thing. If X interferes with that physical thing, A may have a claim against X (if A did not consent to the interference) and B may be able to force A to make such a claim, but B has no direct claim against X.

It has been suggested that this group of rights that can bind A's successor in title, but not a stranger, is comprised of equitable property rights; it

---

[137] The word 'freedom' (rather than liberty) is used here as, in a strict Hohfeldian sense, even C's liberty as against B to use C's land (eg, to build on it) is held by C independently of C's ownership of the land. After all, *as against B*, C had a liberty to build on the land even when that land still belonged to A.

[138] Land Registration Act 2002, ss 29 and 30.

[139] See the authorities listed above (n 114).

[140] *Shell UK Ltd v Total UK Ltd* [2010] EWCA Civ 180, [2011] QB 86, discussed at pp 25–26 above.

has further been argued that such rights operate in this way as they arise whenever A is under a duty to B in relation to a specific right held by A.[141] So if, for example, A holds a freehold on trust for B, the object or target of B's right is not the land itself, but is rather A's right to the land.[142] The different effect of B's right on a successor in title and a stranger depends on the fact that when C acquires A's right, C has acquired the object or target of B's right. In contrast, where X simply interferes with the land, X may have breached a duty to A, but X has not dealt at all with A's right: in other words, X has left the object or target of B's right untouched. While this argument cannot be discussed in detail here, it is important to note that if correct, it provides a powerful rebuttal of the argument made by Hill's counsel. First, English law does not contain a group of rights that cannot bind A's successor in title but can bind a stranger; secondly, in fact, English law does contain a group of rights that can bind A's successor in title but not a stranger.

CONCLUSION

While the *numerus clausus* is a well established feature of many civilian codes, it might be thought that evidence for such a doctrine would be harder to find in a common law system. Indeed, neither *Keppell* nor *Hill* refers explicitly to a *numerus clausus* principle; and, owing to the rule of precedent, no single judge or decision could definitively establish such a principle as part of English law. Nonetheless, the structure of English land law can be deduced not only from legislation, but also from its mass of cases, and certain of those cases can serve as landmarks. Indeed, as we lack the road map of a code, we need to pick out certain principles and navigate by reference to them. And, in order to identify such principles, it is helpful to focus on particular exemplary decisions for use as landmarks. *Keppell* can thus represent the limits on A and B's power to impose continuing burdens on successors to A's property; and *Hill* the limits on A and B's power to impose additional burdens on strangers interfering with that property.

---

[141] See, eg, McFarlane, *The Structure of Property Law*, above (n 52) Pt D2; McFarlane and Stevens, above (n 51). This does not mean, of course, that all equitable property rights operate in this way. Exceptionally among such rights, the restrictive covenant has been allowed to bind a party not acquiring a right from A: see *Re Nisbet & Potts Contract* [1906] 1 Ch 386. If such rights are to operate in the future as legal property rights, under the land obligation scheme proposed in Law Com No 327 (2011), this anomaly would disappear.

[142] See, eg, R Chambers, *An Introduction to Property Law in Australia*, 2nd edn (Sydney, Lawbook Co, 2008) [13.90]; L Smith, 'Philosophical Foundations of the Proprietary Remedies' in R Chambers et al (eds), *Philosophical Foundations of the Law of Unjust Enrichment* (Oxford, OUP, 2009) 281.

Relatively recent decisions such as *Manchester Airport plc v Dutton*[143] and *Shell UK Ltd v Total UK Ltd*[144] may demonstrate the dangers of overlooking these limits. They serve not just as technicalities, but perform the important task of preserving our freedoms to act. In the absence of those limits, land law (and indeed the law of tort) would look very different.

---

[143] *Manchester Airport plc v Dutton* [2000] QB 133 (CA), discussed at p 24 above.
[144] *Shell UK Ltd v Total UK Ltd* [2010] EWCA Civ 180, [2011] QB 86, discussed at p 24 above.

2

Todrick v Western National Omnibus Co Ltd *(1934)*

The Interpretation of Easements

PETER BUTT

DR TODRICK'S BIG PROBLEM—AND A BUS COMPANY'S DILEMMA

The Protagonists

T HIS IS THE story of one man's fight against big business. The man was Dr Archibald Todrick, who practised medicine in St Ives, Cornwall. The big business was the Western National Omnibus Company. It had been formed in 1929 as a joint venture between the Great Western Railway Company and the National Omnibus and Transport Company.[1] It had a large fleet of buses and substantial landholdings. Its bus routes ran the length and breadth of South West England.[2] As we would say today, it had deep pockets.

The Title History

In 1927, Dr Todrick purchased Skidden House, fronting Skidden Hill, St Ives. Skidden Hill had once been the main road down to the harbour at

---

[1] This followed the enactment of the Great Western Railway (Road Transport) Act 1928, which allowed the Great Western Railway to take a share in bus companies operating within its territory.

[2] At least two books have been written about the Western National Omnibus Company. One is Colin Morris, *Western National Omnibus Company* (Ian Allan Publishing, 2008); this is essentially a collection of the bus company's minutes of meetings—conveying a sense of the company's commercial importance in the South West, but hardly scintillating reading. The second is RJ Crawley and FD Simpson, *The Years Between, 1909–1969 (vol 3): The Story of Western National and Southern National from 1929* (Carlton Promotions, 1990); this is more of a social history of the company, and contains much of interest.

St Ives. It was (and still is) a steep and narrow street, in the style of steep and narrow streets in English seaside villages.[3] It runs at right angles downhill from a street on much higher ground, The Terrace, which is now one of the main roads into St Ives.

Skidden House is of some historic interest. It was initially a public house. In that capacity, it was the first public house in England to sell Guinness on tap. An owner in the 1700s, Captain Sampson would sail to Dublin with a load of pilchards and return to St Ives with barrels of Guinness.[4] Much later, when St Ives became an internationally-renowned centre for artists, Skidden House became the home of John Douglas and his wife Mabel. John Douglas was a leading photographer of the time, and Mabel was a portrait miniaturist of some quality. They lived in Skidden House from 1901 to 1915.[5] After the First World War, Skidden House was lived in for a short time and altered significantly by George Turland Goosey, an architect who had made his name in America, and who came to paint and etch in St Ives in 1921.[6]

For our purposes, however, Skidden House is of interest because its title included a laneway which became the battle ground for the case we know today as *Todrick v Western National Omnibus Co.*

The laneway (called in the law report a 'private roadway') ran in from Skidden Hill, along the side of Dr Todrick's house, and continued past his house until it reached his garages, about 35 yards in from Skidden Hill. Dr Todrick used the laneway for vehicular access to the garages. The laneway in fact continued past the garages for a further five or six yards, to reach neighbouring land (called in the law report, the 'blue land').

A right of way over the laneway had been created by way of reservation in 1921 when a certain Dr Nicholls sold Skidden House to Dr Todrick's predecessor in title. Dr Nicholls reserved the right of way as a means of access to the blue land, which he owned. Dr Nicholls also owned another nearby property, known as Penwyn, which fronted The Terrace and overlooked Skidden House. He later converted Penwyn into a hotel named The Regent.

The right of way was drafted in the manner often found in rights of way of that period. It was a right to use the laneway 'at all times and for all purposes with or without vehicles and animals'. Unusually, the reservation

---

[3] The name Skidden Hill is said to derive from the method of bringing carts down the steep slope to the waterfront at the bottom of the street. To prevent the carts from rolling off the narrow street, metal skids were place in front of the cartwheels and then edged forward (*St Ives Times & Echo*, 25 March 1988). It is related to the obsolescent verb 'to skid', meaning 'to apply or fasten a skid or brake to (a wheel) in order to retard its motion' (OED).

[4] The story is told in the *St Ives Times & Echo* (25 March 1988).

[5] Information on file with author, from David Tovey, author of *St Ives (1860–1930)—The Artists and the Community: A Social History* (Wilson Books, c2008).

[6] Ibid.

was expressed to allow the dominant owner to 'extend' the right of way over the five or six yards to reach the blue land; but in truth that additional length was part of the reservation itself—that is, it was a right of way over the entire length of the laneway, to reach the blue land.

Dr Nicholls later sold the blue land. The purchaser of the blue land then bought additional land (which we may call the north land) which abutted the blue land. Later, that purchaser thought it beneficial to vary the direction of the 'extension' component of the right of way, so that it would run directly to the north land. And so in 1926 the owners of the dominant and servient lands by deed varied the right of way. Essentially, the dominant owner surrendered the right to extend the right of way to the blue land, and in its place was granted a right to extend the right of way to the north land. If extended in this manner, the right of way would lead directly to the north land, and would only marginally touch the blue land (that is, the original dominant land). Where it would reach the north land, it would meet a stone wall five feet high. On the further side of that wall, where the north land began, lay a dip or gully; only by traversing the dip or gully could access be gained to the blue land.[7] Importantly, the parties intended the right of way (as varied) still to be appurtenant to the blue land only (and not to the north land). Importantly also, no actual use seems to have been made of the extension (to either the blue land or the north land). It remained unmade.

The Bus Company's Plans

Dr Todrick's problems began in 1930, when the Western National Omnibus Co Ltd purchased the blue land and the north land. Those parcels of land lay at the foot of a very steep slope, at the top of which ran The Terrace. The bus company also purchased land in The Terrace for use as its prospective bus station in St Ives. The bus company planned to use the topography to its advantage. It would build a platform at street level in The Terrace to serve as its bus station and ticket office. The platform would project out over the steep slope. In the void beneath lay the blue land and the north land, on which the company would build garages for housing its buses. It seemed a practical solution to the dual needs of bus station and garaging facilities.

There was a slight problem, in that the garages would lack direct access to The Terrace—the slope was far too steep for buses to navigate

---

[7] This is made clear in the law report, but is not clear on a present-day inspection of the land—because the gully has been filled in. A current inspection shows the laneway as level for most of its length.

directly down. But that would be solved by using the right of way across Dr Todrick's laneway. Buses would be driven in from Skidden Hill, along the laneway past Dr Todrick's garages, along the (new) extension to the north land and then across the north land to reach the blue land. True, to make the right of way accessible for buses, it would be necessary to build a ramp to surmount the stone wall; and that ramp would have to turn at an angle to reach the proposed bus garage; but engineers could solve those problems relatively easily.

The bus company's building plans immediately raised the ire of local inhabitants. The St Ives council, though obliged to pass the plans, strongly opposed them.[8] Dr Nicholls complained that the building operations would interfere with his hotel business.[9] Other inhabitants sought help from their local MP.[10] But the bus company's most obstinate opponent was Dr Todrick. He owned the laneway that was so crucial to the company's plans. This was to be his trump card.

Here we must introduce some further evidence of the physical nature of the laneway.[11] The laneway was nine feet wide, with a rocky surface. It was in the nature of a 'short country lane'. At its entrance point from Skidden Hill, it passed between stone pillars that were seven feet nine inches apart—so any vehicle using the laneway would need to be no wider than seven feet nine inches. Now, buses of the 1930s were a standard width—seven feet six inches; so a bus would have a mere one and a half inches clearance on each side. Also, the laneway (on its side that adjoined Dr Todrick's house) was supported by a retaining wall, which was clearly strong enough to bear the weight of cars using the laneway, but less clearly so to bear the weight of buses (which at the time weighed at least three tons).

Below is a picture (taken in 2011) of the entrance to the laneway, off Skidden Hill. Dr Todrick's house, Skidden House, is on the left. The original stone pillar on the left hand side of the laneway has gone, replaced with a newer breeze block substitute. Close inspection reveals two pillars on the right hand side, abutting each other. Presumably the furthest one to the right was the one from which the entrance width of seven feet nine inches was measured; but in either case, the entrance is barely wide enough for a small van. Buses clearly would have had great difficulty navigating into the laneway.

---

[8] Crawley and Simpson, above (n 2) 21.
[9] Ibid.
[10] Ibid.
[11] This evidence comes from the judgment of Farwell J at first instance: see [1934] Ch 190, 194–95, 207.

The Court Case

The Grounds

The bus company built the ramp. Dr Todrick objected, because (he said) it made it difficult for him to drive cars in and out of his own garages; it also made it difficult for him to wash his cars on a concrete apron he had built in front of his garages.[12] He sued the bus company, making two chief claims:

1. There was no valid right of way over the laneway. This was because the servient and dominant lands were not contiguous. The servient land was the laneway; the dominant land was the blue land. As now extended, the right of way in fact led to the north land, from which access was then had to the blue land.
2. If there was a valid right of way, the bus company's conduct in using it for buses, and in building the ramp, was excessive.

---

[12] Dr Todrick may have built the apron only after the dispute arose, to justify ex post facto his allegation that the bus company's proposed use would inconvenience his car-washing activities: Crawley and Simpson, above (n 2) 21.

In short, Dr Todrick claimed that buses could not use the laneway, and the ramp should be demolished.

The Decision

At first instance, Farwell J found for Dr Todrick on both counts.[13] The right of way as varied did not lead directly to the dominant tenement, and was invalid for lack of contiguity. And if it was valid, its use by buses would be excessive. Also excessive was the building of the ramp; the laneway could have been extended and made useable for vehicles (although not buses) without erecting a permanent structure of this kind.

The bus company appealed. The Court of Appeal reversed Farwell J on the issue of contiguity.[14] No principle of the law of easements required contiguity between dominant and servient tenements as a condition of validity, as long as the easement in fact benefits the dominant tenement.

However, the Court of Appeal agreed with Farwell J that the ramp was an excessive user of the easement. The right of way did not permit the erection of such a substantial structure, particularly when (as Farwell J had found) it was not clear that access could not be provided (if not for buses, then at least for ordinary vehicles) by a less substantial and intrusive structure. Maugham LJ considered that the bus company's ramp would make it difficult, perhaps even dangerous, for Dr Todrick to park his cars in his garages.[15] Lord Hanworth MR considered that it was a question of balancing the rights of both parties, but that the bus company's action in building the ramp on the site of the easement was an unwarranted intrusion into Dr Todrick's rights.[16]

Having failed on the question of the ramp, the bus company did not press on appeal their more general claim to use the laneway for buses. However, all members of the Court of Appeal agreed with Farwell J's judgment on this point. Lord Hanworth MR regarded as key that the buses would need to drive through the entrance gateway, with minimal clearance on each side. This meant, he said, that 'it is quite plain that the right of way was never intended for such vehicles'.[17] Romer LJ said that he had nothing to add to that.[18] Maugham LJ said that the bus company had been right not to argue against Farwell J's conclusion on that point.[19]

---

[13] *Todrick v Western National Omnibus Co Ltd* [1934] Ch 190 (Ch D).
[14] *Todrick v Western National Omnibus Co Ltd* [1934] Ch 561, 572–74 (Lord Hanworth MR); 579–85 (Romer LJ); 589–91 (Maugham LJ).
[15] Ibid, 592.
[16] Ibid, 575–76.
[17] Ibid, 576.
[18] Ibid, 577.
[19] Ibid, 592.

The Relevance of the Physical Circumstances of the Site

The judgments of Farwell J and the Court of Appeal draw heavily on the physical limitations of the site of the right of way. The extent of permissible user—even though expressed in the widest terms—was to be interpreted in the light of the surrounding circumstances, particularly the physical nature of the *locus in quo*. Farwell J said this (and the Court of Appeal must be taken to agree):

> In considering whether a particular use of a right of this kind is a proper use or not, I am entitled to take into consideration the circumstances of the case, the situation of the parties and the situation of the land *at the time when the grant was made* ...; and in my judgment a grant for all purposes means for all purposes having regard to [those considerations]. ... A grant [for all purposes] must be construed as a grant for all purposes within the reasonable contemplation of the parties at the time of the grant (emphasis added).[20]

Other Decisions on the Relevance of the Physical Circumstances of the Site

This approach taken in *Todrick* to the relevance of the physical circumstances of the site of a right of way was hardly new. Courts had traditionally looked to the physical circumstances of a right of way to illuminate the rights granted. The 1870s case of *Cannon v Villars*[21] gives the best-known illustration: consider the grant of a 'right of way', the precise extent of which is not specified in the grant. If the way is paved, with a footpath along the side, and leads to a place where vehicular access is required, the way is presumed to be intended not only for persons on foot but also for vehicles; but if the way is paved merely with flagstones and is only a few feet wide, so that vehicles cannot drive along it, the way is presumed to be intended as a right of footway only.[22] In short, an easement cannot be used in a manner beyond the use that the terms of the grant, viewed in the light of the physical circumstances, indicate objectively was contemplated by the parties at the time of its creation.[23]

---

[20] [1934] Ch 190, 206–07 (Ch D).

[21] *Cannon v Villars* (1878) 8 Ch D 415 (Ch D).

[22] Ibid, 420–21. Applications of this principle include *Gregg v Richards* [1926] Ch 521, 532 (CA); *St Edmundsbury and Ipswich Diocesan Board of Finance v Clark (No 2)* [1975] 1 WLR 468, 473–77 (CA); *Bond and Leitch v Delfab Investments Pty Ltd* (1980) 26 SASR 462, 471; *Hutchinson v Lemon* [1983] Qd R 369, 374–75.

[23] *Jelbert v Davis* [1968] 1 WLR 589, 595 (Lord Denning MR); *Todrick v Western National Omnibus Co Ltd* [1934] Ch 190, 206–07 (Ch D); *Gallagher v Rainbow* (1994) 179 CLR 624, 639–42; *Finlayson v Campbell* (1997) 8 BPR 15,703, 15,708; *Corinne Court (Owners of) 290 Stirling Street Perth Strata Plan 12821 v Shean Pty Ltd* (2000) 23 WAR 1, 21, 22–23 (reversed on other grounds, *Shean Pty Ltd v Owners of Corinne Court, 290 Stirling Street Perth, Strata Plan 12821* (2001) 25 WAR 65).

That said, some easements are granted in terms so generous in their description of the nature and permissible use of the easement, that extrinsic evidence cannot be allowed to qualify them.[24] The terms of the grant then necessarily override any limiting effect inherent in the physical nature of the site of the easement.[25] For example, where the grant of a right of way clearly referred to a way of a certain width and the way was otherwise suitable for the vehicles claimed to be entitled to use it, the permissible use was not to be restricted by the narrowness of the entrance gate at the date of the grant.[26] Again, a right of way granted 'for all purposes' when the dominant tenement was a farm could still be used as a right of way when the dominant tenement was changed to a sand mine.[27] And a 'free and unrestricted right-of-way' granted when the dominant tenement contained several cottages in a market area could be used by large construction vehicles when the dominant tenement was being developed as a 10-storey inner-city building.[28] The cases on this point are not always easily reconcilable with the principle derived from *Todrick*. Certainly, though, one point is clear: courts rarely limit the permissible use of an easement by reference to the use to which the dominant land was put at the time of the grant. We return to this point, later.

THE MODERN PRINCIPLES OF INTERPRETATION

A New Start

Into this difficult area we must now introduce the modern, contextual principles of legal interpretation. These widen somewhat the former ambit of admissible evidence in interpretation cases. The contextual approach finds bold expression in the restatement of principle by the House of Lords in *Investors Compensation Scheme Ltd v West Bromwich Building Society*.[29]

The most cited judgment is that of Lord Hoffmann. His Lordship referred to the 'fundamental change' that had overtaken the interpretation

---

[24] *Scarfe v Adams* [1981] 1 All ER 843, 851 (CA).

[25] *St Edmundsbury and Ipswich Diocesan Board of Finance v Clark (No 2)* [1975] 1 WLR 468, 477 (CA); *West v Sharpe* (1999) 79 P & CR 327, 332 (Mummery LJ): '[T]he language of the grant may be such that the topographical circumstances cannot properly be regarded as restricting the scope of the grant according to the language of it'.

[26] *Bulstrode v Lambert* [1953] 1 WLR 1064, 1069 (Ch D); *Keefe v Amor* [1965] 1 QB 334, 344–45 (CA). See also *Corinne Court (Owners of) 290 Stirling Street Perth Strata Plan 12821 v Shean Pty Ltd* (2000) 23 WAR 1, 28: 'one cannot allow the presence of a barrier to override the explicit language of the instrument' (reversed on other grounds, *Shean Pty Ltd v Owners of Corinne Court, 290 Stirling Street Perth, Strata Plan 12821* (2001) 25 WAR 65).

[27] *South Eastern Railway v Cooper* [1924] 1 Ch 211 (CA).

[28] *Kyren Pty Ltd v Cinema Place Pty Ltd* [2006] SASC 93 (SAFC).

[29] *Investors Compensation Scheme Ltd v West Bromwich Building Society* [1998] 1 WLR 896 (HL).

of contracts. Generally, contractual documents were to be interpreted in accordance with 'common sense principles by which any serious utterance would be interpreted in ordinary life'. Almost all the old 'intellectual baggage' of legal interpretation had been discarded. He summarised the modern principles of interpretation in five propositions. For our purposes, propositions (1) and (2) are key:

> (1) Interpretation is the ascertainment of the meaning which the document would convey to a reasonable person having all the background knowledge which would reasonably have been available to the parties in the situation in which they were at the time of the contract.
>
> (2) The background was famously referred to by Lord Wilberforce as the 'matrix of fact', but this phrase is, if anything, an understated description of what the background may include. Subject to the requirement that it should have been reasonably available to the parties and to the exception to be mentioned next, it includes absolutely everything which would have affected the way in which the language of the document would have been understood by a reasonable person.[30]

These principles have been widely accepted in most common law countries, and are now the conventional starting point in decisions on interpretation. Lord Hoffmann's proposition (2), that 'absolutely everything' is part of the admissible background, has been criticised on a number of occasions for its tendency to increase both uncertainty and the costs of litigation.[31] In later pronouncements, Lord Hoffmann defended this proposition by explaining that it was to be tempered by considerations of 'relevance'—that when saying that the background material included 'absolutely everything', he meant everything that a reasonable person would have regarded as *relevant*.[32]

'Ambiguity' as Gateway to Admissibility?

Despite Lord Hoffmann's expansive statement of principle, courts in some jurisdictions refuse to allow resort to background unless the text of the document is 'ambiguous' or 'unclear' in some way. Under this approach, if the text is clear on its face, background is not admissible to establish that the parties meant something else by the words they used. This seems to be

---

[30] Ibid, 912–13.

[31] Eg, S Price, 'Commercial Contract Interpretation through the Looking Glass' (1998) 142 *Solicitors Journal* 176; Sir Christopher Staughton, 'How do the Courts Interpret Commercial Contracts?' [1999] *CLJ* 303; *LMI Australasia Pty Ltd v Baulderstone Hornibrook Pty Ltd* [2003] NSWCA 74, [34]–[36], [50]–[53] (Young CJ in Eq). See also JJ Spigelman, 'Extrinsic Material and the Interpretation of Insurance Contracts' (2011) 22 *Insurance Law Journal* 143, 145.

[32] *Bank of Credit and Commerce International SA v Ali* [2002] 1 AC 251, 269 (HL); *Chartbrook Ltd v Persimmon Homes Ltd* [2009] UKHL 38, [2009] AC 1101, [32].

the law in, for example, Australia[33] and Canada.[34] In contrast, in England, Lord Hoffmann's five principles allow evidence of the background to be admitted to show that what appears on the face of the contract to be clear is not in fact clear. The English approach is also followed in New Zealand,[35] Ireland[36] and South Africa.[37] In these countries, as in England, if the background shows that the parties meant by their words something different from the face meaning of those words, then the court interprets their words accordingly.[38]

THE EFFECT OF REGISTRATION

Nature and Relevance

Now we must turn to a key consideration in any discussion of modern land law: the effect of registration. Legislation in many common law countries provides a system of title registration. Under this legislation, registration does more than merely record a title that must be established by other means. Rather, registration itself *creates* the title, conferring on the person registered as proprietor a title that did not previously exist.[39] Additionally,

---

[33] This seems to be the Australian position since *Western Export Services Inc v Jireh International Pty Ltd* [2011] HCA 45, [3]–[5] (Gummow, Heydon and Bell JJ). However, the precise status of *Jireh* is uncertain. It was the disposition of a special leave application only, and so lacks the formal status of binding precedent: see D Wong and B Michael, 'Western Export Services v Jireh International: Ambiguity as the Gateway to Surrounding Circumstances?' (2012) 86 *Australian Law Journal* 57. Before *Jireh*, Australian High Court dicta seemed *not* to require ambiguity or uncertainty of meaning as a precondition for introducing extrinsic evidence. Examples include: *Codelfa Construction Pty Ltd v State Rail Authority of NSW* (1982) 149 CLR 337, 352 (Mason J); *Toll (FGCT) Pty Ltd v Alphapharm Pty Ltd* (2004) 219 CLR 165, [40]; *Pacific Carriers Ltd v BNP Paribas* (2004) 218 CLR 451, 461–62; *International Air Transport Association v Ansett Australia Holdings Ltd* (2008) 234 CLR 151, [8] and [54]. From these dicta, a number of Australian intermediate appellate courts assumed that ambiguity or uncertainty of meaning was not a precondition for introducing extrinsic evidence. But *Jireh* has influenced Australian intermediate appellate courts to adopt the more conservative approach of rejecting extrinsic evidence in the absence of ambiguity or uncertainty: eg, *McCourt v Cranston* [2012] WASCA 60, [23]; M Walton, 'Where now Ambiguity?' (2011) 35 *Australian Bar Review* 176.

[34] *Milano's Dining Room & Lounge* (1989) *Ltd v CTDC No 1 Alberta Ltd* (1994) 19 Alta LR (3d) 171 (Alta QB); *Ahluwalia v Richmond Cabs Ltd* [1996] 1 WWR 656 (BCCA).

[35] *Vector Gas Ltd v Bay of Plenty Energy Ltd* [2010] NZSC 5.

[36] *Analog Devices v Zurich Insurance* Co [2005] IESC 12; *Emo Oil Ltd v Sun Alliance & London Insurance* Co [2009] IESC 2; *McCabe Builders v Sagamu Developments* [2009] IESC 31.

[37] *Masstores (Pty) Ltd v Murray & Roberts Construction Pty Ltd* 2008 (6) SA 654 (SCA).

[38] These developments are discussed in the Scottish Law Commission's Discussion Paper No 147, *Review of Contract Law Discussion Paper on Interpretation of Contract* (February 2011) paras [4.6]ff.

[39] *Commonwealth v State of New South Wales* (1918) 25 CLR 325, 342; *Hemmes Hermitage Pty Ltd v Abdurahman* (1991) 22 NSWLR 343, 344–45; *Peldan v Anderson* (2006) 227 CLR 471, [20].

the register is seen as the central repository of information about that title. A fundamental premise is the conclusiveness of the register. As was famously said of the Torrens system: 'The cardinal principle of the [legislation] is that the Register is everything'.[40] In short, the register is both conclusive and exhaustive.

These registration systems conventionally provide for the registration of easements. This leads us to a crucial issue: does the nature of registration preclude recourse to the physical circumstances—or indeed, recourse to any evidence outside the register—when interpreting an easement?

Early Decisions

Initially, the answer seemed to be 'no'. Going beyond the register was seen as inevitable if the court is to glean the parties' intentions at the time of the grant.[41] A clear statement of this approach is that of McHugh J in the Australian High Court in *Gallagher v Rainbow*.[42] In his view, the principles of construction that apply to the grant of an easement at common law apply equally to the grant of an easement over Torrens title land. Other Australian decisions were to the same effect.[43] However, all that has changed with the decision of the Australian High Court in *Westfield Management Ltd v Perpetual Trustee Co*.[44]

The *Westfield* Case

The Facts

In the middle of the central business district of Sydney, Australia, runs a pedestrian mall, known as the Pitt Street Mall. Until the 1980s, it was a busy road, Pitt Street. In the 1980s, the owner of a city building around the corner from Pitt Street granted a right of way over part of the building's basement (the servient tenement) to provide subterranean access to the

---

[40] *Fels v Knowles* (1906) 26 NZLR 604, 620; *Waimiha Sawmilling Co Ltd v Waione Timber Co Ltd* [1926] AC 101, 106 (PC). Both of these cases dealt with the Torrens system as introduced into New Zealand.

[41] *S S & M Ceramics Pty Ltd v Kin* [1996] 2 Qd R 540, 548 (McPherson JA); *Yip v Frolich* (2004) 89 SASR 467, 480.

[42] *Gallagher v Rainbow* (1994) 179 CLR 624, 629–30.

[43] Eg, *Finlayson v Campbell* (1997) 8 BPR 15,703, 15,707; *Middleton v Arthur* (2002) 11 BPR 20, 263, [27]; *Kyren Pty Ltd v Cinema Place Pty Ltd* [2006] SASC 93, [81].

[44] *Westfield Management Ltd v Perpetual Trustee Co Ltd* [2007] HCA 45, (2007) 233 CLR 528. Discussions of *Westfield* include: L Griggs, 'To and From—but not Across: The High Court—Easements, Torrens and Doctrinal Purity' (2008) 15 *Australian Property Law Journal* 260; M Weir, 'The Westfield Case: A Change for the Better?' (2009) 21 *Bond Law Review*, issue 2, article 10.

basement of an adjoining building (the dominant tenement), which fronted Pitt Street. The right of way was in these terms:

> *Full and free right of carriageway for* the grantee its successors in title and registered proprietors for the time being of an estate or interest in possession of *the land herein indicated as the lots benefited or any part thereof* with which the rights shall be capable of enjoyment and every person authorised by it, *to go, pass and repass* at all times and *for all purposes* with vehicles *to and from the said lots benefited* or any such part thereof *across the lots burdened* (emphasis added).

The self-evident purpose of the grant was to give the owner of the dominant tenement underground access to its property, so that it would no longer need vehicular access at Pitt Street level. This was in line with the City Council's plans to make Pitt Street a pedestrian mall. The grantor had in mind that the right of way might also provide subterranean access to the basements of two other properties which lay beyond the dominant tenement. Those remoter properties were at that time owned by third parties, but the grantor hoped that the prospect of this linked underground access might persuade the Council to look favourably on the grantor's wish to increase the allowable floor space of its (the grantor's) building. The grantor even wrote to the Council and to the third parties, raising the possibility of this extended underground access. However, the grantor apparently did not raise this possibility with the grantee of the easement. And, importantly, the easement as granted made no reference to this possibility. It was expressed merely as a right of carriageway to 'pass and repass at all times and for all purposes' to and from the dominant tenement.

Later, the dominant and servient owners sold their respective tenements. Later again, the new owner of the dominant tenement acquired the two other properties. It then claimed the right to access these additional properties from the dominant tenement, using the easement, and thus arose the issue: could the dominant owner use the right of way to access also the remoter properties?

Decision at First Instance

The trial judge held that the owner of the dominant tenement could access the remoter properties via the easement.[45] He based his decision on what (in his view) the parties to the grant of the easement—and certainly the grantor—must have contemplated as permissible use under the easement. He found that the grantor had contemplated that the dominant tenement would be used for access to the remoter properties, even if not immediately; and, against these background circumstances, he held that the wording of the easement was appropriate to give effect to that intention.

---

[45] *Westfield Management Ltd v Perpetual Trustee Co Ltd* [2006] NSWSC 716 (Brereton J).

Court of Appeal

The New South Wales Court of Appeal reversed this decision.[46] Speaking for the Court, Hodgson JA held that in construing the grant of an easement, the Court was entitled—indeed, compelled—to take into account the circumstances surrounding the grant. However, wide statements in some authorities that a court construes the grant so as to enable the easement to be used in the manner contemplated by the parties at the time of the grant were to be applied with care. Considering what was 'contemplated by the parties' was *not* a separate exercise from construing the grant itself. No separate investigation was permissible into the use subjectively contemplated by the parties.[47] In particular, it was not appropriate to admit evidence of what was subjectively known to one party alone. Rather, what must be found is 'the intention of both parties as manifested by the grant'.[48]

Turning then to the registered instrument itself: did it manifest an intention to extend the benefit of the easement to properties remoter than the dominant tenement? The normal rule, of course, is that a grant of easement does not extend the benefit to remoter properties. For this, *Harris v Flower*[49] is generally cited. In particular, the general 'rule' as stated by Romer LJ in that case is generally cited: 'If a right of way be granted for the enjoyment of close A, the grantee, because he owns or acquires close B, cannot use the way in substance for passing over close A to close B'.[50]

Now, this general 'rule' has exceptions. But always the use authorised by an easement must be for the benefit of the dominant tenement. In those decisions where courts have interpreted easements as permitting access to properties additional to the dominant tenement, the additional use remained beneficial to the dominant tenement.[51] On the facts of *Westfield*, Hodgson JA was satisfied that the extended use to remoter properties was not for the benefit of the dominant tenement. A potential benefit might have been the right to extract a toll payment from persons using the dominant tenement to access the remoter properties;[52] but nothing in the admissible evidence suggested that a benefit of that kind was anticipated. Another benefit might

---

[46] *Perpetual Trustee Co Ltd v Westfield Management Ltd* [2006] NSWCA 337, (2007) 12 BPR 23,793, [2007] NSW ConvR 56–170.

[47] Ibid, [27].

[48] Ibid, [26], [34].

[49] *Harris v Flower* (1904) 74 LJ Ch 127 (CA).

[50] Ibid, 132.

[51] As in *Shean Pty Ltd v Owners of Corinne Court* (2001) 25 WAR 65, [2001] WASCA 311, where the dominant tenement (Lot 19) was an office block. Persons visiting that office block by car passed over a right of way to Lot 19 and then parked their cars on another lot (Lot 20). The Western Australian Court of Appeal held that this was within the purpose of the grant of the right of way. The right of way had been granted 'for all purposes connected with the use and enjoyment of' Lot 19, and those who parked on Lot 20 did so only for the purpose of visiting Lot 19.

[52] *Perpetual Trustee Co Ltd v Westfield Management Ltd* [2006] NSWCA 337, [48], [50].

have been some kind of bargaining tool with the Council for planning concessions; but any evidence of that was inadmissible. In short, the trial judge had erred in '[looking] for the intention or contemplation of the parties outside what was manifested by the grant itself'.[53]

High Court

The owner of the dominant tenement then appealed further, to the High Court. The High Court affirmed the Court of Appeal's decision.[54] The High Court's close analysis of the terms of the easement drew out three main points.

First, the easement spoke only of access 'to and from' the benefited land, not 'across' the benefited land—in particular, it did not speak of access 'across' the benefited land to get to some other land. (In contrast, the easement spoke of access 'across' the burdened land.) If the parties had intended the grant to authorise others to go across the dominant tenement to further properties, they could easily have added the words 'and across'.[55]

Secondly, the easement was expressed to be 'for all purposes'. But this of itself did not authorise a use for the benefit of properties beyond the dominant tenement. Rather, it meant for all purposes within the limitation (common to all easements) of conferring some benefit on the dominant tenement (as distinct from merely a personal benefit on the owner of the dominant tenement).[56]

Thirdly, when construing an easement, the 'starting point' is that a right of way may be used only for access to the dominant tenement. That starting point can yield to another construction. But on the terms of this easement it did not. In addition to the key words quoted above, the Court considered the provisions in the easement governing obligations to repair and to insure, for the easement cast many of these obligations on the servient owner. This would make it 'unduly burdensome' on the servient owner if access were to be allowed to remoter properties.

Crucially, the High Court made some telling general points about the admissibility of extrinsic evidence in the construction of easements. The conventional view (as we have seen) was that, in construing an easement one may look to the circumstances surrounding the grant—as in *Cannon v Villars*.[57] The High Court noted McHugh J's remark, mentioned above,

---

[53] Ibid, [69].

[54] *Westfield Management Ltd v Perpetual Trustee Co Ltd* [2007] HCA 45; (2007) 233 CLR 528.

[55] Ibid, [18], approving *Westfield Management Ltd v Perpetual Trustee Co Ltd* [2006] NSWCA 337, [65].

[56] *Westfield Management Ltd v Perpetual Trustee Co Ltd* [2007] HCA 45, [19]–[30].

[57] *Cannon v Villars* (1878) 8 Ch D 415, 420 (Ch D).

that this principle applied in construing easements over Torrens title land.[58] However, the High Court disagreed: McHugh J's statement was 'too widely expressed' in relation to Torrens land. Torrens title depended on a public register. A central aim of the Torrens system was that a person enquiring about the extent of an easement registered on the title should not have to resort to extrinsic information to establish facts or circumstances existing at the time the easement was created.[59] This rendered inadmissible detailed evidence of what might have been in the contemplation of the parties to the grant of the easement, except to the extent that it was reflected in the terms of the easement itself.

The Court made one concession to the admissibility of extrinsic information when interpreting an easement: it is possible to call evidence to explain what the Registrar means by terms and expressions found in the register (for example, the surveying terms and abbreviations which appear in registered plans).[60] But beyond that, the Court gave no further hint.

Australian Cases on Easements Post-*Westfield*

The High Court's discussion of the 'Torrens title point' in *Westfield* was relatively brief. But of course when the highest court in the land opines on a topic, even briefly, lower courts must take notice. And so it has been in later Australian cases on the interpretation of registered easements. Later cases have consistently rejected evidence about what the parties to the grant of an easement actually intended, unless that intention can be deduced from the terms of the grant itself viewed in the light of the limited additional evidence allowed by the High Court in *Westfield*.

Sertari Pty Ltd v Nirimba Developments Pty Ltd[61]

A right of way provided access to a former airfield, comprising some 550 acres. The right of way was expressed in wide, general terms: 'full and free right ... to go, pass along and re-pass at all times ... with or without vehicles ... both to or from the said dominant tenement or any part thereof'. Unusually, the terms of the easement threw the cost of maintaining the easement onto the owner of the servient land. The dominant owner proposed developing its land for residential purposes, comprising 236 units and parking for 351 vehicles. This would greatly increase the traffic on the

---

[58] *Gallagher v Rainbow* (1994) 179 CLR 624, 639–40.
[59] *Westfield Management Ltd v Perpetual Trustee Co Ltd* [2007] HCA 45, [5], [37], [39].
[60] Ibid, [44].
[61] *Sertari Pty Ltd v Nirimba Developments Pty Ltd* [2007] NSWCA 324, [2008] NSW Conv R 56–200.

servient land; it would also increase the maintenance costs on the servient land. The servient owner claimed that the increased use was inconsistent with the purposes for which the easement was granted and was therefore impermissible. However, the New South Wales Court of Appeal held that the increased use was permissible.

The Court of Appeal considered that the High Court's decision in *Westfield* required that, in construing an easement, courts are limited to '[1] the material in the folio identifiers,[62] [2] the registered instrument [of easement], [3] the deposited plans, and [4] the physical characteristics of the tenements' (numbers added).[63] If one may interpolate here, the material in items [1], [2] and [3] is found in Australian Torrens registers; the material in item [4] is not. These four heads of admissible evidence would not include, for example, evidence such as planners' reports and the terms of development consents—evidence that might otherwise throw light on the purpose of an easement. On the facts, the Court held that the admissible material provided no justification for reading down the wide, general terms of the easement.

The reference to the court being able to take into account *the physical characteristics of the tenements* (item [4]) has been repeated in later first instance decisions.[64] However, it may go further than the evidence the High Court would regard as admissible. The High Court in *Westfield* made no mention of the 'physical characteristics' of the land. What the High Court did say was that the permissible user under a registered easement 'may change with the nature of the dominant tenement'.[65] But that was in the context of a different principle, namely, that generally an easement remains exercisable even though the use of the dominant tenement may change—as where a right of way remains exercisable for its expressed purpose even though the residence to which it originally led is later converted to an hotel[66] or where the farm to which it originally led is converted to a caravan park.[67] The High Court was not, it is suggested, allowing back into the centrality-of-registration principle an exception that reference can be

---

[62] This term is used in the New South Wales Torrens legislation to mean, in effect, the certificate of title to the land.

[63] *Sertari Pty Ltd v Nirimba Developments Pty Ltd* [2007] NSWCA 324, [16].

[64] eg, *Neighbourhood Association DP No 285220 v Moffat* [2008] NSWSC 54, [41]; *Van Brugge v Hare* [2011] NSWSC 1364, [33]–[36].

[65] *Westfield Management Ltd v Perpetual Trustee Co Ltd* [2007] HCA 45, [42].

[66] *White v Grand Hotel, Eastbourne, Ltd* [1913] Ch 113, 116 (CA).

[67] *British Railways Board v Glass* [1965] Ch 538 (CA). Australian cases on this point include: *Finlayson v Campbell* (1997) 8 BPR 15,703 (grantee of right of way 'for all purposes' not confined to using the way for purposes prevailing at the time of the grant, but could use it for any reasonable different purpose); *Timpar Nominees Pty Ltd v Archer* [2001] WASCA 430, [37].

made to the physical circumstances at the time of the grant, or the physical circumstances at the time of the dispute between the parties.[68]

Neighbourhood Association DP No 285220 v Moffat[69]

A registered easement was expressed to be 'for pipeline and irrigation'. The site of the easement was 100 metres long and one metre wide, leading from the dominant tenement to an area within the servient tenement. It was clear from background material—if admissible—that the parties to the grant of the easement intended it for pumping sewage from the dominant tenement and discharging it onto the servient tenement. Also, a licence issued by an environmental authority—if admissible—showed that the easement was for that purpose. However, the judge held that *Westfield* precluded recourse to the parties' subjective intent or the environmental licence. The easement was to be construed solely from its own terms. Happily for the dominant owner, the express terms of the easement sufficiently indicated that the purpose was to discharge *water* onto the servient tenement, and this would include both potable and waste water—and so would include effluent from a sewage system constructed on the dominant land.

Berryman v Sonnenschein[70]

A registered right of way provided steep vehicular access across the servient tenement and up to the dominant tenement. The owner of the dominant tenement planned to improve the access by constructing a turning circle where the right of way reached his property. The judge held that the right to construct a turning circle in these circumstances was a right ancillary to the easement. He rejected (on *Westfield* grounds) evidence that the grantor had stated, at the time of the original subdivision, that no turning circle was intended for the right of way.[71]

Van Brugge v Hare[72]

A registered right of way gave a right of use 'with or without vehicles'. The right of way had been granted after the installation on the servient tenement of an inclinator, which provided access to the residences on both servient and dominant tenements down a steep cliff face. No other convenient

---

[68] This more limited view of the High Court's comment on this point seems to be accepted (correctly, in my view) in *Davison v Elkington* [2011] WASC 29, [30].
[69] *Neighbourhood Association DP No 285220 v Moffat* [2008] NSWSC 54.
[70] *Berryman v Sonnenschein* [2008] NSWSC 213.
[71] Ibid, [30].
[72] *Van Brugge v Hare* [2011] NSWSC 1364.

access was available. The inclinator was the only 'vehicle' that could possibly use the right of way. The servient owner argued that the dominant owner needed his consent to use of the inclinator, because this 'vehicle' (and its infrastructure) was a fixture on the servient tenement and so belonged to the servient owner—and you cannot use another person's vehicle without their consent. The judge rejected this argument. The dominant owner was entitled to use the easement according to its terms, which required no consent to use. He held (following *Westfield*) that evidence of the parties' actual use of the easement was inadmissible—regardless of whether that use was before, at the time of, or after the grant of the easement.[73] But evidence was admissible of the physical nature of the site (steep and sloping), pointing to the intended 'vehicle' as the inclinator. In his view, *Westfield* allowed evidence of the physical circumstances of the site.[74]

Chick v Dockray[75]

The question was whether the dominant owner was entitled to exit from a registered right of way before reaching its end point, so as to reach the dominant tenement by crossing other land that he owned. The early exit point was necessary because a substantial land slip on the right of way some years ago had blocked access along its full length. The servient owner claimed that this 'truncated' use of the right of way was not permitted, and sought to block the dominant owner from exiting the easement at the early point. He sought to rely on evidence that this truncated use was not within the contemplation of the parties to the grant of the easement. Specifically, he sought to show that when the easement was created, the owner of the dominant tenement did not own the land onto which he would pass if leaving the right of way at the early exit point (and so would be trespassing), and that the landslip had not then occurred. The Tasmanian Full Court held that the dominant owner was entitled to divert from the right of way at the early point. Under the doctrine of indefeasibility of title, a third party inspecting the register was not expected to look for extrinsic material which might establish facts or circumstances existing at the time of the creation of the easement.[76] *Westfield* established that the only admissible extrinsic evidence in interpreting a registered easement was that necessary to make sense of terms or expressions identified in the register, such as surveying terms or abbreviations that appear on a plan.[77] This meant that evidence was not admissible to show that, at the time of the creation of the easement,

---

[73] Ibid, [31].
[74] Ibid, [33]–[35], [40], [46], [47].
[75] *Chick v Dockray* [2011] TASFC 1.
[76] Ibid, [19], [20].
[77] Ibid, [20].

the now-owner of the dominant tenement did not own the diversion land and that the landslip had not occurred. The language of the grant of easement was paramount; and nothing in that language suggested that the owner of the dominant tenement could not exit the right of way somewhere along its length in order to reach the dominant tenement via a diversion.

Kitching v Phillips[78]

A Western Australian council imposed a planning condition on a residential subdivision that the developer was to set aside part of the land (lot 81) for dog-training uses. The purchasers of a parcel of land (lot 61) in the subdivision assumed that they would have dog-training rights over lot 81. However, for some reason the Council's dog-training condition was never implemented, and the title to lot 81 bore no reference to any dog-training uses binding the land. The developer sold lot 81 to a purchaser, who later on-sold part to another person. The owners of lot 61 claimed an easement for dog-training purposes over the on-sold part of lot 81. They based their claim on common law or equitable principles under which easements can arise from the circumstances surrounding the transfer of land (such as under the principle of non-derogation from grant, or the implication of terms into contracts). However, to establish an easement under these principles would require evidence of the circumstances surrounding the transfer to them of lot 61. The Western Australian Court of Appeal held that these circumstances were inadmissible in interpreting the transfer to them: extrinsic evidence of matters known to the purchasers and the developer could not be used to aid the interpretation of a registered transfer. Nothing on the face of the registered transfer justified the implication of an easement of the kind alleged.[79]

Fermora Pty Ltd v Kelvedon Pty Ltd[80]

A registered easement provided for the discharge of treated waste water from an abattoir on the dominant tenement onto the neighbouring servient tenement. The easement specified that that 'the rights and easements created by *the Deed* and this Grant of Easement' (italics added) would be surrendered if the benefited land ceased to be used as an abattoir. The reference to 'the Deed' was a reference to a separate, unregistered deed made between the parties on the same day as the formal grant of the easement. Unfortunately, the terms in the Deed about surrender of the easement differed somewhat from the terms in the registered easement. That raised

---

[78]   *Kitching v Phillips* [2011] WASCA 19.
[79]   Ibid, [68].
[80]   *Fermora Pty Ltd v Kelvedon Pty Ltd* [2011] WASC 281.

the question: were the terms in the Deed admissible in the interpreting the registered easement? Certainly, under normal principles of interpretation they would have been admissible, as the provisions of the Deed would be regarded as incorporated by reference into the provisions of the easement. But the land here was under the Torrens system, and the easement was registered. The judge held that this made all the difference. Under *Westfield* principles, the contents of the unregistered deed were inadmissible. Unregistered documents could not be allowed to add to, amend or alter rights in a registered document.[81] Therefore, the unregistered deed was inadmissible in interpreting the indefeasible rights contained in the registered deed.

THE EXTENSION OF *WESTFIELD* BEYOND EASEMENTS

The above cases show the growth of something of a '*Westfield* industry' in the interpretation of registered easements in Australia. They demonstrate a substantial narrowing of the kinds of evidence that would traditionally be admitted in interpreting easements. Logically, however, there is no reason to limit *Westfield* to the interpretation of *easements*. At the basis of *Westfield* lies a concern over the conclusiveness of the land register. A person should be able to find, by a search of the register, all that is needed to understand the rights granted by registered interests. Thus, the *Westfield* principle should apply in the interpretation of registered instruments of any kind.

And so it has proved to be. Australian judges have applied *Westfield* not merely to the interpretation of registered easements, but to the interpretation other kinds of registered instruments.

Restrictive Covenants

Miller v Evans[82]

A restrictive covenant, recorded on the title to residential land in Perth, Western Australia, limited the height of 'buildings' on the land. The servient owner built a retaining wall which was higher than the allowable height (and which obstructed water views from the dominant tenement). Was the retaining wall a 'building' for the purposes of the covenant? The parties agreed that the test was: what would a reasonable person

---

[81] Ibid, [40].
[82] *Miller v Evans* [2010] WASC 127.

understand from the language used in the covenant, having regard to the objective surrounding circumstances and the purpose and object of the document.[83] There was evidence that the original covenantee's advisers intended the covenant to regulate fences, not retaining walls. However, the judge held that *Westfield* precluded reference to subjective intentions at the time of creation of the covenant. The covenant used the general term 'building', and nothing in the admissible evidence warranted giving the term a restricted meaning. The term included a retaining wall. The covenant had been breached, and the wall should be lowered to the height allowed by the covenant.[84]

Prowse v Johnstone[85]

A restrictive covenant, recorded on title, prohibited the erection of 'more than one house' on the burdened land. The owner of the burdened land wished to demolish the existing large house on the land and erect a single building containing 18 residential apartments. Would this breach the covenant? The burdened land was a lot in a subdivision; the covenant referred to the registered plan of subdivision; that plan was obtainable by searching the public (Torrens) register; and a search would show that all the other lots in the subdivision were affected by similar covenants. There was no departure from *Westfield* in taking these other covenants into account in deducing that the purpose of the covenant was to preserve the quality of the subdivision.[86] In that context, this proposed building was not a 'house' within the meaning of the covenant.

Leases

Phoenix Commercial Enterprises Pty Ltd v City of Canada Bay Council[87]

In New South Wales, local councils are planning authorities, whose consent is needed for the erection of structures in the municipality. A council granted to a tenant a registered lease for the erection of several large roadside advertising billboards. The lease entitled the tenant to a reduction in

---

[83] As expressed in the Australian High Court's decision in *Toll (FGCT) Pty Ltd v Alphafarm Pty Ltd* (2004) 219 CLR 165.

[84] An appeal to the Court of Appeal was dismissed, though it turned not on the interpretation of the covenant but on the judge's exercise of discretion to order the demolition the offending structure: *Evans v Miller* [2011] WASCA 89.

[85] *Prowse v Johnstone* [2012] VSC 4.

[86] Ibid, [58]–[59].

[87] *Phoenix Commercial Enterprises Pty Ltd v City of Canada Bay Council* [2010] NSWCA 64.

rent if the council, in its capacity as consent authority, later granted other persons the right to erect 'general advertising structures'. The Council later granted to another company permission to erect bus shelters that were designed to accommodate advertising structures. This raised the issue: were the bus shelters 'general advertising structures'? The lease did not define the term. Was it permissible to go outside the registered lease to admit evidence of the meaning of the term?

Campbell JA (with whom Spigelman CJ and Handley AJA, in separate judgments, essentially agreed) drew attention to the 'modern' view that the interpretation of a document involves considering not only the text of the document, but the surrounding circumstances known to the contracting parties, and to the purpose of the transaction.[88] Applying those considerations to leases, the 'background circumstances' that a reader would understand as relevant would include the fact that a lease is to endure for a long time, is assignable, is to be registered under the Torrens system and may well on occasions need to be understood and acted on by people other than the original parties to its creation.[89]

However, *Westfield* limits the admissible surrounding circumstances to those 'that one can know without evidence from outside the terms of the document itself'.[90] How, then, could one decide the meaning of 'general advertising structures' without going outside the terms of the lease, when the lease itself did not define or explain the term? The answer (Campbell JA held) was to be found in the regulatory framework in which the lease was drawn. That framework was part of the background that a reasonable reader would understand as relevant to interpreting the document. The statutory concept of 'general advertising structure' was thus relevant and admissible in interpreting the term in this lease. And that meaning was to be found in the Council's planning ordinances, for the lease clearly contemplated Council's power to approve structures when acting in its capacity as consent authority. Therefore, the expression *'general advertising structure'* was to be given the meaning it had in the relevant planning instrument; and that meaning would include the bus shelters.[91]

---

[88] Citing *Reardon Smith Line Ltd v Hansen-Tangen* [1976] 1 WLR 989, and *Pacific Carriers Ltd v BNP Paribas* (2004) 218 CLR 451.

[89] *Phoenix Commercial Enterprises Pty Ltd v City of Canada Bay Council* [2010] NSWCA 64, [154].

[90] Ibid, [166].

[91] Ibid, [185]. See also *Alliance Engineering Pty Ltd v Yarraburn Nominees Pty Ltd* [2011] NSWCA 301, where the New South Wales Court of Appeal held that evidence of the legislative framework of a lease of a hotel was admissible to show that hotels commonly carried poker machine licences.

Springrange Pty Ltd v Australian Capital Territory & ACT Planning and Land Authority[92]

An assignee of long-term registered lease proposed developing the leased site in accordance with a provision in the lease. The provision left it unclear whether the assignee could redevelop only the existing building, or redevelop the entire site by adding additional buildings. The court held that the former construction was correct.[93] In construing the lease, *Westfield* rendered inadmissible extrinsic material which might cast light on the intention of the original parties to the lease.[94] This included even ignoring the nature and presence of the existing building at the time the lease was granted.[95] The answer had to be found by construing the lease terms alone.

Westfield and the Limits of Indefeasibility

The Issue

Does the *Westfield* principle apply to *all* provisions of registered instruments, or only to some? The question arises because, by well-established Australian case law, the conclusive effect of registration does not necessarily attach to all aspects of a registered instrument; rather, it attaches only to those covenants or provisions that are so intimately connected with the estate or interest created by the registered instrument that they are to be regarded as part of that estate or interest.[96]

This has led an Australian appellate judge to suggest that extrinsic circumstances might yet play a part in the construction of those provisions in a registered instrument that cannot be regarded as intimately connected to the estate or interest in land created by the instrument.[97] The rationale seems to be that since those provisions do not enjoy the conclusiveness of the register—that is, do not confer indefeasibility—then evidence beyond the register, if otherwise admissible on general grounds, is admissible in construing those provisions. If correct, this suggestion would introduce significant difficulty into the interpretation of registered

---

[92] *Springrange Pty Ltd v Australian Capital Territory & ACT Planning and Land Authority* [2010] ACTCA 17.
[93] Ibid, [44].
[94] Ibid, [12].
[95] Ibid, [47].
[96] *Mercantile Credits Ltd v Shell Co of Australia Ltd* [1976] HCA 9, 136 CLR 326, 343 (Gibbs J); *PT Ltd v Maradona Pty Ltd* (1992) 25 NSWLR 643, 679 (Giles J); *Perpetual Trustees Victoria Ltd v English* [2010] NSWCA 32, [68], [92]–[98] (Sackville AJA) (with whom Allsop P and Campbell JA agreed).
[97] *Alliance Engineering Pty Ltd v Yarraburn Nominees Pty Ltd* [2011] NSWCA 301, [54] (Sackville AJA).

instruments. Courts would be required, first, to determine which aspects of a registered instrument conferred indefeasibility and which did not; and then, secondly, to exclude extrinsic evidence when interpreting the indefeasibility-conferring part of the instrument, but admit it when interpreting other aspects of the instrument. This seems, with respect, a step too complex.

An Illustration: Restrictive Covenants

The issue would be particularly acute in the case of restrictive covenants. In most Australian Torrens statutes, restrictive covenants are not 'registered', but merely 'recorded'. Recording a restrictive covenant in the register does not warrant its efficacy in the way that the indefeasibility of title provisions of the statutes warrant the efficacy of registered dealings.[98] A restrictive covenant stands or falls by its own inherent efficacy, tested by the general principles concerning the validity and enforceability of restrictive covenants. And the application of those general principles invariably requires going beyond the register.

An area of particular difficulty is the relationship between indefeasibility and the need to establish the existence of a common building scheme (or scheme of development). Proof of the existence of a common building scheme requires evidence of circumstances attending the sale of the lots in the subdivision.[99] In *Re Martyn*,[100] the New South Wales Full Supreme Court held that a deficiency in identifying the land allegedly benefited by a restrictive covenant could not be overcome by recourse to the extrinsic fact of a scheme of development. Behind the decision lay the premise that rights and obligations over Torrens title land cannot be allowed to arise by implication from material extraneous to the register. On the contrary, the register must contain the information necessary to enable a person who searches the title to become aware of the nature and extent of the restrictive covenant, and must refer in some way to the circumstances on which the enforceability of the covenant depends.[101]

However, in *Re Louis and the Conveyancing Act*[102] the majority of a differently constituted New South Wales Court of Appeal reached a somewhat different conclusion. The Court held that schemes of development can exist over Torrens title land, provided the instruments which create them express on their face the *intention* to confer the benefit of the restrictive covenants

---

[98] *Re Louis and the Conveyancing Act* [1971] 1 NSWLR 164, 181; *Pirie v Registrar-General* (1962) 109 CLR 619, 642.
[99] *Elliston v Reacher* [1908] 2 Ch 374 (CA).
[100] *Re Martyn* (1965) 65 SR (NSW) 387.
[101] Ibid, 396.
[102] *Re Louis and the Conveyancing Act* [1971] 1 NSWLR 164.

on every part of the land in the scheme.[103] The court can then go behind the register to find the facts that would establish the existence of the scheme. The premise behind this conclusion was that the operation of restrictive covenants must depend ultimately on the general principles governing their enforceability; and some of these principles require information beyond the confines of the register. For example, to establish whether a restrictive covenant benefits the dominant land, it is necessary to enquire into such matters as whether the land expressed to be benefited is too large to be benefited, a factual enquiry that may require evidence not only of the area of the land, but also of its topographical features.[104] Again, it may be necessary to establish that the distance between benefited and burdened parcels is not too great to preclude actual benefit from the covenant.[105] Enquiries of that kind may require a search beyond the register, seeking the facts needed to establish validity of the covenant. To that extent at least, extrinsic information would be admissible.

WHAT MIGHT ENGLISH COURTS DO WITH *WESTFIELD*?

The Issue

We now come to the crux of the matter for English courts: what to do with *Westfield*? While Australian courts traditionally apply English decisions— even though no longer bound to do so—rarely do English courts apply Australian decisions.[106] The traffic is mostly one-way. But Australia and England (including for these purposes, Wales) now have land registration systems with similar features. The English Land Registration Act 2002 reflects many of the concepts found in the Australian Torrens system. A key concept is that registration confers a title that is essentially immune from defects in the anterior title—what Australians call an 'indefeasible' title. Another, related, concept is that the register is central and conclusive. If the English system's reliance on the register as the repository of key information about title is similar to that of the Australian Torrens system, then it ought to follow that the *Westfield* logic—specifically, the Australian High Court's views about the non-admissibility of evidence beyond the register—should appeal to English courts.

---

[103] Ibid, 177–82.

[104] As in *Re Ballard's Conveyance* [1937] Ch 473 (Ch D); *Lane Cove Municipal Council v H & W Hurdis Pty Ltd* (1955) 55 SR (NSW) 434.

[105] As in *Baramon Sales Pty Ltd v Goodman Fielder Mills Ltd* [2001] FCA 1672.

[106] There are of course notable exceptions: eg, *Radaich v Smith* (1959) 101 CLR 209 on the importance of exclusive possession in the law of leases, followed in *Street v Mountford* [1985] 1 AC 809 (HL).

Cherry Tree v Landmain

In fact, English courts are now beginning to see the parallels. This is seen starkly in the English Court of Appeal decision in *Cherry Tree Investments Ltd v Landmain Ltd*.[107] It involved a registered charge over land. Under s 101 of the Law of Property Act 1925, a power of sale was implied into the charge, but only if the borrower had defaulted in payment. The same section allows the power of sale to be varied by the deed of charge. The lender and borrower had indeed agreed to vary the terms of the power of sale, to make it exercisable even without default; but they had done so by a side agreement (called a 'facility agreement') which remained *un*registered. The variation should have been included in the (registered) deed of charge—but it was not. This raised the question of whether the court should take into account the unregistered facility agreement in interpreting the registered deed of charge.[108]

In a magisterial but dissenting judgment, Arden LJ held that the unregistered facility agreement could be taken into account in interpreting the registered deed. To use the language we have adopted so far, 'extrinsic evidence' (namely, the terms of the unregistered document) was admissible in interpreting the registered document. Relevant extrinsic evidence was admissible when interpreting a registered document, as long as the interpretation reached by its use would not prejudice the rights of third parties.[109] On the facts (which we need not canvass in more detail) Arden LJ concluded that no third party's rights would be affected by admitting this evidence.

However, the majority (Lewison and Longmore LJJ) held that the unregistered facility agreement was *not* admissible in interpreting the registered deed. For Lewison LJ, a key consideration was the Land Registration Act 2002. The purpose of that Act was to create a system where the register was 'a complete and accurate reflection of the state of the title at any given time, so that it is possible to investigate title on line, with the absolute minimum of additional enquiries and inspections'.[110] Title was conferred by registration, and registration alone. Further, section 120(2) of the Act required the registered instrument to be presumed both to be correct and to contain all the material parts of the document. Despite the occasional differences between the Land Registration Act 2002 and the Australian Torrens system, the approach taken by the Australian High Court in *Westfield*

---

[107] *Cherry Tree Investments Ltd v Landmain Ltd* [2012] EWCA Civ 736.
[108] No claim was made for rectification of the registered deed.
[109] *Cherry Tree Investments Ltd v Landmain Ltd* [2012] EWCA Civ 736, [36], [39], [41], [54], [56].
[110] Ibid, [105], quoting from the Law Commission Report No 271, *Land Registration for the Twenty-First Century: A Conveyancing Revolution* (2001) para 1.5.

ought to be followed in England.[111] Indeed, for Lewison LJ there was no conflict between this approach and the principles in *Investors Compensation Scheme*. This was because the question remained: what weight would the reasonable person with all the background knowledge of the parties attribute to background material which did not appear on the face of the charge itself? The reasonable person's background knowledge would include, said Lewison LJ, knowledge that the charge would be registered in a public register, that the registered document was to be taken to contain all the material terms, and that matters which the parties chose to keep private should not influence the parts of the bargain which they chose to make public.[112]

This is remarkably similar to the approach of Campbell JA in the New South Wales Court of Appeal in *Phoenix Commercial Enterprises Pty Ltd v City of Canada Bay Council*,[113] already noted above. Indeed, Lewison LJ adopted Campbell JA's 'elegant' discussion of the matter.[114] And so, on this general matter of the approach to the interpretation of registered instruments, we may conclude that English and Australian courts are at one.

THE CONTINUED RELEVANCE OF THE PHYSICAL CIRCUMSTANCES EXISTING AT THE TIME OF THE GRANT

Changes in Physical Circumstances

The facts of *Cherry Tree* are, of course, very different from those of *Todrick*. There was in *Cherry Tree* no question of looking to the physical characteristics of the land. Nevertheless, Lewison LJ seemed to contemplate that in cases involving the interpretation of easements, recourse to the physical characteristics would continue to be relevant. Courts (he said) would continue to allow the physical features of the land to influence the interpretation of a transfer or conveyance, because the physical features of land are 'capable of being seen by anyone contemplating dealing with the land and who takes the trouble to inspect'.[115]

That is fine if the physical characteristics of the land remain constant. But the characteristics of land can change. Land is bulldozed, landscaped, developed, consolidated and subdivided; structures on the land are demolished and rebuilt. A third party contemplating dealing with the land today may discern little or no hint of its condition, say, 100 years ago when a right of way was created over it.

---

[111] Ibid, [127].
[112] Ibid, [130].
[113] *Phoenix Commercial Enterprises Pty Ltd v City of Canada Bay Council* [2010] NSWCA 64, [151].
[114] *Cherry Tree Investments Ltd v Landmain Ltd* [2012] EWCA Civ 736, [128], [130].
[115] Ibid, [130].

Take the circumstances of *Todrick* itself. The terms of the easement make no reference to the stone entrance pillars, or to the retaining wall, or to the unmade nature of the laneway. Yet these were all important in the judicial decisions not to permit buses to use the laneway. But the entrance pillars will not remain there forever; they may fall down, or be demolished, or be rebuilt in a different position. The unmade track could be surfaced. The weak retaining wall could be strengthened. Other physical evidence mentioned in the case has indeed disappeared. Thus, the stone wall over which buses would need to pass at the end of the laneway is no longer there; and the dip or gully has been filled in. So a prospective purchaser inspecting the site today may not be able to see some of the physical evidence that swayed the court to read down the extent of permissible use under easement. And unless the prospective purchaser knew of the decision, he or she would be completely unaware of the way the court back in 1934 had interpreted the easement.[116]

An Example

This poses a dilemma. The true meaning of an easement cannot change with later changes in the physical character of the *locus in quo*. To illustrate: consider the grant of a vehicular right of way through a tunnel under a railway line. The right of way would necessarily be limited to the height of the tunnel, even if the grant made no reference to that height. The physical circumstances at the time of the grant would limit the upwards extent of the grant.[117] Now suppose that, some years later, the railway line is removed and the tunnel demolished. The demolition would not remove the height limitation. If the easement was limited at the time of grant, it remains limited—even if a later inspection of the site shows no indication of the former tunnel. The permissible use now *seems* open to the sky, but the grant of easement *means* the same as it meant when first made. So, for example, tall vehicles or cranes could not use the way, as that kind of use could not have been within the (objective) contemplation of the parties at the time of the grant.

Of course, those practical problems have always been present in the interpretation of easements, regardless of whether the easement is registered or not. The introduction of a formal register has not changed this problem. But it has heightened our awareness of a larger problem—one that goes

---

[116] In 2011, the author interviewed the present owner of Dr Todrick's land. She acquired the land by inheritance. Although a lawyer, she was unaware that her land had been the subject of this key case in the 1930s. The present owner of part of the benefited land was aware of the general history of the case, although not of the detailed legal arguments.

[117] An example is an Australian case, where a right of footway was granted over a passageway that was roofed-over. The height of the roof was held to be the maximum height of the right of footway: *Chiu v Healey* (2003) 11 BPR 21, 241, [57].

beyond the mere physical characteristics of the site of the easement. It is the problem of the extent to which *any* circumstances not discoverable on a search of the register, or indeed an inspection of the site, should be allowed to aid the interpretation of the instrument.

Knowledge of Changed Physical Circumstances

Finally, what if the current servient and dominant owners know of information beyond the register that sheds light on the actual intention of the original parties to the grant of the easement? Should it be admitted in interpreting the easement? The conventional approach is to reject it, on the basis that the search for meaning has always been a search for objective meaning: the purpose of interpretation is to seek not what the parties *intended to agree*, but what the instrument *means*.[118] The *Westfield* approach is also to reject it, because it cannot be found on a search of the register. But that seems counter-intuitive if the result is to interpret an easement in a way we know that the parties actually did not intend.[119] As Carnwath LJ has said: 'Where relevant evidence is not available, the court has to do its best on what there is. I cannot see this as a principled reason for excluding such evidence in a case where it is available'.[120]

And so, to return to the example of the railway tunnel: if a person buying the servient or dominant land today in fact had evidence of the existence of the historic tunnel—for example, from old photos or survey reports—then why not use it, even if that information is extrinsic to the register? It seems unrealistic in the extreme to say that you must ignore it, because the current owners *might not* have had access to it. After all, Lord Hoffmann did say that *everything* is admissible, if relevant.

A New Zealand Approach

This brings us, finally, to a leading decision of the New Zealand Court of Appeal: *Big River Paradise Ltd v Congreve*.[121] True to its tradition of careful

---

[118] *Cherry Tree Investments Ltd v Landmain Ltd* [2012] EWCA Civ 736, [99] (Lewison LJ).

[119] It would be reminiscent of the principle of prescription, where the law requires a presumption that a grant was made but has been lost, even though it is clear beyond doubt that no grant was ever in fact made: *Dalton v Angus* (1881) 6 App Cas 740, 765, 767, 813, 814 (HL); *Tehidy Minerals Ltd v Norman* [1971] 2 QB 528, 547–52 (CA); *Golding v Tanner* (1991) 56 SASR 482, 493.

[120] *KPMG LLP v Network Rail Infrastructure Ltd* [2007] EWCA Civ 363, [41].

[121] *Big River Paradise Ltd v Congreve* [2008] NZLR 402. Leave to appeal to the Supreme Court was refused: *Big River Paradise Ltd v Congreve* [2008] NZSC 51.

scrutiny of judicial trends on the other side of the Tasman, that Court expressed reservations about the *Westfield* doctrine.

In *Congreve*, a restrictive covenant precluded the subdivision of the burdened land into more than three separate allotments, with only one dwelling per allotment. The covenant was notified on the Torrens register. The servient owner proposed developing the land by creating 52 leasehold interests; this, he argued, would not be a 'subdivision' in technical sense of that word. The Court of Appeal found that the proposed development was a 'subdivision' in the sense that the parties must have intended. In reaching this conclusion, the Court said that whether *Westfield* should be applied in New Zealand was 'open to question'.[122] The Court said that *Westfield* left some 'unresolved and perhaps troublesome issues'.[123] They were:[124]

a.   Should so narrow an approach as *Westfield* be taken as between the initial parties to a restrictive covenant or easement?
b.   If not, when should the narrow approach kick-in—when one of the original parties sells or when both sell?
c.   What if the subsequent parties are well aware of the relevant extrinsic evidence? For example, what if the extrinsic evidence relates to a particular pattern of use, which (1) existed at the time the document was executed and (2) was continuing when the subsequent party became affected by the easement or restrictive covenant?

These considerations led the Court of Appeal to conclude that the restrictive covenant was to be construed not in the abstract but, at the very least, by reference to the location of the properties which were affected by it. Here the location of the properties—open land, on opposite sides of a large river—showed that the purpose of the covenant was to preserve the benefited land from the adverse effects of intensive development of the burdened land. A division of the burdened land into 52 smaller allotments, even on a leasehold basis, with all the necessary access roads and infrastructure, went well beyond what the covenant intended.

A POSTSCRIPT: THE SEQUEL TO TODRICK'S CASE

As we have seen, Dr Todrick won his case. The local newspaper reported the decisions at length, both at first instance and on appeal.[125] It appears

---

[122] *Big River Paradise Ltd v Congreve* [2008] NZLR 402, [19]. The same doubts were expressed in a later Court of Appeal decision, *Thomson v Battersby* [2008] NZCA 84, [21].
[123] *Big River Paradise Ltd v Congreve* [2008] NZLR 402, [22].
[124] Ibid, [22].
[125] 'St Ives Doctor Wins Case against Omnibus Company' *St Ives Times* (27 October 1933); and (Court of Appeal), 'St Ives' Doctor's Actions Against Bus Company' *St Ives Times* (13 April 1934).

that, after the decision in the Court of Appeal, the bus company and the doctor reached some kind of 'settlement', but no details have survived.[126] Certainly, the bus company was saddled with the costs of substantially altering the ramp,[127] and it doubtless had to pay large legal costs. And of course it was unable to use the right of way for the passage of its buses. One source says that the only use the bus company made of the garage was for storing materials;[128] another says that it was unable to use the garage for any purpose at all.[129] In any event, the garage became a white elephant.[130] That was to the detriment not only of the company, but also of the local population, who paid a penalty in having their bus services curtailed.[131] In the early years of this century, applications were made to convert the void under the bus station platform (which remains the main bus station in St Ives to this day) into a restaurant or café, to take advantage of the excellent sea views.[132]

And what of Dr Todrick? All that we know is that he sold Skidden House in 1935 to Ernest Garbutt, a Lancashire comedian.[133] Mr Garbutt also purchased The Regent and another St Ives hotel, The York.[134] He was a reputed bigamist; it was said that he installed one wife and family in The Regent, and another wife and family in The York.[135]

But we have not quite reached the end of our story. During the Second World War, the Regent Hotel, which still overlooks Skidden House from The Terrace above, became the headquarters of the US 29th Division.[136] General Omar Bradley planned Operation Overlord from there. He used the garage space under the bus station platform to store army jeeps, stacked one on top of another, hidden by the platform from the prying eyes of the Luftwaffe.[137] The only access for the jeeps was along the laneway, beside Skidden House. And so it came to pass that Dr Todrick's laneway, so jealously guarded against bus traffic, became a regular route for American jeeps.

---

[126] Crawley and Simpson, above (n 2) 21.

[127] Ibid.

[128] Ibid.

[129] *St Ives Times & Echo and Hayle Times* (15 April 1983).

[130] In September 1934, the bus company succeeded in having its rates reduced because that part of its land could not be used for its intended purpose: *St Ives Times & Echo and Hayle Times* (15 April 1983).

[131] Ibid.

[132] *St Ives Times & Echo* (14 November 2003).

[133] By conveyance dated 10 July 1935; copy viewed in St Ives Study Centre: www.stivestrust .co.uk.

[134] Source: handwritten notes on file at St Ives Study Centre.

[135] Source: conversation between author and current owner of The Regent, Mr Keith Varnals.

[136] Ted Lever and Nigel Jeyes, *Memories of Wartime St Ives* (St Ives Historical Trust, 2005) 43.

[137] *The Cornishman* (3 June 2004).

3

Re Ellenborough Park *(1955)*

A Mere Recreation and Amusement

ELIZABETH COOKE*

INTRODUCTION

IN THE FILM *Notting Hill* the hero and heroine, walking though London late at night, climb over the locked gate of a town square garden; anyone watching the film who is familiar with *Re Ellenborough Park*[1] must find that it comes to mind at that point. In the film the town square takes on a brief but poignant role as a symbol of peace, privacy and an unexpected love.

The litigants in *Re Ellenborough Park* might certainly have regarded the importance of the case in English property law as something of an unexpected love. How could a squabble over compensation for wartime requisitioning have generated a decision that has made itself indispensable to land lawyers ever since? This chapter looks very briefly at the social and legal story of the English town square garden generally and of this garden in Weston-super-Mare in particular; it then looks briefly at the significance of the Court of Appeal's decision in 1955, while endeavouring to avoid reinventing the wheel of the extensive existing commentary. Finally it considers the importance of the case in the context of twenty-first century law reform.

THE ENGLISH TOWN SQUARE GARDEN

The roots both of the jewel-like peace of the square in *Notting Hill*, and of the legal importance of *Re Ellenborough Park*, lie in the contemplations and ambitions of post-medieval and in particular Georgian town planners,

---

* I am grateful to my colleague Stefan Liberadzki for research assistance in connection with the preparation of this chapter.

[1] *Re Ellenborough Park* [1956] Ch 131; this is the reference both for the decision of Dankwerts J in the High Court and for the decision of the Court of Appeal.

a century or so before Ellenborough Park[2] itself was laid out. The thinking behind the development of town squares has been described thus:

> The features of Georgian domestic architecture and town design that so appeal to present tastes, its simplicity, austerity and regularity, were as much solutions to economic problems as a self-conscious search for aesthetic effect. The geometrical symmetries and harmonies of the patterns result in part from the regular rectangular arrangement of streets in a grid created as the easiest means of dividing and filling space and the cheapest means of providing public access ...

> The basic geometry of the ensemble was determined by the building block and the street frontage. The optimum size of the former was determined by maximising the number of units with street frontage, while the frontage was kept as narrow as possible to reduce service costs. The terrace of 6–10 units was about ideal but the monotony of a constant repetition of this resulted in a certain progression in experimentation with different geometrical figures. The most obvious and earliest was the square (eg, Queens Square, Bath, the Bloomsbury/Bedford and Mayfair squares in London, Merrion and Mountjoy Squares in Dublin etc). There was also the 'circus' (most notably London and Bath), the crescent (eg, Royal Crescent, Bath), the oval (eg, Richmond Place, Limerick) and many complex multi-curves (notably Landsdown Crescent, Bath).[3]

The town square thus combined economies of space with aesthetic considerations; and from the point of view of the householder the town square garden must have been an important ingredient in the amenity of the home in the built-up, urban environment. Town square gardens were a compromise between public and private space, being shared, but not open to everyone. They were a kind of private village green, prevalent in London, but also widely used elsewhere.

Typically the London garden squares began life as a private shared garden for residents; privacy entailed a locked gate, and residents were—and still are in some cases—keyholders. The houses around the square were developed as an ensemble, and then each sold together with a right to hold a key and use the garden, in return for a share in the payment for its upkeep. Whether or not the word 'easement' was used, the fact that land lawyers know about *Re Ellenborough Park* from their (legal) cradles means that that is how we now think of these arrangements.

Ellenborough Park itself is described in the headnote to the report of the Court of Appeal decision:[4]

> The park and the road round it, Ellenborough Crescent or Crescent Road, was a rectangular area measuring 350 yards from East to West and about 100 yards

---

[2] I use this expression to refer to the garden itself, although it is not now known by that name; see below.

[3] GJ Ashworth, 'The Georgian City: The Compact City as Idealised Past or Future Ideal' (2005) 4 *Global Built Environment Review* 43–44.

[4] *Re Ellenborough Park* [1956] Ch 131, 133.

from North to South, its western boundary facing the sea. A right was granted to the purchasers of each of the plots of land in Crescent Road, which faced the park, to use it as a leisure ground. A similar right was granted in respect of nine or 10 other plots not actually facing on to the park but separated only from Crescent Road by houses so fronting.[5]

The land surrounding the park was sold in building plots in the 1860s,[6] and each plot benefited from easements[7] including the right to use the garden; the vendor retained the park and took on obligations not only to allow the use of the garden, but also to maintain it. The nature of the owner's obligations is perhaps a little unclear. They had to be framed as covenants, as can be seen from the commitments entered into by the freehold owners of Ellenborough Park;[8] but those covenants were positive (to maintain the garden) as well as negative (not to build on the garden).[9] So the only guarantee of its performance was the benefit-and-burden principle[10] applied to the receipt of the frontagers' payments.[11]

Such arrangements, private and reciprocal, have not proved to be durable over time, because they depended on the willingness of the owner of the square to carry out the garden maintenance, with the costs covered but without profit. Once the owner's immediate interest in the newly created square waned there can have been little incentive to carry on. Various different legal transformations have taken place over the years. Statute intervened relatively early on to enable the transfer of gardens to local authorities, and byelaws to be made for their public use.[12] Some gardens have passed to the ownership of bodies that have their own reasons for maintaining them and opening them to the public: for example, Gordon Square in London, originally provided for the private use of residents, is now owned by University College London and is open for public use.[13]

A different solution was provided by the Kensington Improvement Act 1851; its effect is that the upkeep of the garden—whatever its ownership—is funded from council tax, and that the residents of the houses fronting the

---

[5] These must be in Albert Avenue.

[6] The court used a conveyance of 1864 for reference, with the parties accepting that the rest of the plots were sold on the same terms.

[7] They were so described in the conveyance.

[8] *Re Ellenborough Park* [1956] Ch 131, 138: the owners 'covenanted … to keep as an ornamental pleasure ground the plot of land thereinbefore referred to'.

[9] 'Except any grotto, bower, summer-house, flower-stand, fountain, music-stand or other ornamental erection': ibid.

[10] *Halsall v Brizell* [1957] Ch 169 (Ch D).

[11] The Ellenborough Park householders covenanted 'to pay a fair proportion of the expenses of making and at all times keeping in good order and condition and well stocked with plants and shrubs the pleasure ground' (*Re Ellenborough Park* [1956] Ch 131, 138); but that level of detail was not set out in the obligations of the owner: see n 8 above.

[12] Eg, Recreation Grounds Act 1859; Public Improvement Act 1860; Open Spaces Act 1906.

[13] www.opensquares.org/detail/Gordon.html.

square are constituted, by the statute, a garden committee to manage the gardening. It also provides that those who have access to the garden shall be the freeholder (if identifiable—many are not); persons to whom the freeholder has given rights; and the occupiers of the houses encompassing the garden. The freehold ownership remains separate (and indeed marketable).[14] The Open Spaces Act 1906 enables the occupiers—the garden committee—to grant rights to others; but they do not have to do so, as two house purchasers found to their cost recently. In 2008, Mr and Mrs Herrmann, an American couple, moved to London and bought a house in a terrace adjoining Ovington Square. They could see the garden from their windows. Their solicitor assured them that they would have access to the garden, which was managed under the 1851 statute; but the garden committee refused to give them a key. Litigation ensued, and in *Herrmann and others v Royal Borough of Kensington and Chelsea and another*[15] Sir William Blackburne (sitting as a judge of the High Court) held that the Herrmanns were not entitled to access, because their house was not 'in' and did not 'encompass' the square—those being the two expressions used in the Act to define those who had what was referred to in the case as 'garden right'.[16]

Still other squares were the subject of privately evolved management arrangements, once the original setup became uncongenial. The Ellenborough Park estate—meaning the garden, and any unsold houses— was purchased by William Davies in 1879, subject to the residents' rights to use the garden. He died in 1880 and the trustees of his will administered the garden until 1924, when the residents formed a committee and took over the garden management (as well as receiving the householders' payments for its upkeep)—thereby achieving privately what the Kensington Improvement Act 1851 had done for the squares to which it applied.

ELLENBOROUGH PARK

Anyone can play in Ellenborough Park nowadays. Indeed, you can walk around the outside of the park without leaving your desk, because Google Street View will take you there. You can almost hear the seagulls. You can potter at will along the roads that bound the green space, which is rectangular but curved along its eastern edge: Ellenborough Park North,

---

[14] Eg, www.auction.co.uk/residential/LotDetails.asp?A=641&MP=84&ID=641000428&S= L&O=A.

[15] *Herrmann and others v Royal Borough of Kensington and Chelsea and another* [2010] EWHC 1706 (Ch), [2010] NPC 82.

[16] That right of course is not an easement, as it is granted by statute and not by deed nor by the owner of a dominant tenement.

Ellenborough Crescent around the eastern curve, Ellenborough Park South and Beach Road, otherwise the A370. The latter runs parallel to the sea and there are no buildings directly opposite the park; the other roads are residential. Properties range from the stately Georgian-style terraces on Ellenborough Crescent,[17] to spacious Victorian villa-type properties reminiscent of North Oxford, to a fearsomely modern looking church and some incongruous blocks of flats. Some of the older properties are no longer family homes; they include a care home and a school. The park is dissected by Walliscote Road, which runs north to south.

Thus there is a western area of grassland and trees; it is a Site of Special Scientific Interest[18] because it is the habitat of a number of rare plants (the area comprised coastal sand dunes, of course, before development).[19] The roadside signs label it 'Corpus Christi Playing Fields'. It seems to be owned by the town council[20] and part of it is used as a playing field by Corpus Christi school.[21] It is open to the public and features grass, trees and commissioned woodwork.[22] To the east of Walliscote Road is a smaller area, again nowadays open to the public and containing a playground for children. Shared privacy has given way to shared and public recreation.

However, in 1941 Ellenborough Park—a sizeable space, as we have seen—became temporarily the subject of a very different use for the benefit of the public. It was requisitioned by the War Office and occupied until 1946. As a result, compensation became payable under the Compensation (Defence) Act 1939.

The Compensation (Defence) Act 1939 governed compensation for, among other things, the requisitioning of land under regulation 51 of the Defence (General) Regulations 1939. That regulation enabled the Government to take possession of and use land in the interests of the public safety, the defence of the realm or the efficient prosecution of war, or for maintaining supplies and services essential to the life of the community. The power could be exercised regardless of any enactment or instrument imposing a restriction on the use of land.

Compensation for the requisitioning of land was payable under section 2 of the Compensation (Defence) Act 1939 under four heads. The first was a sum equal to the rent that the landowner could have obtained for the land assuming that the tenant paid the costs of repair, insurance etc; next, 'a sum

---

[17] But built in the nineteenth century according to the report of the case.

[18] www.sssi.naturalengland.org.uk/special/sssi/sssi_details.cfm?sssi_id=1005488.

[19] However, it does not seem to be on the National Register of Historic Parks and Gardens, maintained by English Heritage and searchable at: list.english-heritage.org.uk.

[20] www.parksandgardens.ac.uk/index2.php?option=com_parksandgardens&task=site&id=3906&preview=1&Itemid=293.

[21] archive.catholicherald.co.uk/article/26th-may-1961/7/new-primary-for-weston-super-mare.

[22] www.somersetwoodrecycling.co.uk/commissions.html.

equal to the cost of making good any damage to the land ... no account being taken of fair wear and tear or of damage caused by war operations'; for agricultural land, whatever the incoming tenant would have paid in respect of crops etc planted before the tenancy; and finally compensation for expenses incurred by the landowner in order to comply with the requisitioning authority's directions.

To a generation that has not experienced wartime requisitioning it is perhaps a surprise that these levels of compensation were paid. Section 2 of the 1939 Act states that the compensation was payable to 'the person who for the time being would be entitled to occupy the land but for the fact that possession thereof is retained in the exercise of [the relevant] powers'.

Accordingly, the War Office paid what the headnote to the case describes as a 'compensation rental' of £150 per year during the occupation, and a further sum eventually for dilapidations. Both sums were paid to the trustees who still owned the park; and the trustees spent much of it on rehabilitation and replanting. But what were they to do with the surplus, some £1770?[23] Should they pay it to the trust beneficiaries? Or were the householders entitled to have the sum placed in the garden fund and put towards the maintenance of the garden by the residents' committee? And that issue generated a question of pure property law: to whom did the garden belong? Clearly the freehold was vested in the trustees, but did the residents who had the right to use the garden have a proprietary interest in it, such as to give them an interest in the land and in the compensation?

THE COURT OF APPEAL DECISION IN 1955

The answer to the legal question that arose from the compensation squabble is history so far as lawyers are concerned: the houses around the park were held to benefit from easements over the garden. That meant that they had an entitlement to at least some of the accumulated rental payments—to be determined by a further inquiry, but in fact the parties settled that aspect of the case. Moreover the compensation for dilapidations, insofar as it had not already been spent, was to be used by the freeholder trustees for the upkeep of the garden and not paid out to their beneficiaries. That commonsense result was achieved by an interesting route in which the nature of an easement was explored and indeed crystallised. Probably most land law students do not notice that the case was 'about' compensation for wartime requisitioning; for all of us it is a crucial case 'about' easements.

---

[23] The report of the High Court decision is a little unclear as to whether the figure related to the total left over from rent and compensation together, or to the original compensation payment. The figure given here follows what Dankwerts J says: *Re Ellenborough Park* [1956] 1 Ch 131, 151.

Yet this is curious. Why should the entitlement to compensation have depended on whether or not the householders held easements, when the Compensation (Defence) Act 1939 stated that it was payable to occupiers? And granted that it did, why had the nature of the right to use the garden (let us call it the 'garden right' by analogy with the Kensington householders, even though the rights of the latter were not easements)[24] never been authoritatively determined[25]—standard though it was throughout the country and described as an easement in the conveyance that created it.

We cannot answer the latter question, save to say that the point had simply never come before the courts. There were cases where the validity of an easement to use a town square garden was clearly assumed by the court: neither *Duncan v Louch*[26] nor *Keith v Twentieth Century Club Ltd*[27] made sense without that background assumption. But the logic of the common law tradition is such that neither was authority for that proposition. As to the former question, about entitlement to compensation, the link is not clearly explained by Dankwerts J in the High Court; and the Court of Appeal did not have to look at the issue of compensation because by that stage the parties had agreed how the funds were to be divided between the trustees of the freehold of the garden and the residents' repair fund, if the beneficiaries' appeal failed in the Court of Appeal. The necessity of establishing that the householders had an easement was assumed, or taken as obvious background, by everyone involved.

What Dankwerts J said about the surplus rent was that it was clearly payable to the trustees because they were the occupiers of the land (the owners of the dominant tenements had only an incorporeal hereditament; so they were not in occupation, even though they were the ones who actually spent time there). However, Dankwerts J reasoned that although the rental element was payable to the occupier, that did not determine 'the position as regards persons who were all interested in the land in question'. He continued: 'in relation to compensation or compulsory purchase the rights of owners of easements are recognised and such persons are entitled to compensation if their rights are taken away'. He gave no authority for that, and it may be that in the aftermath of the war and in a context where a lot of compensation cases were being sorted out it was too obvious to require authority. So what remained of the rental payments was to be divided between the trustees and the residents, and Dankwerts J directed an inquiry—presumably by a surveyor—to determine the proportions. Furthermore, what remained of the compensation for dilapidations was to be held for the benefit of the residents, who were obliged to pay for the maintenance of the garden; by

[24] See text to n 16 above.
[25] As Evershed MR commented: *Re Ellenborough Park* [1956] Ch 131, 161.
[26] *Duncan v Louch* (1845) 6 QB 904 (QBD).
[27] *Keith v Twentieth Century Club Ltd* (1904) 73 LJ Ch 545 (Ch D).

implication, said Dankwerts J, the freeholder trustees were obliged to carry out that maintenance and were obliged to use the dilapidations payment for that purpose, seeking no further contributions from the dominant owners until the money was exhausted.

The reasoning about the rent is thus based on established compulsory purchase principles and makes sense although the authorities are not cited. By contrast, the reasoning about the dilapidations payment does not require the householders to have an easement, or indeed anything more than a contractual obligation to pay for the upkeep of the garden. So we are perhaps fortunate that the compensation problem did generate a decision on easements. There might have been other approaches to the dispute.

But a case about easements it was. The most important function of *Re Ellenborough Park* is that it enshrined in an authoritative judgment the four characteristics by which we still assess the validity of an easement:

1. there must be a dominant and a servient tenement;
2. an easement must accommodate and serve the dominant tenement, that is, be connected with its enjoyment and for its benefit;
3. the dominant and servient owners must be different persons; and
4. the right claimed must be capable of forming the subject matter of a grant.[28]

But the authority for this arises from agreement—counsel for both parties adopted them as correct. Their source was the seventh edition of Cheshire's *Modern Real Property*,[29] and the four characteristics represent the author's analysis of the case law at that date. Strictly, *Re Ellenborough Park* is not therefore authority for the four characteristics; yet we treat it as such. The authority of a textbook—such is at was, and the citation of textbooks was still at this date rather a contentious matter[30]—was thus blessed with the authority of the Court of Appeal and has become unambiguous law.[31] The law of easements was therefore tidied, while Dr Cheshire's authority was yet more deeply entrenched.[32]

---

[28] *Re Ellenborough Park* [1956] Ch 131, 163 (Lord Evershed MR).

[29] Cheshire, *Modern Law of Real Property*, 7th edn (London, Butterworths, 1954) 456–63.

[30] For a discussion of the evolution of attitudes, see P Birks, 'Adjudication and Interpretation in the Common Law' (1994) 14 *Legal Studies* 156. *Re Ellenborough Park* is noted at fn 48.

[31] Cheshire's 8th edition expounds the four characteristics (447–54). The text is almost unchanged from the 7th edition, save for the citations of *Re Ellenborough Park* at the start of the discussion and interspersed throughout; but the discussion of what can form the subject-matter of a grant has been abbreviated so as to exclude part of the discussion in the 7th edition about easements of light and support (7th edition, 460–61). The account of the definition of an easement in *Gale on Easements* changed substantially as a result of the case; whereas the 12th edition (p 10) and following listed seven qualities of easements (referred to by Evershed MR at [1956] Ch 131, 163), the corresponding text in the 13th edition that followed the case (pp 5ff) has been rewritten so as to be based on the Ellenborough characteristics.

[32] Cheshire's *Modern Law of Real Property*, which becomes Cheshire and Burn in 1972, has been much studied and commented on. See M Doupé and M Salter, 'Approaching the

A further important function of the case may have been its approach to the problem of the *ius spatiandi*. It was argued for the trustees that the right could not be an easement because it was a mere *ius spatiandi*: this is referred to as a right to wander at will, and the expression derives from Paulus, the Roman jurist: 'ut spatiari, et ut coenare in aliena possumus, servitus imponi non potest', roughly translated as 'it is not possible to impose a servitude that enables the dominant owner to wander or to dine (picnic?) on someone else's land'.[33] The phrase found its way into English law by being mentioned by Farwell J in two cases, *International Tea Stores v Hobbs*[34] and *Attorney-General v Antrobus*.[35] But those mentions were *obiter*; in each case the judge stated that a mere *ius spatiandi* could not be an easement, but without any English authority to that effect.

Dankwerts J dealt with the point by reference to *Duncan v Louch*[36] and to *Keith v Twentieth Century Club Ltd*,[37] which he took as establishing that the garden right could be an easement. Lord Evershed MR in the Court of Appeal went into the issue more deeply, noting that the reason for the prevalence of maxims of Roman law in the law of easements arose from the fact that the latter was a late developer in English law; by the nineteenth century, when the Industrial Revolution made it important to have clear rules for 'such easements as ways, watercourses, light, and support'[38] there was no body of English principle ready to hand and the courts fell back upon what the Romans had worked out.

The Court of Appeal held *both* that Paulus' proposition had no authority in English law *and* that the garden right was not a right of 'mere recreation and amusement'. It was, said Lord Evershed MR, a pleasure, but 'not a right having no quality either of utility or benefit as those words should be understood'. The double negative is perhaps a symptom of the difficulty of sustaining this argument. Indeed,

[i]ts use for the purposes, not only of exercise and rest but also for such domestic purposes as … taking out small children in perambulators or otherwise … is not fairly to be described as one of mere recreation or amusement and is clearly beneficial to the premises to which it is attached.[39]

Nature and History of Property Law: The Limits of the '"Cheshire Worldview"' (2000) 11 *King's College Law Journal* 49 and the works cited therein.

[33] The verb 'spatiari' is not particularly common but it is found in the classical writers, and it can mean anything from 'process' to 'potter'. Virgil uses it of a crow hopping along on the sand (Georgics 1, 398) and of Dido, queen of Carthage, walking (doubtless in a stately fashion) before the altars of the gods (*Aeneid* 4, 62). It can also mean to 'spread', in the sense of spreading wings (Ovid, *Metamorphoses* 4, 364), so there is more to it than walking.

[34] *International Tea Stores v Hobbs* [1903] 2 Ch 165 (Ch D).

[35] *Attorney-General v Antrobus* [1905] 2 Ch 188 (Ch D).

[36] *Duncan v Louch* (1845) 6 QB 904.

[37] *Keith v Twentieth Century Club Ltd* (1904) 73 LJ Ch 545.

[38] *Re Ellenborough Park* [1956] Ch 131, 162.

[39] Ibid, 179.

A different way of putting it would be to say that the ability to use the park for recreation and amusement is beneficial to the premises to which it is attached (because it enhanced the ownership and use of that land). But that apparently would not do; a rejection of the authority of the Roman principle is combined with a lingering respect for it. There is perhaps here a gut feeling about the balance to be achieved between neighbours. We cannot manage land ownership—particularly on a small island—without neighbour rights and obligations; but there is a limit to the extent to which my rights can be imposed on my neighbour's land, and a sense that certain things would be too much of a limitation of his ownership. A right to do something useful on his land is one thing, a right to have fun is quite another and that gut feeling might be so strong as to be relevant even if the servient land is in fact a park.[40]

The legal expression of that gut feeling is the fourth of the *Re Ellenborough Park* characteristics, which embodies a group of ideas, and it is to those characteristics that we now turn.

RE ELLENBOROUGH PARK AND THE LAW REFORM PERSPECTIVE

Property law reform is something of a recurring fixation among the property lawyers of England and Wales. The difficulty we face is that we have to make a journey towards straightforward law, but we would not have chosen to start from here; every effort to improve our land law is hampered by the long period over which it developed and the untidy accumulation of ideas. Prescription is the obvious example; previous reformers did not tidy up as they went along, and so we now have three methods, none of them particularly straightforward.

Much has been written about the four characteristics enshrined in *Re Ellenborough Park* and to analyse them afresh here would be uncalled for. What is new, however, is the application of the characteristics in the context of modern law reform efforts.

My preoccupation with this aspect of the case is inevitable because after I started work as a Law Commissioner in summer 2008 I spent three years living and breathing easements (among other projects) until the publication in June 2011 of our report, *Making Land Work: Easements, Covenants and Profits à Prendre* ('the Easements Report').[41] In the Easements Report we recommended a number of adjustments to the law relating to easements, of which the most significant were the streamlining of prescription

---

[40] For a thorough discussion of this point see A Baker, 'Recreational Privileges as Easements: Law and Policy' [2012] *Conv* 37.

[41] Law Commission Report No 327, *Making Land Work: Easements, Covenants and Profits à Prendre* (2011) (Easements Report).

and implication.[42] Some of our recommendations adjusted the four *Re Ellenborough Park* characteristics, but not by a great deal. We also recommended the creation of a new legal interest in land—the land obligation—so as to enable both positive and negative obligations to be attached to land. It is well-established that although new legal easements can be recognised by the courts, wholly new interests that are not easements cannot be created by case law.[43] Consistent with this, the courts have refused to allow positive covenants to run with land;[44] if it is to happen,[45] it can only be done by statute, and the Law Commission's draft Bill[46] provides a way of doing this.

As a legal interest, the land obligation would behave in the same way as an easement in many ways, although it could not be created by prescription or implication.[47] The decision in *Re Ellenborough Park* is not strictly relevant to the land obligation, as the case was concerned only with easements; but the characteristics of an easement have their parallels in the conditions for the validity of a land obligation: they cannot exist in gross, they must touch and concern the dominant land, they must be capable of being the subject matter of a grant (whatever that means: see below), and the dominant and servient land must be in different hands (save where title to both plots is registered—again, see below). The *Re Ellenborough Park* characteristics, ill-defined as they are, say something about a legal instinct, namely the extent to which one person's land can be burdened for the sake of another's, and so their relevance beyond the immediate context of easements is unsurprising.

The four characteristics in *Re Ellenborough Park* are flawed and questionable. Those numbered (1) and (3) above are neither logically nor practically necessary characteristics of easements; they are simply hard-edged policy decisions that might have gone otherwise. Those numbered (2) and (4) are extremely imprecise. This means that the category of valid easements is a subset, subjectively defined (by characteristics (2) and (4)), of a set of rights

---

[42] Easements Report, above (n 41) Pt 3.

[43] See, eg, the discussion of this point in AJ McClean, 'The Nature of an Easement' (1966) 5 *Western Law Review* 32, 32–34. The article also contains a detailed analysis of the four characteristics of an easement.

[44] *Rhone v Stephens* [1994] 2 AC 310 (HL).

[45] The arguments in favour of it happening are to be found in Pt 5 of the Easements Report. Most significant among those arguments is that fact that there are already a number of ways by which positive obligations can be attached to land, in particular the estate rentcharge, and—most obviously—the long lease and commonhold.

[46] Easements Report, above (n 41) Appendix A.

[47] So really the principle that new easements can be recognised but new interests cannot be created collapses into a matter of labelling—or, rather, a choice about levels of generalisation. Do we classify land obligations and easements as a subset of—say—servitudes? Or do we prefer a lower level of generalisation and call them a different sort of interest? This is a bit like deciding whether we want to talk about apples and oranges or about fruit—and the decision depends very much on practical criteria: which level of generalisation is more practically useful? It is useful to discuss land obligations separately from easements because of the differences in the way they behave, although the similarities are also important.

(arbitrarily delineated by characteristics (1) and (3)) in land belonging to another. From a law reform perspective, (1) and (3) are rules and the question when addressing possible law reform is whether or not those rules should be varied or abrogated. On the other hand, (2) and (4) are not rules (although at least (2) pretends to be) and they therefore present two conundrums: first, if a certain reform is proposed, does it run counter to either of these principles? That is a matter of judgement and not of objective determination. Secondly, if a proposed reform does offend either principle, does that matter?

So—reverting now just to easements—how did the four characteristics emerge from the Commission's deliberations?

As to (1), a number of other jurisdictions have easements in gross, and the view we hear from them is that there is no need for a dominant tenement; easements work well without. Profits à prendre (rights to take something from the land of another) exist in gross, and there are powerful arguments in favour of English law taking this approach towards easements.[48] The Law Commission in the Easements Report nevertheless recommended that the principle should stand, stating that 'the introduction of easements in gross would lead to a proliferation of adverse interests in land, unlimited by the needs of the dominant land'.[49] This was also the view of a majority of the respondents to the Consultation Paper.[50] Likewise, land obligations would not be able to be created in gross; they must be created for the benefit of an estate in land.[51]

As to (3), being the other clear rule, there is no reason why one person should not own two plots of land, the one benefiting from an easement over the other. If an easement accommodates and serves *the dominant tenement* then it must be possible for us to conceive of two pieces of land related in this way. No one can exercise an easement over his own land because what he does is done as owner;[52] but the law might allow the owner to create such an easement in order then to sell one plot; and that might be useful where in fact several plots were to be sold off,[53] or where part of the land

---

[48] M Sturley, 'Easements in Gross' (1980) 96 *LQR* 557; G Morgan, 'Easements in Gross Revisited' (1999) 28 *Anglo-American Law Review* 220.

[49] Easements Report, above (n 41) para 2.24.

[50] See Law Commission Consultation Paper No 186, *Making Land Work: Easements, Covenants and Profits à Prendre* (Consultation Analysis) (2011) paras 3.1–3.12 (lawcommission.justice.gov.uk/areas/easements.htm).

[51] Easements Report, above (n 41) paras 5.69 and 6.14–6.21, and clause 1(2)(a) of the draft Bill at Appendix A.

[52] Assuming that neither plot is let, in which case obviously different points arise.

[53] If related easements are created in a sequence, it is important that they be created in the right order; where a number of transactions are taking place it is impossible to prevent what was supposed to be a later sale from being registered prior to an earlier sale, so that it is all too easy for a conveyance to grant a right to use an easement that does not yet exist at law: see the Easements Report, above (n 41) paras 4.25–4.33.

was to be mortgaged.[54] Equally, where a dominant owner buys the servient tenement, say, he might wish to keep the easement alive with a view to selling off one or other plot. The Law Commission in the Easements Report therefore recommended that the law allow both these things where title to dominant and servient land is registered,[55] and made the same recommendation for land obligation.[56]

Turning to characteristic (2), we move into something less precise. What does 'accommodate and serve' mean, and why does an easement have to do this? The second question is easier than the first, although the answer is not always very precise. The Law Commission stated in its 2008 Consultation Paper, *Easements, Covenants and Profits à Prendre*, that the requirement is imposed 'to ensure that capricious personal rights do not run with and bind the land and thereby constitute unnecessary incursions on the title'.[57] The concern here is with overburdening, in the sense of avoiding the creation of easements that are too many in number or that are on some way related to people rather than to the land itself. As discussed above, this is a very fine line to draw, and the test is imprecise. It is not, for example, the case that the benefit conferred cannot be any good to anyone except the benefited owner—in other words, that it cannot be unique to that particular plot of land; that follows from *Re Ellenborough Park* itself, where lots of houses enjoy the same easement. Nor is it the case that the benefit must be useless to anyone except a landowner (generically), since a right of way might be handy for others, as might the use of gardens in a square. Nor is it essential that the easement increase the value of the land.[58] The Court of Appeal in *Ellenborough* did say that it must be 'connected with the normal enjoyment of the property'; that criterion at least rules out the usual counter-examples of the box at the Royal Albert Hall or the right to attend matches at Lord's Cricket Ground.[59] But it is not a definition, not least because it is clear that an easement may enhance the business use of land, which may or may not be the 'normal enjoyment' of the land.[60]

---

[54] As the law stands, it is not possible to create a mortgage over part of one's land if that land cannot be sold independently without an easement over the retained, non-charged land; the mortgagor cannot create an easement over his own land, and the mortgagee cannot create an easement when it takes possession and sells: see the Easements Report, above (n 41) paras 4.34–4.38.

[55] Easements Report, above (n 41) para 4.44.

[56] Ibid, para 6.83.

[57] Law Commission Consultation Paper No 186, *Easements, Covenants and Profits à Prendre: A Consultation* (2008) para 3.25.

[58] *Re Ellenborough Park* [1956] Ch 131, 173: enhancement of value is 'in no way decisive of the problem'.

[59] Ibid, 174 and (in argument) 156.

[60] *Copeland v Greenhalf* [1952] Ch 488 (Ch D) is the obvious example. Greenwood (1956) 24 *CLJ* 24 comments that the test as propounded by the Court of Appeal in *Re Ellenborough Park* would have validated the right in *Hill v Tupper* (1863) 2 H & C 121.

The Commission made no proposal to adjust or remove the requirement, in the Consultation Paper or the 2011 Report. It did discuss at some length the related idea, that a restrictive covenant (under the current law) must 'touch and concern' the benefited land. This is, I suggest, impossible to distinguish from the 'accommodate and serve' test. Its virtue is the same; it prevents the attachment of too many burdens, or the wrong sort of burdens, to land, and that is important despite its imprecision. The test becomes all the more important if positive obligations are to be able to attach to land, as the Commission has recommended.[61] The Consultation Paper took some steps towards spelling out the meaning of 'touch and concern';[62] the Report and draft Bill wisely relied on the well understood phrase and did not attempt to define the indefinable.[63]

Finally, characteristic (4): the right must be capable of being the subject matter of a grant. It is very tempting when teaching this to students to explain that this means 'it has to be the right sort of thing', so subjective is this characteristic when examined. This is the expression of the gut feeling, mentioned above; this is the characteristic that can be used to outlaw purported easements that somehow do not feel right to the court. It encapsulates a number of ideas, of which the Court of Appeal in *Re Ellenborough Park* examined three: the right must not be too vague, it must not be inconsistent with the possession of proprietorship of the servient owner and it must not be a right of mere recreation and amusement. The Court of Appeal was able to dispose of all three questions, noting that the right given in the deed to the first purchaser of each plot was 'both well-defined and commonly understood';[64] and that the freeholders could certainly do things on the land, in particular cutting and selling timber and indeed to maintain it as a garden. The issue about recreation and amusement is discussed above.

The Law Commission made something of an inroad into the ideas bundled in this characteristic in its examination of parking easements. An easement to park is a practical and economic benefit, adding considerably to the value of property and to the convenience of life in our crowded

---

[61] The American Law Institute in its Restatement of the Law Third: Property (Servitudes) (2000), at § 3.2, took a different approach, recommending the abandonment of the "touch and concern" requirement on the basis that sufficient control is provided by the ability to apply to have the burden discharged or modified. The Law Commission recommended the extension of s 84 of the Law of Property Act 1925 so as to enable positive as well as negative obligations to be modified or discharged by the Lands Chamber of the Upper Tribunal, but it did not regard that as sufficient reason to abandon the 'touch and concern' requirement, preferring prevention to cure: Easements Report, above (n 41) paras 5.55–5.57.

[62] Law Commission Consultation Paper No 186, *Easements, Covenants and Profits à Prendre: A Consultation* (2008) para 8.80.

[63] Easements Report, above (n 41) para 6.20, and clause 1(2)(b) of the draft Bill at Appendix A.

[64] *Re Ellenborough Park* [1956] Ch 131, 176.

suburbs. Many are created. Many are registered as 'exclusive' rights to park, and it is not clear in such cases whether what is meant is that only the grantee has to right to park on the space (if a single space is involved) or whether something rather more exclusive is implied, perhaps bordering dangerously on exclusive possession. Exclusive possession is the hallmark of an estate in land;[65] an easement cannot grant exclusive possession. But the practical importance of the validity of parking easements is such that the Commission recommended the abolition of the rule that an easement must not confer such extensive rights on the dominant owner that the servient owner is left with no reasonable use for the land. We took the view that so long as the servient owner can access the land, however minimally and for purposes however limited, the easement is valid as the parties clearly intended. In practical terms, of course, this is not very far from the actual result in *Re Ellenborough Park*, where the Court of Appeal was prepared to find that the 'ouster principle' was not infringed by the rights of the dominant owners even though the servient owner could do little except tend the garden and manage the timber. The test is a subjective one; the Court of Appeal took a very liberal approach to it and the Law Commission's recommendation[66] arguably does little more than formalise that liberality.

CONCLUSIONS

What is striking in examining the issues within *Re Ellenborough Park* is the imprecision of the decisions made in the High Court and the Court of Appeal, and also in the four characteristics that the Court of Appeal's judgment made authoritative. That imprecision makes the decision vulnerable to attack, and yet also makes it useful material for the law reformer: it embodies some useful legal instincts without being so rigid that it has to be overruled in order for the law to move on. Just as Ellenborough Park itself has evolved, from sand dunes to a private space to a public amenity, so the decision in *Re Ellenborough Park* has proved itself to be a landmark that is all the more useful for its flexibility.

---

[65] *Street v Mountford* [1985] 1 AC 809 (HL); and see the discussion in the Easements Report, above (n 41) paras 3.188–3.211.
[66] Easements Report, above (n 41) para 3.209, and clause 24 of the draft Bill at Appendix A.

4

Taylors Fashions Ltd v Liverpool Victoria Trustees Co Ltd; Old & Campbell Ltd v Liverpool Victoria Friendly Society (1979)

Stitching Together Modern Estoppel

MARTIN DIXON

22 Westover Road, Bournemouth, 1975–78

INTRODUCTION

IT WAS ALL the fault of Mr Justice Buckley. To the continuing incomprehension of law students, in *Beesly v Hallwood Estates Ltd*,[1] Buckley J held that a tenant's option to renew a lease, enshrined in a covenant in that lease, was an 'estate contract' within the meaning of section 10(1) of the Land Charges Act 1925 (LCA 1925)[2] and thus was

---

[1] *Beesly v Hallwood Estates Ltd* [1960] 1 WLR 549 (Ch D).
[2] See now Land Charges Act 1972, s 2(4)(iv).

required to be registered as a land charge in order to be enforceable against a purchaser of the reversion.[3] It mattered not in *Beesly* that such an option might be thought to be an obligation that touched and concerned the land and so able to run with the reversion automatically under section 142 of the Law of Property Act 1925 (LPA 1925). It was, for Buckley J, simply a matter of construction of the LCA 1925 and there was no pressing reason to read that statute consistently with section 142 of the LPA 1925, which otherwise might be thought to make such registration unnecessary. This was not an obligation which passed with the reversionary interest per se. Understandably, and with some justification,[4] the view of the legal profession prior to *Beesly* had been otherwise; and no doubt many tenants were in the same position as Taylors Fashions Ltd in that their apparently valuable option to renew a lease was in fact precarious if it had not been registered against the name of the relevant estate owner. Indeed, despite the apparent approval of *Beesly* in *Greene v Church Commissioners for England*[5] and *Kitney v MEPC Ltd*,[6] both decided before *Taylors Fashions Ltd v Liverpool Victoria Trustees Co Ltd; Old & Campbell Ltd v Liverpool Victoria Friendly Society*,[7] it appears that none of the parties in *Taylors Fashions* (or their legal advisers) appreciated the significance of *Beesly* until 1975 when Liverpool Victoria began to grasp that they might not, after all, be obliged to renew the lease in favour of Taylors Fashions. Moreover, it then dawned that this might, in turn, enable them to determine a lease of part of the same building held by Old & Campbell, as this was linked to Taylors Fashions' lease, and, further, to escape renewal of a third lease held by Old & Campbell of yet another unit in the building.

Today, the decision in *Taylors Fashions* is regarded by many as providing the impetus for a sea change in the way that proprietary estoppel can be established. The judgment of Oliver J is seen as distilling estoppel into an assurance, reliance and detriment in circumstances of unconscionability. Yet, while no doubt it was a case of great moment for the parties, at first it seemed to involve no issue of profound importance, no unresolved question of statutory interpretation and no weighty issue of public policy. An option to renew a lease had not been registered when it should have been; and now it was void under the clear provisions of the LCA 1925 with adverse consequences for the tenant under that lease and those with linked

---

[3] Land Charges Act 1925, s 13(2). See now Land Charges Act 1972, s 4(6).

[4] See text to n 27 below.

[5] *Greene v Church Commissioners for England* [1974] Ch 467 (CA).

[6] *Kitney v MEPC Ltd* [1977] 1 WLR 981.

[7] *Taylors Fashions Ltd v Liverpool Victoria Trustees Co Ltd; Old & Campbell Ltd v Liverpool Victoria Friendly Society* [1982] QB 133 (Ch D). Although not reported in the official law reports until 1982, judgment was handed down on 27 February 1979. For post-*Taylors Fashions* approval, see *Phillips v Mobil Oil Ltd* [1989] 1 WLR 888 (CA). The Landlord and Tenant (Covenants) Act 1995, s 3(6)(b), preserves the *Beesly* rule for post-1995 leases.

tenancies. This was unfortunate for the parties, and perhaps their legal advisers,[8] but not unforeseeable given the earlier decision in *Beesly*. In this sense, the result in *Taylors Fashions* should have been predictable and much of the judgment does indeed represent what was then a thoroughly conventional analysis of the relevant principles of property law. So it was, almost it seems in desperation, that the plaintiffs raised the estoppel argument because, they alleged, the defendants had acquiesced in or encouraged the plaintiffs' beliefs that the options were enforceable and the leases would be renewed.[9]

As the authorities then stood, the argument appeared to have little chance of success. The law of estoppel appeared to require a plaintiff to prove a great deal—represented by the five probanda of *Willmott v Barber*[10]—and the scales seemed weighted in favour of the freehold reversioner who, after all, was relying on nothing less than the clear words of the LCA 1925. But, perhaps Oliver J was more open to persuasion than might otherwise have been the case, noting at the outset of his judgment that the 'defendants' case is not one which impresses itself upon one immediately as overburdened with merit and the first impression is not significantly improved by a closer examination of the background'.[11] In any event, Oliver J felt able to step outside the strict confines of existing authority and saw instead 'a much wider equitable jurisdiction to interfere in cases where the assertion of strict legal rights is found by the court to be unconscionable'.[12] However, what is not clear is whether Oliver J intended to dismantle the rather limited doctrine of estoppel then recognised by the courts and to fashion in its stead a broader equitable principle. Much of *Taylors Fashions* is conventional; and, if Oliver J was minded to be revolutionary, he could have taken the simple and bolder step of declining to follow *Beesly*.[13] As will be seen, counsel provided him with a good line of argument to this end and it would not have involved even appearing to compromise the policy of the LCA 1925. In other words, it was not necessary to reformulate the law of estoppel and depart from *Willmott v Barber* in order to protect Old & Campbell; and one wonders whether Oliver J thought he was doing anything other than applying conventional estoppel law to the unusual facts before him. In fact, taking a longer view, one might argue that *Taylors Fashions* did not become a pivotal case in the development of estoppel until the strong affirmation of

---

[8] I have been unable to discover whether any solicitors were held liable in negligence for failing to appreciate the change brought about by *Beesly*.

[9] For Old & Campbell the relevant issue was whether the leases would be renewed, rather than the option being enforceable. This meant that Old & Campbell were not directly challenging the requirements of registration under the Land Charges Act: see p 90 below.

[10] *Willmott v Barber* (1880) LR 15 Ch D 96.

[11] *Taylors Fashions* [1982] QB 133, 135.

[12] Ibid, 147.

[13] This route—attacking *Beesly*—would also have saved Taylors Fashions.

it in *Jones v Stones*;[14] and it did not become widely pleaded until the Law of Property (Miscellaneous Provisions) Act 1989 brought a new emphasis on formality by abandoning the doctrine of part performance in favour of a requirement of writing for most contracts disposing of an interest in land. Seen through the prism of time, and the status quo of *Gillett v Holt*[15] and *Thorner v Major*,[16] *Taylors Fashions* is a landmark case, but the judgment does not give the sense that Oliver J intended a grand statement of the modern law of proprietary estoppel. Perhaps it just turned out that way.

TAYLORS FASHIONS: THE FACTUAL BACKGROUND

Taylors Fashions involved a relatively long hearing for the Chancery Division,[17] and the trial judge and two of the counsel would one day sit in the House of Lords.[18] Old & Campbell had been the freehold owners of the building and their sale of that freehold to Liverpool Victoria[19] in 1949 was part of a wider commercial rearrangement whereby Old & Campbell would lease back part of the building (21 Westover Road) in order to carry on their established business. In its turn, Liverpool Victoria would acquire an appreciating asset and an income stream, which was to include the rent from a new lease of 22 Westover Road (part of the same building), which had been granted to Taylors Fashions' predecessor in title by Old & Campbell before they sold the freehold to Liverpool Victoria. It is clear that the new lease of No 22 was part of the overall package and was intended to have been granted at the same time as the sale of the freehold to Liverpool Victoria; but in fact it was granted just before that sale. Indeed, had the lease been granted by Liverpool Victoria on acquiring the freehold, there would never have been a dispute to go before Oliver J: the option in the lease would not have required registration as a land charge in order to be enforceable against Liverpool Victoria as grantor. Consequently, however, when Liverpool Victoria acquired the freehold, it was subject to two leases: a lease of No 21 in favour of Old & Campbell for 42 years granted by itself; and a lease of No 22 in favour of (now) Taylors Fashions for

---

[14] *Jones v Stones* [1999] 1 WLR 1739 (CA).

[15] *Gillett v Holt* [2001] Ch 210 (CA).

[16] *Thorner v Major* [2009] UKHL 18, [2009] 1 WLR 776.

[17] Seven days in January 1979. Judgment was handed down on 27 February 1979.

[18] Oliver J, Peter Millet QC, who appeared for Liverpool Victoria in both cases, and Richard Scott QC, who appeared for Taylors Fashions. Lord Scott, as he became, would give the leading judgment in *Yeoman's Row Management Ltd v Cobbe* [2008] UKHL 55, [2008] 1 WLR 1752, which takes a narrower view of estoppel than that in *Gillett v Holt*, but perhaps not narrower than that in *Taylors Fashions*.

[19] *Liverpool Victoria Trustees Co Ltd* was the trustees of the Liverpool Victoria Friendly Society.

28 years granted by Old & Campbell,[20] with a right to renew for a further 14 years (also therefore potentially 42 years). Crucially, the two leases were tied together, so that Liverpool Victoria could terminate Old & Campbell's lease of No 21 after 28 years if Taylors Fashions did not renew its lease of No 22 for a further 14 years.[21] The final piece of the puzzle then came in 1963 when, in order to complete the transformation of the building and enhance its business, Old & Campbell took a new 14 year lease of No 20 Westover Road, specifically to merge the unit physically with its premises at No 21. This lease, although standing on its own, was capable of renewal for a further 14 years, again however on condition that Taylors Fashions exercised its option to renew the lease of No 22. Both Liverpool Victoria and Old & Campbell understood that the renewal of the new lease of No 20 was tied to the option to renew No 22, just like Old & Campbell's existing lease of No 21. However, it was also clear that both parties assumed that Taylors Fashions' option could (and most likely would) be exercised against Liverpool Victoria; and Old & Campbell undertook renovations of its units at No 21 and No 20 on the footing that its leases would be renewed.[22]

An appreciation of this background is more than a matter of interest. It is material because it demonstrates that Liverpool Victoria could not deny that it was aware that Old & Campbell had a long-term plan for the premises, as witnessed by the fact that it had been freehold owner with a thriving business, that it now had a long lease and a second lease, and that initially it had stipulated for a right of pre-emption to protect its position in respect of the lease of No 22 should the original tenants decide to dispose of the premises. There could be little doubt that Liverpool Victoria knew that Old & Campbell expected the leases to continue for 42 years; and until 1975 so did they. Taylors Fashions was in much the same position in respect of its own dealings with Liverpool Victoria, save only that the evidence—critical as it turned out—was less clear that Liverpool Victoria

---

[20] In 1958 Taylors Fashions had taken an assignment of the lease of No 22 from the original tenants, Mr and Mrs Murray. The right to renew remained unregistered, as well it might given the perceived state of the law at that time, but in any event registration would have been too late as Liverpool Victoria was already a purchaser of the reversion within the meaning of the Land Charges Act.

[21] In order to protect itself, Old & Campbell had a right of first refusal to purchase the lease from the original tenants of No 22 if they proposed to assign. As events turned out, Old & Campbell waived this right of pre-emption when Taylors Fashions took an assignment of the lease of No 22. It seems that Old & Campbell took no further steps to protect itself against non-exercise of the option in the lease No 22, which today seems careless given that their own lease (of No 21) was thus left at the mercy of persons over whom they had no control. One might have expected Old & Campbell to have extracted (at least) some kind of contractual guarantee from Taylors Fashions when it waived its right of pre-emption in relation to the lease of No 22.

[22] There seems to have been no provision for Old & Campbell to exercise the option to renew its leases if Taylors Fashions simply chose not to exercise its own option—a provision perhaps equally as valuable as the right of pre-emption it once enjoyed and surrendered.

had ever addressed the question of renewal with Taylors Fashions directly. In this sense, however, the plaintiffs and defendants in *Taylors Fashions* were not unconnected parties that came to the business table cold. They were not unknown to each other before the question of estoppel arose, unlike the parties in *Yeoman's Row Management Ltd v Cobbe*.[23] They were parties to a dispute that arose out of a pre-existing legal relationship that had generated its own expectations. *Taylors Fashions* was therefore like so many cases that would come later, where the potential estoppel related back to an arrangement between the parties that, in circumstances unforeseen, did not turn out as expected.[24] In the result, Taylors Fashions could not establish the elements of estoppel and the invalidity of the option under the LCA 1925 was upheld. But Old & Campbell's position was 'very different' and they succeeded.[25]

THE ISSUES

The *Beesly* Principle

An easy answer to Oliver J's apparent dilemma—and one that would have resulted in a favourable outcome for both Taylors Fashions and Old & Campbell—would have been to decline to follow *Beesly*. This was not out of the question. Oliver J recognised that Richard Scott QC's argument against *Beesly* in this case, cast as it was in a different way from previous cases, had not been fully tested, and further that there was something to commend the pre-*Beesly* view of the law. Further still, although there was some precedential support for *Beesly*—in the sense that it had been followed in subsequent cases without argument—it was clear that this amounted to no more than the '*Rhone v Stephens*[26] defence'—that conveyancing practice had proceeded on the basis of an assumption about the law that it was now to unwise to challenge, even if that understanding was dubious. There was, of course, a difference: acceptance that positive obligations could not run outside a lease had been operative for decades when *Rhone* was decided; by contrast it had been a mere 18 years since *Beesly*.[27] This defence of *Beesly*, not based on principle, is a conveyancer's answer—and a conservative answer.

---

[23] *Yeoman's Row Management Ltd v Cobbe* [2008] UKHL 55, [2008] 1 WLR 1752.

[24] In fact, the plaintiffs' case was closer to the plea that estoppel operated as a bar to action by the landowner (a shield against termination), rather than the modern emphasis on estoppel as a sword. It links to the past and foreshadows the future role of estoppel.

[25] *Taylors Fashions* [1982] QB 133,157.

[26] *Rhone v Stephens* [1994] 2 AC 310 (HL).

[27] Buckley J in *Beesly* had felt no qualms about disturbing the then existing practice and creating the potential problems that materialised in *Taylors Fashions*.

Strictly, therefore, Oliver J did not have to follow *Beesly* at all. In that case the new lease was held to have been validly granted *despite* the fact that, in the view of Buckley J, the plaintiff was not entitled to exercise the option to renew because it amounted to a land charge and was unregistered. On one view, the ratio of *Beesly* concerns the requirements for a valid grant by deed,[28] the issue on which it was affirmed on appeal. Likewise, the precedents were weak: the point was not material in *Greene v Church Commissioners for England*[29] and in fact the Court of Appeal was keener to disagree with Buckley J's analysis of what a 'contract' was, rather than ever agreeing that this option in a lease was a land charge. So too in *Kitney v MEPC Ltd*,[30] where the decision was that, assuming the option to renew was void as an unregistered land charge, it could not (of course) be revived on first registration of title. Neither of these cases even considered Richard Scott QC's argument raised in *Taylors Fashions* and, with respect, Oliver J did not refute it as opposed to merely note it and not follow it. Essentially, Scott QC argued that the point of the LCA 1925 was to replace the doctrine of notice—on which few would disagree—and therefore the touchstone of what should be registrable under the Act were those things that required 'notice' to bind a purchaser (save where the statute is explicit, as for example by including puisne mortgages).[31] A proprietary covenant in a lease, prior to 1925, was regarded less of a third party burden and more as an inherent attribute of the estate granted—*Muller v Trafford*.[32] It did not require 'notice' to bind but rather passed as an attribute of the estate when the estate passed. That, Scott QC argued, is why we have sections 141 and 142 of the LPA 1925, which now find even more generous expression in the Landlord and Tenant (Covenants) Act 1995.[33] Thus, he concluded that the proper approach to the LCA 1925 is to read it consistently with the LPA 1925 and to honour its purpose, especially since, as Oliver J himself notes, this accords 'with the view of the original authors of *Wolstenholme and Cherry's Conveyancing Statutes*'.[34]

The force of Scott QC's argument, never really tested in court, remains today. In the well known case of *Phillips v Mobil Oil Ltd*,[35] *Beesly* was of

---

[28] Aspects of which have since been disapproved by the Court of Appeal in *Bolton MPC v Torkington* [2003] EWCA Civ 1634, [2004] Ch 66 (CA).

[29] *Greene v Church Commissioners for England* [1974] Ch 467.

[30] *Kitney v MEPC Ltd* [1977] 1 WLR 981.

[31] This is entirely explicable because usually another mortgagee has the title deeds and a purchaser will not know that this second, puisne mortgage exists—hence the availability of registration.

[32] *Muller v Trafford* [1901] 1 Ch 54 (Ch D).

[33] Under the 1995 Act the covenant need not 'touch and concern' the land, although this has raised eyebrows; see *BHP Petroleum Great Britain Ltd v Chesterfield Properties Ltd* [2002] Ch 12; [2001] EWCA Civ 1797, [2002] Ch 194.

[34] *Taylors Fashions* [1982] QB 133, 143.

[35] *Phillips v Mobil Oil Ltd* [1989] 1 WLR 888.

course confirmed by a powerful Court of Appeal (who also noted Oliver J's acceptance of it in *Taylors Fashions*); and some consideration is given to the legislative history of the LCA 1925 to see if renewal covenants in leases could fall outside the registration requirement and simply 'run' with the estate per se. But, for that court, at that time, with (by then) over 30 years of practice following *Beesly*, it was dealt with as a matter of statutory construction and not as a matter of policy. The *Beesly* rule is now unchallengeable and has been confirmed by the Landlord and Tenant (Covenants) Act.[36] In the context of *Taylors Fashions* though, the interesting question is, why did Oliver J brush aside Scott QC's argument so easily when he—perhaps unlike the court in *Phillips v Mobil Oil*—really did have a choice? Whatever the answer, it is interesting that in neither *Beesly* itself nor in *Taylors Fashions* did the lack of registration actually cost the deserving plaintiff. As noted, in *Beesly* it was held that a new lease had been granted anyway; and in *Taylors Fashions* estoppel rescued Old & Campbell. Indeed, in *Beesly* the plaintiffs ran an argument based on *promissory* estoppel, but this was rejected for two reasons: first, there appears to have been no detriment; and, secondly, because it 'cannot ... be invoked to render enforceable a right which would otherwise be unenforceable, nor to negative the operation of a statute'.[37] That issue, of course, is one of the sharp points of disagreement about the proper role of the modern law of *proprietary* estoppel and, one might say, is exactly the effect (but not the purpose) of what Oliver J did in *Taylors Fashions*. That Oliver J had another route to a solution for at least one of the plaintiffs in *Taylors Fashions* may well explain his brief dismissal of Scott QC's submission that *Beesly* was wrong. Perhaps it was an opportunity missed, although perhaps now only rued by some tidy minded property lawyers who have to explain it to baffled students.

The Registration Question

Taylors Fashions was not the first case where Oliver J had applied the full force of the voidness rule found in the LCA 1925 to an unregistered land charge. Although the House of Lords' decision in *Midland Bank Trust Co Ltd v Green (No 1)*[38] was yet to come,[39] Oliver J had tried the case at first instance in October 1977; and he was already well aware of how the legislation, if applied unremittingly, could appear to favour those who stood on their strict rights at the expense of those being stood on. In response to a plea by Leonard Hoffmann QC in *Green* not to be swayed by an emotional

---

[36] Landlord and Tenant (Covenants) Act 1995, s 3(6)(b).
[37] *Beesly v Hallwood Estates Ltd* [1960] 1 WLR 549, 561 (Buckley J).
[38] *Midland Bank Trust Co Ltd v Green (No 1)* [1981] AC 513.
[39] For discussion of *Midland Bank Trust Co Ltd v Green (No 1)*, see ch 7.

view of the merits,[40] Oliver J had applied section 13 of the LCA 1925 and declared Geoffrey's unregistered option void, as he was later to do with that of Taylors Fashions Ltd. When it came to the decision in *Taylors Fashions* itself, Oliver J did not seek to rely on his own judgment in *Green*—by then subject to an unresolved appeal[41]—but the rationale is essentially the same: the clear provisions of the LCA 1925 cannot be compromised simply because they appear to favour the less deserving at the expense of the more innocent.

In fact, the similarity with *Green* does not end there. In both cases Oliver J expressed sympathy with the holder of the unprotected option. In *Taylors Fashions*: 'the defendants' case is not one which impresses itself upon one immediately as overburdened with merit and the first impression is not significantly improved by a closer examination of the background';[42] in *Green*: 'it seems to me that the merits are all one way. The conclusion I have reached therefore is one which I reach with regret'.[43] In both cases, Oliver J accepts that he may not stray beyond the judicial function into the unchartered waters of morality or deploy his own sense of fairness; and that his role is to apply the law. In *Taylors Fashions*: 'But if they are right in law and if there is no equity which assists the plaintiffs, it is no part of a judge's function to seek to impose upon a party to litigation his own idiosyncratic code of commercial morality';[44] and in *Green*: 'I cannot, with the best will in the world, allow my subjective moral judgment to stand in the way of what I apprehend to be the clear meaning of the statutory provisions'.[45] But, unlike *Green*, in *Taylors Fashions*, Oliver J could see a way out and one must wonder what it was that made the situation in *Taylors Fashions* unconscionable when it was not in *Green*. Why was it that the option in *Green* could not be saved, but one plaintiff could succeed in *Taylors Fashions*?[46] One possibility is that Oliver J recognised that estoppel was not a remedy for general unconscionability (as might be thought to characterise the factual matrix in *Green*), even though its operation turned on a finding of specific unconscionability as stipulated in *Taylors Fashions*. Indeed,

---

[40] Presumably, Minerva's Owl had had its wings clipped.

[41] The Court of Appeal in *Green* allowed the appeal, but was itself reversed on appeal to the House of Lords.

[42] *Taylors Fashions* [1982] QB 133,135.

[43] *Midland Bank Trust Co Ltd v Green (No 1)* [1979] Ch 590, 614.

[44] *Taylors Fashions* [1982] QB 133,135. There is also the cryptic comment, based on who knows what observation during the trial, that 'I would not wish to be thought to be voicing a criticism of those who have the conduct of the defendants' affairs [presumably Peter Millet QC]. Those who undertake a fiduciary responsibility for management of the affairs of others are not always free to follow their own personal inclinations in the performance of that responsibility': ibid.

[45] *Midland Bank Trust Co Ltd v Green (No 1)* [1979] Ch 590, 614.

[46] As is well known, Geoffrey's estate successfully pursued other remedies in contract and tort against his father and in negligence against the original solicitors.

a similar view was adopted by Lord Scott (as he had become) in *Yeoman's Row Management Ltd v Cobbe*;[47] and Oliver J had already made it clear that he did not see a judge's function to deliver 'palm-tree justice'.[48]

It seems that Oliver J's conception of estoppel, even after stepping outside the confines of *Willmott v Barber*, was not that it was based on a broad notion of equitable fairness, nor that it provided a way out of an inconvenient statutory rule, but that it was the application of well-worn principles in a new context. Thus, while the judgment in *Taylors Fashions* now might be seen as breaking with the past and casting estoppel in a different direction, it is not certain that Oliver J saw it that way. After all, if that were his mind set, if he were thinking Denning-like, *Green* had already provided the perfect opportunity.[49] Indeed, on one view, *Taylors Fashions* and *Green* are not that different. In *Green*, the holder of the unregistered option failed; in *Taylors Fashions* the holder of the unregistered option failed. Both cases upheld the voidness rule of the LCA 1925. The difference is that in *Taylors Fashions* Old & Campbell won its case on estoppel, but it was not Old & Campbell who had failed to register the option and was directly subject to the rule of statutory voidness under the LCA 1925. Indeed, Old & Campbell could never have registered the option because it had not been granted an option: Old & Campbell was caught by the failure of others.[50] On those facts, therefore, being rescued by estoppel does not directly compromise the principles of charge registration. Perhaps Oliver J did not regard estoppel in *Taylor Fashions* as detracting from principles of charge registration at all, and so did not see it as being used 'to negative the operation of a statute' as feared by Buckley J in *Beesly*.[51] It was an example of specific unconscionability that did not cross the sovereignty of Parliament.

The Estoppel

The ability of all three leases to continue or (as was the case) to be renewed for the maximum period contemplated by the parties when the leases were negotiated depended on the exercise of the option by Taylors Fashions Ltd.[52] If the option were not exercised, or rather were not capable of being

---

[47] *Yeoman's Row Management Ltd v Cobbe* [2008] UKHL 55, [2008] 1 WLR 1752, 1762.
[48] *Taylors Fashions* [1982] QB 133, 157.
[49] Lord Denning MR led the Court of Appeal which overturned Oliver J in *Green*, and whose judgment was not well received by Lord Wilberforce in the House of Lords.
[50] It remains surprising that Old & Campbell would tie their leases so closely to those held by others, even with the initial right of pre-emption. Perhaps this had been demanded by Liverpool Victoria, but the risks seem obvious.
[51] *Beesly v Hallwood Estates Ltd* [1960] 1 WLR 549, 612.
[52] There was a subsidiary question whether 'exercised' meant validly and effectively exercised, or 'purported to be exercised' even though frustrated by the general law. If the latter, Old & Campbell would have prevailed irrespective of lack of registration and estoppel because

exercised because it was void against Liverpool Victoria for want of registration, both tenants would suffer, even though Old & Campbell had always been powerless in respect of the registration and even if the *Beesly* rule had been understood. So, in play was a statutory voidness rule; and today courts are wary of using estoppel where that would appear to contradict the requirements of a statute, whether as to formality or registration.[53] In fact, Oliver J spends little time considering the interplay between estoppel and statutory formalities—perhaps because he did not see it as raising a question of principle[54] or perhaps because, as noted above, the successful plaintiff was not directly within the reach of the LCA 1925. Of course, this is speculation, but it is certain that the identification of the modern criteria for estoppel arose in a case where a successful claim *appeared* to circumvent statutory formalities but no eyebrows were raised.

Apart from the issue of principle about the interplay between statute and estoppel, the difficulty faced by both plaintiffs was the conventional and apparently required approach to establishing proprietary estoppel prescribed in *Willmott v Barber*.[55] That case emphasised that the beliefs, knowledge and actions of the landowner were paramount. It was, in essence, his mistake which founded the estoppel; and he had to know that he was mistaken in order to be held to the assurance and that he encouraged the claimant in the mistaken belief. Unconscionability per se was not highlighted, although an equity lawyer at the time would certainly have regarded the landowner as engaging in 'sharp practice' if he had behaved within the *Willmott v Barber* formula. As Fry J said, immediately before setting out his famous five probanda:

> It has been said that the acquiescence which will deprive a man of his legal rights must amount to fraud, and in my view that is an abbreviated statement of a very true proposition. A man is not to be deprived of his legal rights unless he has acted in such a way as would make it fraudulent for him to set up those rights.[56]

The five probanda were, in essence, the factual elements necessary to establish the 'near fraud' sufficient to prevent the legal owner asserting his rights. In cases of estoppel by acquiescence—broadly equated in Oliver J's

---

Taylors Fashions would have 'exercised' the option by relying on it, even if it was not in the end enforceable. Oliver J was not sympathetic to this ingenious argument, *Taylors Fashions* [1982] QB 133, 160.

[53] *Herbert v Doyle* [2010] EWCA Civ 1095; *Kinane v Mackie-Conteh* [2005] EWCA Civ 45; *Brightlingsea Haven Ltd v Morris* [2008] EWHC 1928 (QB), [2009] 2 P & CR 11. But see *Whittaker v Kinnear* [2011] EWHC 1479 (QB).

[54] Certainly, it is this author's view that the 'problem' of the relationship of estoppel to statutory requirements is illusory and arises only when no proper consideration is given to the principles on which estoppel is based (as opposed to a search for factual criteria to establish it).

[55] *Willmott v Barber* (1880) LR 15 Ch D 96. The Olympic Park in London now incorporates the site of the saw mill at the heart of the dispute in *Willmott v Barber*.

[56] Ibid, 105.

judgment with what we now regard as the modern doctrine of proprietary estoppel—authority appeared to establish that an essential ingredient was that the landowner knew of the true position and that the plaintiff had made a mistake as to his rights over the land, which the landowner had not dispelled. This was certainly true in 'standing by cases'[57] and there was 'high authority'[58] that it applied also to cases of encouragement of the plaintiff in that belief by the landowner. This was, indeed, to be contrasted with cases of promissory estoppel (apparently the issue in *Beesly* and also described in this case as estoppel by representation) where the landowner did not need to be aware of the true position. However, no one needed reminding in *Taylors Fashions* that promissory estoppel merely permits the enforcement of an otherwise unenforceable contract and does not extinguish rights. If the plaintiff wished to establish a claim to the land irrespective of the existence of a contract, or wished to extinguish the landowner's rights, proprietary estoppel was needed and *Willmott v Barber* had decided that the landowner must have been aware of the true legal position in order to generate the 'near fraud' that could cement a claim. In *Taylors Fashions* there was a common mistake as to the need for registration—and thus whether the leases could be renewed automatically—but there was no sense in which Liverpool Victoria could have be said to have been even tinged with a fraud. They *may* have acquiesced in a false position, but certainly innocently: so how could that equate to an estoppel under *Willmott v Barber*?

Oliver J recognised the force of the submission that the establishment of proprietary estoppel required the landowner to be aware of the true legal position and, on the whole, did not appear to regard *Willmott v Barber* as imposing such a high hurdle that it strangled the equitable nature of the doctrine. Indeed, he thought that the five probanda might still be applicable in their entirety in the 'standing by' cases.[59] He was less sure, however, whether the five probanda were always to be adhered to in cases where the landowner had encouraged the plaintiff in his mistake. In such cases, he thought, perhaps the emphasis should be on the *effect* of the encouragement on the claimant, rather than on the state of mind or knowledge of the landowner.[60] After all, even if the landowner did not know the true

---

[57] *Armstrong v Sheppard & Short Ltd* [1959] 2 QB 384 (CA).

[58] *Taylors Fashions* [1982] QB 133, 147.

[59] As it turned out, *Taylors Fashions* changed this also; see *Lester v Woodgate* [2010] EWCA Civ 199, [2010] 2 P & CR 359.

[60] 'This is the principal point on which the parties divide. Mr Scott and Mr Essayan contend that what the court has to look at in relation to the party alleged to be estopped is only his conduct and its result, and not—or, at any rate, not necessarily—his state of mind. It then has to ask whether what that party is now seeking to do is unconscionable. Mr Millett contends that it is an essential feature of this particular equitable doctrine that the party alleged to be estopped must, before the assertion of his strict rights can be considered unconscionable, be aware both of what his strict rights were and of the fact that the other party is acting in the belief that they will not be enforced against him': *Taylors Fashions* [1982] QB 133, 144.

position, it could still be unconscionable to insist on the enforcement of strict legal rights against the plaintiff when the landowner had encouraged that expectation, whether he knew of the true position or not.[61] In this sense, Oliver J saw unconscionability not as a function of the actions and beliefs of the landowner, but as turning on the effect the encouragement had on the plaintiff. Thus,

> [T]he inquiry which I have to make therefore, as it seems to me, is simply whether, in all the circumstances of this case, it was unconscionable for the defendants to seek to take advantage of the mistake which, at the material time, everybody shared.[62]

This led to what we now regard as a rejection of the prescriptive quality of *Willmott v Barber*, at least in encouragement cases, and in turn to the identification of a broader principle of estoppel, focusing more on the impact of the landowner's action on the claimant, than on what the landowner was doing or believed. Even so, this was still located within the relatively traditional boundaries established by *Willmott v Barber* and *Ramsden v Dyson*;[63] but the recognition that proprietary estoppel in fact encompasses 'a much wider equitable jurisdiction to interfere in cases where the assertion of strict legal rights is found by the court to be unconscionable', both freed estoppel from the *Willmott v Barber* limitations and placed unconscionability at the heart of the doctrine. It led to the now common mantra that estoppel is founded on assurance, coupled with detrimental reliance in circumstances of unconscionability—even though such a precise formulation is not adopted by Oliver J himself, albeit that it echoes (but not perfectly) that put forward by counsel for the plaintiffs.[64]

On the facts *Taylors Fashions Ltd* was unsuccessful. Although it believed that the option was enforceable against Liverpool Victoria, its conduct in relation to its leasehold unit—the renovation works and the installation of the lift to which the right of renewal was tied—was based on the assumption that renewal would be available and it intended to take up the opportunity. For its part, Liverpool Victoria gave all necessary permissions as landlord for these works to take place, including reasonably detailed discussions about the installation of the lift. Nevertheless, the evidence before Oliver J did not reveal that Liverpool Victoria had encouraged Taylors Fashions to believe that the option was valid, nor encouraged it to spend time and money (ie, undertake detriment) *because* it was valid. It was a perfectly understandable assumption on the part of Taylors Fashions; but the

---

[61] A different way of looking at it is that the plaintiff should not be the only one who bears the risk of a mistake having been made.

[62] *Taylors Fashions* [1982] QB 133, 155.

[63] *Ramsden v Dyson* (1866) LR 1 HL 129.

[64] *Taylors Fashions* [1982] QB 133, 144.

landowner had done nothing to foster or encourage it. Thus, Oliver J could

> find nothing in the defendants' conduct which can properly be said to have encouraged Taylors to believe in the validity of the option to any greater extent than they had already been encouraged to do so by what they had previously been told by their legal advisers.[65]

Simply, there had been no assurance. Moreover, there was little evidence that the work undertaken by Taylors Fashions was 'on the faith' of the assumption. All the work could be explained on the basis that Taylors Fashions was improving the premises for the benefit of the residue of the lease, the unexpired term, rather than in the expectation of a new lease. Thus, there was no reliance. Absent assurance and reliance, there was no unconscionability.

By way of contrast, Old & Campbell was successful in its plea of estoppel because Liverpool Victoria did encourage it to believe that its leases would continue to their full term or be renewed, albeit that (as once required by *Willmott v Barber*) Liverpool Victoria did not know that there had been a mistake. Oliver J thought its position to be very different, largely because of Old & Campbell's extended business relationship with Liverpool Victoria. He took the view that both parties believed the lease would continue, a belief that Liverpool Victoria had itself 'fostered by the terms of the lease,' and in light of which Old & Campbell was 'encouraged by the defendants to expend a very large sum on the premises and to take a lease of the adjoining premises'.[66] Of course, one might wonder here how this was different from the position of Taylors Fashions, who also might be thought to have been encouraged 'by the terms of the lease' to think that the option was enforceable. There are perhaps two points that explain the difference.

First, as noted above, as a simple matter of evidence, Oliver J was not clear that Liverpool Victoria had ever encouraged Taylors Fashions to believe that the lease would continue *apart* from the fact that there was an option to extend it. It might—I surmise—have been different if Liverpool Victoria had promised that it would not rely on the lack of registration of the option, knowing that it was required; but it had not.[67] It was a mistake by both parties with no encouragement by the landowner, active or passive, to the contrary. Note here the suggestion that the landowner *does* need to know of the mistake *in some cases*, as *Willmott v Barber* suggests. Where there is a statutory rule that invalidates a transaction or event, this is deemed to be known to all, so that estoppel can only save a transaction

---

[65] Ibid, 155.

[66] Ibid, 157.

[67] In the same way that a person cannot rely on a 'subject to contract' clause if they then assure the other party that they will not insist on such, all other elements of estoppel being established.

that does not comply with the statutory rule if the defendant (ie, he who is said to be subject to the estoppel) has explicitly addressed himself to it. On that basis *Willmott v Barber* is not wrong, just illustrative rather than definitive.

Secondly, as noted above but not highlighted by Oliver J, there is a real difference between the estoppel claims made by Taylors Fashions and Old & Campbell. In relation to Taylors Fashions, the effect of the estoppel would have been to circumvent the requirement of the LCA 1925 as to registration. But in relation to Old & Campbell, Liverpool Victoria was not encouraging the belief that the option need not be registered, but that the leases would last as long as had been anticipated by both parties. Of course, underlying this was Liverpool Victoria's mistaken belief that the option was valid against it, but this was not the assurance operating on Old & Campbell. Old & Campbell was at risk of early termination and non-renewal (respectively) of its two leases not because of *its* failure to utilise the statutory machinery provided by Parliament in the LCA 1925, but because of the effect of that legislation on another party. Thus, to allow Old & Campbell to utilise estoppel need not be seen as allowing a party to avoid prescriptive legislation which *it* should have observed. Indeed, the first lease contained no option, and no question of registration arose in respect of the second lease because Liverpool Victoria was seeking to rely on the condition attached to the option reserved to it as grantor. It was not seeking to plead its status (as against Old & Campbell) as purchaser under the LCA 1925. Or to put it another way, Old & Campbell's successful estoppel was not one that contravened the policy of the LCA 1925, but Taylors Fashions' would have been.

THE LEGACY

At first blush, Oliver J's judgment in relation to the preliminary issues which brought the plea of estoppel to the fore looks more conventional than ground breaking. Oliver J preferred to follow *Beesly* for frankly not particularly good, or at least not convincingly articulated, reasons and despite being provided with some compelling arguments by Richard Scott QC. Perhaps, in the grand scheme of things, this missed opportunity to return to what most conveyancers at the time thought was the law is not such a matter of great moment, although it adds to the schizophrenic way in which our law of property deals with the landlord and tenant relationship.[68] Similarly, there was not much chance that Oliver J would favour a solution that would directly and blatantly sidestep the voidness rule of land charges

---

[68] Is it contractual; is it proprietary; is it both?

registration. Not having done it in *Green*, he was unlikely to do it in this case. Nor in truth could he have done so without undermining the raison d'être of the legislation, a point made with clarity by the House of Lords in *Green* when restoring his judgment in preference to that of the Court of Appeal. Departing from *Beesly* would barely have rippled the water; but, having declined to do so, he was hardly likely to whip up a typhoon.

Even then, when it came to the estoppel question, Oliver J's premise was that the earlier cases—*Ramsden v Dyson* in particular—supported his more holistic approach. He saw the five probanda as one way (rather than the only way) to establish the existence of the inequity, the unconscionability, and as never having been a definitive statement of the ingredients of estoppel by acquiescence. Indeed, in the earlier case of *Shaw v Applegate*,[69] both Goff J and Buckley LJ (obiter) had expressed doubts that all the probanda need be met, with Buckley LJ noting (in a more relaxed frame of mind than perhaps in *Beesly*) that

> the real test, I think, must be whether upon the facts of the particular case the situation has become such that it would be dishonest or unconscionable for the plaintiff, or the person having the right sought to be enforced, to continue to seek to enforce it.[70]

The different result for Taylors Fashions and Old & Campbell was itself an expression of a narrow view of unconscionability and perhaps the relationship between estoppel and the rigour of 'formality' rules. It was, of course, influenced by the different facts, but even these illustrate a holistic but grounded view of unconscionability. It is then—perhaps as it is with many cases that turn out to be seminal—that Oliver J did not see his judgment as the clear break with the past in the way that we are now tempted to see it.

Having said that, however, does not detract from the influence that *Taylors Fashions* has had on the development of proprietary estoppel. Certainly, this was not the last of *Willmott v Barber*: years after *Taylor Fashions* it featured prominently in *Matharu v Matharu*[71] but its influence (in the many cases in which it is cited) is illustrative rather than definitive of estoppel. In *Habib Bank Ltd v Habib Bank AG Zurich*[72] Oliver LJ (as he had then become), in the context of a passing off claim, repeated his broad approach to estoppel by acquiescence that he had identified in *Taylors Fashions*. And in *Jones v Stones*[73] Aldous LJ (who had appeared before

---

[69] *Shaw v Applegate* [1977] 1 WLR 970.

[70] Ibid, 978 (Buckley LJ). See also *Electrolux Ltd v Electrix Ltd* (1953) 71 RPC 23 (Evershed MR) and (the customary verve of Lord Denning MR) in *Moorgate Mercantile Co Ltd v Twitchings* [1976] QB 225, 241.

[71] *Matharu v Matharu* [1994] P & CR 93 (CA).

[72] *Habib Bank Ltd v Habib Bank AG Zurich* [1981] 1 WLR 1265 (CA).

[73] *Jones v Stones* [1999] 1 WLR 1739 (CA).

Oliver LJ in *Habib* and learnt the hard way not to rely on 'archaic and arcane' distinctions) made it clear in a real property context that Oliver J's dicta in *Taylor Fashions*, repeated in *Habib*, encapsulated the modern law. He added, possibly in frustration:

> As I have pointed out before in this court, the five elements referred to in *Willmott v Barber* can be important considerations, but the modern approach to acquiescence and estoppel is that laid down in *Habib Bank Ltd v Habib Bank AG Zurich*.[74]

Lest there be any doubt, Lord Scott returned to the matter, over 30 years later. In *Blue Haven Enterprises Limited v Tully*,[75] on behalf of the Privy Council, he said:

> Oliver J's concentration on unconscionable behaviour on the part of the defendant rather than on the *Willmott v Barber* five probanda was implicitly approved by Lord Templeman in giving the judgment of the Privy Council in *Attorney General of Hong Kong v Humphrey's Estate (Queen's Gardens) Ltd* [1987] AC 114 123 and is referred to in *Snell's Equity*, 31st ed (2005), para 10.16 as 'the most important authoritative modern statement of the doctrine'. Their Lordships are of the same opinion. Fry J's five probanda remain a highly convenient and authoritative yardstick for identifying the presence, or absence, of unconscionable behaviour on the part of a defendant sufficient to require an equitable remedy, but they are not necessarily determinative.[76]

So it is that *Taylors Fashions* explains *Ramsden v Dyson*, and leads to the holistic approach of *Gillett v Holt*,[77] itself confirmed wholeheartedly in *Thorner v Major*. It places unconscionability at the heart of the doctrine and is 'the most important authoritative modern statement of the doctrine'. Moreover, as Morgan J said in *Avocet Industrial Estates LLP v Merol Ltd*, '[e]stoppels are highly fact sensitive';[78] and *Taylors Fashions* allows the sensitivity in the particular facts and the sensitivity in going outside the strict confines of the law to be accommodated. That we have come far from the confines of *Willmott v Barber* is no better illustrated than the recent case of *Lester v Woodgate*.[79] The issue was whether the claimant was estopped from enforcing a right of way (and the Court of Appeal held that it was), but the Court went from *Ramsden*, through *Willmott v Barber*, citing the same cases as in *Taylors Fashions,* and ending with Oliver LJ's formulation of his judgment in *Habib* and its approval in *Stones*. In the view of

---

[74] Ibid, 1743.
[75] *Blue Haven Enterprises Limited v Tully* [2006] UKPC 17.
[76] Ibid, [23].
[77] *Gillett v Holt* [2001] Ch 210 (CA).
[78] *Avocet Industrial Estates LLP v Merol Ltd* [2012] L & TR 13, [83]. *Taylors Fashions* was not cited to Morgan J in *Avocet* but he relied on it still.
[79] *Lester v Woodgate* [2010] EWCA Civ 199, [2010] 2 P & CR 359.

the Court of Appeal, the Recorder had applied the *Taylors Fashions* test; and the Court of Appeal would not disturb it. In the words of Patten LJ, 'These authorities, I think, indicate the need to take a flexible and very fact-specific approach to each case in which an estoppel by acquiescence is relied upon'.[80] This is the legacy of *Taylors Fashions*.

[80] Ibid, [39].

5

Federated Homes Ltd v Mill Lodge Properties Ltd *(1979)*

Annexation and Intention

NIGEL P GRAVELLS

INTRODUCTION

FEDERATED HOMES LTD v Mill Lodge Properties Ltd[1] (*Federated Homes*) merits the designation of a landmark case on a number of levels. Most significantly, the Court of Appeal[2] adopted an interpretation of section 78 of the Law of Property Act 1925 that first recognised the concept of statutory annexation of the benefit of covenants affecting freehold land. The decision contradicted the long-standing judicial interpretation of section 78;[3] but it provided some welcome simplification in the law relating to the transmission of the benefit of restrictive covenants, not least by rendering largely redundant some of the traditional methods of transmission. Even though the original decision has been qualified and refined, it continues to have significant impact on the effect of existing covenants and on the drafting of new covenants. Moreover, the decision also contributed to (or at least prompted) the clarification of the law on a range of other matters relating to covenants affecting freehold land.

FEDERATED HOMES: THE FACTS

In 1970, Mackenzie Hill, the owner of a development site, which comprised four areas of land (the green land, the red land, the blue land and the pink land), obtained outline planning permission to build 1250 houses (and

---

[1] *Federated Homes Ltd v Mill Lodge Properties Ltd* [1980] 1 WLR 594 (CA).
[2] Brightman, Megaw and Browne LJJ.
[3] In 1984 the Law Commission observed that *Federated Homes* 'has made radical and controversial changes in what was thought to be the law about annexation': Law Commission Report No 127, *Transfer of Land: The Law of Positive and Restrictive Covenants* (1984) para 4.10.

associated amenities) on the site. The permission was stated to be valid for three years. In 1971, Mackenzie Hill sold the blue land to the defendant, Mill Lodge Properties Ltd, who covenanted

> with the vendor that in carrying out the development of the blue land [the defendant] shall not build at a greater density than a total of 300 dwellings so as not to reduce the number of units which the vendor might eventually erect on the retained land under the existing planning consent.

(By a simultaneous conveyance Mackenzie Hill sold the pink land to another purchaser, subject to a similar covenant.) The plaintiff, Federated Homes Ltd, subsequently became owner of the green land and the red land by different routes. The green land was conveyed to purchaser A and then to the plaintiff, each conveyance containing an express assignment of the benefit of the defendant's covenant. The red land was also conveyed to purchaser A, then to purchaser B and finally to the plaintiff; the first two conveyances of the red land each contained an express assignment of the benefit of the defendant's covenant; but the final conveyance to the plaintiff did not. The plaintiff then discovered that the defendant had obtained planning permission to develop the blue land at a higher density than that permitted by the 1971 restrictive covenant, and that such development would be likely to prejudice the plaintiff's planned development of the red and green land. The plaintiff accordingly brought an action to restrain the defendant from building on the blue land at a density that would be in breach of the restrictive covenant.

RESTRICTIVE COVENANTS AND PLANNING CONTROL

The first line of defence, which comprised two alternative but interrelated limbs, was that the restrictive covenant was inextricably linked to the outline planning permission so that (i) the 1970 planning permission and the benefit of the 1971 covenant were personal to Mackenzie Hill and could not be assigned and/or (ii) the 1971 covenant was spent (and ceased to be enforceable) when the 1970 planning permission lapsed in 1973. This defence obviously raised issues as to the relationship between public law development control through the planning process and private law development control through restrictive covenants.

In order to appreciate the arguments, it is necessary to consider in more detail the terms and conditions of the 1970 planning permission, which was granted by Newport Pagnell Urban District Council, acting as agent for Buckinghamshire County Council, the planning authority. First, the outline planning permission could only be exploited following detailed approval on such matters as the siting, design and external appearance of the proposed buildings. Secondly, if such approval were not applied for within three years, the permission would become void. Thirdly, the permission was stated to be for the benefit of Mackenzie Hill and its subsidiaries only. Mackenzie Hill also entered into an agreement with Newport Pagnell UDC, under which the construction of the houses on the development site would be phased over a period of ten years.[4] The terms of the phasing agreement clearly contemplated that, as indeed happened, Mackenzie Hill might sell (part of) the site to another developer rather than develop the site itself. Moreover, the conveyances of the blue land and the pink land were expressed to be subject to, and with the benefit of, the phasing agreement; and, to that end, Mackenzie Hill covenanted with the purchasers that it would not develop the green land and the red land until the respective purchasers had developed the blue land and the pink land.

The 1970 outline planning permission lapsed in 1973 because the required detailed approval had not been applied for within three years. However, the defendant had proceeded with the development of the blue land under new planning permissions granted in 1971, 1972 and 1975 (the last permission in its terms effectively allowing the number of houses to be built on the blue land to exceed the 300 specified in the covenant with Mackenzie Hill).

Turning to the first limb of the defendant's submission, it was pointed out that the 1970 planning permission was expressed to be for the benefit of Mackenzie Hill and its subsidiaries only. Whatever the reason for that restriction, it meant that an unconnected purchaser from Mackenzie Hill could not rely on the planning permission to develop the site. The defendant sought to argue from this that the covenant in the conveyance to the defendant was personal to Mackenzie Hill and that the benefit was not assignable: it was designed to protect a non-assignable planning permission and therefore should itself be treated as non-assignable. The defendant further argued that the covenant was expressed to be 'with the vendor' and made no reference to the vendor's assigns or other successors in title.

Brightman LJ rejected both arguments. First, he noted that the planning permission was not exclusive to Mackenzie Hill because it was available to a subsidiary; and to that extent it was clearly assignable. Secondly, he found that it was not necessary nor natural nor sensible to read the covenant as personal to Mackenzie Hill since the benefit of a contract between businessmen is generally assignable without any mention of assignability, unless the contract is of a personal nature, which the restrictive covenant was not. Thirdly, the conveyance to the defendant stated that the blue land was sold subject to, and with the benefit of, the phasing agreement and that agreement

---

[4] Brightman LJ was of the view that, since it was Newport Pagnell UDC that had granted the planning permission (albeit in its capacity as agent for the planning authority), the planning permission should be read in conjunction with the phasing agreement, which was made on the same date.

clearly contemplated that Mackenzie Hill might sell the development site in whole or part. For those reasons, he held that the restrictive covenant was not personal but was assignable—a conclusion which corresponded with the business realities.[5]

In the alternative, the defendant argued that the covenant to limit the number of houses to be built on the blue land 'so as not to reduce the number of units which [the plaintiff] might eventually erect on the retained land *under the existing planning consent*' (emphasis added) had lost its purpose and was spent. Since detailed approval had not been obtained for the whole development site and the 1970 outline planning permission had therefore lapsed, no houses could be constructed in reliance on the original planning consent. Brightman LJ concluded, admittedly largely as a matter of impression, that 'it seemed a little unlikely' that the parties intended to tie the restrictive covenant to the original planning permission so that the covenant and the permission should stand or fall together. First, there would seem to be no purpose in such rigidity. Secondly, there must always have been a strong possibility that a developer would have to apply for a new planning permission at some stage (as happened) because the three-year deadline for seeking detailed approval might not fit easily into the ten-year phasing of the development. Thirdly, the covenant would be of limited value if it were linked to, and co-terminous with, the 1970 planning permission. Mackenzie Hill was selling off and therefore not itself developing the blue and the pink land. Consequently—quite apart from the fact that the outline planning permission was granted to Mackenzie Hill and its subsidiaries only—it was unlikely that Mackenzie Hill would apply for detailed approval for the development of land which was going to be developed by others. Furthermore, since the defendant did not covenant to apply for detailed approval within the three-year period, it made no sense to link the duration of the covenant to the 1970 planning permission. Again, looking to the business realities, Brightman LJ construed the reference in the covenant to the existing planning consent as explanatory and not as controlling.[6]

Although Brightman LJ based his decision largely on the construction of the planning permission, the phasing agreement and the covenant, more generally the conclusion on the defendant's first line of defence would seem to provide clear confirmation of the principle that public law development

---

[5] *Federated Homes* [1980] 1 WLR 594, 601–02. Brightman LJ also stated that s 78 of the Law of Property Act 1925, in providing that a covenant relating to any land of the covenantee shall be deemed to have been made with the covenantee and his successors in title, presupposes assignability. That argument seems to assume that s 78 cannot be excluded, a view which was arguably adopted by Brightman LJ in *Federated Homes* but which is no longer tenable in light of *Roake v Chadha* [1984] 1 WLR 40 (Ch D) and *Crest Nicholson Residential (South) Ltd v McAllister* [2004] EWCA Civ 410, [2004] 1 WLR 2409, discussed below, pp 119–21.

[6] *Federated Homes* [1980] 1 WLR 594, 602–03.

control through the planning process and private law development control through restrictive covenants are complementary. Restrictive covenants are seen as having an indispensable role, especially in the context of residential property developments, regulating many matters that cannot be the legitimate concern of planning control. Consequently, even where the planning authority, in the exercise of its public law powers, has authorised a particular use of land, as a matter of private law that permission cannot authorise that use if the landowner has covenanted that he will not so use the land. In other words, a landowner who has covenanted with his neighbour not to build on his land cannot escape that covenant by obtaining planning permission from the planning authority.[7]

PASSING THE BENEFIT OF RESTRICTIVE COVENANTS

Having held that the restrictive covenant was capable of assignment and had not become spent, Brightman LJ turned to the defendant's second line of defence, namely that the benefit of the covenant had not passed to the plaintiff—with the result that it could not enforce the covenant against the defendant. On the assumption that the benefit of the defendant's covenant was assignable, it was common ground that, as owner of the green land, the plaintiff had acquired the benefit of the covenant through the unbroken chain of assignments from Mackenzie Hill to the plaintiff; and that was sufficient to entitle the plaintiff to an injunction restraining breach of the covenant by the defendant. However, both the trial judge[8] and the Court of Appeal also considered the position of the plaintiff as owner of the red land.

As noted above, there was no complete chain of assignments in the case of the red land. The trial judge therefore considered whether the benefit of the covenant had been annexed to the red land—if so, any subsequent assignment of the benefit would have been unnecessary and the incomplete chain of assignments would have been irrelevant.

Annexation of the Benefit of Restrictive Covenants

Annexation is the permanent fixing of the benefit of a restrictive covenant to the land of the covenantee at the time of the covenant so that from that

---

[7] See Law Commission Report No 11, *Transfer of Land: Report on Restrictive Covenants* (1967) para 19; Law Com No 127, *The Law of Positive and Restrictive Covenants*, above (n 3) paras 2.5–2.7; Law Commission Consultation Paper No 186, *Easements, Covenants and Profits à Prendre: A Consultation* (2008) para 7.34.

[8] John Mills QC, sitting as a Deputy High Court Judge.

time onwards the benefit of the covenant is effectively part of the land and passes automatically when the land is transferred. However, annexation is only one element in the legal rules according to which the benefit of a covenant between freehold owners may 'run with' the land of the covenantee so that subsequent owners of that land may enforce the covenant.

The orthodox view on the pre-*Federated Homes* position is that the benefit of a freehold covenant may run with the land of the covenantee pursuant to common law or equitable rules. Where the person seeking to enforce the covenant is a successor in title of the original covenantee but he is seeking to enforce the covenant against the original covenantor, he can (but need not) rely on the common law rules for the passing of the benefit. The covenant must 'touch and concern' the land of the covenantee;[9] and the covenantee and the successor in title must both have a legal estate in the land.[10] Although there seems to be clear authority for an additional requirement that the original parties to the covenant must have intended that the benefit of the covenant should run with the land of the covenantee,[11] this has been questioned.[12]

However, reliance on the common law rules is generally regarded as not permissible where the original covenantor has disposed of his land so that the person seeking to enforce the covenant has to show that the burden has passed to the successor in title of the original covenantor under the equitable doctrine in *Tulk v Moxhay*.[13] In such circumstances it seems that, if the person seeking to enforce the covenant is a successor in title of the original covenantee, he must show that the benefit of the covenant has passed to him according to the equitable rules,[14] although in one such case the court

---

[9] The covenant must 'affect the land as regards mode of occupation, or it must be such as per se, and not merely from collateral circumstances, affects the value of the land': *Congleton Corporation v Pattison* (1808) 10 East 130, 135 (Bayley J) adopted by Farwell J in *Rogers v Hosegood* [1900] 2 Ch 388, 395.

[10] In relation to covenants entered into prior to 1926 it is possible that the covenantee and the successor in title must have the same legal estate: *Westhoughton UDC v Wigan Coal & Iron Co Ltd* [1919] 1 Ch 159. Any such requirement seems to have been removed by s 78 of the Law of Property Act 1925: see *Smith and Snipes Hall Farm Ltd v River Douglas Catchment Board* [1949] 2 KB 500.

[11] *Rogers v Hosegood* [1900] 2 Ch 388, 396; *Smith and Snipes Hall Farm Ltd v River Douglas Catchment Board* [1949] 2 KB 500, 506, 511; and *Williams v Unit Construction Co Ltd* (1955) 19 Conv 262, 265.

[12] Law Com No 186, *A Consultation*, above (n 7) para 7.22, referring to C Harpum, *Megarry and Wade, The Law of Real Property*, 6th edn (London, Sweet & Maxwell, 2000) para 16-012. See now C Harpum, SN Bridge and MJ Dixon (eds), *Megarry and Wade, The Law of Real Property*, 8th edn (London, Sweet & Maxwell, 2012) para 32-012, noting the absence of any such requirement in *Dyson v Forster* [1909] AC 98 and *Westhoughton UDC v Wigan Coal & Iron Co Ltd* [1919] 1 Ch 159 and in the restatement of the common law rules in *P & A Swift Investments v Combined English Stores Group plc* [1989] AC 632, 639–40.

[13] *Tulk v Moxhay* (1848) 2 Ph 774 (Ch D).

[14] See *Re Union of London and Smith's Bank Ltd's Conveyance; Miles v Easter* [1933] Ch 611, 630 (CA).

permitted reliance on the common law rules.[15] However, it is accepted that a successor in title of the original covenantee must satisfy the equitable rules for passing the benefit where he acquires part only of the land of the original covenantee[16] or where he acquires only equitable ownership of the land[17] or where he seeks injunctive relief or some other equitable remedy.

In order for the benefit of a covenant to pass in equity so as to enable the successor in title of the original covenantee to enforce the covenant, it must be established (i) that the covenant touches and concerns the land of the covenantee; and (ii) that the benefit has passed to the successor in title (a) by express or implied annexation, (b) by assignment or (c) through the operation of a scheme of development.[18]

Express annexation depends upon appropriate words in the document creating the covenant, demonstrating the intention that the benefit should be permanently fixed to the land of the covenantee. The covenant must be stated to be made for the benefit of the covenantee's land or for the benefit of the covenantee in his capacity as owner of the land or for the benefit of the covenantee and his successors in title to the land.[19] Implied annexation, according to which the relevant intention may be implied from surrounding circumstances alone, is more controversial;[20] and there seems to have been a retreat from more extreme formulations of the doctrine—with the result that it remains necessary at least to anchor the finding of intention in the creating document;[21] and that may make the doctrine indistinguishable from the modern, more flexible, operation of express annexation.

[15] *Rogers v Hosegood* [1900] 2 Ch 388, 394, 404 (CA).

[16] *Re Union of London and Smith's Bank Ltd's Conveyance; Miles v Easter* [1933] Ch 611, 630 (CA).

[17] Eg, *Lord Northbourne v Johnston* [1922] 2 Ch 309 (Ch D); *Newton Abbott Co-operative Society Ltd v Williamson & Treadgold Ltd* [1952] Ch 286 (Ch D); *Marten v Flight Refuelling Ltd* [1962] Ch 115 (Ch D).

[18] Assignment and schemes of development are not considered further.

[19] *Rogers v Hosegood* [1900] 2 Ch 388 (CA) is usually cited as providing a classic formula for express annexation: the covenantor covenanted 'with intent that the covenant may enure to the benefit of the vendors their successors and assigns and others claiming under them to all or any of the adjoining lands'. There is no effective annexation where the covenant is made merely 'with the vendors their heirs executors administrators and assigns' since such a formulation contains no reference to the land of the covenantee: see *Renals v Cowlishaw* (1878) 9 Ch D 125 (Ch D) and *Reid v Bickerstaff* [1909] 2 Ch 305 (CA).

[20] Contrast HWR Wade, 'Covenants—"A Broad and Reasonable View"' [1972B] *CLJ* 157, 168–70, who supported the notion of implied annexation in principle, with PV Baker, 'The Benefit of Restrictive Covenants' (1968) 84 *LQR* 22, 30, who argued that there was no compelling basis for the concept in the principal case relied on (*Marten v Flight Refuelling Ltd* [1962] Ch 115 (Ch D)).

[21] *Shropshire County Council v Edwards* (1982) 46 P & CR 270, 277 (Ch D); *J Sainsbury plc v Enfield LBC* [1989] 1 WLR 590, 595–96 (Ch D); *Jamaica Mutual Life Assurance Society v Hillsborough Ltd* [1989] 1 WLR 1101, 1106, 1108 (PC); *Re MCA East Ltd* [2002] EWHC 1684 (Ch), [2003] 1 P & CR 118, [24]–[28].

Federated Homes: Express and Implied Annexation

Although the plaintiff was seeking to enforce the covenant against the original covenantee—so that it would seem that the common law rules could have been applied—the conclusion of the trial judge on annexation clearly suggests that the case was argued by reference to the equitable rules for the running of the benefit.[22] He stated:

> Submissions were made about express annexation, implied annexation, that is to say, annexation implied from surrounding circumstances, and annexation by assignment. In my judgment, there was in this case no 'annexation' of the benefit of the covenant to the retained land or any part of it. Section 78, in particular, of the Law of Property Act 1925 does not have the effect of annexing the benefit of the covenant to anything. It is simply a statutory shorthand for the shortening of conveyances, which it perhaps has done to some extent in this case. Annexation depends upon appropriate drafting, which is not here in this case, in spite of a recent process which can perhaps be called 'a widening of the law' in these matters. The attendant circumstances, moreover, positively militate against annexation because, as [counsel for the defendant] rightly pointed out to me (though he did so in the course of his argument on construction) the restriction in this particular case is of limited duration and plainly not applicable to ultimate purchasers of plots of the land intended to be benefited. 'Annexation', in my judgment, is for the parties to the covenant itself to achieve if they wish to, and (though parties may no doubt provide for annexation at a later stage) I am not satisfied or prepared to hold that there is any such thing as 'delayed annexation by assignment' to which the covenantor is not party or privy.[23]

The trial judge clearly dismissed the submission that there had been express or implied annexation (although he noted that a 'good deal of argument' was addressed to him by both parties). That conclusion would seem to be consistent with the orthodox operation of express and implied annexation. The complete silence of the Court of Appeal on the issue is perhaps rather surprising, since their Lordships can hardly have been oblivious to the revolutionary switch to statutory annexation; but it may suggest agreement with the trial judge.

The Court of Appeal did not refer to the conclusion of the trial judge that the surrounding circumstances militated against a finding of annexation; but that finding clearly did not affect the conclusion of the trial judge on section 62 of the Law of Property Act 1925[24] nor the conclusion of the

---

[22] The author has been unable to find any record of the submissions before the trial judge or the Court of Appeal.

[23] *Federated Homes* [1980] 1 WLR 594, 603.

[24] See pp 109–11 below.

Court of Appeal on section 78 of the 1925 Act.[25] It seems clear that both courts were of the view that the covenant should be enforceable.

Delayed Annexation

The trial judge also rejected the concept of 'delayed annexation by assignment', which blurs the distinction between annexation and assignment as methods of transmitting the benefit of a covenant. As noted above, according to the othodoxy, annexation permanently affixes the benefit of the covenant to the land of the original covenantee at the time of the covenant so that from that time onwards the benefit of the covenant is effectively part of the benefited land and passes automatically when the benefited land is transferred. By contrast, assignment simply transfers the benefit of the covenant to the assignee personally at the time of the subsequent transfer of the covenantee's land; and from that it would seem to follow that, if the current owner of the original covenantee's land is seeking to enforce the covenant, he must establish that the benefit of the covenant has been assigned on every intermediate transfer of the benefited land.[26]

However, there are dicta in older cases which seem to support the view that, where there has been no initial annexation by the creating document but, on a subsequent transfer of the benefited land to a successor in title, the original covenantee assigns the benefit of the covenant, that assignment effects what has been termed 'delayed annexation' (thereby removing the need for any further assignment on subsequent transfers).[27] More recent cases are more equivocal, seeming to support the need, in the absence of initial annexation, for a complete chain of assignments linking the original covenantee and the successor in title seeking to enforce the covenant.[28] There is support from some academic commentators for the

---

[25] See pp 112ff below.

[26] The basis of the trial judge's suggestion that the original parties to the covenant may provide for annexation 'at a later stage' (after the date of the original covenant) is unclear. Presumably the parties could 'renew' the covenant so as to ensure the annexation of the benefit of the renewed covenant *from the date of the renewal*; but it is difficult in principle to see how the benefit of the original covenant as such could be annexed after the date of the covenant.

[27] In *Rogers v Hosegood* [1900] 2 Ch 388, 404, Collins LJ said: 'Where there is no indication in the original conveyance, or in the circumstances attending it, that the covenant is imposed for the benefit of the land reserved, or any particular part of it, then it becomes necessary to examine the circumstances under which any part of the land reserved is sold, in order to see whether a benefit, not originally annexed to it, has become annexed to it on the sale, so that the purchaser is deemed to have bought it with the land'. See also *Renals v Cowlishaw* (1878) 9 Ch D 125, 130–31; *Reid v Bickerstaff* [1909] 2 Ch 305, 320.

[28] In *Re Pinewood Estate, Farnborough* [1958] Ch 280 (Ch D) the need for a chain of assignments was assumed, although the point appears to have been conceded and the three cases referred to in n 27 above were not cited. The judgment of Ungoed-Thomas J in *Stilwell v Blackman* [1968] Ch 508 (Ch D) contains dicta that seem to support both views.

concept of delayed annexation;[29] but the Law Commission seems to have rejected the concept and has asserted the need for an unbroken chain of assignments.[30]

Although in *Federated Homes* Brightman LJ did not comment on the trial judge's rejection of the concept of delayed annexation,[31] the reasoning of the Court of Appeal, in respect of both the green land and the red land, would seem implicitly but incontrovertibly to reject the concept. In finding that the benefit of the covenant had passed to the plaintiff as owner of the green land, Brightman LJ stressed the unbroken chain of assignments; by contrast, despite the express assignment of the benefit of the covenant on the first transfer of the red land from the original covenantee, it was the absence of an unbroken chain of assignments passing the benefit of the covenant to the plaintiff as owner of the red land that necessitated consideration of annexation. Such consideration would have been wholly unnecessary if the express assignment of the benefit of the covenant on the first transfer of the red land had effected annexation. The reasoning on both issues would therefore seem to be inconsistent with the concept of delayed annexation.[32]

---

[29] SJ Bailey, 'The Benefit of a Restrictive Covenant' (1938) 6 *CLJ* 339, 360–61, expressed the view (i) that it was 'highly probable' that the law recognised delayed annexation, although he accepted that there was no unequivocal judicial authority; but (ii) that delayed annexation may require the intention of the assignor not merely to pass the benefit to the assignee but further to annex the benefit to the land from the date of the assignment. Baker, above (n 20) 29–32, and DJ Hayton, 'Restrictive Covenants as Property Interests' (1971) 87 *LQR* 539, 564–68, noted the lack of consistency in the case law but argued (i) that assignable restrictive covenants are property interests (and not merely contractual rights) and (ii) that it is inconsistent with property principles to insist on an express assignment each time the benefited land is transferred. The views of Baker and Hayton were endorsed by Wade, 'Covenants', above (n 20) 166.

[30] Law Com No 186, *A Consultation*, above (n 7) paras 7.24, 7.31. Earlier views of the Law Commission were less clear: Law Com No 11, *Report on Restrictive Covenants*, above (n 7) para 10, was ambiguous; and Law Com No 127, *The Law of Positive and Restrictive Covenants*, above (n 3) para 3.28, referred to the 'possibility' of delayed annexation but concluded that this was not clear from the cases.

[31] CHS Preston and GH Newsom, *Restrictive Covenants Affecting Freehold Land*, 8th edn (London, Sweet & Maxwell, 1991) para 2-16, point out that Brightman LJ referred to the 'proposition' of delayed annexation. Moreover, in *Allen v Veranne Builders Ltd* [1988] EGCS 2 Browne-Wilkinson V-C referred to the 'supposed doctrine' of delayed annexation.

[32] See also *Crest Nicholson Residential (South) Ltd v McAllister* [2004] EWCA Civ 410, [2004] 1 WLR 2409, [27]; *Rees v Peters* [2011] EWCA Civ 836, [12]. It is difficult to make sense of the statement of Proudman J in *Cygnet Healthcare Ltd v Greenswan Consultants Ltd* [2009] EWHC 1318 (Ch), [14]: 'I accept Mr Davies's submission on behalf of the claimant that although the assignment of the benefit of the roadway covenants did not comply with s 136 of the Law of Property Act 1925 … it was nevertheless an effective assignment for the purposes of s 78 of that Act, which operated to annex the covenant to every part of Mr and Mrs Gates's retained land: see *Federated Homes v Mill Lodge Properties Limited* [1980] 1 WLR 594'.

Effect of Section 62 of the Law of Property Act 1925

Although the trial judge concluded that there had been no annexation of the benefit of the covenant to the red land, he held that on the transfer of the red land to the plaintiff the benefit of the covenant (which had been transferred to the plaintiff's predecessor in title by two successive assignments) passed to the plaintiff by virtue of section 62 of the Law of Property Act 1925. Section 62(1) provides:

> A conveyance of land shall be deemed to include and shall by virtue of this Act operate to convey, with the land, all buildings, erections, fixtures, commons, hedges, ditches, fences, ways, waters, watercourses, liberties, privileges, easements, rights, and advantages whatsoever, appertaining or reputed to appertain to the land, or any part thereof, or, at the time of conveyance, demised, occupied, or enjoyed with, or reputed or known as part or parcel of or appurtenant to the land or any part thereof.

An analogous argument had been considered but viewed with some doubt in *Rogers v Hosegood*.[33] The question in that case concerned the effect of a conveyance which was executed before the enactment of section 62 and its predecessor, section 6 of the Conveyancing Act 1881, but which contained a general words clause in similar terms to section 6 of the 1881 Act. Farwell J doubted whether the benefit of the covenant could be said to 'belong or be reputed to belong' to the covenantee's land; and since then the courts have tended to reiterate the early dicta, stressing the need for annexation or express assignment.

There is no indication of the precise reasoning of the trial judge (or the argument of counsel) in *Federated Homes*. However, the defendant might have been expected to take advantage of the wider wording of section 62 of the 1925 Act (as compared with section 6 of the 1881 Act) and argue that at the very least the benefit of assignable covenants are 'rights enjoyed with the land'.[34]

Apart from the reference to the decision of the trial judge and his reliance on section 62, the Court of Appeal made no comment. Although their Lordships' interpretation of section 78 made a decision on section 62 strictly unnecessary, the defendant appealed against the decision of the trial judge and again it is unfortunate that they did not express a view on the issue.[35]

---

[33] *Rogers v Hosegood* [1900] 2 Ch 388 (CA).

[34] This was the view of Hayton, above (n 29) 570–73, expressing the hope that the conclusion was 'not too startling'. Wade, 'Covenants', above (n 20) 175, observed that, once it is accepted that restrictive covenants are first and foremost interests in land, there was 'at least some strength' in Hayton's view.

[35] In *Shropshire County Council v Edwards* (1982) 46 P & CR 270 (Ch D) Judge Rubin expressly decided to follow the example of the Court of Appeal in *Federated Homes* and 'to remain silent on this highly debatable point'.

The argument based on section 62 was subsequently considered in *Roake v Chadha*[36] and in *Kumar v Dunning*.[37] In *Roake v Chadha* Judge Paul Baker QC stated:

> This argument is directed to the conveyances or transfers conveying the alleged benefited land to the predecessors of the plaintiffs, and ultimately to the respective plaintiffs themselves. In each of these transfers, so I am prepared to assume, there is to be implied the general words of section 62 of the Act of 1925 ....

> The argument is that the benefit of the covenant contained in the original transfer to the predecessor of the defendants ... was carried by the words 'rights and advantages whatsoever appertaining or reputed to appertain to the land, or any part thereof'. It seems an argument on these lines was accepted by ... the deputy judge who gave the decision at first instance in the *Federated Homes* case [1980] 1 WLR 594, but I have not seen it, and so cannot comment on it. The proposition now contended for is not a new one. In *Rogers v Hosegood* [1900] 2 Ch 388, it was similarly put forward as an alternative argument to an argument based on annexation. In that case however it was decided that the benefit of the covenant was annexed so that the point on section 6 of the Conveyancing Act 1881, the forerunner of section 62 of the Law of Property Act 1925, did not have to be decided. Nevertheless, Farwell J, sitting in the Chancery Division, said, at p 398:

> 'It is not necessary for me to determine whether the benefit of the covenants would pass under the general words to which I have referred above, if such covenants did not run with the land. If they are not in fact annexed to the land, it may well be that the right to sue thereon cannot be said to belong, or be reputed to belong, thereto; but I express no final opinion on this point'.

> In the Court of Appeal the point was canvassed in argument but not referred to in the judgment of the court, which was given by Collins LJ.

> In the present case, the covenant in terms precludes the benefit passing unless it is expressly assigned. That being so, as it seems to me, it is not a right 'appertaining or reputed to appertain' to land within the meaning of section 62 of the Law of Property Act 1925. As to whether the benefit of a covenant not annexed can ever pass under section 62, I share the doubts of Farwell J. [Counsel for the defendant] suggested—and there may well be something in this—that the rights referred to in section 62 are confined to legal rights rather than equitable rights which the benefit of restrictive covenants is. But again I place it on construction. It cannot be described as a right 'appertaining or reputed to appertain to land' when the terms of the covenant itself would seem to indicate the opposite.[38]

---

[36] *Roake v Chadha* [1984] 1 WLR 40 (Ch D).
[37] *Kumar v Dunning* [1989] QB 193 (CA).
[38] *Roake v Chadha* [1984] 1 WLR 40, 46–47.

And in *Kumar v Dunning* Browne-Wilkinson V-C stated:

The main intention of section 62 was to provide a form of statutory shorthand rendering it unnecessary to include such words expressly in every conveyance. It is a matter of debate whether, in the context of the section, the words 'rights ... appertaining to the land' include rights arising under covenant as opposed to strict property rights. However, I will assume, without deciding, that rights under covenant are within the words of the section. Even on that assumption, it still has to be shown that the right 'appertains to the land'. In my judgment, a right under covenant cannot appertain to the land unless the benefit is in some way annexed to the land. If the benefit of a covenant passes under section 62 even if not annexed to the land, the whole modern law of restrictive covenants would have been established on an erroneous basis.

Section 62(1) replaces section 6(1) of the Conveyancing Act 1881. If the general words 'rights ... appertaining to land' operate to transfer the benefit of a restrictive covenant, whether or not such benefit was expressly assigned, it would make all the law developed since 1881 unnecessary. It is established that, in the absence of annexation to the land or the existence of a building scheme, the benefit of a restrictive covenant cannot pass except by way of express assignment. The law so established is inconsistent with the view that a covenant, the benefit of which is not annexed to the land, can pass under the general words in section 62.[39]

A number of observations may be made. First, in both *Roake v Chadha* and *Kumar v Dunning* the Court considered only whether the benefit of a restrictive covenant could be categorised as a right 'appertaining or reputed to appertain to land'; in neither case did the Court consider whether the benefit of a restrictive covenant could be categorised more broadly as a 'right enjoyed with the land'.[40] Secondly, in both cases the judges seemed to suggest that annexation is a *precondition* to the operation of section 62; but annexation would make section 62 unnecessary. Thirdly, in *Roake v Chadha* the stipulation that the benefit of the covenant could only pass by assignment could be regarded as constituting an expressed contrary intention, which, pursuant to section 62(4), would render the section inapplicable. Fourthly, against the background of the decision in *Federated Homes* it is perhaps ironic that in *Kumar v Dunning* Browne-Wilkinson V-C should have rejected the section 62 argument on the ground that it would undermine the received law on restrictive covenants.

---

[39] *Kumar v Dunning* [1989] QB 193, 198 (CA). Similar reasoning was adopted in rejecting an argument that the benefit of a restrictive covenant had passed to a successor in title by virtue of s 63 of the Law of Property Act 1925: see *Sugarman v Porter* [2006] EWHC 331 (Ch), [2006] 2 P & CR 274, [31]–[44].
[40] See also *Briggs v McCusker* [1996] 2 EGLR 197, 200 (Ch D).

Thus, while there would seem to be a significant tide of judicial opinion against the section 62 argument, it cannot be said to have been conclusively rejected.[41]

The Effect of Section 78 of the Law of Property Act 1925

Section 78 of the Law of Property Act 1925 provides:

> (1) A covenant relating to any land of the covenantee shall be deemed to be made with the covenantee and his successors in title and the persons deriving title under him or them, and shall have effect as if such successors and other persons were expressed.

> For the purposes of this subsection in connexion with covenants restrictive of the user of land 'successors in title' shall be deemed to include the owners and occupiers for the time being of the land of the covenantee intended to be benefited.

The trial judge summarily rejected the argument that the benefit of the covenant had been annexed to the retained land by virtue of section 78; but, contrary to this undoubtedly orthodox view of section 78, the Court of Appeal concluded that the benefit of the covenant had indeed been annexed to the covenantee's retained land by virtue of section 78. Brightman LJ stated:

> If, as the language of section 78 implies, a covenant relating to land which is restrictive of the user thereof is enforceable at the suit of (1) a successor in title of the covenantee, (2) a person deriving title under the covenantee or under his successors in title, and (3) the owner or occupier of the land intended to be benefited by the covenant, it must, in my view, follow that the covenant runs with the land, because ex hypothesi every successor in title to the land, every derivative proprietor of the land and every other owner and occupier has a right by statute to the covenant. In other words, if the condition precedent of section 78 is satisfied—that is to say, there exists a covenant which touches and concerns the land of the covenantee—that covenant runs with the land for the benefit of his successors in title, persons deriving title under him or them and other owners and occupiers.[42]

This interpretation of section 78 demands more detailed analysis.

Automatic Annexation

The orthodox view of section 78 is that the section is a word saving provision operating within the context of a covenant that otherwise demonstrates

---

[41] Law Com No 127, *The Law of Positive and Restrictive Covenants*, above (n 3) para 3.28, mentioned the 'possibility' that s 62 might pass the benefit of a restrictive covenant; but there was no reference to the section in the discussion of covenants in Law Com No 186, *A Consultation*, above (n 7).

[42] *Federated Homes* [1980] 1 WLR 594, 605.

an intention to annex the benefit to the covenantee's land. By contrast, the Court of Appeal stated in the clearest terms that the section itself effects the annexation of any covenant that relates to (or touches and concerns) the land of the covenantee. As will be discussed, subsequent decisions have made clear that such 'automatic' statutory annexation is subject to conditions and qualifications. Nonetheless, this interpretation of section 78 undoubtedly represents a significant and unexpected change from the previous understanding of the rules relating to the passing of the benefit of restrictive covenants.[43]

The central feature of all methods of passing the benefit of a covenant is the expressed or inferred intention of the parties that the benefit should be passed.[44] Although there is some argument as to the strictness of this requirement in the context of the common law rules,[45] the equitable rules for annexation reflect the acceptance of the importance attached to the element of intention as a necessary condition for the transmission of the benefit of a covenant—the intention on the part of the original parties to a covenant that the benefit of the covenant should attach to the land so that future owners of the covenantee's land can enforce the covenant.[46]

In its terms *Federated Homes* itself seems to discard the requirement of expressed or inferred intention; and, even though subsequent cases have demonstrated that intention is not wholly irrelevant,[47] it is clear that the developed *Federated Homes* interpretation of section 78 reverses the burden of proof by applying a presumption of intention which can only be rebutted by positive evidence that annexation was not intended.

Brightman LJ based his departure from the orthodoxy on the views of a number of academic commentators, who had championed the new interpretation and who, moreover, had expressed surprise that that interpretation

---

[43] See pp 103–05 above.

[44] S Gardner, *An Introduction to Land Law*, 3rd edn (Oxford, Hart Publishing, 2012) 317ff, rejects this 'standard account', arguing that the only requirement for passing the benefit of covenants at law and in equity is the 'touch and concern' requirement. However, it emerges that, according to Gardner, the 'touch and concern' requirement is only satisfied if the benefit of the covenant is intended to run with the land of the covenantee. This 'realignment' of the rules for passing the benefit of covenants would appear to leave no scope for assignment: the benefit of a covenant can only be assigned if the covenant touches and concerns the land of the covenantee; but, on Gardner's view, if a covenant satisfies the 'touch and concern' requirement, that is sufficient to make the benefit run with the land.

[45] See n 12 above.

[46] The common law rules have largely been applied in relation to positive covenants, where the intention to benefit the covenantee's land has usually been obvious from the circumstances: such intention is less obvious in the case of restrictive covenants.

[47] See *Roake v Chadha* [1984] 1 WLR 40 (Ch D); *Crest Nicholson Residential (South) Ltd v McAllister* [2004] EWCA Civ 410, [2004] 1 WLR 2409; *Sugarman v Porter* [2006] EWHC 331 (Ch), [2006] 2 P & CR 274.

had not been seriously argued in the courts.[48] He also stated that his interpretation was consistent with two decisions of the Court of Appeal— *Smith and Snipes Hall Farm Ltd v River Douglas Catchment Board*[49] and *Williams v Unit Construction Co Ltd*.[50] However, it is difficult to see how he was able to make that assertion. First, both cases involved the enforcement of *positive* covenants, involving recurrent obligations of repair. In respect of such covenants it is arguable that a less strict approach may be appropriate because the intention to confer benefit for the future is generally obvious. Secondly, in neither case does the Court appear in fact to have considered, much less adopted, the new interpretation of section 78.[51] On the contrary,

---

[48] GRY Radcliffe, 'Some Problems of the Law Relating to Restrictive Covenants' (1941) 57 *LQR* 203, 204–06, suggested that s 78(1) might have altered the law after 1925 so as 'of necessity to comprise in every covenant sufficient evidence of intention that the benefit should attach to the covenantee's land'. Wade, 'Covenants', above (n 20) 171–75, expressed the view that, where a covenant relates to (touches and concerns) any land of the covenantee, s 78(1) should be (and s 58 of the Conveyancing Act 1881 should have been) interpreted as raising a presumption that his successors in title are intended to benefit; and he regarded it as 'extraordinary' that this interpretation of s 78(1) had previously been virtually ignored by judges, counsel and textbook writers. On the other hand, Wade does not appear to have regarded intention as irrelevant. He stated (ibid, 172–73): 'Whether a covenant is capable of touching and concerning land is an objective matter of law, independent of the intention of the parties. Whether, if so capable, it actually does relate to any given land'—and that is the precondition for the operation of s 78(1)—'is a matter of intention, to be collected from the deed and the surrounding circumstances'. (These comments led PN Todd, 'Annexation after *Federated Homes*' [1985] *Conv* 177, to conclude that *Federated Homes* did not decide that s 78(1) has the effect of automatic annexation independently of intention, arguing, inter alia, that Brightman LJ's reliance on Wade must have included acceptance of the element of intention in the operation of the section.) RE Megarry and HWR Wade, *The Law of Real Property*, 4th edn (London, Sweet & Maxwell, 1975) 765, stated (contrary to the view expressed in the 3rd edition): 'Inserting these prescribed words, including the reference to land, produces what is tantamount to a formula of annexation closely similar to the classic formula [for express annexation]'. Following the decision in *Federated Homes*, DJ Hurst, 'The Transmission of Restrictive Covenants' (1982) 2 *Legal Studies* 53, argued that s 78(1) (and s 58 of the Conveyancing Act 1881) should always have been interpreted as transmitting the benefit of covenants relating to land without any expression of intention. By contrast, GH Newsom, 'Universal Annexation?' (1981) 97 *LQR* 32, argued that the parliamentary history of s 78(1) (the Conveyancing Act 1881, the Law of Property Act 1922, the Law of Property (Amendment) Act 1924 and the Law of Property Act 1925) demonstrates that the section did not alter the pre-1881 position that (i) annexation is a matter of intention; and (ii) that the intention to annex must be found from something other than statutorily implied references to successors in title. GH Newsom, 'Universal Annexation? A Postscript' (1982) 98 *LQR* 202, sought to reinforce his views by contrasting the wording of s 78 with the express and unambiguous annexation formula in s 76 (covenants for title) and s 77 (implied covenants in conveyances subject to rents). Sections 76(6) and 77(5) provide: 'The benefit of a covenant implied as aforesaid shall be annexed and incident to, and shall go with, the estate or interest of the implied covenantee, and shall be capable of being enforced by every person in whom that estate or interests is, for the whole or any part thereof, from time to time vested'.

[49] *Smith and Snipes Hall Farm Ltd v River Douglas Catchment Board* [1949] 2 KB 500 (CA).

[50] *Williams v Unit Construction Co Ltd* (1951) (CA), noted at (1955) 19 *Conv* 262.

[51] Although the reasoning has been questioned, it has been argued that in the two cases the Court of Appeal did rely on s 78 to permit the tenant of a successor in title to enforce the covenant, on the basis that the section abrogated the former restriction that a successor in title could only enforce a covenant at common law if he had the same legal estate as the original covenantee.

in both cases there are statements that appear wholly inconsistent with the interpretation adopted by Brightman LJ. In *Smith* Tucker LJ stated:

> It is first necessary to ascertain from the deed that the covenant is one which 'touches or concerns' the land ... *and it must then be shown that it was the intention of the parties that the benefit thereof should run with the land....* In my view the language of the deed satisfies both tests (emphasis added).[52]

In *Williams* Tucker LJ referred to the argument of counsel that had relied on the emphasised words, analysed the wording of the covenant and concluded:

> I think this covenant is one which clearly relates to the land of the covenantee within the meaning of section 78 of the Law of Property Act 1925 *and was intended to enure for the benefit of [the plaintiff]* (emphasis added).[53]

More generally, direct reliance on these cases does raise the question whether Brightman LJ was applying the common law rules or the equitable rules for the passing of the benefit. As noted above, the application of the common law rules would have been possible since the plaintiff was seeking to enforce the covenants against the original covenantor; but the terminology and the overall tenor of the judgment seems more consistent with the application of the equitable rules.

Annexation to the Whole and/or Parts of the Benefited Land

The defendant in *Federated Homes* suggested that, even if section 78 had the effect of annexing the benefit of the covenant to the retained land of the covenantee, the benefit was annexed to the whole of the land and not to each and every part of the land.[54] This issue—and a number of related supplementary questions—had been widely discussed by the courts following the decision in *Re Ballard's Conveyance*;[55] and, although the solution seemed clear—that a covenant could be expressed to be for the benefit of the whole or any part or parts of the covenantee's land[56]—the question remained as to the proper construction of a covenant where no such express formula was used. Brightman LJ regarded the answer as clear. He stated:

> I find the idea of the annexation of a covenant to the whole of the land but not to a part of it a difficult conception fully to grasp. I can understand that a covenantee

---

[52] *Smith and Snipes Hall Farm Ltd v River Douglas Catchment Board* [1949] 2 KB 500, 506 (CA).

[53] *Williams v Unit Construction Co Ltd* (1955) 19 Conv 262, 265 (CA).

[54] It is not clear how this argument could have assisted the defendant since, if statutory annexation operated in the circumstances of the present case, it presumably operated in relation to the whole of the plaintiff's retained land, comprising both the green land and the red land.

[55] *Re Ballard's Conveyance* [1937] Ch 473 (Ch D).

[56] See *Marquess of Zetland v Driver* [1939] Ch 1 (CA).

may expressly or by necessary implication retain the benefit of a covenant wholly under his own control, so that the benefit will not pass unless the covenantee chooses to assign; but I would have thought, if the benefit of a covenant is, on a proper construction of a document, annexed to the land, prima facie it is annexed to every part thereof, unless the contrary clearly appears.[57]

In fact the view that annexation to the whole of the land prima facie includes annexation to every part thereof seems to be inconsistent with earlier authority;[58] and in *Bridges v Harrow LBC*,[59] decided after *Federated Homes*, Stuart-Smith J expressed the view that annexation to each and every part of the covenantee's land was a matter of intention and that it was necessary that some indication of that intention should be found in the creating document itself. However, the position adopted in *Federated Homes*—that, in the absence of a clear contrary intention, annexation (whether express or statutory) enures for the benefit of every part of the land—was endorsed in *J Sainsbury plc v Enfield LBC*[60] and in *Small v Oliver & Saunders (Developments) Ltd*;[61] and it seems that the contrary former position is no longer seriously argued.

Identification of the Benefited Land

Assuming that section 78 does have the potential to effect automatic annexation in relation to covenants that relate to the covenantee's land (contrary to the defendant's first possible view of the section), the question remains as to how far that land must be identified in the creating document. In *Federated Homes* the defendant suggested two possibilities (respectively the defendant's second and third possible views of section 78): first, that the section effects annexation only where the land intended to be benefited is identified in the document by express words or necessary implication; and secondly, that the section effects annexation if the covenant in fact touches

---

[57] *Federated Homes* [1980] 1 WLR 594, 606. Similarly, Megaw LJ, who only addressed this issue in his concurring judgment, stated: 'I find great difficulty in understanding how, either as a matter of principle or as a matter of practical good sense in relation to a legal relationship of this sort, it can be said that a covenant, which *ex hypothesi* has been annexed to the land as a whole, is somehow or other not annexed to the individual parts of that land'. A presumption in favour of annexation to each and every part was proposed by the Law Commission in 1967: Law Com No 11, *Report on Restrictive Covenants*, above (n 7) proposition 4(b).

[58] See *Re Union of London and Smith's Bank Ltd's Conveyance; Miles v Easter* [1933] Ch 611, 628 (CA).

[59] *Bridges v Harrow LBC* [1981] 2 EGLR 143 (QBD).

[60] *J Sainsbury plc v Enfield LBC* [1989] 1 WLR 590, 595 (Ch D).

[61] *Small v Oliver & Saunders (Developments) Ltd* [2006] EWHC 1293 (Ch), [2006] 3 EGLR 141, [30]. Mark Herbert QC concluded that the statements of Brightman and Megaw LJJ were statements of principle, which did not depend on the wording of s 78 and which therefore applied without distinction to both statutory and express annexation and, in the case of the latter, irrespective of when annexation took place.

and concerns the land of the covenantee, whether the identity of that land be gleaned from the document itself or from evidence outside the document. On the facts of *Federated Homes* Brightman LJ did not find it necessary to choose between those two possibiities: the covenant was stated to be for the protection of 'the retained land' and, although there was no formal definition in the creating document, he was prepared to equate that designation with a reference elsewhere in the conveyance to 'any adjoining or adjacent property retained by the vendor'.[62]

In *Robins v Berkeley Homes (Kent) Ltd*[63] Judge Colyer QC adopted a view close to the second of those possible views (what he termed a 'modified view three').[64] He concluded that section 78 effects annexation

> if the relevant covenant in fact does touch and concern the land of the covenantee, whether that be gleaned from the document itself or from extrinsic evidence, provided that one is not permitted by the section to redraw the covenant so as, for example, to make what was specifically a personal covenant into a restrictive covenant or so as to defeat an express stipulation that the covenant benefits some but not all of the vendor's land which otherwise might seem to be affected, or that it be annexed specifically to the vendor's estate as a totality and not to each and every part (which in my view would require an express stipulation).

However, to the extent that that view would permit the benefited land to be identified *exclusively* from extrinsic evidence, it is now untenable following the decision of the Court of Appeal in *Crest Nicholson Residential (South) Ltd v McAllister*.[65] In that case, Chadwick LJ expressed the view that the question left open in *Federated Homes* had already been answered by the Court of Appeal in *Marquess of Zetland v Driver*:[66] 'the land which is intended to be benefited must be so defined as to be easily identifiable'. It is not necessary for the benefited land to be identified exclusively by reference to the creating document itself. It is sufficient that the land can be identified 'from a description, plan or other reference in the conveyance itself, but aided, if necessary, by external evidence to identify the land so described, depicted or otherwise referred to'.[67] However, extrinsic evidence will not be admissible to identify the benefited land when the creating document itself is completely silent.

---

[62] In *Rogers v Hosegood* [1900] 2 Ch 388 (CA) a similar formulation was held to be sufficient to identify the benefited land for the purposes of express annexation: see n 17 above.

[63] *Robins v Berkeley Homes (Kent) Ltd* [1996] EGCS 75 (Ch D).

[64] In preference to the inelegant 'view two-and-a-half' or 'view two-and-three-quarters'.

[65] *Crest Nicholson Residential (South) Ltd v McAllister* [2004] EWCA Civ 410, [2004] 1 WLR 2409.

[66] *Marquess of Zetland v Driver* [1939] Ch 1, 8 (CA).

[67] *Crest Nicholson Residential (South) Ltd v McAllister* [2004] EWCA Civ 410, [2004] 1 WLR 2409, [45]. See also *Stocks v Whitgift Homes Ltd* [2001] EWCA Civ 1732, [104]–[105].

Moreover, there are good reasons for this requirement, which were seemingly overlooked in *Federated Homes*. Chadwick LJ stated:

> It is obviously desirable that a purchaser of land burdened with a restrictive covenant should be able not only to ascertain, by inspection of the entries on the relevant register, that the land is so burdened, but also to ascertain the land for which the benefit of the covenant was taken—so that he can identify who can enforce the covenant. That latter object is achieved if the land which is intended to be benefited is defined in the instrument so as to be easily ascertainable. To require a purchaser of land burdened with a restrictive covenant, but where the land for the benefit of which the covenant was taken is not described in the instrument, to make enquiries as to what (if any) land the original covenantee retained at the time of the conveyance and what (if any) of that retained land the covenant did, or might have, 'touched and concerned' would be oppressive. It must be kept in mind that (as in the present case) the time at which the enforceability of the covenant becomes an issue may be long after the date of the instrument by which it was imposed.[68]

This clarification is important. Without the qualification as to the identification of the benefited land, the *Federated Homes* principle was probably unworkable. It had the potential to generate insurmountable problems in practice—in particular, a proliferation in the number of potential unidentified enforcers of restrictive covenants and, as a consequence, the inevitable increase in indemnity insurance premiums.[69] On the other hand, *Crest Nicholson* itself has prompted some criticism. Even where the requirements set out in that case are met at the time of the covenant, there may be practical problems of identifying qualifying enforcers many years later after the land has been divided.[70] Moreover, the *Crest Nicholson* requirement does

---

[68] *Crest Nicholson Residential (South) Ltd v McAllister* [2004] EWCA Civ 410, [2004] 1 WLR 2409, [34].

[69] The difficulty of identifying the person(s) holding the right to enforce restrictive covenants was the most common problem commented on by those who responded to the Law Commission consultation on covenants: Law Commission Consultation Paper No 186, *Making Land Work: Easements, Covenants and Profits à Prendre (Consultation Analysis)* (2011) para 7.5. The recommendation of the Law Commission that, for the future, (restrictive) covenants should take effect as legal interests in land—land obligations—would have the practical advantage that, in the context of registered land, the extent and ownership of the benefited land would be discoverable from the register of title: Law Commission Report No 327, *Making Land Work: Easements, Covenants and Profits à Prendre* (2011) paras 5.10, 5.61–5.62, 6.2. However, the initial proposal—that the creation of a land obligation would require for its validity the inclusion in the instrument creating the land obligation of a plan identifying the land to be benefited (Law Com No 186, *A Consultation*, above (n 7) paras 8.39–8.41)—became a recommendation that the requirement of identification should be imposed through Land Registry procedures on an application for the registration of a land obligation: Law Com No 327, *Making Land Work*, paras 6.48–6.51.

[70] See *R v Westminster CC Ex p Leicester Square Coventry Street Association Ltd* (1989) 59 P & CR 51 (QBD) (where the original covenantee was a member of the Tulk (as in *Tulk v Moxhay*) family).

not assist the owner of the burdened land in identifying assignees of the benefit of covenants.

Contrary Intention

In *Roake v Chadha*[71] the question for the Court was whether, if the requirements of section 78 as set out in *Federated Homes* are satisfied, the section effects annexation automatically and irrespective of any contrary intention of the parties. It is submitted it would be wholly unacceptable if the operation of section 78 could not be excluded by the parties; and Judge Paul Baker QC refused to accept that that was the inevitable effect of the *Federated Homes* interpretation of section 78, insisting that it is still necessary to construe the covenant as a whole to see whether the benefit is annexed to the covenantee's land. He was supported in this view by the fact that in *Federated Homes* itself Brightman LJ seemed to indicate that the covenantee may elect to retain the benefit wholly under his own control.[72] On the facts of *Roake v Chadha* the covenantee had done precisely that by formulating the covenant in terms that 'it shall not enure for the benefit of any owner or subsequent purchaser of [the land of the covenantee] *unless the benefit of this covenant shall be expressly assigned*'(emphasis added).

The issue was raised again in *Crest Nicholson Residential (South) Ltd v McAllister*.[73] Having referred to *Roake v Chadha*, Chadwick LJ continued:

> I respectfully agree ... that it is impossible to identify any reason of policy why a covenantor should not, by express words, be entitled to limit the scope of the obligation that he is undertaking, nor why a covenantee should not be able to accept a covenant for his own benefit on terms that the benefit does not pass automatically to all those to whom he sells on parts of his retained land. As Brightman LJ pointed out, in the passage cited by Judge Paul Baker QC,[74] a developer who is selling off land in lots might well want to retain the benefit of a building restriction under his own control. Where, as in *Roake* and in the present case, development land is sold off in plots without imposing a building scheme, it seems to me very likely that the developer will wish to retain exclusive power to give or withhold consent to a modification or relaxation of a restriction on building that he imposes on each purchaser; unfettered by the need to obtain the consent of every subsequent purchaser to whom (after imposing the covenant) he has sold off other plots on the development land. I can see no reason why, if the original

---

[71] *Roake v Chadha* [1984] 1 WLR 40 (Ch D).
[72] See text to n 57 above.
[73] *Crest Nicholson Residential (South) Ltd v McAllister* [2004] EWCA Civ 410, [2004] 1 WLR 2409; and see *Rees v Peters* [2011] EWCA Civ 836.
[74] See text to n 57 above.

covenantor and covenantee make clear their mutual intention in that respect, the legislature should wish to prevent effect being given to that intention.[75]

Indeed, Chadwick LJ regarded this issue and the identification of the benefited land as part of the same issue. He continued:

[I]t is important to keep in mind that, for the purposes of its application to restrictive covenants—which is the context in which this question arises where neither of the parties to the dispute were, themselves, party to the instrument imposing the covenant or express assignees of the benefit of the covenant—section 78 of the 1925 Act defines 'successors in title' as 'the owners and occupiers for the time being *of the land of the covenantee intended to be benefited*'. In a case where the parties to the instrument make clear their intention that land retained by the covenantee at the time of the conveyance effected by the transfer is to have the benefit of the covenant only for so long as it continues to be in the ownership of the original covenantee, and not after it has been sold on by the original covenantee unless the benefit of the covenant is expressly assigned to the new owner, *the land of the covenantee intended to be benefited* is identified by the instrument as: (i) so much of the retained land as from time to time has not been sold off by the original covenantee; and (ii) so much of the retained land as has been sold off with the benefit of an express assignment; but as not including (iii) so much of the land as has been sold off without the benefit of an express assignment. I agree with the judge in *Roake* that, in such a case, it is possible to give full effect to the statute and to the terms of the covenant.[76]

According to Chadwick LJ, this approach also provides the basis for reconciling the much debated apparent discrepancy between sections 78 and 79 in relation to the issue of contrary intention.[77] Although section 78 (unlike section 79) makes no express reference to a contrary intention, such a qualification is implicit in the definition of 'successors in title' that appears in the section, namely 'the owners and occupiers for the time being of the land of the covenantee *intended to be benefited*' (emphasis added). If the terms of the covenant show—as they did in *Marquess of Zetland v Driver* and in *Roake v Chadha*—that the land of the covenantee intended to be benefited does not include land that may subsequently be sold off by the original covenantee in circumstances where (at the time of that subsequent sale) there is no express assignment of the benefit of the covenant, then the owners and occupiers of the land sold off in those circumstances are not 'successors in title' of the original covenantee for the purposes of section 78.

By contrast, the counterpart in section 79 of 'land of the covenantee intended be benefited' is 'any land of the covenantor or capable of being

[75] *Crest Nicholson Residential (South) Ltd v McAllister* [2004] EWCA Civ 410, [2004] 1 WLR 2409, [41].
[76] Ibid, [42]. See also *Norwich City College of Further and Higher Education v McQuillin* [2009] EWHC 1496 (Ch).
[77] *Crest Nicholson Residential (South) Ltd v McAllister* [2004] EWCA Civ 410, [2004] 1 WLR 2409, [43]–[44].

bound by him'. But section 79 imposes the qualification that there must be no expression of contrary intention. The section could have described the land as 'land of the covenantor (or capable of being bound by him) intended to be burdened'. But the effect would have been the same. If the parties did not intend that that land, burdened while in the ownership of the covenantor, should continue to be subject to the burden in the hands of its successors (or some of its successors), they could say so. On a true analysis, there is no difference in treatment in the two sections. There is a difference in the drafting technique used to achieve the same substantive result; but that may well simply reflect the legislative history of the two sections.[78]

IMPACT OF FEDERATED HOMES

There is no doubt that the decision in *Federated Homes* was at the time controversial; and it prompted a range of responses. Although welcomed by some commentators, its critics included one of the leading practitioners in the field.[79] Some commentators sought to sideline the decision, pointing out that the unexpected interpretation that overturned over 50 years' understanding was contained in an extempore judgment. Others asserted that the interpretation of section 78(1) was strictly obiter: the plaintiff was clearly entitled to enforce the covenant as owner of the green land so that consideration of its entitlement to enforce the covenant as owner of the red land was unnecessary. However, since the issue was fully argued before the Court, the suggestion was never wholly convincing; and it has been expressly rejected by the courts.[80] More subtlely, it was argued that, since the defendant was the original covenantor, the *Federated Homes* principle should properly be confined to the situation where enforcement is sought against the original covenantor. On that basis, it was argued that it may no longer be appropriate to draw a distinction between legal annexation and equitable annexation of the benefit where enforcement is sought against the original covenantor;[81] but that, where enforcement is sought against a successor in title of the original covenantor under the doctrine in *Tulk v*

---

[78] S 78(1) of the 1925 Act reformulated s 58 of the Conveyancing and Law of Property Act 1881; s 79 was a new provision, first introduced in the 1925 Act.

[79] Newsom, 'Universal Annexation?' and 'Universal Annexation? A Postscript', above (n 48). See also Preston and Newsom, above (n 31).

[80] *Roake v Chadha* [1984] 1 WLR 40, 45 (Ch D); and see *Allen v Veranne Builders Ltd* [1988] EGCS 2 (Ch D).

[81] Brightman LJ purported to support his decision by reference to *Smith and Snipes Hall Farm Ltd v River Douglas Catchment Board* [1949] 2 KB 500 (CA) and *Williams v Unit Construction Co Ltd* (1951) (CA), noted at (1955) *Conv* 262, both cases involving the passing of the benefit of positive covenants at law.

Moxhay, so that legal annexation is not available,[82] it may be defensible for equity to continue to apply the stricter pre-*Federated Homes* requirements for annexation.[83] However, this argument has also been rejected: the decision in *Federated Homes* has been applied, albeit subject to the qualifications discussed, both in the English courts[84] and in other Commonwealth courts;[85] and in all those cases enforcement was sought against a successor in title of the original covenantor.

Subject to a contrary ruling from the Supreme Court,[86] therefore, the question is not whether *Federated Homes* sets out the law on the annexation of the benefit of (restrictive) covenants but what is the law that *Federated Homes* sets out and what are the practical implications.[87]

For existing covenants entered into before 1926 (and that is no insignificant number, as the case law demonstrates), except in relation to one matter, the law is unaffected by the decision in *Federated Homes*, since the interpretation of section 78 has been held not to apply to its predecessor, section 58 of the Conveyancing Act 1881.[88] It follows that in relation to such covenants, a successor in title of the original covenantee must continue to confront 'the unnecessary mystique and semantics'[89] which have accumulated around express and implied annexation and assignment. Most significantly, successful annexation will depend on the manifestation of a positive intention to annex. The exception is that there is now a presumption (albeit rebuttable by evidence of a contrary intention) that, where annexation occurs, the benefit of the covenant is annexed to each and every part of the benefited land.

---

[82] See pp 104–05 above.

[83] Todd, above (n 48).

[84] *Roake v Chadha* [1984] 1 WLR 40 (Ch D); *Jalnarne Ltd v Ridewood* (1989) 61 P & CR 143 (Ch D); *Robins v Berkeley Homes (Kent) Ltd* [1996] EGCS 75 (Ch D); *Stocks v Whitgift Homes Ltd* [2001] EWCA Civ 1732; *Crest Nicholson Residential (South) Ltd v McAllister* [2004] EWCA Civ 410, [2004] 1 WLR 2409; *Mohammadzadeh v Joseph* [2006] EWHC 1040 (Ch), [2008] 1 P & CR 107, [34]–[46].

[85] In New Zealand the High Court applied the *Federated Homes* principle in *Randle v Contact Energy Ltd* (2000); and the principle is now contained in s 301 of the Property Law Act 2007. In Australia the *Federated Homes* principle has been adopted at State level (see, eg, *Midland Brick Co Pty Ltd v Welsh* (2006) 32 WAR 287, 339–40), although the Australian High Court has left the question open: see *Forestview Nominees Pty Ltd v Perpetual Trustees WA Ltd* (1998) 193 CLR 154, 171.

[86] *Federated Homes* was referred to with apparent approval by the House of Lords in *Rhone v Stephens* [1994] 2 AC 310, 322 (HL).

[87] Existing restrictive covenants would not be affected by the implementation of the Law Commission's recommendations for Land Obligations: Law Com No 327, *Making Land Work*, above (n 69) paras 5.82–5.89.

[88] *J Sainsbury plc v Enfield LBC* [1989] 1 WLR 590, 601 (Ch D); *Re MCA East Ltd* [2002] EWHC 1684 (Ch), [2003] 1 P & CR 9, [20]; *Seymour Road (Southampton) Ltd v Williams* [2010] EWHC 111 (Ch), [21].

[89] Harpum, Bridge and Dixon (eds), above (n 12) para 32-064.

For existing covenants entered into after 1925, the position of a successor in title of the original covenantee will be determined in accordance with the developed *Federated Homes* principle; and few would question that the law has been simplified. It is no longer necessary positively to demonstrate an intention that the benefit should be annexed to the original covenantee's land. Provided (i) that the covenantee's land is identified in accordance with the principles in *Crest Nicholson*, (ii) that the covenant relates to (touches and concerns) that land and (iii) that the covenant does not manifest an intention positively to exclude or limit annexation, then section 78 will effect automatic statutory annexation. Moreover, provided that there is no clear intention that the benefit of the covenant is to be annexed only to the whole of the benefited land, the benefit will be annexed to each and every part. On the one hand, the application of *Federated Homes* may remedy defective drafting that failed to effect annexation under the pre-*Federated Homes* law; on the other hand, annexation may be found to have been effected contrary to the parties' intentions because they relied on deliberate omission in relation to the pre-*Federated Homes* requirement of a positive intention to annex.

For practitioners responsible for drafting new covenants, they must do so in the light of the developed *Federated Homes* principle.[90] This will almost certainly require more proactive and discriminating drafting to ensure that intended consequences are achieved and, equally importantly, that unintended consequences are avoided. Paradoxically, this is may reduce the scope (and need) for the operation of section 78 as draftsmen adopt a more sophisticated approach to express annexation and express non-annexation.

The future of assignment is uncertain. Rumours of its demise following *Federated Homes* have almost certainly proved to be premature: the lesser incidence of statutory annexation under the developed *Federated Homes* principle would seem to leave greater scope for assignment as a response to a failure of annexation.[91] More proactively, assignment can provide a useful tool where covenantees wish to exclude annexation but also wish to keep their options open as to the future transmission of the benefit of covenants.[92]

---

[90] The *Federated Homes* principle will continue to apply to restrictive covenants entered into before any implementation of the recommendations of the Law Commission.

[91] However, Law Commission has stated that it is now 'rare' for it to be necessary to transmit the benefit of a covenant made after 1925 other than by statutory annexation: Law Com No 186, *A Consultation*, above (n 7) para 7.30.

[92] Exemplified by *Roake v Chadha* [1984] 1 WLR 40 (Ch D).

FEDERATED HOMES AS A LANDMARK CASE

Reverting to the question of the status of *Federated Homes* as a landmark case, from one point of view such designation may be judged by the change in the law brought about by the case from the previous legal position; and the designation may be more deserved if that change is not only significant but also unexpected. Assessing *Federated Homes* against those criteria is not without its difficulties because commentators have articulated a range of different views, both as to the pre-*Federated Homes* position on the passing of the benefit of a restrictive covenant and as to the post-*Federated Homes* position. Nonetheless, landmark case status can legitimately be based on the new interpretation of section 78 and the judicial recognition of the concept of statutory annexation, which in its developed version has the effect of presuming an intention to annex. The consequences of that development for existing and new covenants have been outlined above. In addition, *Federated Homes* both in itself and in its developed version has provided welcome confirmation or clarification of many other aspects of the law relating to freehold covenants.

6

Williams and Glyn's Bank Ltd v Boland *(1980)*

The Development of a System of Title by Registration

ROGER SMITH

IN THE BEGINNING

FOR MANY STUDENTS today, overriding interests form the heart of their analysis of land registration. That may well produce a very lopsided impression of land registration, but overriding interests are central to the never-ending quest to establish a balance between certainty in land transactions and, on the other hand, the need to reflect justice in individual cases. Overriding interests may be justified where, as the Law Commission states,[1] it is 'either not reasonable to expect nor sensible to require any entry on the register'.

It is remarkable that for many decades the area received little attention. In the 1950s, Curtis and Ruoff[2] described overriding interests as a 'miscellany of minor liabilities' and this reflected opinion at that time.[3] Actual occupation had been introduced as an overriding interest by the 1925 legislation and was given quite cursory treatment: there was no hint of its modern

---

[1] Law Commission Report No 254, *Land Registration for the Twenty-First Century: A Consultative Document* (1998) para 4.17. It is frequently overlooked that this is intended as a minimum requirement for overriding interest status rather than a qualification for such.

[2] G Curtis and T Ruoff, *The Law and Practice of Registered Conveyancing* (London, Stevens & Sons, 1958) 156.

[3] Three decades earlier, see C Brickdale and J Stewart-Wallace, *Land Registration Act 1925*, 3rd edn (London, Stevens & Sons, 1927) 253.

application to family home disputes. It was thought likely to apply to those who had not yet registered dispositions[4] and to rights of tenants.[5]

It must be remembered, however, that the number of titles involving joint ownership of the family home was relatively small at the time Curtis and Ruoff were writing. A combination of (i) larger numbers of owner-occupiers (ii) more partners (mostly wives, at least in the earlier cases) in employment, but not on the register (or title deeds) and (iii) the development of the common intention constructive trust in cases such as *Gissing v Gissing*[6] was the catalyst for the litigation in *Williams and Glyn's Bank Ltd v Boland*.[7] Perhaps the first case raising the now familiar conflict between contributing partner and subsequent mortgagee was the unregistered land case of *Caunce v Caunce*[8] in 1969. In this connection, it should be recalled that land registration involved a relatively small proportion of titles until recent decades. Thus, the total of registered titles—now standing at over 23 million and around 95 per cent of all titles—amounted to 7.2 million in 1981 and just 1.48 million in 1959.[9]

BOLAND

It was against the above background that *Williams and Glyn's Bank Ltd v Boland* fell to be decided. Mrs Boland claimed an interest in the family home by reason of her contributions. Mr Boland later borrowed money for his company and secured the loan on the family home—a procedure that is very common for small businesses and a vital way of providing finance for them.[10] This charge on the house was registered. When Mr Boland defaulted on loan repayments, the bank sought possession in order to sell the house. This raised the question whether registration of the charge had the effect of defeating Mrs Boland's equitable interest in the house, which quickly became a question as to whether she could assert an overriding interest.

---

[4] An example of this type of claim (though it was based on a contract rather than unregistered transfer) is provided by *Bridges v Mees* [1957] Ch 474 (Ch D) (as an alternative to an adverse possession claim).

[5] Well illustrated by *Webb v Pollmount Ltd* [1966] Ch 584 (Ch D) in which a tenant was able to assert an overriding interest to protect an option to purchase a freehold. Though the lease was an overriding interest as a short legal lease, this protects only covenants which, unlike that option, touch and concern the land: today, see Land Registration Act 2002 (hereafter LRA; unless otherwise indicated, references are to this Act) sch 3, para 1.

[6] *Gissing v Gissing* [1971] AC 886 (HL); the recognition of its constituting a constructive trust (as opposed to a resulting trust) is much more recent.

[7] *Williams and Glyn's Bank Ltd v Boland* [1981] AC 487 (HL).

[8] *Caunce v Caunce* [1969] 1 WLR 286 (Ch D).

[9] Land Registry Annual Reports, 1958–59; 1980–81; 2011–12.

[10] Fully recognised by the House of Lords in *Royal Bank of Scotland plc v Etridge (No 2)* [2001] UKHL 44, [2002] 2 AC 773, [34].

Boland is an extremely well known case[11] and no attempt will be made to describe the arguments and decision in full detail. Rather, the principal focus for discussion will be the extent to which *Boland* set land registration on a new path, largely free from property rules applying to unregistered land (at least those relating to priority issues regarding two competing interests). *Boland* can be seen as part of a development of land registration as a free-standing area of property law, a development which is evident from Law Commission Reports 254 and 271, which led to the Land Registration Act 2002 (LRA).

Before these wider questions can be investigated, a brief review of the issues in *Boland* is required. There are always two basic requirements before an actual occupation overriding interest can be shown: an interest in land capable of binding a purchaser[12] and actual occupation. Both of these were in issue in *Boland*. The first was vitally important, as it raised the question as to how far beneficial interests under trusts can be overriding interests.[13] The House of Lords (with the leading judgment being delivered by Lord Wilberforce) held that such interests are overriding when combined with actual occupation. However, it is not necessary to go into the reasoning in depth. The most troublesome point concerned the question whether an overlap between minor interests and overriding interests should be recognised. The LRA 2002 no longer employs the category of minor interests, so much of the difficulty falls away. It might be argued that interests which may be protected by notice or restriction should fall outside the actual occupation overriding interest, but in that event it is difficult to comprehend what rights would ever qualify! Another problem discussed in *Boland* concerned the status of interests under a trust for sale,[14] given that the doctrine of conversion treated such interests as being in money rather than in the land. However, section 3 of the Trusts of Land and Appointment of Trustees Act 1996 effectively abolishes the doctrine of conversion.

The second issue—the one which will be concentrated on—concerns the meaning of actual occupation. The interesting question in *Boland* is the

---

[11] It attracted a fair amount of attention in journals, examples being J Martin, 'Section 70(1)(g) and the Vendor's Spouse' [1980] *Conv* 361; RJ Smith, 'Overriding Interests, Wives and the House of Lords' (1981) 97 *LQR* 12; S Freeman, 'Wives, Conveyances and Justice' (1980) 43 *MLR* 692 and MJ Prichard, 'Registered Land—Overriding interests—Actual Occupation' [1980] *CLJ* 243. It is fair to say that overreaching, both in *Boland* and *City of London Building Society v Flegg* [1988] AC 54 (HL) attracted the greatest attention.

[12] Established by *National Provincial Bank Ltd v Ainsworth* [1965] AC 1175 (HL) and never subsequently challenged (despite an argument by L Tee, 'The Rights of Every Person in Actual Occupation: An Enquiry into Section 70(1)(g) of the Land Registration Act 1925' [1998] *CLJ* 328, that a broader view should be adopted).

[13] These issues are further explored by Nicholas Hopkins in ch 9.

[14] This appears to have been the primary basis on which Templeman J rejected the overriding interest argument at first instance: (1978) 36 P & CR 448 (Ch D). This goes far to explain the earlier failure of commentators to anticipate the modern scope of the actual occupation overriding interest.

extent to which its meaning is influenced by the doctrine of notice. It is a commonplace observation that actual occupation is the registration counterpart of the unregistered land principle[15] that occupation of land provides constructive notice of the interests of the occupier. Indeed, the House of Lords notes that Lord Loughborough LC used 'actual possession' in 1794[16] and the leading 1853 Privy Council decision in *Barnhart v Greenshields*[17] employed the term actual occupation.

There was very little earlier authority analysing the role of actual occupation in the overriding interest context. The single full analysis of occupation by spouses is found in the first instance unregistered land case of *Caunce v Caunce*.[18] Stamp J held there to be no constructive notice:[19] 'She was there, ostensibly, because she was the wife, and her presence there was wholly consistent with the title offered to the bank'. Problems with inquiries of spouses were one reason for rejecting any proprietary status for the deserted wife's equity in *National Provincial Bank Ltd v Ainsworth*[20] and Stamp J thought this to be equally applicable to requiring inquiries of spouses in the present case. He described such inquiries as being 'as embarrassing to the inquirer' as 'intolerable to the wife and the husband'. It is fair to add that earlier authorities had stressed that notice applied where the vendor was not in occupation—but the inferences to be drawn naturally differ where spouses (or partners) are involved. In any event, soon afterwards the Court of Appeal in *Hodgson v Marks*[21] (not a husband and wife case: the elderly claimant had transferred title to her lodger) rejected the argument that the vendor's being in possession precluded constructive notice. Many issues were left open by the Court of Appeal, including the question of whether spouses are in a special position (as the occupation of one might be taken to be the occupation of the other) and the general question whether registered land employed the same tests as unregistered land. Nevertheless, the dicta of Russell LJ constitute a clear warning to purchasers and mortgagees that they take a real risk if they fail to make inquiries of occupiers. Unfortunately, the warnings appear to have gone largely unheeded.

It was nearly a decade later that the position of spouses in registered land arose in litigation. The first decision was that of Templeman J in *Bird v Syme-Thompson*,[22] curiously decided just four days before the same judge

---

[15] *Hunt v Luck* [1902] 2 Ch 428 (CA) is frequently quoted as authority in this context; it restated the law in the light of the Conveyancing Act 1882 provisions regarding notice (now Law of Property Act 1925, s 199).

[16] *Taylor v Stibbert* (1794) 2 Ves Jun 43, 440.

[17] *Barnhart v Greenshields* (1853) 9 Moo PC 18, 34.

[18] *Caunce v Caunce* [1969] 1 WLR 286 (Ch D).

[19] Ibid, 293.

[20] *National Provincial Bank Ltd v Ainsworth* [1965] AC 1175, especially 1248.

[21] *Hodgson v Marks* [1971] Ch 892 (CA); the leading judgment was delivered by Russell LJ.

[22] *Bird v Syme-Thompson* [1979] 1 WLR 440 (Ch D); it is not mentioned by Templeman J in *Boland*.

heard *Boland* at first instance. Without citing *Hodgson v Marks* (though it had been cited in argument) *Caunce* was applied: there was no actual occupation. Unsurprisingly, Templeman J took a similar approach in *Boland*.[23] The effects of a contrary decision on purchasers and lenders weighed heavily on the judge: any contrary result would provide an 'impossible situation' with 'wide and almost catastrophic results'.

Such broad assertions (with little attempt to justify them by rigorous analysis) not infrequently prove to contain more bluster than substance. As is well known, a contrary conclusion was reached by both the Court of Appeal and the House of Lords in *Boland*. In the Court of Appeal the riposte of Lord Denning MR[24] was unambiguous:

> I profoundly disagree ... I see no reason why this should cause any difficulty to conveyancers. Nor should it impair the proper conduct of businesses. Anyone who lends money on the security of a matrimonial home nowadays ought to realise that the wife may have a share in it. He ought to make sure that the wife agrees to it, or to go to the house and make inquiries of her. It seems to me utterly wrong that a lender should turn a blind eye to the wife's interest or the possibility of it—and afterwards seek to turn her and the family out—on the plea that he did not know she was in actual occupation.

As the Court of Appeal and House of Lords were in agreement, however, it is most profitable to investigate the reasoning in the House of Lords.

Lord Wilberforce delivered the leading judgment; Lord Scarman delivered a concurring judgment.[25] Lord Wilberforce observes that a wife living in a home would naturally be treated as being in actual occupation—living in a house is one of the most obvious forms of actual occupation. He is emphatic that actual occupation should not be construed so as to operate in the same fashion as the doctrine of notice. Though it may well be accepted that the origins of actual occupation lie in the old doctrine of notice, as recognised in *National Provincial Bank Ltd v Ainsworth*,[26] it does not follow that it should operate in an identical manner. As he observes, one of the objectives of registration was to side-step the problems with applying notice (though it might be countered that this is less clear as regards notice arising from occupation). In a famous dictum, he concludes:

> In the case of registered land, it is the fact of occupation that matters. If there is actual occupation, and the occupier has rights, the purchaser takes subject to them. If not, he does not. No further element is material.[27]

---

[23] (1978) 36 P & CR 448.

[24] [1979] Ch 312, 332.

[25] [1981] AC 487; Lord Roskill also delivered a very short judgment but did not deal with actual occupation.

[26] *National Provincial Bank Ltd v Ainsworth* [1965] AC 1175, 1259, approving Lord Denning MR's analysis in the Court of Appeal: [1964] Ch 665, 689.

[27] [1981] AC 487, 504.

Similarly, Lord Scarman rejects an argument that actual occupation requires

> an occupation, which by its nature necessarily puts a would-be purchaser (or mortgagee) upon notice of a claim adverse to the registered owner. On the contrary, I expect to find—as I do find—that the statute has substituted a plain factual situation for the uncertainties of notice, actual or constructive, as the determinant of an overriding interest.

In coming to his conclusion, Lord Wilberforce considered three arguments in favour of the contrary view. The argument that actual occupation operates only if the vendor is not in occupation was rejected, approving *Hodgson v Marks*. It might be convenient for purchasers and mortgagees, but has little else to commend it. Next, a special rule for spouses was suggested by counsel—based on the earlier first instance cases and the dicta in *Hodgson*. This was rejected on the basis that a special rule based on unity of husband and wife was seriously outdated. It might be observed that Templeman J had stressed that the same principle would apply regardless of whether it was the husband or the wife who was the legal owner, but it is difficult to argue that an analysis applicable only to husband and wife (and not, for example, an unmarried couple) is fit for purpose in modern society.

Counsel's most compelling argument was that occupation should not suffice where it is consistent with the vendor's (or mortgagor's) title. Somebody buying land is not surprised to see a spouse, parent or child of the vendor living there—it is not a factor which naturally shouts out that there is a likely problem. However, quite apart from the fact that it is not what the statute states, Lord Wilberforce stresses that it would be difficult to operate in practice. Without going into the detail of the relationship between the parties, the consistency test cannot be operated. *Hodgson* provides a good example. The vendor told the purchaser that the occupier was a lodger. The truth was very different—the vendor was a lodger who had persuaded the claimant occupier to transfer title to him on trust for her. In truth, no purchaser or mortgagee can make assumptions without making enquiries of occupiers.

In common with Lord Denning MR, both Lord Wilberforce and Lord Scarman thought that the practical problems for purchasers and mortgagees were exaggerated. Lord Wilberforce accepted that an additional burden was being imposed, but stressed that this was largely a result of shared beneficial ownership becoming much more prevalent.

The Impact of *Boland* on Conveyancing

Whether the views expressed in the Court of Appeal and House of Lords were unduly sanguine may be gauged by the experience over the past thirty years. Initial response was hostile, with the Law Commission issuing something of a knee-jerk recommendation that *Boland* be reversed (though with other protections for spouses to be implemented).[28] Within five years, that recommendation was withdrawn by the Law Commission.[29] It had already been rejected by the Government; it had become apparent that conveyancers had quickly become accustomed to making enquiries of occupiers.[30] Indeed, these enquiries performed the highly desirable role of involving occupiers in decisions to sell or mortgage: something which could not readily be guaranteed otherwise (whatever duties of consultation may be imposed on trustees of land). There is no evidence that conveyancing is made measurably slower or more expensive as a result; indeed it was a period in which conveyancing costs were tending to fall.[31] Of course, it still happens from time to time that enquiries are not made. However, this is today viewed as a substantial failing by the purchaser or mortgagee and the courts are untroubled when this leads to liability.[32]

When assessing the risks to purchasers and mortgagees, it is important to note that most purchasers face no significant risk. Nearly always the purchaser will be taking vacant possession and this will almost always be inconsistent with actual occupation—certainly in the central case where the actual occupier is living there as their home. Meanwhile, even a trusting spouse or partner is likely to regard it as odd if prospective purchasers visit the house and start measuring up for carpets and curtains! Nevertheless, *Chhokar v Chhokar*[33] is an example of a wife's overriding interest binding a purchaser. However, the facts were exceptional; the wife was in hospital having a baby and it was not a normal purchase (among other factors, the sale was at a 30 per cent undervalue). Some purchasers may be purchasing property as an investment and not be worried if there is a tenant paying rent, but this factual situation will look very different from a spouse or partner living with the vendor. *Hodgson v Marks*, where the vendor passed the occupier off as a lodger, might be cited as an example of a purchaser being bound. However, it is not clear that this was a normal purchase. Ungoed-Thomas J noted at first instance 'disturbing circumstances which might suggest that the transaction might not at any rate be just a plain sale'.[34]

---

[28] Law Commission Report No 115, *Property Law: The Implications of Williams & Glyn's Bank v Boland* (1982); WT Murphy, 'After *Boland*: Law Com No 115' (1983) 46 *MLR* 330.
[29] Law Commission Report No 158, *Property Law: Third Report on Land Registration* (1985).
[30] Ibid, paras 1.3, 2.63.
[31] RJ Smith, 'Land Registration: White Elephant or Way Forward?' [1986] *CLP* 111, 112.
[32] *Thompson v Foy* [2009] EWHC 1076 (Ch), [2010] 1 P & CR 308 (on the facts, there was no beneficial interest); *Link Lending Ltd v Bustard* [2010] EWCA Civ 424, [2010] 2 EGLR 55.
[33] *Chhokar v Chhokar* [1984] FLR 313 (CA).
[34] *Hodgson v Marks* [1971] Ch 892, 910.

Mortgagees, on the other hand, are at greater risk because they do not take possession at the time of the mortgage. This means that it is quite possible that there is a claimant in actual occupation. Even so, first mortgagees (those who fund a purchase) will take priority over any claims arising on the purchase of the land and this means they will defeat a spouse or partner who partly funds the purchase.[35] It follows that the mortgagee at real risk is a second mortgagee, one who lends money after the purchase. Though such mortgages are common and frequently perform a useful function (in *Boland*, it financed the proprietor's business) it is difficult to treat a relatively infrequent loss to such mortgagees (coupled with the burden of a duty of enquiry) as more compelling than the potential loss of the home of the co-owning spouse or partner. Even if there is a minimal increase in interest rates in such loans to take account of the added risk and expenditure, that can be justified.

A rather different point concerns the likely outcome for the occupier. The result in *Boland* was that the bank's claim to possession failed, so that the bank could not exercise its power of sale as mortgagee. That does not necessarily represent the final result. A mortgagee possesses two further remedies, either of which will see the occupier losing their home. It has been clear since *Alliance and Leicester plc v Slayford*[36] that the bank can sue the borrower for the sums due. Given that the borrower is defaulting on payments (the reason why possession was sought in *Boland*) it is virtually inevitable that the borrower will be unable to pay and will be bankrupt. The trustee in bankruptcy can apply to the court for sale. Applying the principles in section 335A of the Insolvency Act 1986, sale will be ordered after one year save in the rare case in which there are exceptional circumstances. Somewhat more directly, the mortgagee can apply to the court for sale under section 14 of the Trusts of Land and Appointment of Trustees Act 1996. Section 15(1)(d) provides that the interests of secured creditors (which covers the mortgagee, of course) should be taken into account. Vitally, the courts are inclined to order sale in such cases,[37] at least unless the occupier can pay interest on a loan equal to the borrower's share.[38] This last possibility will be unusual. Accordingly, whether or not the bankruptcy route is adopted, it is likely that the occupier will lose the house.

---

[35] *Abbey National Building Society v Cann* [1991] 1 AC 56 (HL); *Re North East Property Buyers Litigation* [2012] EWCA Civ 17, [2012] 1 WLR 1521.

[36] *Alliance and Leicester plc v Slayford* (2000) 33 HLR 743 (CA) (the wife had consented to the mortgage, but this was ineffective because of undue influence by the borrower: *Barclays Bank plc v O'Brien* [1994] 1 AC 180 (HL)).

[37] *Bank of Ireland Home Mortgages Ltd v Bell* [2001] 2 FLR 809 (CA); *First National Bank plc v Achampong* [2003] EWCA Civ 487, [2004] 1 FCR 18. In neither case was the mortgagee bound by an overriding interest, but *Achampong* (where the wife's signature had been forged) is a good example of the charge binding the borrower, but not the occupier resisting sale.

[38] *Mortgage Corporation v Shaire* [2001] Ch 743 (Ch D).

Nevertheless, it is very important to realise that the occupier will receive a proportionate part of the proceeds. Typically, the sale proceeds will have to be used first to pay off any acquisition mortgage:[39] it is the net proceeds which will be shared. Unless the borrower's share is large enough to pay off the debt, the probability is that the lender will be unable to recover the balance of the loan.

THE LEGACY OF *BOLAND*

Introduction

It has been seen that *Boland* denies the application of the old notice rules to the actual occupation overriding interest. This supports an argument that land registration should be seen as a free-standing system, rather than one which simply applies a new procedure for buying and selling houses. The remainder of this chapter will examine this argument.

The discussion will be split into two areas. First (and most obviously) is an investigation of the extent to which actual occupation, in the years since *Boland*, has developed independently of ideas based upon notice.

The second area will be much wider: studying the extent to which registration generally is developing its own property principles, so that it operates as a self-contained system. A full investigation of this question would require a detailed review of several complex areas of law.[40] Given constraints of space, this chapter will consider one specific area: obligations personally undertaken by a registered transferee. One general point will be made at this stage—that we should be alert to an obvious danger. It would be naive to suppose that all the old common law (or equitable) rules are inadequate and should be avoided. It may be entirely appropriate to operate land registration in a manner similar to unregistered land, where this is both consistent with the legislation and provides the most workable and coherent system. Rejecting rules because they are old common law rules (whether or not related to the doctrine of notice) is just as silly as assuming that all the old rules should apply to registered land.

Developing the Meaning of Actual Occupation

Schedule 3, Paragraph 2(c)

Lord Wilberforce asserted that no element other than occupation is material. How far has this been fully accepted? The earlier cases (especially

---

[39] *Abbey National Building Society v Cann* [1991] 1 AC 56 (HL), discussed above.
[40] As explained below, these include the effect of forgeries and rectification of the register.

Hodgson v Marks) discussed the question whether the occupation must be actual and apparent, though Russell LJ did not think such wording 'adds to or detracts from the words in the section'. In any event LRA, schedule 3, paragraph 2(c) provides a defence where the 'occupation would not have been obvious on a reasonably careful inspection of the land' (assuming no actual knowledge of the interest).

Whatever the merits of the decision in *Boland* on the 1925 legislation, paragraph 2(c) seems well justified. Much as we may wish to protect purchasers from the vagaries and uncertainties of notice, there can be little justification for binding them when occupation cannot reasonably be discovered.[41] The Law Commission is at pains to stress that it is the occupation which must be apparent, not the interest of the occupier.[42] They go out of their way to stress that the doctrine of notice is not being applied, not even to the question whether there is actual occupation. Let us consider how paragraph 2(c) applies to *Boland*. The central issue turned on whether it should be material whether it looked as though Mrs Boland had an interest in the land. The House of Lords denied any such requirement and the new provision makes no change to this. When Mrs Boland was living in the house as her home there could be no question but that she was in actual occupation. Similarly, her occupation would be obvious to a purchaser: the outcome would be unaffected by the 2002 Act.

It is difficult to predict the impact of paragraph 2(c). It is in fact difficult to find any pre-2002 case in which the occupation was not obvious. One possibility might be the obiter suggestion in *Kingsnorth Finance Ltd v Tizard*[43] that a wife who had left the family home but kept clothes there and returned regularly to help look after children (and sometimes staying overnight) was in actual occupation.

There has been relatively little assistance from the cases since 2002. In *Mehra v Mehra*,[44] it was said (unsurprisingly) that occupation would not be obvious where a house appeared not to be lived in and to be unfurnished (actual occupation was not satisfied in any event). More interesting is *Thompson v Foy*,[45] in which the claimant's furniture remained in the property, though she had removed personal belongings and valuables. She had no intention of returning and Lewison J held this to be fatal to her

---

[41] Perhaps the strongest assertion of this argument had been in *Kling v Keston Properties Ltd* (1983) 49 P & CR 212, 222 (Vinelott J).

[42] Law Commission Report No 271, *Land Registration for the Twenty-First Century: A Conveyancing Revolution* (2001) para 5.73.

[43] *Kingsnorth Finance Ltd v Tizard* [1986] 1 WLR 886 (Judge Finlay QC). Title was not registered.

[44] *Mehra v Mehra* [2008] 3 EGLR 153 (Central London County Court).

[45] *Thompson v Foy* [2009] EWHC 1076 (Ch), [2010] 1 P&CR 308. In the similar case of *Link Lending Ltd v Bustard* [2010] EWCA Civ 424, [2010] 2 EGLR 55, the chargee did not argue that occupation was not obvious.

argument that she was in actual occupation. However, he also considered that any actual occupation would have been obvious from a reasonable inspection—the furnished state of the premises was the crucial factor. The facts of *Thompson* prompt a thought as to when the new provision might operate. Suppose the proprietor had surreptitiously removed the furniture (or the clothes in *Tizard*), could it then be argued that the occupation is not obvious? This might be a case where actual occupation might continue (especially if the furniture is replaced after the mortgagee's inspection) but the overriding interest might fail under paragraph 2(c).

One aspect of *Thompson* is that Lewison J states that a purchaser is protected against non-obvious occupation even if no inspection is in fact made.[46] Though this surprises Bogusz,[47] it fits the wording of the legislation. Plainly, an alternative legislative approach could have been justified, though the doctrine of notice similarly protects purchasers who do not make enquiries.[48]

The fullest analysis of paragraph 2(c) is found in the recent decision of Ramsey J in *Thomas v Clydesdale Bank plc*.[49] The facts were very similar to those in *Lloyds Bank plc v Rosset*,[50] some 20 years earlier. In each case the claimant was supervising extensive building work, prior to moving in to a newly purchased house. Given that a majority of the Court of Appeal in *Rosset* held that this constituted actual occupation, it is unsurprising that Ramsey J held that the claimant had a reasonable prospect of proving actual occupation at trial. Since *Rosset*, of course, the 2002 Act has introduced the obvious on reasonable inspection test. Ramsey J considered this in the following terms:

> In my judgment the concept of inspection strongly suggests that what has to be obvious is the relevant visible signs of occupation upon which a person who asserts an interest by actual occupation relies. It is clear from what is said above that, in order to determine whether somebody is in actual occupation it is necessary to determine not only matters which would be obvious on inspection but matters which would require enquiry to ascertain them. That includes such things as the permanence and continuity of the presence of the person concerned, the intentions and wishes of that person and the personal circumstances of the person concerned.

---

[46] *Thompson v Foy* [2009] EWHC 1076 (Ch), [2010] 1 P&CR 308, [132].

[47] B Bogusz, 'Defining the Scope of Actual Occupation Under the Land Registration Act 2002: Some Recent Judicial Clarification' [2011] *Conv* 268, 279–80.

[48] *Carter v Williams* (1870) LR 9 Eq 678 (no notice where a conveyance had not been inspected, but the relevant right was not apparent from it).

[49] *Thomas v Clydesdale Bank plc* [2010] EWHC 2755 (QB).

[50] *Lloyds Bank plc v Rosset* [1989] Ch 350 (CA); in the House of Lords [1991] 1 AC 107 it was held that the wife had no beneficial interest and so it was unnecessary to consider the actual occupation issue.

... I find it difficult to read into the objective phrase 'reasonably careful inspection' a requirement that the person inspecting would have any particular knowledge or that, in the absence of any express provision, the term 'inspection' would also require the person inspecting to make reasonable enquiries. On that basis, it is the visible signs of occupation which have to be obvious on inspection.[51]

To stress visible signs of occupations seems, with respect, to be fully in line with both the approach adopted by Lord Wilberforce in *Boland* and the policy of the 2002 Act. It should be relatively straightforward to apply.

A final observation on the new provision is entirely speculative. In the past, courts were reluctant to extend actual occupation too far, in order to be fair to purchasers. This is further discussed below. Now that we have the requirement that the occupation be obvious, the courts may be tempted to broaden the meaning of actual occupation. This would be of most obvious importance to a purchaser who is aware of the interest.

Notice and *Boland*

It was surprising that, despite the very clear dicta of Lord Wilberforce, some judges remained attracted to the approach adopted by first instance judges before *Boland*—the approach which sought to link the operation of actual occupation to the doctrine of notice. To avoid confusion, it should be stressed that no judge has suggested that a spouse or partner living in the family home is not in actual occupation; the issue has arisen in less clear cut situations. Thus, in *Rosset*,[52] Purchas LJ stated that: 'two things must be established: (a) was she in actual occupation? and (b) would appropriate inquiries made by the bank have elicited the fact of her interest?'

It is very difficult to reconcile these dicta with *Boland*. *Rosset* was doubtless a borderline case, but to require both actual occupation and elements of the doctrine of notice appears unjustified—the more so as the enquiry is as to the interest and not as to the occupation itself. It is not identical to the test introduced by paragraph 2(c), but it is to be hoped that this provision renders it unnecessary to add the *Rosset* gloss to actual occupation in future cases.

The Meaning of Actual Occupation

This chapter is not undertaking a thorough investigation into how actual occupation applies to specific factual situations—that is too large a question

---

[51] *Thomas v Clydesdale Bank plc* [2010] EWHC 2755 (QB), [38]–[40].
[52] *Lloyds Bank plc v Rosset* [1989] Ch 350, 404 (CA).

for the space available. Rather, the investigation is as to the nature of actual occupation. It should be remembered that, since 2002, finding actual occupation is not conclusive in favour of the occupier—it has already been seen that the 'obvious' test may protect the purchaser, resulting in less pressure to limit the scope of actual occupation.

An initial point is that actual occupation is not limited to houses; it applies just as well to commercial property (shops, factories)[53] and agricultural land.[54] Just as living in a house clearly suffices, so will operating offices and factories or running farms. Nor are these categories exhaustive, as shown by parking a car in a garage in *Kling v Keston Properties Ltd*.[55] In these cases, *Boland* can readily be applied. However, with any form of property there may be claims to occupation that are different from the paradigm examples of actual occupation (for houses, living in them). Examples have been seen in the cases already discussed: half moving out of property in *Thompson v Foy* (and *Link Lending Ltd v Bustard*,[56] in which the Court of Appeal approved the approach of Lewison J) and renovating semi-derelict property in *Rosset* and *Thomas v Clydesdale Bank plc*. These are situations in which it is by no means obvious whether there is or is not actual occupation. Nevertheless, there are some useful pointers. As stressed in *Rosset*, the nature of the property must be taken into account. What is required for actual occupation of a normal house is quite different for a semi-derelict house. This may be seen as analogous to adverse possession, where again the nature of the property can be crucial.[57]

The modern application of actual occupation is well illustrated by *Malory Enterprises Ltd v Cheshire Homes (UK) Ltd*.[58] The case involved an uncompleted and derelict block of flats. The sole use of them was for a limited amount of temporary storage; the land was fenced and the ground floor windows boarded up. Arden LJ was faithful to authority in holding that the nature and state of the property are relevant and (as held in *Abbey National Building Society v Cann*)[59] there must be some degree of permanence and continuity. Arden LJ then states that 'The requisite physical presence must, as it seems to me, in fairness be such as to put a person inspecting the land on notice that there was some person in occupation:

[53] *London & Cheshire Insurance Co Ltd v Laplagrene Property Co Ltd* [1971] Ch 499 (Ch D); *Ferrishurst Ltd v Wallcite Ltd* [1999] Ch 355 (CA).

[54] *Blacklocks v JB Developments (Godalming) Ltd* [1982] Ch 183 (Ch D).

[55] *Kling v Keston Properties Ltd* (1983) 49 P & CR 212 (Ch D).

[56] *Link Lending Ltd v Bustard* [2010] EWCA Civ 424, [2010] 2 EGLR 55.

[57] One of many examples is *Red House Farms (Thorndon) Ltd v Catchpole* [1977] 2 EGLR 125 (CA).

[58] *Malory Enterprises Ltd v Cheshire Homes (UK) Ltd* [2002] EWCA Civ 151, [2002] Ch 216.

[59] *Abbey National Building Society v Cann* [1991] 1 AC 56 (HL).

see generally per Lord Oliver in *Cann's* case'. She concluded that actual occupation was present on the facts:

> [N]o one visiting the rear land at the time of the sale to Cheshire could have drawn the conclusion that the land and buildings on the rear land had been abandoned; the evidence of activity on the site clearly indicated that someone claimed to be entitled to be on it.

This analysis is very similar to that employed by the Court of Appeal in *Rosset* and fits other cases well.[60] It must be stressed that the concept of 'putting on notice' is not being used as a test in addition to actual occupation; in this respect it is quite different (and far more acceptable) from what was said by Purchas LJ in *Rosset*, discussed above. Though *Boland* works very readily when one has a straightforward case of living in a house or farming agricultural land (the 'plain meaning' of actual occupation, as Lord Wilberforce expressed it) there has to be some basis for resolving less obvious cases. As Lord Oliver observed in *Cann*,[61] 'even plain English may contain a variety of shades of meaning'. The extent of physical activity is plainly relevant (this is what caused the difficulty in *Malory*) but this has to be balanced against the type of property. In this context, to use a test analogous to notice can be justified in providing coherence and predictability to the actual occupation test.

It is this approach which is central to an understanding of how actual occupation functions today. It helps to explain the apparently inappropriate dicta of Purchas LJ in *Rosset*. It also explains why the new 'obvious' test in the 2002 Act is unlikely to have much practical effect. It would be rare indeed that standard examples of actual occupation, such as living in a house, will not be obvious (absent exceptional circumstances such as hiding evidence of the occupation, as suggested above). In situations where occupation is a more arguable, the test adopted by Arden LJ comes to the same result as the 'obvious' test.

A final point concerns a development observed in *Thomas v Clydesdale Bank plc*. In the quotation above,[62] it is observed that actual occupation depends on factors other than physical actions which can be observed. One example is the *Cann* requirement that the occupation possess 'some degree of permanence and continuity'. This was applied so as to exclude acts (such as moving in furniture) which were preparatory to completion. In some cases, 'permanence and continuity' may be seen from the objective facts, at least if observed over a period of time, but we are moving away from sole reliance on the actions of the claimant.[63] This it might suffice to

---

[60] Examples include *Epps v Esso Petroleum Co Ltd* [1973] 1 WLR 1071 (Ch D) and *Abbey National Building Society v Cann* [1989] 2 FLR 265 (CA); [1991] 1 AC 56 (HL).
[61] *Abbey National Building Society v Cann* [1991] 1 AC 56, 93.
[62] See text preceding n 51 above.
[63] Described by Bogusz, above (n 47) as a contextual approach.

move in furniture *after* completion, even if the claimant was (like Mrs Cann) away on holiday at the time. The second example is more telling. In each of *Thompson v Foy*[64] and *Link Lending Ltd v Bustard*[65] the claimant had left the relevant house, but some of their belongings remained there. In *Thompson v Foy*, the claimant had no intention of returning. The result was that there was no actual occupation four days after she had left with her personal belongings, even though her furniture, etc remained there. In contrast, in *Link Lending*, absence for over a year did not prevent actual occupation when the claimant had been confined to hospital (because of mental illness) and intended to return when and if that proved possible; she had no other home. This last factor explains the contrary result in *Stockholm Finance Ltd v Garden Holdings Inc.*[66] In that case the claimant had another home in Saudi Arabia; Robert Walker J treated absence for a year as far too long for actual occupation to continue, despite the house being fully furnished.

The crucial element distinguishing these cases lies in the intention to return in *Link Lending*, coupled with the absence of any other home. Quite clearly, there is nothing on the facts of either *Thompson* or *Link Lending* which indicated to a purchaser whether or not there was an intention to return. These cases really do seem to introduce elements which lie outside a simple objective assessment of the facts. Should this be a concern? It does not appear to operate to the prejudice of purchasers. It seems to be saying that activities which are indicative of actual occupation will not always have that quality: in other words, intention is used to limit actual occupation rather than to extend it. This is illustrated by the finding in *Thompson v Foy* that, had there been actual occupation, it would have been obvious on a reasonably careful inspection. Certainly, this limitation on actual occupation is not an application of ideas based on the doctrine of notice. It might also be noted that the dicta in *Thomas v Clydesdale Bank plc*, quoted above, state that the paragraph 2(c) test is based only on 'visible signs of occupation': there is no scope for the subjectivity found in *Thompson* and *Link Lending*.

Perhaps it should be added that the presence of furniture does not by itself signify actual occupation. This was clearly stated by the Court of Appeal in *Strand Securities Ltd v Caswell*.[67] However, that was a case where the claimant did not live on the premises and another person did. It does not prevent furniture from being a significant factor when coupled with normal residence—the occupier's temporary absence at the time of the disposition is not conclusive.

---

[64] *Thompson v Foy* [2010] 1 P & CR 308.
[65] *Link Lending Ltd v Bustard* [2010] 2 EGLR 55.
[66] *Stockholm Finance Ltd v Garden Holdings Inc* [1995] NPC 162 (Ch D).
[67] *Strand Securities Ltd v Caswell* [1965] Ch 958, 985 (CA).

The Legacy of *Boland*: Personal Obligations—How Far do we Break Free from Unregistered Land Principles?

Harpum has argued that 'registered conveyancing should be developed according to its own logic and potential, unconstrained by whatever the position might be in relation to unregistered conveyancing'.[68] This fits well with the approach in *Boland* that actual occupation should not be seen as a simple shorthand for notice from occupation.

It is plain that registered conveyancing cannot be completely isolated from general legal principles. In particular, the range of interests in land is determined by common law and statutory principles established over the centuries. This was made very clear by the House of Lords in *National Provincial Bank Ltd v Ainsworth*.[69] Nevertheless, there is scope for development. Thus, the LRA[70] makes provision for estoppels, pre-emptions and certain equities. One suspects that a more subtle development may be an adjustment of the criteria for proprietary status, as outlined in *Ainsworth*,[71] so as to remodel them according to the needs of registered conveyancing and what it can offer claimants and purchasers.

However, the most obvious area in which registered land principles may be expected to be dominant is that of priorities: the competition between two or more claims to land. This is enhanced by the 2002 Act because section 28 makes express provision (for the first time) for the priority of unregistered interests. Priorities is, of course, the area within which overriding interests operate. A number of different issues arise within the broad priorities area. One of them concerns the effect of registration in guaranteeing the title of the registered proprietor. This is especially important as regards void transfers, with forgeries forming the basis for much of the discussion. This was the area investigated by Harpum.[72] Another area concerns rectification principles: how far should we treat unregistered priorities as the 'right' result so as to justify rectification? This provides the background for the Scottish Law Commission to refer to 'bijural inaccuracy': contrasting the legal position as recorded on the register with that as it would be if title were unregistered. Their solution to the problems in this area is to diminish the impact of registration: a very different approach to that seen in the 2002 Act in England.[73]

---

[68] C Harpum, 'Registered Land—A Law Unto Itself?' in J Getzler (ed), *Rationalizing Property, Equity and Trusts* (UK, LexisNexis, 2003) 188. Harpum bases this proposition on Law Com No 254, *Land Registration for the Twenty-First Century*, above (n 1) para 1.6.

[69] *National Provincial Bank Ltd v Ainsworth* [1965] AC 1175 (HL).

[70] ss 115 and 116.

[71] *National Provincial Bank Ltd v Ainsworth* [1965] AC 1175, 1247–48 (Lord Wilberforce).

[72] Harpum argues in favour of protecting an innocent purchaser, but note the very different approach of the Scottish Law Commission in Scot Law Com No 222.

[73] Ibid. However, those subsequently relying on the register would still be protected.

Void transfers and rectification provide excellent material from which one can assess the extent to which registration can be seen to provide a free-standing and comprehensive solution of priority disputes. However, the remainder of this chapter will concentrate on a question which has received little attention from English courts: can an interest which has not been protected on the register (and which is not an overriding interest) be enforced against a purchaser because of some personal obligation? Normally, of course, section 29 ensures that an unprotected interest will not be binding on a purchaser, once the purchaser has been registered as the new proprietor (the same protection applies to tenants and mortgagees). Although there was some support under the pre-2002 law for saying that the purchaser had to be in good faith in order to gain that protection,[74] the 2002 Act is differently worded and clearly designed to avoid any such requirement. Bad faith (or fraud) provides one particular setting in which it is likely to be argued that the purchaser is bound by a personal obligation.

The two principal questions which will be investigated in this section will concern (a) the meaning and scope of personal obligations affecting purchasers of registered land and (b) the effect of personal obligations.

What are Personal Obligations?

Property rights bind purchasers automatically, at least if protected on the register. However, proprietary status is just one of several routes whereby a purchaser may be attacked. Take contractual licences—a good example of a non-proprietary right. It is today impossible to argue that a purchaser is bound by such a licence by virtue of either an entry on the register or actual occupation.[75] However, one can contemplate a number of ways in which a purchaser might be held liable. The cases recognise that a purchaser who induces the transfer by promising (to the vendor) to give effect to the contract will be bound by a constructive trust in order to avoid an unconscionable result.[76] Liability would also be present if the purchaser contracted to respect the licence[77] or if there were a representation to the licensee, which the licensee relied on to his or her detriment (estoppel).

---

[74] *Peffer v Rigg* [1977] 1 WLR 285 (Ch D), relying on LRA 1925, s 59(6).

[75] The leading case is *Ashburn Anstalt v Arnold* [1989] Ch 1 (CA).

[76] *Binions v Evans* [1972] Ch 359 (CA); *Lyus v Prowsa Developments Ltd* [1982] 1 WLR 1044 (Ch D); *Ashburn Anstalt v Arnold* [1989] Ch 1 (CA) (limiting the applicability of the constructive trust).

[77] Either directly with the licensee or with the licensor/vendor (applying the Contracts (Rights of Third Parties) Act 1999. S Bright, 'The Third Party's Conscience in Land Law' [2000] *Conv* 398 argues that the contractual analysis should be employed rather than a constructive trust).

The contractual licence has been considered because it is not proprietary in nature and yet there are ways in which a purchaser may be attacked. It is important to note that what binds the purchaser is not the original licence standing by itself—rather, a new obligation undertaken by the purchaser (or imposed on him) is being enforced. In principle, there is no reason why a similar analysis should not be employed where there is a proprietary interest, but one that does not bind a purchaser as it is not entered on the register. Indeed, the courts have indicated willingness to recognise a personal obligation in such a case.[78]

How do personal obligations fit into the registration system? In the Torrens registration systems operating in many Commonwealth jurisdictions, they have long been recognised as an exception to the protection accorded to registered purchasers. Their status is beyond argument, although it will be seen that the scope of their application remains controversial. In English cases, their development and application have been minimal. However, they are recognised by the Law Commission, which fully approves of them.[79] The Law Commission identifies four examples: the constructive trust imposed on those who knowingly receive property in breach of trust, the constructive trust imposed on those who have promised to give effect to a claim (as recognised in *Ashburn Anstalt*), tort liability (perhaps for conspiracy or inducing breach of contract) and equitable liability for undue influence or misrepresentation on the part of the registered purchaser (inducing the relevant transfer).

Technically, how does personal liability fit the statutory protection of purchasers? That protection is conferred by LRA, section 29, which provides that 'completion of the transaction by registration has the effect of postponing to the interest under the disposition any [unprotected] interest affecting the estate immediately before the disposition'. It is important to note that the legislation does not say that no claims whatsoever bind the purchaser; rather it postpones interests which affect the estate prior to the purchase. If a new claim based on the conduct of the purchaser has arisen, there is nothing in the Act which purports to protect the purchaser against it. Though this is most obvious when there is no proprietary interest affecting the seller (as with the contractual licence example),[80] it also appears to

---

[78] *Lyus v Prowsa Developments Ltd* [1982] 1 WLR 1044 (Ch D), though there was considerable reliance on the presence of fraud. The facts were unusual in that the proprietary interest (an estate contract) was not binding on the vendor (a mortgagee, whose mortgage predated the estate contract entered into by the mortgagor). See also *Chattey v Farndale Holdings Inc* (1996) 75 P & CR 298 (CA).

[79] Law Com No 254, *Land Registration for the Twenty-First Century*, above (n 1) para 3.48; see also Law Com No 271, *Land Registration for the Twenty-First Century*, above (n 42) paras 4.11, 7.7 (fn 31).

[80] See also *Lyus v Prowsa Developments Ltd* [1982] 1 WLR 1044 (Ch D).

be applicable if the substance of the new claim appears to be the same as the interest which is defeated by section 29.

The existence of some forms of personal liability should not be surprising: it would be extraordinary if the purchaser could avoid a contract, for example. However, what is more controversial is whether all the types of claims suggested by the Law Commission should operate as personal obligations. There is also difficulty concerning the effect of a personal claim (assuming that it has survived the registration of the purchaser).

Why is the range of personal obligations controversial? One might wish to split them into three categories. The first is where there is no interest binding the seller. In such a case it seems difficult to understand how any objection could be made to the recognition of a personal obligation: it simply does not relate to the quality of the seller's title. Few would argue that registration should exclude claims which would be effective in unregistered land. For example, a purchaser should not be able to deny a constructive trust of the family home under the principles in cases such as *Gissing v Gissing*[81] and *Stack v Dowden*[82] merely because title is registered. The same may be applicable if there is a common intention constructive trust outside the family home context, as in *HSBC Bank plc v Dyche*[83] where it gave effect to an intention that the legal estate be held by way of security only.

The second category is where the purchaser has expressly (or by necessary inference) agreed to give effect to an existing interest (which itself is defeated by section 29). So long as the facts suffice to satisfy the requirements of contract, estoppel or constructive trust,[84] it would be pedantic to argue that defeating the interest binding the seller should be inconsistent with the recognition of a fresh obligation. Neither policy nor principle points against the recognition of the personal obligation.

The third category is more troublesome. Some obligations are imposed because it is perceived that the conduct of the defendant is culpable in some manner. Examples are provided by tort liability for inducing breach of contract or a constructive trust imposed in order to counter unconscionable conduct. Should this be enough to recognise personal liability where section 29 protects the purchaser against an unprotected interest? It may be thought that registration law and tort or equity are answering the same question: should a purchaser be bound? That they come to different answers provides cause for concern. Much of the problem arises because of the insistence of the Law Commission that an unprotected interest should be

---

[81] *Gissing v Gissing* [1971] AC 886 (HL).

[82] *Stack v Dowden* [2007] UKHL 17, [2007] 2 AC 432.

[83] *HSBC Bank plc v Dyche* [2009] EWHC 2954 (Ch), [2010] 2 P & CR 58, [23] (relying on *Lyus v Prowsa Developments Ltd* [1982] 1 WLR 1044, discussed above).

[84] The difficulties faced by claimants who rely on 'subject to' promises by the purchaser are illustrated by *Chaudhary v Yavuz* [2011] EWCA Civ 1314, [2012] 1 P & CR 206, especially [61]–[62].

defeated by registration regardless of bad faith or actual notice of interest.[85] Yet these are the very situations in which personal remedies are likely to arise, as the Law Commission recognises. Indeed, the Law Commission argues that the presence of personal liability helps to justify the rejection of any role for bad faith or actual notice.

The cornerstone of the Law Commission's defence of its position is that personal liability is quite different from proprietary liability. In their eyes, there is no inconsistency in denying proprietary liability while recognising personal liability, as the two have quite different consequences. Before the scope of personal obligations can be fully assessed, we need to investigate their effect.

The Effect of Personal Obligations

There are two quite different ways in which personal obligations may be understood to be 'personal' (they are not mutually exclusive). The first underpins much of the analysis above: an obligation may be said to be personal if it is accepted by a person or imposed on him or her by virtue of their conduct. By contrast, a proprietary obligation binds a purchaser simply because it is on the register (or is overriding, where relevant). This is the distinction made in *Binions v Evans*,[86] of course. Though the contractual licence was not binding on the purchaser (it was not a proprietary claim), this did not preclude a new obligation arising as a result of the purchaser's promise. *Binions* involved unregistered land, but the same reasoning should apply in registered land. Accordingly, it is the source of the obligation which is personal.

The second meaning—that adopted by the Law Commission—is that the obligation is personal in nature and effect. The liability is imposed on the purchaser personally. This means that it does not affect the land, which can therefore be resold free of any claim (regardless of any entry on the register). We will return later to the question whether this justifies allowing the personal obligation, but is it correct? As a matter of principle, one would expect that the proprietary status of the obligation should depend on the nature of the right claimed.[87] Suppose that the personal obligation is based on contract. If there is a contract for a licence, one would certainly not expect this to be proprietary in nature. By contrast, suppose that the

---

[85] Law Com No 254, *Land Registration for the Twenty-First Century*, above (n 1) para 3.46.

[86] *Binions v Evans* [1972] Ch 359 (CA).

[87] Strongly supported by B McFarlane, 'Constructive Trusts Arising on a Receipt of Property *Sub Conditione*' (2004) 120 *LQR* 667, 671 (fn 23). McFarlane criticises an apparent suggestion by the present author (in fact unintended) that the obligation is personal in nature. See also E Cooke and P O'Connor, 'Purchaser Liability to Third Parties in the English Land Registration System: A Comparative Perspective' (2004) 120 *LQR* 640, 649.

claimant has estate contract. Though this is not protected on the register, suppose that a purchaser chooses, as part of the purchase of the land, to enter into a fresh contractual obligation (enforceable by the claimant) to give effect to the estate contract. In this scenario, it would appear natural that this should be proprietary in nature—as in any other case in which a person contracts to create an estate in land.

The contrary conclusion—favouring the position of the Law Commission—is, however, supported by dicta of Norris J in *Halifax plc v Curry Popeck*.[88] One aspect of the case was rather special—the purchaser was also one of the vendors and as such had taken part in the creation of the interest. In the more normal situation, the purchaser has no other involvement, so that there is more of a separation between the proprietary interest which is defeated by section 29 and the personal obligation; and it can be more readily said that there is 'a *new* right ..., arising at the time of transfer'.[89] Leaving that on one side, Norris J employed the following analysis:

> If A, as personal representative, contracts to sell Blackacre to X and he then for valuable consideration transfers Blackacre into his own name and then contracts to sell Blackacre to Y, X will not be able to assert an equitable title to Blackacre against Y; but the contract that had made will continue to bind him; he will be liable for damages for such breach.[90]

This analysis is difficult to follow. As Norris J recognised, specific performance would have been available against A, prior to the sale to Y. Does not that right to specific performance confer an equitable interest on X? It is the availability of specific performance that results in the proprietary status of estate contracts.[91]

We have seen that another example of a personal obligation is a tort—inducing breach of contract may be the best example. The nature of tortious liability is that we do not normally recognise it as giving rise to proprietary status. This appears to justify the Law Commission's approach. However, the court may make an order reversing the effect of the tort[92] and this might lead to a credible argument that a proprietary right has been created (ie, even before the court order).

---

[88] *Halifax plc v Curry Popeck (A Firm)* [2008] EWHC 1692 (Ch).

[89] McFarlane, above (n 87) 671.

[90] [2008] EWHC 1692 (Ch), [51]. The facts of the case involved two trustees transferring to one of them as part of a complex mortgage fraud. The issue discussed in text is obiter, the case being decided on the absence of valuable consideration (as required by s 29).

[91] The thrust of this argument can be maintained even if S Gardner, 'Equity, Estate Contracts and the Judicature Acts: *Walsh v Lonsdale Revisited*' (1987) 7 *OJLS* 60 is correct in arguing that proprietary status may apply even if specific performance is not available.

[92] As in *Esso Petroleum Co Ltd v Kingswood Motors (Addlestone) Ltd* [1974] QB 142 (QBD).

The Law Commission also uses misrepresentation or undue influence on the part of a borrower (exerted on the chargor) as an example of a personal obligation affecting the registered chargee. While it is clear that the chargee may be bound,[93] it is a strange example of a personal interest. The person committing the wrong is the borrower: it is the notice of the chargee (a very special use of notice) which causes the charge to be affected.[94] Given the lack of cases involving a subsequent transfer of the registered charge, there appears to be no authority on the proprietary nature of the right to set the charge aside. However, might it not be an example of a 'mere equity' that section 116 of the LRA declares to be capable of binding purchasers?

The final type of personal obligation identified by the Law Commission is the constructive trust. One example is provided by a purchaser who promises the seller that the interest will be given effect to: the cases (including *Binions v Evans*) show that a constructive trust will be imposed on the purchaser for the benefit of the holder of the interest. Such a trust needs to be proprietary before a *subsequent* purchaser can be bound. *Chattey v Farndale Holdings Inc*[95] involved a claim against a subsequent purchaser, but it is tantalisingly unclear. The purchaser was not bound, but this appears to be because the right was not entered on the register—the inference might be that a purchaser would be bound if there were such an entry (or actual occupation).

Constructive trusts are also imposed on those who receive trust property and unconscionably retain it.[96] This liability is regarded as personal in that it provides liability where the recipient no longer holds the property.[97] However, this is only part of the story. The background is one where there is clear proprietary liability arising from receipt: the personal liability operates to extend that liability to situations in which the recipient has disposed of the property. Whether personal liability can be divorced from initial proprietary liability (as where the latter is precluded by registration rules) is less clear. This relates to receipt based trusts. Those imposed where there is

---

[93] *Barclays Bank plc v O'Brien* [1994] 1 AC 180 (HL); *Royal Bank of Scotland plc v Etridge (No 2)* [2001] UKHL 44, [2002] 2 AC 773.

[94] As stressed by Lord Hoffmann in *Barclays Bank plc v Boulter* [1999] 1 WLR 1919, 1924: 'There was no prior interest which the bank needed to defeat'.

[95] *Chattey v Farndale Holdings Inc* (1996) 75 P & CR 298, 313–17 (CA) (the subsequent purchaser would have be liable if he had made a fresh promise).

[96] *BCCI (Overseas) Ltd v Akindele* [2001] Ch 437 (CA) (based on the first head of liability in *Barnes v Addy* (1874) 9 Ch App 244, 251–52).

[97] As explained by Megarry V-C in *Re Montagu's ST* [1987] Ch 264 (Ch D). See also Lord Browne-Wilkinson in *Westdeutsche Landesbank Girozentrale v Islington LBC* [1996] AC 669, 707 (HL). This element is stressed by M Conaglen and A Goymour, 'Knowing Receipt and Registered Land' in C Mitchell (ed), *Constructive and Resulting Trusts* (Oxford, Hart Publishing, 2010) 162.

dishonest assistance[98] less clearly relate to receipt and so are more obviously personal, even if trust property is in fact received.

The recent decision of the Privy Council in *Arthur v Attorney-General of the Turks and Caicos Islands*[99] concerned a claim to a receipt based constructive trust. The Privy Council recognised the difference between personal and proprietary claims, but proceeded to allow both on the basis of legislation which permitted the enforcement of trusts (construed to include a trust arising from knowing receipt). The existence of that legislation (no equivalent provisions are found in the LRA) makes it difficult to draw inferences as to whether the personal liability can survive statutory protection against proprietary liability.

These categories of personal claims are almost certainly not exclusive. Thus, a victim of misrepresentation or mistake can assert rights notwithstanding registration and these rights are capable of binding purchasers.[100] Indeed, the acceptance of 'mere equities' as property rights (LRA, section 116) supports this. In addition, claims may be brought where there is unjust enrichment.[101]

As has been observed, Torrens systems have long recognised personal claims, despite taking very seriously the principle that the register should be conclusive (usually described as 'indefeasibility'). It seems quite clear that they are regarded as being capable of being proprietary in nature (obviously, this would not apply to a monetary remedy). At first sight, some of the dicta appear to support the personal remedy analysis of the Law Commission. A particularly notable example is the decision of the Privy Council in *Frazer v Walker*,[102] stating that indefeasibility 'in no way denies the right of a plaintiff to bring against a registered proprietor a claim in personam, founded in law or in equity, for such relief as a court acting in personam may grant'. However, it seems widely agreed that the personal nature of the claim relates to its source rather than its nature. Thus, there are plentiful references to the land being held on trust (where a trust is appropriate for the claim in question).[103] Even allowing for the point that in Torrens systems personal claims encompass those arising after as well as

---

[98] As articulated by *Royal Brunei Airlines Sbn Bhd v Tan* [1995] 2 AC 378 (PC).

[99] *Arthur v Attorney-General of the Turks and Caicos Islands* [2012] UKPC 30.

[100] For rectification, see *Blacklocks v JB Developments (Godalming) Ltd* [1982] Ch 183 (Ch D). See also the discussion of fraud, p 151 below.

[101] Explored by E Bant, 'Registration as a Defence to Claims in Unjust Enrichment: Australia and England Compared' [2011] *Conv* 309.

[102] *Frazer v Walker* [1967] 1 AC 569, 585 (PC).

[103] Eg, see *Taitapu Gold Estates Ltd v Prouse* [1916] NZLR 825; *Loke Yew v Port Swettenham Rubber Co Ltd* [1913] AC 491, 505–06 (PC) and *Executive Seminars Pty Ltd v Peck* [2001] WASC 229, [237]–[239]. In *Bahr v Nicolay (No 2)* (1988) 164 CLR 604, 638, Wilson and Toohey JJ refer to an 'equitable estate' as one possibility. The point is strongly put by K Low, 'The Nature of Torrens Indefeasibility: Understanding the Limits of Personal Equities' (2009) 33 *Melbourne University Law Review* 205, 208.

before registration,[104] it seems clear that the Law Commission's analysis is impossible to square with Australian thinking.

Should the Law Restrict the Range of Personal Claims?

If, contrary to the views of the Law Commission and *Curry Popeck*, personal claims may be proprietary in their effect, then this weakens the case for their recognition. It should be stressed that this is not a black-and-white issue. Some forms of personal obligations can be defended whether or not they have proprietary effect—the first two categories identified above.[105] It is the third category—where the personal claim is based on the conduct of the purchaser—that is most difficult.

If there is proprietary liability, then in this third category there is an apparent inconsistency between the outcome as mandated by the legislation (primarily LRA, section 29) and the personal obligation. This is not so clear with obligations that are purely personal in effect, as where a monetary remedy is awarded. Under the Torrens system, this has been used to argue that such personal remedies are permissible.[106] However, there is much to be said for the dominant view expressed by Wu[107] that 'it is a hollow victory for the registered proprietor to retain the land if they have to pay a sum equivalent to the value of the land in terms of equitable compensation to the defendant'. In England, Conaglen and Goymour[108] have argued that it would 'subvert the function that section 29 was designed to perform, even though it might be formally consistent with the language used in the section'. It certainly follows that the purchaser is not safe in relying on the register!

There are two related questions. The first is whether there should be any constraint on personal claims. The second is what the substance of any such constraint should be. What is alarming about the analysis of the Law Commission is that it appears not to recognise any need for constraints. The label of personal obligation, coupled with its alleged non-proprietary effect, is thought sufficient to justify its enforcement.

---

[104] *Bahr v Nicolay (No 2)* (1988) 164 CLR 604, 613, Mason CJ and Dawson J. *Barry v Heider* (1914) 19 CLR 197 is a leading authority on such subsequent claims. Under the English land registration system there have never been doubts about the proprietary status of these subsequent claims.

[105] See p 143 above.

[106] M Harding, '*Barnes v Addy* Claims and the Indefeasibility of Torrens Title' (2007) 31 *Melbourne University Law Review* 343.

[107] T Wu, 'Beyond the Torrens Mirror: a Framework of the In Personam Exception to Indefeasibility' (2008) 32 *Melbourne University Law Review* 672, 691.

[108] Conaglen and Goymour, 'Knowing Receipt and Registered Land', above (n 97) 177.

This is to be contrasted with the position in Torrens jurisdictions, in which almost every analysis stresses the need to balance personal actions against the competing benefits of indefeasibility.[109] It is treated as of paramount importance that the statutory protection against unprotected interests should not be compromised by personal obligations. One of the concerns in the earlier cases was that a constructive trust might be used where a purchaser knows about an unprotected interest. By way of contrast, the recognition of such a trust where the purchaser has agreed to give effect to the interest has received general approval, as being in the nature of a new obligation agreed to by the purchaser.[110]

More recently, there has been a flurry of Torrens system cases based on the *Barnes v Addy*[111] constructive trust imposed on those who receive (or keep) trust property when they are aware of a breach of trust. This is, of course, much more problematic because the purchaser has not undertaken any obligation. Though Torrens systems exclude protection where the purchaser has been guilty of fraud, it should be stressed that Australian cases are very clear that simple knowledge of an interest does not constitute fraud.[112] The earlier cases display differing approaches as to whether the constructive trust defeats indefeasibility, with the judges frequently reaching split decisions.[113] We now have a decision of the High Court of Australia in *Farah Constructions Pty Ltd v Say-Dee Pty Ltd*,[114] which means that those earlier cases are of less significance. The High Court concludes that the knowing receipt trust cannot be enforced. This appears to be based upon two primary factors. The first is that receipt is by reference to the effect of registration rather than the transfer.[115] This might be thought a rather technical analysis[116] and a more broadly based analysis is that a trust is justified where 'the defendant was the primary wrongdoer, attempting to ignore an obligation to share or convey the land with or to the plaintiff'. In contrast,

---

[109] An early example is provided by L Stevens, 'The In Personam Exceptions to the Principle of Indefeasibility' (1969) 1 *Auckland University Law Review* 29.

[110] *Bahr v Nicolay (No 2)* (1988) 164 CLR 604, 638–39 (Wilson and Toohey JJ) and 653 (Brennan J). *Binions v Evans* [1972] Ch 359 and *Lyus v Prowsa Developments Ltd* [1982] 1 WLR 1044 (Ch D) (pp 142, 144 above) are relied on.

[111] *Barnes v Addy* (1874) 9 Ch App 244. See p 146 above.

[112] *Bahr v Nicolay (No 2)* (1988) 164 CLR 604 provides one quite recent example: see 613 (Mason CJ and Dawson J), 630 (Wilson and Toohey JJ) and 652–53 (Brennan J).

[113] The earlier cases are usefully discussed by Cooke and O'Connor, above (n 87).

[114] *Farah Constructions Pty Ltd v Say-Dee Pty Ltd* (2007) 230 CLR 89; and see P Butt, 'Knowing Receipt of Trust Property as an Exception to Indefeasibility' (2007) 81 *Australian Law Journal* 713 and M Conaglen and R Nolan, 'Recipient Liability in Equity' [2007] *CLJ* 513.

[115] *Macquarie Bank Ltd v Sixty-Fourth Throne Pty Ltd* [1998] 3 VR 133 (Tadgell J at 156–57) is quoted. For discussion whether a similar analysis could apply to LRA 2002, s 29, see Conaglen and Goymour, 'Knowing Receipt and Registered Land', above (n 97) 167–70.

[116] It is relied on by Wu, above (n 107) but less so by Low, above (n 103) 229.

there should be no liability where 'the defendant is a party who merely had notice of an earlier interest or notice of third party fraud'.[117]

Say-Dee demonstrates that care needs to be taken in asserting personal claims. The dangers are well illustrated by the New Zealand decision in *Smith v Hugh Watt Society Inc*.[118] Here, the court accepted a very wide view of receipt liability, based on constructive and imputed notice, and then proceeded to allow it as a personal claim. This really does look inconsistent with the objective of protecting registered purchasers. It may be more acceptable to recognise receipt based liability as recognised in *BCCI (Overseas) Ltd v Akindele*,[119] given its basis in unconscionability. However, even this is difficult to square with the insistence of the Law Commission that ideas of actual notice and good faith should play no role in the protection of purchasers.[120]

Before leaving *Say-Dee*, two points should be noted following from *Arthur v Attorney-General of the Turks and Caicos Islands*.[121] First, the case acts as a reminder that attention must focus on the legislation in question. Though *Arthur* involved Torrens system registration, a knowing receipt claim was allowed because it was permitted by the legislation. The Privy Council stressed that the legislation in Australia is different, as is the Land Registration Act 1925 (and, presumably, the 2002 Act).

The second point—left open in *Arthur*—follows from an analysis that a constructive trust may arise prior to registration, biting on the equitable interest acquired by the purchaser. At that stage the statutory protection of the purchaser has not arisen, so the trust is acceptable. However, the question is whether to allow it to continue after registration. To do so risks challenging the statutory protection; this is the sort of risk that *Say-Dee* sought to exclude.[122]

If this constructive trust raises difficult questions, how far is this also true of some other personal actions? Most obviously, inducing breach of contract raises similar issues. Perhaps the active element of inducing breach could justify liability: it requires more than simply taking a transfer.[123] Another tort based idea relates to fraud. This is less of a problem for *in*

---

[117] Pullin J in *LHK Nominees Pty Ltd v Kenworthy* (2002) 26 WAR 517, 571, quoted and approved in Farah. The distinction may well not be easy to draw: Bant, above (n 101) 317.

[118] *Smith v Hugh Watt Society Inc* [2004] 1 NZLR 537, [66]–[88]. More generally, New Zealand courts have been less inclined to protect the registered proprietor: D Whalan, *The Torrens System in Australia* (Sydney, Law Book Company, 1982) 315.

[119] *BCCI (Overseas) Ltd v Akindele* [2001] Ch 437 (CA).

[120] Law Com No 254, *Land Registration for the Twenty-First Century*, above (n 1) para 3.44.

[121] *Arthur v Attorney-General of the Turks and Caicos Islands* [2012] UKPC 30, discussed above, p 147.

[122] Conaglen and Goymour, 'Knowing Receipt and Registered Land', above (n 97) 179–80 (cited in *Arthur v Attorney-General of the Turks and Caicos Islands* [2012] UKPC 30).

[123] Especially as explained in *OBG Ltd v Allen* [2007] UKHL 21, [2008] 1 AC 1.

personam claims in Torrens systems, as fraud constitutes an express statutory exception to indefeasibility. Whether fraud precludes statutory protection under the LRA is unsettled. While *Lyus v Prowsa Developments Ltd*[124] supports the existence of an exception, the contrary is presumed by Norris J in *Halifax plc v Curry Popeck*.[125] Although it might be thought that a personal obligation based on fraud would make it unnecessary to limit the statutory protection, there is a crucial difference if (as the Law Commission asserts) the personal obligation does not have proprietary effect. If the purchaser is protected by the LRA, should fraud be permitted as a personal action? Given the law's dislike of fraud, it would be surprising if it were not permitted. Nor should we be unduly concerned by this: the nature of fraud is that it is unlikely to have an unacceptably broad application. Fraud may be treated as analogous to constructive trusts imposed in cases of dishonest assistance (mentioned above).[126] This situation fits a fraud analysis very readily.[127] What, however, must be avoided is the description of a purchaser as fraudulent simply because the purchaser is aware of the unprotected interest.

Conclusions

Personal obligations are undeniably problematic. Their recognition by the Law Commission is to be welcomed. It is unsurprising, given that Torrens systems (which have traditionally taken registration more seriously than the English system) had recognised such claims for several decades. This is an area in which the register cannot be taken as conclusive as to the purchaser's obligations: such would enable purchasers to renege on their own obligations in a manner which no legal system could countenance.

However, it has been argued above that to recognise every non-proprietary obligation (in the sense that the obligation does not arise from the simple application of priority rules) as an enforceable personal obligation runs the risk of undermining the protection that we want purchasers to enjoy against unprotected interests. There is a strong public interest in purchasers being able to rely on the register as a conclusive statement of the rights which may affect them. *Boland* indicates that, where registration rules

---

[124] *Lyus v Prowsa Developments Ltd* [1982] 1 WLR 1044 (Ch D).

[125] *Halifax plc v Curry Popeck (A Firm)* [2008] EWHC 1692 (Ch). This explains why the court employed a personal obligation analysis. Cooke and O'Connor, above (n 87) 658–59, also deny any exception.

[126] See p 147 above.

[127] Pullin J in *LHK Nominees Pty Ltd v Kenworthy* (2002) 26 WAR 517, 567. Liability is supported by Conaglen and Goymour, 'Knowing Receipt and Registered Land', above (n 97) 177–81.

establish priorities, then we should have confidence in those rules and not subordinate them to non-registration principles.

The receipt based constructive trust is a leading example of the problems that arise. Conaglen and Goymour[128] have argued that 'although it involves an element of wrongdoing ... the fundamental purpose of the claim seems to be to vindicate the pre-existing property rights'. Although one may doubt whether that distinction will always be a clear one,[129] their conclusion that receipt based liability should not be recognised is to be applauded.

Others may argue that the law should have no sympathy for those who are aware of a breach of trust. That is entirely understandable, but the correct response should be to amend the protection for purchasers in LRA, section 29. This echoes the developments whereby non-obvious occupation was thought to be problem following *Boland*: the entirely appropriate response in 2002 was to remove overriding status from such occupation. What is inappropriate is to have one set of rules indicating a desired result (protection against unprotected interests) and then to discover that there are other rules outside the registration system which effectively negate that carefully structured statutory outcome.

BOLAND AS A LANDMARK CASE

Some years ago, the Law Commission, quoting from an Australian case, stated that the registration system is 'not a system of registration of title but a system of title by registration'.[130] This encapsulates the idea that one is not simply recording what the legal position is in unregistered land. Rather, it is what the register contains that is determinative of legal rights. This, of course, is subject to overriding interests—but here again their scope owes more to the legislation than unregistered land priority principles. *Boland* can be seen as a central authority—probably *the* central authority—in moving to the position espoused by the Law Commission. Rather than accepting ideas based on the old doctrine of notice when assessing priority questions, it applies the direct wording of the legislation. Even though we now have the 'obvious on reasonable inspection' test, this is still a statutory test and not identical to notice.

Important as *Boland* is for actual occupation, its greater impact lies in developing a willingness to move away from traditional ideas of rights to property rights—at least as regards priority disputes. As we have seen, it is

---

[128] Conaglen and Goymour, 'Knowing Receipt and Registered Land', above (n 97) 172.

[129] Is the constructive trust so different from tort liability for inducing breach of an estate contract?

[130] Law Com No 254, *Land Registration for the Twenty-First Century*, above (n 1) para 10.43 (in the context of adverse possession), quoting from *Breskvar v Wall* (1971) 126 CLR 376, 385 (Barwick CJ).

unrealistic to think that all property rules can be found within land registration: the only appropriate role for registration is to govern rival claims to property rights (the subject matter of priority and formality rules). Personal actions form one significant and challenging example of the enforcement of rights that are not entered on the register. Plainly, some recognition of personal actions is inevitable. However, to go too far would be to limit the significance of registration and would be inconsistent with the needs of purchasers. It is here that the bold approach of Lord Wilberforce in *Boland* should guide us, albeit that it is difficult to establish bright-line rules.

So perhaps we should conclude that, while *Boland* is undoubtedly a landmark case, the jury is still out as to how far it goes. This is unsurprising. The needs of clarity and certainly in land law (central to the Law Commission's recommendations) are in tension with concepts of flexibility and fairness. This tension is perpetually enduring: it has been the root of most troublesome issues in land law for centuries. Nevertheless, each generation has to establish its own way to resolve this tension and land registration now forms an important aspect of modern thinking on this. That is the true legacy of *Boland*.

7

Midland Bank Trust Co Ltd v Green *(1980)*

Maintaining the Integrity of Registration Systems

MARK P THOMPSON

INTRODUCTION

O NE OF THE fascinations of the common law is that a small mistake, resulting in a comparatively simple factual matrix, can give rise to legal issues of some complexity and importance. In *White v Jones*,[1] a testator had instructed his solicitor to amend a will to include bequests to two plaintiffs. Negligently, he failed to do so, so that on the testator's death, the will had not been amended and the plaintiffs were excluded from the will. They sued the solicitor in negligence. In the earlier case of *Ross v Caunters*,[2] Sir Robert Megarry V-C had held a solicitor liable in negligence to a disappointed beneficiary who had failed to inherit property owing to the negligent drafting of the will. Lord Goff, commenting on this case, remarked that 'it has been recognised on all hands that [it] raises difficulties of a conceptual nature, and that as a result it is not altogether easy to accommodate the decision within the ordinary principles of our law of obligations'.[3] Notwithstanding these difficulties, Lord Goff led a bare majority in the House of Lords in extending the ambit of *Ross v Caunters* to embrace a negligent omission as well as a negligent commission and held the solicitor liable.

Just as a mistake by a solicitor can have expensive consequences in the context of probate activity, this is also true in the conveyancing context, although the cost and complexity of the consequences of one error in the

---

[1] *White v Jones* [1995] 2 AC 207 (HL).
[2] *Ross v Caunters* [1980] Ch 297 (Ch D).
[3] *White v Jones* [1995] 2 AC 207, 255 (HL).

saga of the Green family would, perhaps, have been hard to foresee, given that it led, directly, to three separate pieces of litigation[4] and, indirectly, to fourth.[5] The purpose of this chapter is to analyse the outcome of the direct litigation to assess the continuing impact of the House of Lords decision in *Midland Bank Trust Co Ltd v Green*.[6]

AN EVERYDAY STORY OF COUNTRY FOLK[7]

The background to what was described by Oliver J, who heard all the cases at first instance, as 'in many ways a tragic and very unhappy family dispute',[8] was that Walter Green, who was married to Evelyn and had five children, owned two farms. In 1960, he sold the larger of the two farms to one of his sons, Robert, at a price of £75 per acre. In 1961, for the purpose of avoiding potential estate duty problems, he entered a different arrangement with his son Geoffrey. In consideration of £1, he granted Geoffrey an option to purchase the second farm—also at a price of £75 per acre. The total purchase price was in the region of £21,000. This option was prepared by a solicitor but, although it was to remain open for a period of ten years, for some unexplained reason the solicitor neglected to protect the option by registering it as a land charge under the Land Charges Act 1925.[9] In 1967, following a discussion with an unidentified lawyer, Walter discovered that the option had not been registered. Shortly afterwards,[10] when the value of the land was in the region of £40,000,[11] he conveyed the farm to his wife, Evelyn, for a consideration of £500. She then made a will, leaving the farm, subject to a life interest in favour of her husband, to the five children, including Robert and Geoffrey. Geoffrey, on discovering what had happened, sought to enforce the option, arguing that notwithstanding the provisions of the Land Charges Act, Evelyn took subject to it.

This part of the litigation raised two issues. First, did the Land Charges Act 1925 lead to the conclusion that a purchaser with notice of an unregistered

---

[4] *Midland Bank Trust Co Ltd v Green (No 1)* [1981] AC 513 (HL); *Midland Bank Trust Co Ltd v Green (No 3)* [1982] Ch 529 (CA); *Midland Bank Trust Co Ltd v Hett, Stubbs & Kemp* [1979] Ch 384 (Ch D).

[5] *Midland Bank Trust Co Ltd v Green (No 2)* [1979] 1 WLR 460 (Ch D), a case concerning the potential personal liability of an executor.

[6] *Midland Bank Trust Co Ltd v Green* [1981] AC 513 (HL).

[7] HE Johnson, 'An Everyday Story of Country Folk ...' [1981] *Conv* 361.

[8] *Midland Bank Trust Co Ltd v Green (No 1)* [1980] Ch 590, 598 (Ch D).

[9] That Act has been superseded by the Land Charges Act 1972, but the relevant provisions of the later Act are identical. References in this chapter are to the relevant sections of the 1972 Act.

[10] According to Lord Denning MR ([1980] Ch 590, 621), '[n]ever in the history of conveyancing has anything been done so rapidly'.

[11] When the case reached the Court of Appeal, the estimated value of the land was £454, 500—in the words of Lord Denning MR ([1980] Ch 590, 623), 'a prize worth a fight'.

land charge would take free from it? Secondly, if the answer to that was in the affirmative, was there some principle of equity, normally expressed in the terms of the maxim that equity will not allow a statute to be used as an instrument of fraud (a maxim which has been described as proverbial)[12] that would prevent her from relying on the Act to take free of the unprotected right. The House of Lords, unanimously reversing the majority decision of the Court of Appeal and restoring the decision of Oliver J at first instance,[13] held that Evelyn took free from the unregistered land charge, notwithstanding that she actually knew of its existence[14] and had bought the land at a significant undervalue. So, although it had been held that as a matter of property law Evelyn was not bound by the unregistered option, the question remained whether Geoffrey had any other redress available to him—an important matter on which, unfortunately, the House expressed no opinion.

CONSTRUCTION OF THE LAND CHARGES ACT

A central issue in the litigation was whether or not the provisions of the Land Charges Act included the requirement that a purchaser must act in good faith. It was common ground that an option to purchase is an estate contract registrable as a C(iv) land charge. Section 4(6) of the Act provides that 'an estate contract ... shall be void as against a purchaser for money or money's worth ... unless the land charge is registered'. Section 199 of the Law of Property Act 1925 provides that '[a] purchaser shall not be prejudicially affected by notice of any ... matter capable of registration under ... the Land Charges Act ... which is void or not enforceable as against him under that Act ... by reason of the non-registration thereof'. Not surprisingly, in the light of these provisions, Lord Wilberforce thought that 'the case appears to be a plain one'.[15] He then concluded that the appearance was the reality and the Act was clear and definite. The meaning of the two statutory provisions was that a purchaser who actually knew of the existence of an unregistered land charge nevertheless took free from it.

The majority of the Court of Appeal had sought to avoid this, seemingly inescapable, conclusion by a combination of two factors. First, it was recognised that under section 17 of the Land Charges Act, 'purchaser' is defined to mean a person who, for valuable consideration, takes any interest

---

[12] *Steadman v Steadman* [1976] AC 536, 540 (Lord Reid) (HL).

[13] Writing extra-judicially, Sir Peter Oliver said of the Court of Appeal decision that it 'must have caused the late Sir Benjamin Cherry, the architect of the 1925 legislation, to turn in his grave at a rate of several thousand revolutions a minute': 'The Green Saga', Child & Co Oxford Lecture (1983).

[14] See also *Hollington Brothers Ltd v Rhodes* [1951] 2 All ER 578 (Ch D).

[15] *Midland Bank Trust Co Ltd v Green (No 1)* [1981] AC 513, 527.

in land, and noted that there is no requirement that he be in good faith. Secondly, section 199 of the Law of Property Act 1925 provides that a purchaser is not to be prejudicially affected by notice of any matter which is void for non-registration. However, the definition of purchaser in section 205 of the latter Act does include a reference to good faith. Reading these provisions together, Lord Denning MR thought that the key to their meaning centred on the adequacy of consideration. He said:

> I know that in the law of contract, we never enquire into the adequacy of the consideration. But this is different. 'Money or money's worth' means a fair and reasonable value in money or money's worth: not an undervalue: particularly a gross undervalue as here.[16]

The focus on the value of the consideration is, at first sight, attractive, but as a general test is unworkable. This can be demonstrated if one changes the figures a little.[17] In the present case the option gave Geoffrey the right to buy the land for £21,000 and the value of it when it was conveyed to Evelyn was £40,000. Suppose that a purchaser, aware of the option and that it had not been protected by registration, had purchased the land for £30,000. If the option were held to be void for non-registration, then he would have bought the land at an undervalue. If, because he had notice of the option, it was binding on him, he would have bought at an overvalue, being compellable to sell land he had bought for £30,000 for £21,000. In this example, an argument based on purchasing at an undervalue would be circular. Of course, on the actual facts this circularity would not arise, but it does point to the potential difficulties involved in having regard to the adequacy of the consideration.

Be that as it may, the premise of Lord Denning MR's judgment was emphatically rejected by the House of Lords. Lord Wilberforce considered that the omission of the requirement of good faith from the Land Charges Act had been deliberate, and that there was no warrant for introducing this requirement, whatever it might mean,[18] as a criterion for deciding whether a purchaser took free from an unregistered interest. He also rejected any argument based on the adequacy or otherwise of the consideration. He refuted any suggestion that the expression 'valuable consideration' should be affected in any way by a definition of the term in the Law of Property Act

---

[16] *Midland Bank Trust Co Ltd v Green (No 1)* [1980] Ch 590, 624. Eveleigh LJ took a rather different approach, which was not fully considered in the House of Lords, and this reasoning will be considered below. Interestingly, no comment was made on the fact that the option itself was granted in consideration of only £1, although see *Mountford v Scott* [1975] Ch 258 (CA).

[17] See also RJ Smith, 'Land Charges and Actual Notice: Justice More or Less Fanciful?' (1980) 96 *LQR* 8, 9.

[18] Interestingly, counsel for Geoffrey did not argue that good faith should be equated with a lack of notice: see *Midland Bank Trust Co Ltd v Green (No 1)* [1981] AC 513, 522 (Jonathan Parker QC).

which excluded nominal consideration. He regarded valuable consideration as a term which did not need definition, because it is a term of art which denotes an advantage conferred or a detriment suffered. He then pointed out that what different statutes do is to exclude certain elements which would otherwise be included within the concept of valuable consideration. The Law of Property Act includes marriage, but not a nominal sum; the Land Charges Act excludes marriage but allows money or money's worth. To refine the latter expression further—to exclude a nominal sum—would, for him, be to rewrite the section.[19] Even were it to be permissible to rewrite the section in this way, Lord Wilberforce said that he would have had great difficulty in accepting that a sum of £500 was nominal consideration. Nominal consideration was, in his opinion, a term of art denoting some sum or consideration which can be mentioned as consideration but is not necessarily paid. He continued: 'To equate "nominal" with "inadequate" or even "grossly inadequate" would embark the law upon inquiries which I cannot think were contemplated by Parliament'.[20]

IMPACT ON UNREGISTERED LAND

The decision in *Green* did, of course, settle the issue, so far as unregistered land is concerned, that a purchaser for money or money's worth (that expression including a purchase at a significant undervalue) would take free from a registrable interest that had not been protected by the registration of a land charge. This finding was consistent with earlier cases where interests had been held to be registrable and purchasers had prior knowledge of the interest, in which it was not even argued that that fact alone would mean that the purchaser would be directly bound by the unprotected interest.[21] Instead, the argument was unsuccessfully raised that the interests in question should not have been regarded as registrable at all. However, the main interest of these cases was not related to the registration point, but to the subsequent acquisition of rights through the medium of estoppel, either against the original purchaser or against a subsequent purchaser of that land.

The only serious attempt in the unregistered land context to escape from the decision in *Green* occurred in *Lloyds Bank plc v Carrick*.[22] Mrs Carrick

---

[19] Ibid, 531.
[20] Ibid, 532.
[21] See *ER Ives Investment Ltd v High* [1967] 2 QB 379 (CA) (equitable easement); *Taylors Fashions Ltd v Liverpool Victoria Trustees Co Ltd* [1982] QB 133 (Ch D) (option to renew a lease).
[22] *Lloyds Bank plc v Carrick* [1996] 4 All ER 630 (CA).

orally agreed[23] to buy a maisonette from her brother-in-law. She paid the money in full. He moved out and she moved in. This transaction appeared to have been effected without any legal advice,[24] as no conveyance was ever executed in her favour[25] and, in the light of this, it should occasion little surprise that the contract was not protected by the registration of a land charge. Subsequently, Mr Carrick mortgaged the property to the bank which, astonishingly,[26] appeared to have made no enquiries of or about Mrs Carrick, despite her being in sole occupation. When Mr Carrick defaulted on the mortgage and the bank sought possession Mrs Carrick argued that she had a beneficial interest binding on the mortgagee. This argument was rejected, the case being regarded as indistinguishable from *Green*. While this is open to criticism in that, unlike the situation in *Green*, Mrs Carrick was actually the sole beneficial owner of the property and was not relying solely on her rights under the antecedent contract,[27] the decision does demonstrate the continuing strong effect of the decision in *Green*.

REGISTRATION AND FRAUD[28]

It is, of course, true that *Midland Bank Trust Co Ltd v Green* concerned unregistered land, and the consequences of non-registration of land charges. As registered title has become more widespread, one could view the decision as having little abiding effect, as the issue which arose in that case is increasingly unlikely to recur in the context of the Land Charges Act, although this will still be the case in the context of first registration of title.[29] That would be true, to an extent at least, if the focus of the reasoning was based exclusively on the construction of the Land Charges Act. However, wider arguments of principle were advanced as to why Evelyn should not have been permitted to rely on the seemingly clear provisions of the Land Charges Act, that principle being best summed up by the maxim: 'equity will not allow a statute to be used as an instrument of fraud', and

---

[23] Had the facts of this case occurred after the coming into force of the Law of Property (Miscellaneous Provisions) Act 1989, the result would have been different, as the oral agreement would not have amounted to a valid contract and therefore would not have been registrable.

[24] The significance of legal advice in these types of transaction is considered below.

[25] For the same type of cavalier attitude to the conveyancing process, see K More, *More or Less (An Autobiography)* cited by JT Farrand, *Contract and Conveyance*, 4th edn (London, Oyez Longman, 1983) 6–7.

[26] See P Ferguson, 'Estate Contracts, Constructive Trusts and the Land Charges Act' (1996) 112 *LQR* 549, 550, pointing out that the mortgage occurred at least five years after the decision in *Williams & Glyn's Bank Ltd v Boland Ltd* [1981] AC 487. Presumably, had such enquiries been made, the bank would not have lent the money in the first place.

[27] See MP Thompson, 'The Widow's Plight' [1996] *Conv* 295; Ferguson, ibid.

[28] See MP Thompson, 'Registration, Fraud and Notice' [1985] *CLJ* 280.

[29] See *Sainsbury's Supermarkets Ltd v Olympia Ltd* [2005] EWHC 1235, [53] (Mann J).

the comments on this jurisdiction are as applicable to the Land Registration Acts 1925 and 2002 as they are to the Land Charges Act.

Shams

Although it has, with some justice, been said of this maxim that, '[a]s with all other maxims of equity and other branches of the law, the meaning of this epitomistic sentence is not self-evident',[30] one uncontroversial manifestation of it would be if the transaction is a sham. The classic definition of a sham is that given by Diplock LJ in *Snook v London and West Riding Investment Co Ltd*,[31] where he said that it consisted of

> acts done or documents executed by the parties to the 'sham' which are intended by them to give to third parties or to the court the appearance of creating between the parties legal rights and obligations (if any) which the parties intended to create.

An excellent illustration of this occurred in *Jones v Lipman*,[32] where a person who had contracted to sell land to the plaintiff sold it to a company which he controlled. The argument that the company took free from the estate contract which had not been registered failed on the ground that the transaction was a sham: the company was 'the creature of the [vendor], a device and a sham which he holds before his face in attempt to defeat the eye of equity'.[33]

However, this route of finding in favour of Geoffrey in *Midland Bank Trust Co Ltd v Green* was dealt a fatal blow at first instance, where Oliver J held that the transaction was not a sham. He said:

> The transaction was not in my judgment a sham in the accepted sense of the word at all. There was a genuine passing of the legal estate by Walter to his wife without any reservation of any interest to Walter. It was, and was intended to be, a beneficial transfer of the legal estate. There was a payment of the expressed consideration of £500 and there was an acceptance of that payment. That there may have been some ulterior motive for the transaction does not as it seems to me make the transaction other that it was. Obviously a substantial and indeed an almost overwhelming element of gift existed here but in my judgment that does not matter.[34]

Although Eveleigh LJ in the Court of Appeal said, somewhat unintelligibly, that 'I do not say that the transaction is a sham. In my opinion, however, the

---

[30] LA Sheridan, *Fraud in Equity* (London, Pitman & Sons Ltd, 1957) 146.

[31] *Snook v London and West Riding Investment Co Ltd* [1967] 2 QB 786, 822 (CA).

[32] *Jones v Lipman* [1962] 1 WLR 832 (Ch D).

[33] Ibid, 836 (Russell J). See also *Ferris v Weaven* [1953] 2 All ER 233 (QBD), approved on the basis of the transaction being a sham in *National Provincial Bank Ltd v Ainsworth* [1965] AC 1175, 1257 (Lord Wilberforce).

[34] *Midland Bank Trust Co Ltd v Green (No 1)* [1980] Ch 590, 613.

consideration of £500 expressed in the conveyance is a sham',[35] this finding by Oliver J effectively precluded this line of argument from prevailing.

Motive Underlying the Transaction

In the Court of Appeal, Lord Denning MR, as well as being able to construe the legislation so as to enable him to hold that Evelyn was bound by the unregistered land charge, had another, more wide-ranging, string to his bow. He cited a dictum of Lord Cozens-Hardy MR in *Re Monolithic Building Co*,[36] where he said: 'The doctrine of the Court in a case of fraud, of course, proceeds upon a different footing, and any security may be postponed if you can find fraud at its inception'. Encouraged by this, he referred to what he himself had said in a completely different context in *Lazarus Estates Ltd v Beasley*,[37] namely that

> [n]o court in this land will allow a person to keep an advantage which he has obtained by fraud. No judgment of a court, no order of a Minister, can be allowed to stand if it has been obtained by fraud. Fraud unravels everything.

In *Green* he asserted: 'Fraud in this context covers any dishonest dealing done so as to deprive unwary innocents of their rights'.[38]

This approach—that, if the purpose of the transaction was simply to cause harm to a person, then that would be fraudulent—appeared to find support in the dissenting judgment of Sir Stanley Rees. In his view, there was evidence that the reason behind the transaction was to redistribute the assets among the family in a way which they considered justified in the family interest. Equally, there was evidence that Walter and Evelyn were acting spitefully and deceitfully to deprive Geoffrey of his contractual right to the farm. In his view, if the latter position had been established and the former displaced by the evidence, then that would have clearly established a finding of fraud.[39] However, on the evidence, and notwithstanding the express finding at first instance that the defeat of the option was the primary motive for the transaction,[40] Sir Stanley Rees concluded that the second position had not been established and so fraud was not present.

Now it is, of course, true that in *Re Monolithic Building Co* Lord Cozens-Hardy MR did refer to the effect of fraud being to disentitle a person from asserting the priority of his interest. However, the case also contains a strong confirmation of the need to apply the wording of the legislation and

---

[35] Ibid, 628.
[36] *Re Monolithic Building Co* [1915] 1 Ch 643, 669 (CA).
[37] *Lazarus v Beasley* [1956] 1 QB 702, 712 (CA).
[38] *Midland Bank Trust Co Ltd v Green (No 1)* [1980] Ch 590, 625.
[39] Ibid, 623–24.
[40] Ibid, 611 (Oliver J).

not to water it down by the introduction of general concepts. In that case, a purchaser had notice of an unregistered interest: indeed Lord Cozens-Hardy MR expressed the view that he had 'never come across a case in which notice was so clearly proved'.[41] The purchaser nevertheless took free from the interest. In coming to this conclusion, the court was keen to give its imprimatur to the trend of not reading into seemingly clear statutes general notions of fairness or conscience. In early days, courts had been quite willing to do this, as evidenced by decisions such as *Le Neve v Le Neve*.[42] This tendency had been strongly checked in *Edwards v Edwards*,[43] another case where it was held that a purchaser was not bound by an unregistered interest of which he had notice. Mellish LJ said:

> Then it is urged that although this instrument ... was not registered it is good against the execution creditor, because he had notice of it when his debt was contracted. Notice he clearly had, but does that take the case out of the Act? I am of opinion that at law it clearly does not.... Then, is a Court of Equity to act differently? I agree ... that we ought not to put such constructions on modern Acts of Parliament ... The Courts of Equity have given relief on equitable grounds from provisions of old Acts of Parliament ... but this has not been done in the case of modern Acts, which are framed with a view to equitable as well as legal doctrines.

These sentiments were strongly endorsed in *Re Monolithic Building Co*,[44] and it is, therefore, easy to appreciate why in *Green* Lord Wilberforce failed to see how this case provided any support at all for the importation of general equitable doctrines such as notice into modern Acts of Parliament. Rather, it supported the general proposition that 'it is not "fraud" to rely on legal rights conferred by Act of Parliament: it confirms the validity of interpreting clear Acts of Parliament as to registration and priority according to their tenor'.[45]

However, Lord Wilberforce did recognise that there was some support for a fraud argument in *Re Monolithic Building Co*. Phillimore LJ said, obiter, that if there was a case where

> the whole inception of the transaction was to create an assurance which would defeat what the party intending to defeat it knew was an honest transaction. In such a case, I assume that the manner in which the matter would be worked would be by making the second person trustee of his advantages in favour of the first where there are third parties to be considered.[46]

[41] *Re Monolithic Building Co* [1915] 1 Ch 643, 662 (CA).
[42] *Le Neve v Le Neve* (1748) 3 Atk 648 (Ch D).
[43] *Edwards v Edwards* (1875) 2 Ch D 291, 297 (CA).
[44] *Re Monolithic Building Co* [1915] 1 Ch 643, 666–67 (Lord Cozens-Hardy MR).
[45] *Midland Bank Trust Co Ltd v Green (No 1)* [1981] AC 517, 531.
[46] *Re Monolithic Building Co* [1915] 1 Ch 643, 670.

Somewhat surprisingly, Lord Denning MR did not refer to this passage, which appeared to adopt much the same approach as to what constitutes fraud as did his own, rather more polemical, articulation. The motive-based approach was considered head-on by Lord Wilberforce. He said:

> But suppose ... the purchaser's motive is to defeat the option, does this make any difference? Any advantage to oneself seems necessarily to involve a disadvantage for another: to make the validity of the purchase depend upon which aspect of the transaction was prevalent in the purchaser's mind seems to create distinctions equally difficult to analyse in law as to establish in fact: avarice and malice may be distinct sins, but in human conduct they are likely to be intertwined. The problem becomes even more acute if one supposes a mixture of motives. Suppose—and this may not be far from the truth—that purchaser's motives were in part to take the farm from Geoffrey, and in part to distribute it between Geoffrey and his brothers and sisters, but not at all to obtain any benefit for herself, is this acting in 'good faith' or not? Should family feeling be denied a protection afforded to simple greed? To eliminate the necessity for inquiries of this kind may well have part of the legislative intention. Certainly there is here no argument for departing—violently—from the wording of the Act.[47]

This reasoning led, unsurprisingly, to an express disapproval of what Phillimore LJ had said,[48] and the rejection of an argument that the motive of the purchaser in effecting the transaction can disallow that person from relying on the priority rules which would otherwise apply. While the present case may seem a paradigm of a situation where the isolation of a motive to harm a person may seem to be easy to do, and Oliver J at first instance did just that, Lord Wilberforce's approach seems more realistic.[49] If the overriding intention had been to cause harm to Geoffrey, one would not have expected him to be named as a beneficiary of Evelyn's will in respect of the farm—which in fact he was. On the facts one could quite easily see what was done as an attempt to make a fairer settlement among the siblings than would have occurred had nothing been done—a consideration which strengthens considerably the justification for the rejection of a motive-based approach as to what constitutes fraud.

FRAUD AND REGISTERED LAND

The decision in *Green* emphatically established that the complementary provisions of the Land Charges Act and the Law of Property Act 1925 were

---

[47] *Midland Bank Trust Co Ltd v Green (No 1)* [1981] AC 513, 530. Contrast *Beerjeraz v Dabee* [2012] UKPC 22, a case dealing with quite different legislation in Mauritius, and *Arthur v Attorney-General of the Turks and Caicos Islands* [2012] UKPC 30, again dealing with differently worded legislation.

[48] *Midland Bank Trust Co Ltd v Green (No 1)* [1981] AC 513, 531.

[49] See also Smith, 'Land Charges and Actual Notice' above (n 17) who considered that the motive behind the transaction was probably to rearrange the finances of the family.

to be given their natural meaning. It also rejected any attempt to read those provisions subject to a general jurisdiction to prevent their being relied on in cases of fraud, at least where the presence of fraud is dependent on the motives of the parties to a transaction. While this aspect of the decision is only directly applicable to the unregistered system, and not to land which is subject to the Land Registration Acts 1925 and 2002, the latter comments should be just as relevant when title is registered. This is because 'although the land charges and land registration systems operate under very different legislation, it would be irrational to treat a mala fide purchaser, or one with actual notice, differently'.[50] It is nevertheless unfortunate that the opportunity was not taken to consider what the position would have been had title been registered,[51] not least because of an earlier decision affecting registered land, which reflected an ethos entirely different from that which underlay the reasoning of the House of Lords in *Green*.

In *Peffer v Rigg*,[52] Mr Peffer and Mr Rigg were married to two sisters. Together they bought a house, partly as an investment, and partly to provide accommodation for their mother-in-law. Mr Rigg was the sole registered proprietor, although it was accepted that he held the house on trust for himself and Mr Peffer; and this was reflected in a trust deed to that effect. As part of a divorce settlement, Mr Rigg transferred the house to his wife in return for payment of £1, and she was registered as the new proprietor. The litigation concerned whether or not she was bound by Mr Peffer's beneficial interest in the property, of which it was accepted that she had actual knowledge. Graham J, for three different reasons, held that she did.

Central to the argument that Mrs Rigg took free of the unregistered notice was section 20 of the Land Registration Act 1925, which provides that a disposition of registered land for valuable consideration shall confer on the transferee an estate in fee simple, subject to incumbrances and entries noted on the register and, unless the contrary is expressed, to overriding interests, but free from all other estates and interests whatsoever. In approaching the case, however, Graham J underpinned his reasoning by articulating an entirely false premise. He said:

It can be argued therefore that the section seems to be saying that a transferee whether he has good faith or not, and whether he has notice or not, takes free of all other interests (other than overriding interests) provided he has given valuable consideration.

This at first sight seems a remarkable proposition and though undoubtedly the property legislation of 1925 was intended to simplify such matters of title as far

---

[50] Ibid, 11.
[51] For a slightly surprising reluctance to have regard to cases on constructive notice in construing the Land Registration Act 1925, s 70(1)(g), see *Williams & Glyn's Bank Ltd v Boland Ltd* [1981] AC 487, 504 (Lord Wilberforce).
[52] *Peffer v Rigg* [1977] 1 WLR 285 (Ch D).

as possible, I find it difficult to think that section 20 of this Act can have been intended to be as broad in scope as this.[53]

Clearly, this sentiment would have spurred the judge to find reasons to avoid what he considered to be an unpalatable outcome. His view on this matter is not really supportable, however, as quite some time before the 1925 Act was passed, the Real Property Commissioners had expressed the view that 'it is on the whole expedient that actual notice of an unregistered interest should not affect the priority of a registered deed for valuable consideration'.[54] Again, albeit subsequent to *Peffer v Rigg*, Lord Wilberforce described the underlying ethos of the Land Registration Act 1925 in trenchant and starkly contrary terms. In his view, '[a]bove all, the system is designed to free the purchaser from the hazards of notice—real or constructive—which, in the case of unregistered land, involved him in inquiries, often quite elaborate, failing which he might be bound by equities'.[55]

Given Graham J's strong, if erroneous, view of the philosophy underlying the Act, it is perhaps unsurprising that he looked for reasons to find for the plaintiff. What is more surprising is that he found three. The first two reasons are either fact specific or manifestly unsupportable and can be dealt with briefly. Noting that section 20 refers to a disposition for valuable consideration, he concluded that this excluded nominal consideration. While this seems to be correct, his view that the payment of £1 was in fact nominal is questionable. In the light of Lord Wilberforce's subsequent comments, the fact that it was a gross undervalue does not mean that it was what the law would regard as nominal.[56] Moreover, as the judge himself recognised, the payment of £1 was part of a wider transaction involving a financial settlement on divorce, and so the consideration might not properly be regarded as nominal.[57] On the assumption that the consideration was not nominal, Graham J moved on to his second reason, which involved a more convoluted, and even less convincing, interpretation of the legislation than that employed by the Court of Appeal in *Green*. He read together sections 20 and 59(6) of the Act to arrive at a conclusion that it required a purchaser to be in good faith, and that a purchaser with notice of an unregistered interest was not such a purchaser. This reasoning was untenable, however, as he neglected to read section 59(6) in its entirety which, had he done so,

---

[53] Ibid, 293.

[54] (1830) Second Report of the Real Property Commissioners, 36.

[55] *Williams & Glyn's Bank Ltd v Boland Ltd* [1981] AC 487, 503.

[56] In *Mountford v Scott* [1975] Ch 258, 264, Russell LJ described an argument that consideration of £1 should not be regarded as valuable consideration as 'a startling proposition'. See also above (n 19).

[57] *Peffer v Rigg* [1977] 1 WLR 285, 293. Contrast E Cooke and P O'Connor, 'Purchaser Liability to Third Parties in the English Land Registration System: A Comparative Perspective' (2004) 120 *LQR* 640, 652.

would have revealed that it specifically provides that a purchaser is to take free from an unprotected interest 'whether he has or has not notice thereof, express, implied or constructive'.

The first two reasons for the decision are treated briefly. The first might be said to turn on the special facts. The second was clearly wrong but it is of historical significance only as no such interpretation is possible in respect of the relevant provision of the Land Registration Act 2002. The third reason—which sought to apply general equitable principles—warrants a little more attention.

Constructive Trust

Graham J said:

> I have found that the second defendant knew ... that the first defendant held the property on trust for himself and the plaintiff in equal shares. The second defendant knew this was so and that the property was trust property when the transfer was made to her, and that therefore she took the property on a constructive trust in accordance with general equitable principles.... This is a new trust imposed by equity and is distinct from the trust which bound the first defendant. Even if, therefore, I am wrong as to the proper construction of sections 20 and 59, when read together, and even if section 20 strikes off the shackles of the express trust which bound the first defendant, this cannot invalidate the new trust imposed on the second defendant.[58]

This idea that the circumstances of the transaction can give rise to a new equitable obligation has subsequently acquired a degree of traction but, on the facts of a case such as *Peffer v Rigg*, cannot be sustained.[59] The reason for this is that, if it is correct, then any protection given by registration statutes becomes completely illusory. This point was authoritatively made in *Assets Co Ltd v Mere Roihi*, where Lord Lindley, giving the judgment of the Privy Council, said:

> Then it contended that a registered proprietor may hold as trustee and be compelled to execute the trusts subject to which he holds. That is true; for, although trusts are kept off the register, a registered owner may not be beneficially entitled to the lands registered in his name. But if the alleged cestui que trust is a rival claimant, who can prove no trust apart from his own alleged ownership, it is plain that to treat him as a cestui que trust is to destroy all benefit from registration. Here the

---

[58] *Peffer v Rigg* [1977] 1 WLR 285, 294. While this reasoning was accepted in *Melbury Road Properties 1995 Ltd v Kreidi* [1999] 3 ELGR 108, 109 (Judge Cowell), this sits very uneasily with other passages in his judgment.

[59] But see B Green, 'Void Land Charges—Literalism Triumphs in the House of Lords' (1981) 97 *MLR* 518, 521, advancing a very similar argument as a means of circumventing the decision in *Midland Bank Trust Co Ltd v Green (No 1)*.

plaintiffs set up an adverse title and nothing else; and to hold in their favour that there is a resulting or other trust entitling them to the property is, in their Lordships' opinion, to the very thing that registration is designed to prevent.[60]

It is plain that the formulation by Graham J is completely at odds with this statement of principle and that 'the imposition of a constructive trust in this case would necessarily lead to the imposition of a constructive trust in every case where a purchaser of registered or unregistered land had actual notice of an unregistered interest'.[61] This state of affairs was not correct then and, in the light of the wider statement of principle in *Green*, should certainly not be considered to be the position today.

More recent judicial statements are, in the main, consistent with this view. Thus, in *Lloyd v Dugdale* Sir Christopher Slade stated:

> There is no general principle which renders it unconscionable for a purchaser of land to rely on a want of registration of a claim against registered land, even though he took with express notice of it. A decision to the contrary would defeat the purpose of the legislature in introducing the system of registration embodied in the 1925 Act.[62]

Halifax plc v Curry Popeck (A Firm)[63] concerned a number of fraudulent transactions. Norris J held that, because the purported transactions were shams, the purported transferee could not take free of an unregistered interest because he was not a purchaser for value. However, he went on to consider what the position would have been had the transactions been genuine and the purchaser had actual notice of the unprotected interest. In this situation, he accepted counsel's argument that the purchaser would not be bound. While he acknowledged that section 29 of the 2002 Act was couched differently from section 20 of the 1925 Act, he considered that the effect of the two sections was the same, namely that equitable interests which were unprotected at the date of registration of a disposition would not be kept alive. In reaching that conclusion, he also accepted an argument, based on the reasoning in *Green*, that this interpretation would allow the system to be manipulated in order to confer benefits on the unworthy but, in an attempt to avoid such an outcome, the plain words of the statute should not be given a contorted construction.[64]

As against these clear, and principled, approaches, mention must be made of *HSBC Bank Ltd v Dyche*,[65] a case involving a not dissimilar issue to that which is currently being discussed, and which might be seen as importing requirements of good faith into conveyancing legislation. Simplifying the

---

[60] *Assets Co Ltd v Mere Roihi* [1905] AC 176, 204–05 (PC).
[61] S Anderson, 'Notice of Unprotected Trusts' (1977) 40 *MLR* 602, 606.
[62] *Lloyd v Dugdale* [2001] EWCA Civ 1754, [50].
[63] *Halifax plc v Curry Popeck (A Firm)* [2008] EWHC 1692 (Ch).
[64] Ibid, [48].
[65] *HSBC Bank Ltd v Dyche* [2009] EWHC 2954 (Ch), [2010] 2 P & CR 58.

facts, D1 and D2 held property on trust for C. As part of their divorce settlement, D1 and D2 transferred the house to D2 in consideration of £5000. D2 then mortgaged it to a bank, the presence of C in the property being explained by reference to a forged document, which falsely indicated that he was a tenant. The issue was whether C's interest was binding on the bank. Judge Purle held that it was. The essential issue was whether the conveyance from D1 and D2 to D2 overreached C's interest. Relying on *City of London Building Society v Flegg*,[66] it was argued that, as the conveyance was executed by two trustees, C's interest was overreached, so that C had no interest capable of binding a mortgagee. Understandably, this argument failed.[67] However, one of the reasons given is that D2 knew that the transfer to her was in breach of trust and that she was therefore not acting in good faith, with the result that overreaching did not occur.[68] Such an importation of the element of good faith is to be regretted; and much the better basis for the decision is that a conveyance from two trustees to one of them will not operate to effect the overreaching of a beneficial interest under the trust. It is hard to see that this case can be seen as providing fuel for the argument that a lack of good faith on the part of a purchaser will prevent him from relying on statutory protection.

While it would appear to be clear that merely having notice of an unprotected third party right will not of itself be sufficient to cause a constructive trust to be imposed on a purchaser, there are circumstances, as Lord Lindley recognised, where such a purchaser may be subject to an equitable obligation. In some situations, such rights can arise as a result of the behaviour of the parties after the purchase has been completed. Thus, in *Taylors Fashions Ltd v Liverpool Victoria Trustees Co Ltd*[69] and *ER Ives Investment Ltd v High*,[70] land charges—in the former case an option to renew a lease and in the latter case an equitable easement—had not been registered as land charges. In both cases the purchaser had actual notice of the relevant interest. Although both cases pre-dated the House of Lords decision in *Green*,[71] they are consistent with it on the land charges point. The interest in the decisions then relates to arguments concerning the acquisition of rights through estoppel. Although the issue in *Taylors Fashions* has subsequently been described as being whether a purchaser should be estopped from

---

[66] *City of London Building Society v Flegg* [1988] AC 54 (HL).

[67] For approval of the result, but with justified criticism of some of the reasoning, see MJ Dixon, 'Constructive Trusts; Mortgagees; Overriding Interests; Possession' [2010] *Conv* 1, and NP Gravells, '*HSBC Bank plc v Dyche*: Getting your Priorities Right' [2010] *Conv* 169.

[68] *HSBC Bank Ltd v Dyche* [2009] EWHC 2954 (Ch), [2010] 2 P & CR 58, [39]–[40].

[69] *Taylors Fashions Ltd v Liverpool Victoria Trustees Co Ltd* [1982] QB 133 (Ch D).

[70] *ER Ives Investment Ltd v High* [1967] 2 QB 379 (CA).

[71] Although *Taylors Fashions* was not officially reported until 1982, it was actually decided in 1979.

denying the right to exercise the option,[72] if by this it is meant that estoppel operated to prevent the purchaser from relying on the Land Charges Act, then this is a misleading way of looking at the case. The main interest in the case is whether an estoppel could arise in circumstances where both parties are mistaken as to the actual legal position. As such the cases are not directly relevant to the present discussion, but instead provide examples of situations when a right can arise against a purchaser who is not bound by an unregistered interest at the instigation of the holder of that interest. Unsurprisingly, the answer to this is that it can. The cases involve situations where there is a direct interaction between the holder of the right and the purchaser. What is germane to the issue being considered here is whether such rights can arise when there is no such direct interaction.

AGREEING TO TAKE SUBJECT TO AN INTEREST

In *Lyus v Prowsa Developments Ltd*,[73] the plaintiff had contracted to sell V's land. That land was subject to a mortgage created prior to the contract. V became insolvent and the mortgagee exercised its power of sale. In doing so, and without securing a reduction in the purchase price as a consequence,[74] it sold the land to D1 'subject to and with the benefit of P's contract'. The land was then sold on to D2, subject to P's contract so far, if at all, as it might be enforceable against the first defendant. It was clear that had the mortgagee not sold the land subject to the plaintiff's contract, there would have been no question of either defendant taking subject to it. As the mortgagee had priority, had it chosen to do so, it could have sold free from any right created subsequent to it.[75] However, because of the agreement to take subject to it, Dillon J held the contract to be binding on D2 and ordered specific performance of it. Digressing slightly, in cases of this sort it is often felt that the merits of the case dictate that a purchaser with actual notice of an interest which would otherwise be void should nevertheless take subject to it.[76] In the instant case, it has been pointed out that that result would actually have damaged the interests of other creditors, as the result of the case was that the plaintiff succeeded in getting the land, as opposed to sharing in the vendor's assets (as was the fate of the other creditors).[77]

[72] *Yeoman's Row Management Ltd v Cobbe* [2008] UKHL 55, [18] (Lord Scott).
[73] *Lyus v Prowsa Developments Ltd* [1982] 1 WLR 1044 (Ch D).
[74] Ibid, 1053 (Dillon J).
[75] See also *Valais v Clydesdale Bank plc* [2011] EWHC 94 (Ch).
[76] See, eg, *Midland Bank Trust Co Ltd v Green* [1980] 590, 614 (Oliver J) and *Taylors Fashions Ltd v Liverpool Victoria Trustees Co Ltd* [1982] QB 133, 135 (Oliver J). In neither case did Oliver J succumb to the temptation to avoid applying the law to reach a result in line with the perceived merits of the case.
[77] See P Jackson, 'Estate Contracts, Trusts and Registered Land' [1983] *Conv* 64, 67.

This is another illustration of the salutary principle that 'doing justice to the litigant who actually appears in the court by the invention of new principles of law ought not to involve injustice to the other persons who are not litigants before the court but whose rights are fundamentally affected by the new principles'.[78]

In determining what these principles are, it is apposite to recognise that Dillon J accepted that, on the basis of *Green*, a person would not be bound by an unregistered interest simply because he had notice of it. What made a difference was the actual agreement to take subject to that interest. In reaching this conclusion, he relied on *Rochefoucauld v Boustead*,[79] *Bannister v Bannister*[80] and the minority judgment of Lord Denning MR in *Binions v Evans*.[81] Since then the courts have recognised the existence of this principle, although they have also sought to construe it narrowly;[82] and it has attracted academic support.[83]

Its scope was considered by the High Court of Australia in *Bahr v Nicolay (No 2)*.[84] To raise funds the plaintiff, the registered proprietor of land, sold it to a purchaser and took a lease back for a period of three years. The contract provided that, at the expiration of the lease, the plaintiff would have the right to enter a contract to buy the land back at an agreed price. The land was then sold to the defendant. It was a provision of that latter contract that the defendant would recognise the plaintiff's contract to re-purchase the land. However, that right had not been protected by an entry on the register of title. When the defendant refused to contract with the plaintiff, the plaintiff sued and the High Court granted him a decree of specific performance.

As in other Commonwealth jurisdictions which have adopted the Torrens system, the relevant statutory provision[85] made clear that, except in case of fraud,[86] a transferee is not to be affected by actual or constructive notice

---

[78] *Re Sharpe* [1980] 1 WLR 219, 226 (Browne-Wilkinson J).

[79] *Rochefoucauld v Boustead* [1897] 1 Ch 196 (CA).

[80] *Bannister v Bannister* [1948] 2 All ER 133 (CA).

[81] *Binions v Evans* [1972] Ch 359 (CA).

[82] See *Ashburn Anstalt v Arnold* [1989] Ch 1, 25–26 (Fox LJ); *Chattey v Farndale Holdings Ltd* (1996) 75 P & CR 298, 317 (Morritt LJ). In *Chaudhary v Yavuz* [2011] EWCA Civ 1314, [61] Lloyd LJ pointed out that he knew of no English case where the principle of *Lyus v Prowsa Developments Ltd* had been used to make a purchaser bound by an interest which was void against him for non-registration.

[83] See B McFarlane, 'Constructive Trusts Arising on a Receipt of Property *Sub Conditione*' (2004) 120 *LQR* 667.

[84] *Bahr v Nicolay (No 2)* (1988) 164 CLR 604.

[85] Transfer of Land 1893 (WA) s 68. For valuable discussions of this type of provision, see Cooke and O'Connor, above (n 57) and M Harding and M Bryan, 'Responding to Fraud in Title Registration Systems: A Comparative Study' in M Dixon (ed) *Modern Studies in Property Law, Volume 5* (Oxford, Hart Publishing, 2009) ch 1.

[86] Interestingly, an Australian commentator thought that, even under such statutes, the question as to whether *Green* would have been decided differently in that jurisdiction was considered to be 'not easy to answer': IJ Hardingham, '*Midland Bank v Green* under the Torrens System' (1982) 2 *OJLS* 138, 140.

of any trust or unregistered interest and that knowledge of any trust or unregistered interest is not to be equated with fraud. Although Mason CJ and Dawson J were prepared to hold that the transaction was fraudulent because its underlying purpose was to defeat an unregistered interest,[87] this, in the light of *Green*, is not an argument which is tenable in this country. The main interest for present purposes is the differing approaches to the creation of a trust in favour of the plaintiff. Applying *Lyus v Prowsa Developments Ltd*, the majority[88] found that the express agreement to take subject to the plaintiff's interest gave rise to a constructive trust, whereas Mason CJ and Dawson J took a different view, and held that a new *express* trust was created. In their words:

> If the inference to be drawn is that the parties intend to create or protect an interest in a third party and the trust relationship is the appropriate means of creating or protecting that interest or of giving effect to the intention, then there is no reason why in a given case an intention to create a trust should not be inferred. The present is just such a case. The trust is express not a constructive trust.[89]

While one might query whether an express trust is the most appropriate way of enforcing what was in effect an option to purchase,[90] it is thought that the minority view is to be preferred. While to an extent the debate is academic, the issue has some theoretical importance, in that it depends in part on what the underlying basis of *Rochefoucauld v Boustead*[91] actually is.

In that case, Lindley LJ famously said:

> It is further established by a series of cases, the propriety of which cannot now be questioned, that the Statute of Frauds does not prevent the proof of a fraud; and that it is a fraud on the part of a person to whom land is conveyed as a trustee, and who knows it was so conveyed, to deny the trust and claim the land himself. Consequently, notwithstanding the statute, it is competent for a person claiming land conveyed to another to prove by parol evidence that it was so conveyed upon trust for the claimant, and the grantee, knowing the facts, is denying the trust and relying upon the form of the conveyance and the statute, in order to claim the land himself.[92]

While, taken at face value, this would support the reasoning of Dillon J in *Lyus v Prowsa Developments Ltd*, as ever context is important. First, the statute in question was one requiring written evidence of the creation of a

---

[87] *Bahr v Nicolay (No 2)* (1988) 164 CLR 604, 615.

[88] Ibid, 638–39 (Wilson and Toohey JJ); 655–56 (Brennan J).

[89] Ibid, 618–19.

[90] For justified criticism of a tendency to use the language of constructive trusts to describe equitable liability, see W Swadling, 'The Fiction of the Constructive Trust' (2012) 64 *CLP* 399, although to argue from this that the concept of a constructive trust is not a coherent entity goes too far.

[91] *Rochefoucauld v Boustead* [1897] 1 Ch 196.

[92] Ibid, 206.

trust; it did not deal with the effect of unregistered interests on a purchaser. Although the maxim that equity will not allow a statute to be used as an instrument of fraud has been applied to different statutes, the underlying basis of what is meant by fraud differs with different statutes.[93] Secondly, in *Rochefoucauld v Boustead* the fraud in question was being practised directly by the defendant on the plaintiff. The plaintiff owned land subject to a mortgage and the mortgagees sold the estate to the defendant. There was, however, a prior agreement between the plaintiff and the defendant that the latter was in effect to buy the mortgage,[94] and the fraud in this case was being directly effected by the defendant on the plaintiff by denying an agreement between the two of them.[95] Although it has been convincingly argued that the reasoning in *Rochefoucauld v Boustead* was that an express trust, and not a constructive trust, had been created,[96] the courts have subsequently treated the rationale of the case as being the imposition of a constructive trust.[97] This is to be preferred because, although in this line of cases the oral agreement is enforced notwithstanding the statute, 'specific performance of an express agreement and compulsory restitution of the consideration for the agreement are fundamentally different things, even in cases where the practical result of the two remedies is the same'.[98] That the remedy is effectively restitutionary rather than the enforcement of an agreement is particularly evident in cases where a third party is involved,[99] as it is not clear why a constructive trust should be imposed in favour of that third party against whom no direct fraud has been perpetrated.

The matter can be illustrated by examples. In the first situation, A transfers property to B. It is clear that B is not intended to take the property beneficially but is to hold the property on trust. However, no trust is declared. The result is that B cannot retain the beneficial interest and the property is held on resulting trust for A.[100] In the second situation, A transfers land to

---

[93] See MP Thompson, 'Using Statutes as Instruments of Fraud' (1985) 36 *NILQ* 358. See also S Bright, 'The Third Party's Conscience in Land Law' [2000] *Conv* 398, 402–03.

[94] *Rochefoucauld v Boustead* [1897] 1 Ch 196, 197.

[95] This is also the case in *Bannister v Bannister* [1948] 2 All ER 133. See also *Banner Homes Group plc v Luff Developments Ltd* [2000] Ch 372 (CA); *Crossco No 4 Unlimited v Jolan Ltd* [2011] EWCA Civ 1619.

[96] See W Swadling, 'The Nature of the Trust in *Rochefoucauld v Boustead*' in C Mitchell (ed), *Constructive and Resulting Trusts* (Oxford, Hart Publishing, 2010) 63.

[97] See, eg, *Bannister v Bannister* [1948] 2 All ER 133, 136 (Scott LJ); *Re Densham* [1975] 1 WLR 1514, 1525 (Goff J). See also N Hopkins, 'How should we Respond to Unconscionability?' in M Dixon and GLH Griffiths (eds), *Contemporary Perspectives on Property, Equity and Trusts Law* (Oxford, OUP, 2007) 1, 5.

[98] JB Ames, 'Constructive Trusts Based upon the Breach of an Express Oral Trust of Land' (1906–07) 20 *Harvard Law Review* 544, 552.

[99] See also TG Youdan, 'Formalities for Trusts of Land, and the Doctrine of *Rochefoucauld v Boustead*' [1984] *CLJ* 306, 335–36, who favours the enforcement of the trust in favour of the third party.

[100] See *Vandervell v IRC* [1967] 2 AC 191 (HL).

his solicitor B, and informs him orally that he is to hold the land on trust for C. In this situation the intended trust in favour of C will fail owing to non-compliance with section 53(1)(b) of the Law of Property Act 1925.[101] If B admits the agreement with A, the outcome would appear to be that he now holds the land on resulting trust for A. The position is substantially the same as in the first situation. However, if B denies the oral undertaking and seeks to claim the property for himself, clearly, once the agreement is proved, equity will not permit him to retain the beneficial interest for himself; but it is not obvious why a constructive trust should now be imposed in favour of C. It would be very strange if C were better off if B acted honestly as opposed to dishonestly. In both situations A has failed to comply with the formalities necessary to create a trust of land and the intended trust should fail. For this reason, I would argue that the use of the constructive trust in *Lyus v Prowsa Developments Ltd* was inappropriate and runs counter to the doctrine of privity of contract which prevailed at the time.[102]

However, this discussion is largely academic, in that the actual result in *Lyus v Prowsa Developments Ltd* can now be justified on other grounds. It was argued that the plaintiff could take advantage of the extended notion of privity of contract provided by section 56 of the Law of Property Act 1925 to establish that he was privy to the contract between the bank and the defendants and therefore able to sue on it. Predictably, this argument failed because, although the contract was for his benefit, it did not purport to be made with him, which is a requirement for that section to have the effect which was argued for.[103] This difficulty would now seem to have been removed by section 1(1)(b) of the Contracts (Rights of Third Parties) Act 1999, which enables a person to sue on a contract if it purports to confer a benefit on him. That would appear to cover the situation in *Lyus v Prowsa Developments Ltd*; and so the problem at the centre of that case would appear to have been solved by legislative intervention rather than by a watering down of the underlying ethos of *Green*.

---

[101] S Gardner, 'Reliance-Based Constructive Trusts' in C Mitchell (ed), *Constructive and Resulting Trusts* (Oxford, Hart Publishing, 2010) 63, 86–87, argues that a constructive trust should be imposed in favour of the third party if A does not know of the legal requirement of writing. This cannot be right since it would be tantamount to judicial repeal of the statute.

[102] See Thompson, 'The Widow's Plight', above (n 27) 288–89 and MP Thompson, 'Leases, Licences and the Demise of *Errington*' [1988] *Conv* 201, 206. This point is also made by Swadling, 'The Nature of the Trust in *Rochefoucauld v Boustead*', above (n 96), although his criticism sits uneasily with his espousal of the express trust argument.

[103] See *Lyus v Prowsa Developments Ltd* [1982] 1 WLR 1044, 1049, applying *White v Bijou Mansions Ltd* [1937] Ch 610, affmd at [1938] Ch 351.

ALTERNATIVE SOURCES OF LIABILITY

The saga involving the Green family was not ended by the decision of the House of Lords, as other arguments were advanced in other litigation. Some of this raised the question as to whether—although Evelyn took free from Geoffrey's option as a matter of land law—she could be liable to Geoffrey on some other basis.[104] This question entails consideration of tortious liability, the possibility of which was raised in the *Green* litigation itself, and other equitable liability, which was not.

Liability in Tort

It is very much to be regretted that in *Midland Bank Trust Co Ltd v Green* the House of Lords did not address the important issue whether Evelyn could be sued in tort. In part, this may be because of an unfortunate concession by counsel, which accepted that an action in tort would have lain against her for inducing breach of contract.[105] This issue loomed large in the judgment of Eveleigh LJ in the Court of Appeal and must be addressed on its merits. Similarly, as part of the Green saga, the issue arose as to whether Walter and Evelyn could be liable to Geoffrey for conspiracy; and in *Midland Bank Trust Co Ltd v Green (No3)*[106] the Court of Appeal accepted that there was no rule of law that precluded a husband and wife from incurring liability for tort, although the assumption that the other ingredients of the tort were present was not challenged. This raises important issues.

In the Court of Appeal Eveleigh LJ started from the premise, which was contrary to his actual view, that Geoffrey's charge was void as against Evelyn. However, he went on to say:

> Nonetheless the mother will have induced a breach of contract and can be sued for this by Geoffrey ... If she can be sued for damages for breach of contract in that she has caused Geoffrey to lose the land, it seems to me that the court should be in a position to order her to convey the land to Geoffrey upon payment by him of the option price provided that no one else has an adverse claim to the land. There is nothing, as I see it, in such a situation which should prevent the court from restoring the status quo before the breach of contract.[107]

It is a great shame that Lord Wilberforce did not comment on this because, if Eveleigh LJ is right, then the actual decision which he arrived at would have

---

[104] See MP Thompson, *Modern Land Law*, 5th edn (Oxford, OUP, 2012) 168–71.
[105] See *Midland Bank Trust Co Ltd v Green (No 1)* [1981] AC 513, 516 (L Hoffmann QC and G Lightman QC).
[106] *Midland Bank Trust Co Ltd v Green (No 3)* [1982] Ch 529.
[107] *Midland Bank Trust Co Ltd v Green (No 1)* [1980] Ch 590, 629. Presumably he meant damages for *inducing* breach of contract.

been pointless. Had the decision gone the other way, Geoffrey could have bought the land at the price stipulated in the option. Eveleigh LJ's reasoning is that, notwithstanding this outcome, the law of tort would allow him to do precisely what, as a matter of land law, the House of Lords held that he could not do. While it has been argued that the result produced by the law of tort is to be preferred on ethical grounds,[108] such a contradiction makes no sense at all; and much the better view is that 'where real property principles accord priority to a contract or a conveyance over an earlier contract, it should not be open to the earlier contracting party to rely on tort'.[109]

To reach this conclusion in a principled way, one must rely to an extent on the defence of justification. In doing this, one should recognise that there is a difference in law between preventing the performance of a contractual obligation and inducing its breach.[110] Action by C that will cause B to be in breach of contract to A is not necessarily tortious. Thus, in *Lyus v Prowsa Developments Ltd*, had the bank sold the land without reference to the plaintiff's contract,[111] as everyone agreed it could have done, then the purchaser would have taken free from it, regardless of whether he knew about its existence beforehand. When the purchaser chose not to allow the plaintiff to buy the property from him, as he would have been entitled to do, he would then have occasioned the breach of the contract between the mortgagor and the plaintiff. Surely it is unarguable that he could then be held to be liable in tort for inducing that breach: he has prevented the performance of the contract between A and B but has not, for the purpose of the law of tort, induced its breach.[112] The situation in *Green* is not identical, in that the option preceded the conveyance between Walter and Evelyn and prior to that conveyance occurring, Geoffrey could, by injunction[113] or more sensibly by registering his option, have prevented that transaction from being completed. However, once the conveyance had occurred, then the order of priority is reversed, so that the refusal of Evelyn to give effect to Geoffrey's option then prevents the performance of the contract between Geoffrey and Walter—but in a way that is justified.

Similar observations can be made concerning liability for conspiracy. In the case of conspiracy to injure by unlawful means, while it is not necessary to isolate a predominant intention to injure, provided that it is known that that will be the outcome of the action, it is necessary for the means to be unlawful. In the type of situation which occurred in *Green*, however,

---

[108] G Battersby, 'Informal Transactions in Land, Estoppel and Registration' (1995) 58 *MLR* 637, 655.

[109] RJ Smith, 'The Economic Torts: Their Impact on Real Property' [1977] *Conv* 318, 329.

[110] *Meretz Investments NV v ACP Ltd* [2007] EWCA Civ 1303, [177] (Toulson LJ). See also *OBG Ltd v Allan* [2008] AC 1, [39] (Lord Hoffmann).

[111] See also *Duke v Robson* [1973] 1 WLR 267 (CA).

[112] *Meretz Investments NV v ACP Ltd* [2007] EWCA Civ 1303.

[113] See *Tophams Ltd v Earl of Sefton* [1965] Ch 119, reversed on the facts at [1967] 1 AC 50.

the action is not unlawful. This was made clear by Arden LJ in *Meretz Investments NV v ACP LTD*:

> The respondents did not have the intention to cause harm ... for the purposes of the tort of inducing breach of contract or the tort of conspiracy to cause harm by unlawful means. They had a firm belief based on the legal advice that they had received, that Britel's rights under the leaseback option would be overreached by the exercise by FP of its power of sale.[114]

This seems equally applicable to the situation in *Green*.

Knowing Receipt

A final method of outflanking the decision in *Green* has been to argue that a person in Evelyn's position should be liable for knowing receipt.[115] With respect, this seems an odd argument. Liability for knowing receipt of trust property is a form of personal liability in equity which arises when the person against whom the claim is made no longer owns the property in question but has disposed of it. The issue does not arise when he still has the property, as then the issue is whether he is bound by the trust interest,[116] which is a matter of title and not personal liability.[117] If that person then disposes of the property, no liability for knowing receipt can arise because the original trust has been rendered void by the preceding transaction.[118] Although this would seem to dispose of an argument based on knowing receipt, it has been argued that liability could ensue for knowing assistance in a breach of trust.[119] The crux of this argument is that the basis of liability could be the motive of the purchaser to do harm to the person who has failed to protect a registrable interest.[120] This fails to convince. It was the difficulty in isolating such an intention to injure that led Lord Wilberforce in *Green* to reject a rationale for the concept of fraud;[121] and the same difficulty arises in the context of other forms of liability.

---

[114] *Meretz Investments NV v ACP Ltd* [2007] EWCA Civ 1303, [2]. See also ibid, [174] (Toulson LJ).

[115] See Law Commission Report No 254, *Land Registration for the Twenty-First Century: A Consultative Document* (1998) para 3.48.

[116] See J Martin, *Hanbury and Martin Modern Equity*, 18th edn (London, Sweet & Maxwell, 2009) 337–45.

[117] See *Creque v Penn* [2007] UKPC 44, [15] (Lord Walker). See also M Conaglen and A Goymour, 'Knowing Receipt and Registered Land' in C Mitchell (ed), *Constructive and Resulting Trusts* (Oxford, Hart Publishing, 2010) 159, 174.

[118] See *Farah Constructions Pty Ltd v Say-Dee Pty Ltd* (2007) 230 CLR 89, [193].

[119] Conaglen and Goymour, above (n 117) 180.

[120] For much the same argument in the context of tortious liability, see Bright, above (n 93) 408.

[121] See (above) n 47.

In short, the argument put here is that the ethos of *Green*, which should apply to both unregistered and registered land, should not be undermined by reference to either tortious or other equitable forms of liability.

A MERITORIOUS LANDMARK?

Sir Peter Oliver, whose professional life seemed at one time to have been dominated by the *Green* saga, said of this case that it 'is now largely without significance in the mainstream of jurisprudence thought, though it remains an interesting example of the registration provisions even in transactions between closely connected persons'.[122] I would disagree. In my view, *Midland Bank Trust Co Ltd v Green* is undoubtedly a landmark case. It established that clear legislative principles which apply the strict sanction of making void an unregistered interest as against a purchaser with actual notice of it are not to be diluted by appeals to general equitable interests. This result has attracted controversy. Thus, while the reasoning has been approved, unease has been felt at the result, which can be seen as unjust.[123] Similar sentiments are expressed by commentators who approve the result in *Peffer v Rigg* but who are highly critical of the reasoning. They seek to support the same result by indirect means, advocating a solution such as personal liability or rectification of the register.[124] For reasons advanced earlier, it is suggested that such siren voices should be resisted. As has aptly been said, '[t]here seems little consistency in first declaring that a registered title is unencumbered and promptly encumbering it'.[125] More directly and, it is suggested, in a more principled way, it has been argued that it would be desirable to amend the legislation to allow for a purchaser to be bound by an unregistered interest of which he has actual notice.[126] The question is asked: 'Would it really cause the collapse of civilised conveyancing if the statutes were altered to make actual notice of an unprotected interest binding upon a purchaser?'[127] It is suggested that the Law Commission was right not to recommend this course of action.[128]

---

[122] Oliver, above (n 13) 15.

[123] See C Harpum, 'Purchasers with Notice of Unregistered Land Charges' (1981) 40 *CLJ* 213, 217.

[124] See, eg, D Hayton, 'Purchasers of Registered Land' [1977] *CLJ* 227, 230–31.

[125] DC Jackson, 'Security of Title in Registered Land' (1978) 94 *LQR* 238, 251.

[126] See J Howell, 'Notice: A Broad View and a Narrow View' [1996] *Conv* 34, 42; Battersby, above (n 108) 655.

[127] Anderson, above (n 61) 606.

[128] Law Commission Report No 271, *Land Registration for the Twenty-First Century: A Conveyancing Revolution* (2001) para 5.16.

Actual Occupation and Professional Liability

In registered land, a person who is in actual occupation of land will have his rights protected against a purchaser,[129] despite it being possible to protect that right by registration.[130] It has been said of this protection that, had it been incorporated into Commonwealth title registration, then the introduction of the provisions relating to fraud would probably not have been necessary.[131] This is an important point because the safety net afforded to occupiers of registered land effects a valuable compromise between an insistence on the integrity of the register and the protection of people who occupy a property and who may, perhaps for that reason alone, be ignorant of registration requirements. Of course, the decisions in *Green* and in *Carrick* would have been different had such protection been available when title was unregistered,[132] since in both cases the persons who held the unprotected rights were in actual occupation of the land in question. This merely highlights the unacceptable difference between the two systems insofar as the importance of actual occupation is concerned—a well-known and almost certainly unintended anomaly.[133] With the spread of registered title, this anomaly will become less evident in practice.

A related point is that, if the person claiming to enforce the right is not in actual occupation of the land, then he is *ex hypothesi* seeking to enforce a proprietary right over land which he does not possess. In such circumstances, it is likely that one is looking at a commercial right in land, which will have been created with the benefit of legal advice. Indeed, in *Green* itself, despite Geoffrey actually farming the land in question, he did take legal advice. A failure to protect that interest in the appropriate manner by registration will inevitably lead to a finding of negligence, for which, as was made clear in *Midland Bank Trust Co Ltd v Hett, Stubbs & Kemp*,[134] there is concurrent liability in both contract and tort—a part of the overall litigation which ensured that Geoffrey was not without a remedy. It seems better to place the liability where it properly lies, without contorting normal principles of property law. It also is consistent with the policy adverted to at the outset of holding solicitors liable for damage caused by their professional failings.

---

[129] Land Registration Act 1925, s 70(1)(g); Land Registration Act 2002, schs 1 and 3.
[130] See *Williams & Glyn's Bank Ltd v Boland Ltd* [1981] AC 487.
[131] Cooke and O'Connor, above (n 57) 656.
[132] See, eg, *Bridges v Mees* [1957] Ch 475.
[133] See HWR Wade, 'Land Charge Registration Reviewed' [1956] *CLJ* 216, 218.
[134] *Midland Bank Trust Co Ltd v Hett, Stubbs & Kemp* [1979] Ch 145, approved in *Henderson v Merrett Syndicates Ltd* [1995] 2 AC 145, 191–93 (Lord Goff).

8

Street v Mountford *(1985)*; AG Securities v Vaughan; Antoniades v Villiers *(1988)*

Tenancies and Licences: Halting the Revolution

STUART BRIDGE

INTRODUCTION

*S*TREET *v* MOUNTFORD[1] is universally cited as the leading authority on the legal distinction between tenancies (or leases)[2] and licences. In a speech with which the other four members of the House of Lords agreed, Lord Templeman set out in uncompromising terms the requirements of a tenancy, namely the grant of exclusive possession for a term at a rent.

The decision of the House of Lords had humble beginnings. In its simplest terms the dispute concerned the level of rent payable by a single person occupying two furnished rooms in a house in Boscombe. Yet the decision provides an important perspective on some of the central issues that have perplexed landlord and tenant lawyers over the last hundred years: the relationship between the parties' bargain and the statutory regimes of security of tenure and rent control; the extent to which parties are free to contract out of statutory protection; and, ultimately, what we mean by a tenancy and how such an interest is to be distinguished from a bare (or contractual) licence.

---

[1] *Street v Mountford* [1985] 1 AC 809 (HL).

[2] Although lawyers refer to the lease/licence dichotomy, the legislation and the case law generally refer to 'tenancies' rather than 'leases'. The terminology of 'tenancies' is adopted in this chapter.

However, it was a decision that was very much 'a product of its times'.[3] First, in order to understand the significance of *Street v Mountford*, we must see it in its historical context—against the background both of the development over the previous 25 years of a new approach to the definition of the landlord and tenant relationship principally advocated by Lord Denning MR and of the prevailing statutory regimes of security of tenure and rent control. Changes in relation to both those matters have to some extent reduced the wider practical importance of the decision. Secondly, while *Street v Mountford* is, in its own right, a landmark in the development of landlord and tenant law, it cannot be fully understood in isolation, as a detailed examination of its central concept exclusive possession was postponed to the later decision of the House of Lords in *AG Securities v Vaughan; Antoniades v Villiers*.[4] For that reason, this chapter focuses on two cases rather than one.

The Tenancy/Licence Issue

Why is the question whether an owner of property has granted a tenancy so important? The simple answer was given by Denning LJ, as he then was, in *Errington v Errington*:[5] 'The difference between a tenancy and a licence is ... that in a tenancy an interest passes in the land, whereas in a licence it does not'.[6]

This strikingly orthodox statement of principle is all the more striking in light of the reasoning advanced as the judgment in *Errington* progresses. But it lays down the position with consummate clarity. A tenancy is an interest (indeed, an estate) in land which can and does bind successors in title of the estate over which the interest prevails. A licence is not an interest in land, and so it cannot and does not bind successors in title, but it is not simply in defining what is—and what is not—property, that the tenancy/licence distinction is central. A tenancy carries a status which a licence does not. A large number of statutes confer a range of rights on those who can establish that they are tenants; and, although there are exceptions, those rights are generally denied to those who cannot establish that they are tenants. It is not being a licensee which is crucial; it is being a non-tenant. It soon becomes clear that in this context it is more difficult, or at least more circuitous, to define 'licence' than it is to define 'tenancy'. The latter is

[3] S Bright, '*Street v Mountford* revisited' in S Bright (ed), *Landlord and Tenant Law: Past, Present and Future* (Oxford, Hart Publishing, 2006) 38.

[4] *AG Securities v Vaughan; Antoniades v Villiers* [1990] 1 AC 417 (HL).

[5] *Errington v Errington & Woods* [1952] 1 KB 290 (CA).

[6] Ibid, 296. But for recognition of the *non-proprietary* tenancy, see *Bruton v London & Quadrant Housing Trust* [2000] 1 AC 406, discussed below, p 202.

defined by reference to what it is; whereas the former is defined by reference to what it is not.

The Rent Acts

The historical context of *Street v Mountford* is immediately apparent from a recital of the facts which gave rise to the litigation between the landlord, Mr Roger Street, a Bournemouth solicitor, and Mrs Wendy Mountford, the occupier of two rooms in his property in St Clements Gardens, Boscombe. The parties entered into a written agreement, which on its face purported to be a licence rather than a tenancy, and Mrs Mountford signed an express declaration as a postscript to the agreement to the effect that she understood and accepted that 'a licence in the above form does not and is not intended to give me a tenancy protected under the Rent Acts'. However, Mrs Mountford subsequently applied to the Rent Officer for the registration of a fair rent, a rent that would no doubt be less than the weekly 'licence fee' of £37 that she had agreed to pay to Mr Street.

The single issue that took the parties all the way to the House of Lords was whether or not their agreement was subject to the protection of the Rent Acts. The resolution of that issue depended in turn on whether the agreement did or did not create a tenancy. Mrs Mountford contended that she had a tenancy regulated under the Rent Act 1977 in that it was a tenancy under which a dwelling-house was let as a separate dwelling which did not fall within any of the statutory exclusions to protected status.[7] Such a 'protected' tenancy would entitle the tenant to apply to the Rent Officer for the registration of a fair rent.[8] The imposition of rent control would be ineffective if landlords were free to terminate the tenancies of those who sought a reduction of their rent by these means and to recover possession. In order to prevent landlords from adopting such practices, the Rent Act 1977 also conferred upon regulated tenants a highly significant degree of security of tenure. It followed that, while the protected tenancy was notionally terminable by the landlord (for example, by giving the requisite notice) the court would be prohibited from making an order for possession except on specified grounds set out in schedule 13 to the Rent Act 1977, and the tenant would be entitled to remain in possession as a statutory tenant pending such an order of the court.[9] Moreover, the landlord would not necessarily be able to recover possession even in the event of the tenant's death because the Rent Act 1977 made generous provision for succession on the death of a regulated (ie, protected or statutory) tenant by a spouse

---

[7] Rent Act 1977, ss 1, 4–16A.
[8] Ibid, ss 66, 67, sch 11.
[9] Ibid, s 98.

and other members of the tenant's family residing with him at the time of his death.[10]

It is not entirely surprising that when Mr Street reflected on his defeat in the House of Lords, he condemned the Rent Acts as 'grossly unfair to landlords' and expressed 'little wonder that over the years landlords and their legal advisers have sought various ways of avoiding the potentially horrendous consequences of being caught by the legislation'.[11] The particular method of avoidance chosen by Mr Street did not involve any attempt to deceive the occupier. Far from it, it was commendably transparent,[12] and Mr Street frankly conceded before the House of Lords that the agreement conferred exclusive possession upon Mrs Mountford. His point was that parties were free to contract on whatever terms they saw fit and that, if it were clear that they did not intend to contract on terms whereby the occupier would become a Rent Act regulated tenant, then the Court should respect the parties' bargain. His argument was based on a number of decisions, largely of the Court of Appeal, over the previous 30 years or so, where the courts had asked the question whether the parties had intended to create a tenancy.

Lord Templeman's speech does not take any hostages. It is bold and uncompromising, and, without some knowledge of the authorities to which he refers, one could be forgiven for thinking that the result in *Street* was a foregone conclusion. Every authority is put in its right place and, while four previous decisions are overruled, the majority of potentially awkward cases are dealt with by way of ex post facto explanation. It is therefore important to remember that Mr Street had won in the Court of Appeal, where the judgment was given by no less a property lawyer than Slade LJ. The strength of Mr Street's arguments derived from a considerable body of authority, which had developed over the previous 25 years, giving greater weight to contractual autonomy and paying less regard to the concerns raised by the disparity of bargaining positions between landlord and occupier in the privately rented sector of residential housing.

LORD DENNING MR'S REVOLUTION

Errington v Errington

In reappraising that body of authority, let us take as our starting point a decision of the Court of Appeal we have already mentioned—*Errington v*

---

[10] Ibid, s 2(1)(b), sch 1.

[11] R Street, 'Coach and Horses Trip Cancelled? Rent Act Avoidance after *Street v Mountford*' [1985] *Conv* 328.

[12] See, eg, the comments of Slade LJ in the Court of Appeal: (1984) 271 EG 1261, 1264.

Errington.[13] Dating from the final year of the reign of King George VI, it is no longer a decision which is much cited by counsel. The action was one for possession of a dwelling-house. Mr Errington had bought the house with the assistance of a mortgage loan. On the marriage of his son he handed the building society payment book to his daughter-in-law and allowed the newly-weds into occupation of the house on the basis that, if and when they repaid the mortgage loan, he would transfer the house to them. The father died, his son and daughter-in-law separated and the father's estate sued for possession from the daughter-in-law, who remained in the house and who was continuing to pay the mortgage instalments. At first instance, the County Court judge held that the son and daughter-in-law were tenants at will, having been granted exclusive possession of the house by the father, and that the action for possession was statute barred because 13 years had elapsed since they went into occupation. The Court of Appeal dismissed the estate's appeal on entirely different grounds. The Court held that the son and daughter-in-law were not tenants at will; they were contractual licensees and as such they were entitled to remain in occupation as long as they continued to pay the mortgage instalments in accordance with the original agreement.

The approach to the tenancy/licence distinction advocated by Denning LJ, like that of Lord Templeman over 30 years later, was firmly based on an analysis of the parties' intentions. But there is a significant difference between the two judges. For Denning LJ what mattered was not whether the parties intended to grant exclusive possession but *whether they intended to grant a tenancy*. If the parties only intended to grant a personal privilege (rather than an interest—or 'a stake'—in the land) the agreement would give rise to nothing more than a licence. Exclusive possession was not therefore the acid test: although a person with exclusive possession was prima facie a tenant, he would not be a tenant if the circumstances negatived any intention to create a tenancy:

> Words alone may not suffice. Parties cannot turn a tenancy into a licence merely by calling it one. But if the circumstances and the conduct of the parties show that all that was intended was that the occupier should be granted a personal privilege, with no interest in the land, he will be held to be a licensee only.[14]

In *Errington*, Denning LJ explained the previous authorities on this basis. There were a number of recent instances in which occupiers in exclusive possession had been held to be licensees not tenants:[15] where a requisitioning authority allowed people into possession at a weekly rent;[16] where a

---

[13] *Errington v Errington* [1952] 1 KB 290 (CA).
[14] Ibid, 298.
[15] Ibid, 297.
[16] *Minister of Health v Bellotti* [1944] KB 298 (CA); *Southgate BC v Watson* [1944] KB 541 (CA); *Ministry of Agriculture v Matthews* [1950] 1 KB 148 (KBD).

tenant was permitted by his landlord to continue living in the property rent-free;[17] where, on the death of a Rent Act statutory tenant, her daughter was allowed to stay on;[18] and where the manager of a shop was permitted by his employer to live in the flat above.[19] In addition, there was the deserted wife who would be allowed by the courts to remain in the former matrimonial home, and to enjoy exclusive possession, as a licensee.[20] The general rule was that all depended on whether the parties' intention, properly analysed, was to grant a tenancy or to confer nothing more than a licence. At most, exclusive possession gave rise to a presumption that a tenancy had been created.

Of the various examples given by Denning LJ, the licence accorded to the wife who had been deserted by her husband—later to be termed 'the deserted wife's equity'—attracted much judicial consideration in the period that followed as Lord Denning MR (as he became) attempted to confer on it the status of property.[21] Sound though the policy reasons may have been for this splendid initiative in judicial law reform, the device was itself given its quietus by the House of Lords in *National Provincial Bank Ltd v Ainsworth*.[22] It was left to Parliament, no doubt appropriately as the sovereign legislative body, to enact the necessary legislation as it sought to give effect to the laudable objectives of the Master of the Rolls.[23]

Developing the New Approach: Intention to Create a Tenancy

In the years following *Errington*, a number of authorities adopted the approach, advocated by Denning LJ, of determining whether the parties had intended to create a tenancy or merely a licence—thereby rendering the test of exclusive possession no longer conclusive. In *Cobb v Lane*,[24] the first such decision, the landlord allowed her brother to occupy her house rent free. The Court of Appeal, led by Denning LJ, held that the agreement could not be a tenancy at will as the parties did not intend a tenancy to be created; and the Court refused to follow the previously well respected decision

---

[17] *Foster v Robinson* [1951] 1 KB 149, 156 (KBD).
[18] *Marcroft Wagons Ltd v Smith* [1951] 2 KB 496 (CA).
[19] *Webb Ltd v Webb*, unreported, 24 October 1951 (CA)
[20] At the time of *Errington v Errington*, the leading decision on this doctrine was *Middleton v Baldock* [1950] 1 KB 311 (CA).
[21] *Bendall v McWhirter* [1952] 2 QB 466 (CA); *Jess Woodcock & Sons Ltd v Hobbs* [1955] 1 WLR 152 (CA).
[22] *National Provincial Bank Ltd v Ainsworth* [1965] AC 1175 (HL)
[23] Matrimonial Homes Act 1967. For the current legislation, see Family Law Act 1996, Part IV.
[24] *Cobb v Lane* [1952] 1 All ER 1199 (CA).

in *Lynes v Snaith*[25] to the effect that the grant of exclusive possession would, without more, give rise to a tenancy:

> The question in all these cases is one of intention: did the circumstances and the conduct of the parties show that all that was intended was that the occupier should have a personal privilege with no interest in the land?[26]

Abbeyfield (Harpenden) Society v Woods[27] was a different case altogether. A 'dear old man', aged 85, was allowed to occupy an unfurnished room in an old people's home run by a charitable organisation; and in return for payment of a weekly sum he obtained various services, including heating, cleaning, house-keeping and the provision of two meals each day. The parties did not sign any formal agreement; but before the defendant went into occupation the charity had sent him a letter, setting out the basis of the arrangement. The letter conceded that the defendant had 'sole occupation' of his room; and it reserved to the charity the right to serve on the defendant one month's notice should it be considered absolutely essential to do so in the interests of the charity and of other occupiers of the home. The Court of Appeal, led by Lord Denning MR, held that the defendant was no more than a licensee and that the charity, which had served notice pursuant to the terms of the letter was entitled to possession of the room: 'The modern cases show that a man may be a licensee even though he has exclusive possession, even though the word "rent" is used, and even though the word "tenancy" is used'.[28]

A similar conclusion was reached nearly ten years later in *Marchant v Charters*,[29] where the landlord had allowed the defendant into occupation of a furnished bed-sitting room, again with extensive services (including daily cleaning) being provided. The case was important as it followed the coming into force of the Rent Act 1974, which extended security of tenure to furnished as well as to unfurnished tenancies, and therefore afforded the courts their first opportunity to consider the effect of the new legislation. The Court of Appeal, once more with Lord Denning MR at the helm, arrived at the same conclusion as in *Abbeyfield v Woods*, holding that the defendant occupier was a licensee rather than a tenant. In doing so, the Court emphasised the significant developments in the law over the previous 25 years, commenting that they were such that the law could almost be said to have been 'revolutionised'.[30] One particular passage stood out as setting

---

[25] *Lynes v Snaith* [1899] 1 QB 486 (QBD).
[26] *Cobb v Lane* [1952] 1 All ER 1199, 1202. See further *Murray Bull & Co Ltd v Murray* [1953] 1 QB 211 (McNair J); *Greene v Chelsea BC* [1954] 2 QB 127 (CA).
[27] *Abbeyfield (Harpenden) Society Ltd v Woods* [1968] 1 WLR 374 (CA).
[28] Ibid, 376.
[29] *Marchant v Charters* [1977] 1 WLR 1181 (CA).
[30] Ibid, 1184.

out how the law had changed, a passage that was subsequently singled out by Lord Templeman in *Street v Mountford*:[31]

> Gathering the cases together, what is the test to see whether the occupier of one room in a house is a tenant or a licensee? It does not depend on whether he or she has exclusive possession or not. It does not depend on whether the occupation is permanent or temporary. It does not depend on the label the parties put upon it. All these are factors which may influence the decision but none of them is conclusive. All the circumstances have to be worked out. Eventually the answer depends on the nature and quality of the occupancy. Was it intended that the occupier should have a stake in the room or did he have only permission for himself personally to occupy the room, whether under a contract or not in which case he is a licensee?[32]

In 1978, the Court of Appeal was confronted with a new phenomenon in the form of the non-exclusive occupation agreement, a device clearly intended to avoid the regulation of the Rent Acts. The first, and best known authority is *Somma v Hazelhurst*,[33] where a landlord had provided identical but separate standard-form agreements for signature by a young unmarried couple who intended to live together in a bed-sitting room. Each individual was required to sign the agreement, accepting that they would share the room in common with such other persons as the landlord might from time to time nominate. In this case, and in two later decisions,[34] the Court held that these agreements were effective to deny the occupiers the protection of the Rent Acts. Neither of the individuals had exclusive possession of the premises; and, while exclusive possession was not determinative of the issue, in the absence of exclusive possession there could be no tenancy. The readiness of the courts to allow landlords to use such devices in order to circumvent the protective legislation was striking; and it meant that by careful drafting it was possible to deny residential occupiers the privileges that Parliament had intended them to have. However, the case law was not all one way. In *Demuren v Seal Estates Ltd*,[35] decided shortly after *Somma v Hazelhurst*, the Court of Appeal felt able to draw distinctions based on the particular terms of the written agreements and the understanding of the occupiers in signing them; and the occupiers were held to be tenants. The same conclusion was reached in *O'Malley v Seymour*,[36] in which there was obvious reluctance to give full weight to a term that the occupier had the 'right to use in common with others' where there was no other visible intending occupier. The issues highlighted in these cases were, first, the

---

[31] *Street v Mountford* [1985] 1 AC 809, 824 (HL).
[32] *Marchant v Charters* [1977] 1 WLR 1181, 1185 (CA).
[33] *Somma v Hazelhurst* [1978] 1 WLR 1014 (CA).
[34] *Aldrington Garages v Fielder* (1978) 37 P & CR 461 (CA); *Sturolson & Co v Weniz* (1984) 272 EG 326 (CA).
[35] *Demuren v Seal Estates Ltd* (1978) 249 EG 440 (CA).
[36] *O'Malley v Seymour* (1978) 250 EG 1083 (CA).

extent to which the courts would be vigilant and intervene where a landlord sought to invoke devices in order to avoid the impact of the protective legislation and, second, the true meaning of the concept of exclusive possession in the context of shared residential accommodation. Only the first of these issues would be substantially resolved in *Street v Mountford*; the second would have to await the later decision of the House of Lords in *AG Securities v Vaughan*; *Antoniades v Villiers*.

Outside the Residential Context

The enactment of Part II of the Landlord and Tenant Act 1954 rendered the distinction between tenancies and licences of central importance where persons or companies were allowed into occupation of premises for the purposes of carrying on their business trade or profession. If the arrangement gave rise to a tenancy, then the occupier would be likely to have a business tenancy pursuant to Part II of the 1954 Act, conferring privileges such as the right to claim a new tenancy on the expiry of the old and the right to claim compensation on quitting the premises in certain circumstances. This new legislation conferred protection on a potentially wide range of business tenants, 'business' being defined so as to include a trade, profession or employment and any activity carried on by a body of persons whether corporate or unincorporated.

The first major decision on the tenancy/licence distinction as it applied to the 1954 Act was that of the Court of Appeal in *Addiscombe Garden Estates Ltd v Crabbe*.[37] The owners of tennis courts and a clubhouse entered into a written agreement with the trustees of a lawn tennis members' club, whereby the owners purported to confer a licence on the club to use and enjoy the premises for a period of two years in consideration of monthly payment of 'court fees'. On the expiry of the two-year period, the owners claimed possession. However, the trustees of the club contended that the agreement had granted a tenancy that fell within the provisions of Part II of the Landlord and Tenant Act 1954; and that, in order to terminate the tenancy and recover possession, the owners must prove proper compliance with that Act. The Court of Appeal emphasised the importance of concentrating on the substance of the agreement rather than its form, and in particular of not giving undue weight to the 'labels' being used. Jenkins LJ, giving the leading judgment, promoted an approach that involved careful analysis of the document as a whole in an attempt to discern whether the rights and obligations imposed were in substance those pertinent to a relationship of landlord and tenant. Three clauses were found to be 'completely

---

[37] *Addiscombe Garden Estates Ltd v Crabbe* [1958] 1 QB 513 (CA).

inconsistent with the document being a licence',[38] namely those (i) permitting the owners to 'enter and inspect' the premises, (ii) imposing upon the owners a covenant for quiet enjoyment and (iii) reserving to the owners the right to enter and determine the agreement in the event of the court fees not being paid. Extensive reference was made to the judgments of Denning LJ in *Errington v Errington*[39] and (in particular) *Facchini v Bryson*;[40] but Jenkins LJ expressed some unease about the lack of prominence given in those cases to exclusive possession, which remained, in his judgment, 'if not decisive against the view that there is a mere licence, as distinct from a tenancy … at all events a consideration of the first importance'.[41]

In 1959, the tenancy/licence issue came before Lord Denning, sitting on the Judicial Committee of the Privy Council in *Isaac v Hotel de Paris Ltd*,[42] an appeal from the courts of Trinidad and Tobago. Mr Isaac managed a hotel bar for his employers. In the course of negotiations over the purchase of shares in the hotel company, Mr Isaac was permitted to run the bar on the basis that he paid the rent for the hotel. This did not give rise to a tenancy pending the outcome of the negotiations. In the Federal Supreme Court Archer J held that the intention of the parties was 'the paramount consideration' and that, while the fact of exclusive possession, together with the payment of rent, was of 'the first importance', it was not conclusive where, as here, the circumstances showed that, to the knowledge of Mr Isaac, the employers never intended to accept him as tenant. Moreover, the payments made by Mr Isaac could not properly be characterised as rent. The Privy Council upheld the decision of the lower court on the ground that the circumstances and the parties' conduct showed that all that they intended was that Mr Isaac would have a personal privilege (to run the hotel bar) and not an interest in the land. *Isaac v Hotel de Paris Ltd* thus required the Privy Council to ascertain the intentions of the parties to a commercial agreement, not all of which had been committed to writing.

In *Shell Mex & BP Ltd v Manchester Garages Ltd*,[43] the Court of Appeal led by Lord Denning MR purported to apply *Addiscombe Garden Estates Ltd v Crabbe* to another commercial agreement where the defendants to a possession action contended that they were protected by Part II of the Landlord and Tenant Act 1954. The label put upon the transaction (in this case 'licence') was held not to be determinative, since what mattered was the nature of the transaction itself. Nor was exclusive possession conclusive,

[38] Ibid, 529 (Parker LJ).
[39] *Errington v Errington* [1952] 1 KB 290 (CA).
[40] *Facchini v Bryson* [1952] 1 TLR 1386 (CA).
[41] *Addiscombe Garden Estates Ltd v Crabbe* [1958] 1 QB 513, 528 (Jenkins LJ).
[42] *Isaac v Hotel de Paris Ltd* [1960] 1 WLR 239 (PC).
[43] *Shell Mex & BP Ltd v Manchester Garages Ltd* [1971] 1 WLR 612 (CA).

Lord Denning MR seizing the opportunity to further the revolutionary cause:

> At one time it used to be thought that exclusive possession was a decisive factor. But that is not so. It depends upon broader considerations altogether. Primarily on whether it is personal in its nature or not: see *Errington v Errington*.[44]

The written agreement (which concerned a petrol filling station) was very different from that in *Addiscombe Garden Estates*. There was no covenant for quiet enjoyment, no proviso for re-entry in the event of breach and the defendants expressly agreed not to impede the officers of the plaintiff company 'in the exercise of the company's rights of possession and control of the premises'. This clause would now seem to be highly significant, intimating that the defendant occupiers did not have exclusive possession of the premises. However, Lord Denning MR refused to deal with the case in such a way. Looking at the transaction as a whole, he held that the defendants had no more than a licence, that is, a 'personal privilege'. Exclusive possession, or the lack of it, was, according to Lord Denning MR, 'no longer decisive'.[45]

Lord Denning was well aware of the wider policy ramifications in distinguishing between tenancies and licences in the commercial context and he was prepared to advance the case for contractual autonomy in such circumstances:

> It seems to me that when the parties are making arrangements for a filling station, they can agree either on a licence or on a tenancy. If they agree on a licence, it is easy enough for their agreement to be put into writing, in which case the licensee has no protection under the Landlord and Tenant Act 1954. But, if they agree upon a tenancy, and so express it, he is protected. I realise that this means that the parties can, by agreeing on a licence, get out of the Act. But so be it. It may be no bad thing. Especially as I see that the parties can now, with the authority of the court, contract out of the Act, even in regard to tenancies: see section 5 of the Law of Property Act 1969.[46]

We shall return later to the question whether residential and commercial transactions should be treated similarly when it comes to deciding whether a tenancy or a licence has been created. First, we must consider in some detail the landmark cases.

STREET V MOUNTFORD IN THE HOUSE OF LORDS

Commencing on 4 March 1985, the same members of the House of Lords (Lord Scarman, Lord Keith, Lord Bridge, Lord Brightman and Lord

---

[44] Ibid, 615.
[45] Ibid, 616.
[46] Ibid.

Templeman) heard two appeals in which the central issue was the distinction between a tenancy and a licence. Argument in *Street v Mountford* was immediately followed by argument in *Eastleigh BC v Walsh*.[47] When it came to the delivery of the judgments, the order was reversed: that in *Eastleigh BC v Walsh* was delivered on 28 March 1985, and that in *Street v Mountford* was delivered on 2 May 1985.

Eastleigh BC v Walsh

Eastleigh BC v Walsh was an action by a local authority landlord for possession of a dwelling-house. As the house in question was in the public sector, the Rent Acts had no application. However, since the implementation of Part 1 of the Housing Act 1980, many public sector tenants had acquired security of tenure pursuant to a secure tenancy; and in this case the court had to decide whether Mr Walsh, the occupier of the council house, was a secure tenant. The accommodation had initially been offered to Mr Walsh and his wife for the benefit of themselves and their dependent children in order to acquit the council of its duties under the Housing (Homeless Persons) Act 1977. In October 1981, a written offer of 'tenancy' was made, and Mr Walsh (possibly with his family, although no specific finding of fact was made in relation to the issue) moved in shortly afterwards. The council soon became aware that Mrs Walsh and the children were not living in the house and that they had in fact moved to Darlington, although Mr Walsh did not trouble to tell the council of this material change in his circumstances. As schedule 3 to the Housing Act 1980 provided that a tenancy granted pursuant to the Housing (Homeless Persons) Act 1977 was not a secure tenancy before the expiry of a period of 12 months beginning with the date the tenant received notification of the grant of a tenancy, the council could and should have proceeded to recover possession within 12 months of Mr Walsh moving in. But it did not. For reasons that were never made clear, proceedings against Mr Walsh were not commenced until February 1983. The judge in the Southampton County Court, applying Lord Denning's test, held that Mr Walsh never held a tenancy as the parties did not intend to create a tenancy of what was obviously temporary accommodation. The Court of Appeal acknowledged that such reasoning was insufficient since, unlike the Rent Acts, the Housing Act 1980 expressly provided that licences conferring exclusive occupation were to be regarded as tenancies and could therefore be treated as secure tenancies. However, the Court still held in favour of the council, expressly on the ground that the temporary nature

---

[47] *Eastleigh BC v Walsh* [1985] 1 WLR 525 (HL).

of the 'emergency shelter' given to Mr Walsh indicated that the council did not intend to create a tenancy in his favour.

In a single speech delivered by Lord Bridge, the House of Lords allowed Mr Walsh's appeal. No reference was made to any authorities; indeed, no authorities had been cited in argument. In Lord Bridge's judgment the position was quite clear. Mr Walsh had been granted exclusive possession of the house on terms which were fully set out in the offer of tenancy and in a document entitled 'Conditions of Tenancy', which was given to him at the outset. Those documents were unambiguous. The Housing Act 1980 made express provision that, where a tenancy was granted in pursuance of a local authority's duties towards the homeless, it would not be a secure tenancy for the first 12 months. That provision was significant in at least two respects. First, it accepted, albeit tacitly, that the provision of temporary accommodation to homeless persons could constitute the grant of a tenancy. Secondly, it offered the landlord an opportunity to recover possession of such temporary accommodation provided that action was taken expeditiously within the first 12 months of the tenancy. While *Eastleigh BC v Walsh* gave little away in terms of their Lordships' views of the numerous authorities on the tenancy/licence distinction, the emphasis on the central importance of exclusive possession was, with the benefit of hindsight, something of a pointer towards the outcome in *Street v Mountford*.

Street v Mountford: The Facts

In *Street v Mountford*, the agreement between the parties was committed to writing and signed by both of them. The consideration was expressed to be a 'licence fee of £37 a week'. The right to occupy was 'conditional on the strict observance of' a number of rules: no heating other than that provided by the landlord to be used; no person other than the licensee to occupy or sleep in the room; the licence not to be assignable; the owner to be entitled at all times to enter and inspect the condition of the room; the room to be kept clean and tidy; damage and breakages to be paid for, or replaced, at once; a deposit of two weeks' licence fee to be paid to the landlord and to be refunded on termination of the licence; no nuisance or annoyance to other occupiers; no children or pets; payment of licence fee to be paid promptly every Monday in advance. The agreement contained two provisions regarding its termination. First, the owner was entitled to re-enter the room (and the licence would thereupon be immediately terminated) if the licence fee or any part of it should be seven days in arrear, if the occupier should be in breach of any of the other terms of the agreement or if (except by arrangement) the room should be left vacant or unoccupied. Secondly, either party was entitled to terminate the licence by 14 days' written notice at any time.

The argument on behalf of Mr Street was that, adopting the 'hallmarks' approach advocated in *Addiscombe Garden Estates Ltd v Crabbe* and other cases, the agreement was a licence rather than a tenancy. Although, as was conceded, Mrs Mountford had exclusive possession of the rooms, that was not a decisive factor in circumstances where the evidence to be distilled from the written agreement was to the effect that the parties did not intend to create a tenancy. The postscript to the agreement, specifically acknowledged by Mrs Mountford's signature, was a clear indication that no tenancy was intended.

The Return to Exclusive Possession

Lord Templeman would have none of this. While he accepted that the parties' intentions are of the first importance, it is the intention to grant exclusive possession—not the intention to grant a tenancy (and not merely a licence)—which is material. This reasoning necessarily involved the rejection of Lord Denning MR's 'revolution' and the reappraisal of the authorities reflecting that approach. Some of the decisions are defensible on other grounds: others are not and must therefore be overruled. So, where does Lord Templeman's speech leave the law? His speech is frequently, but inaccurately, reduced to the tripartite mantra 'exclusive possession for a term at a rent'. While this is what he appears to be saying at several points in his speech, it is necessary to qualify these components, both with reference to what was said in *Street v Mountford* itself and with reference to other authority.

The first question is whether there is a grant of exclusive possession, characterised by the tenant being able to exercise the rights of an owner in relation to the land 'which is in the real sense his land albeit temporarily and subject to certain restrictions'.[48] According to Lord Templeman, there is no difficulty in deciding whether the grant of residential accommodation confers exclusive possession. There was certainly no such difficulty in *Street v Mountford* itself, for the simple reason that Mr Street conceded that Mrs Mountford had exclusive possession. But there may be difficulties, in particular where a landlord has conferred occupational rights in residential accommodation on more than one individual at the same time. As we have already seen from *Somma v Hazelhurst*, landlords had used such circumstances, and devices such as the non-exclusive occupation agreement, as a means to deny that exclusive possession had been granted. In *Street v Mountford* the House of Lords overruled *Somma v Hazelhurst* on the basis that the agreements were sham, in other words 'artificial transactions

---

[48] *Street v Mountford* [1985] 1 AC 809, 816 (HL).

whose only object is to disguise the grant of a tenancy and to evade the Rent Acts'.[49] But continuing resort to such arrangements led to the House of Lord having to revisit the issue of multiple occupiers and exclusive possession in the conjoined appeals of *AG Securities v Vaughan* and *Antoniades v Villiers*.[50]

Lord Templeman contended that an occupier of residential accommodation at a rent for a term 'is either a lodger or a tenant'.[51] This is controversial. As he himself goes on to explain, there are a number of 'exceptional circumstances' where despite the grant of exclusive possession the occupier is not a tenant but is only a licensee. Moreover, it is quite clear, applying Lord Templeman's own definition of 'lodger' ('the landlord provides attendance or services which require the landlord or his servants to exercise unrestricted access to and use of the premises')[52] that the lodger does not have exclusive possession. It would be more accurate to say that an occupier of residential accommodation for a term at a rent is either a tenant or a licensee but that a lodger is only one type of licensee. Indeed, later in his speech Lord Templeman appears to accept this when he says that exclusive possession

> is not decisive because an occupier who enjoys exclusive possession is not necessarily a tenant. The occupier may be a lodger or service occupier or fall within the other exceptional categories mentioned by Denning LJ in Errington v Errington.[53]

The lodger is therefore a licensee and he is exemplified in the pre-*Street* case law by the occupiers in *Abbeyfield (Harpenden) Society Ltd v Woods*[54] and *Marchant v Charters*.[55] Neither of those decisions was based on that reasoning; but the result in both cases can be justified on the ground that the services provided by the landlord were so extensive as to deny exclusive possession to the occupier.

Exceptional Circumstances

The lodger does not have exclusive possession. The tenant does. But the grant of exclusive possession is not necessarily decisive. It is, according to Lord Templeman, the starting point, and it will often be the ending point as well; but there are a number of 'exceptional circumstances' where exclusive possession does not lead inexorably to the finding of a tenancy. First, there

---

[49] Ibid, 825.
[50] See below, p 197.
[51] *Street v Mountford* [1985] 1 AC 809, 817 (HL).
[52] Ibid, 818.
[53] Ibid, 823.
[54] *Abbeyfield (Harpenden) Society Ltd v Woods* [1968] 1 WLR 374 (CA).
[55] *Marchant v Charters* [1977] 1 WLR 1181 (CA).

is the service occupier, the landlord's employee who 'requires the premises he occupies in order the better to perform his duties as a servant'.[56] The occupation of the premises must be necessary for the performance of the services, and the occupier must be required to live there by his employer. There must be something more than mere convenience to the employee.[57] Secondly, the parties may have not intended to enter into any legal relationship, that is, to enter into a contract at all. In such circumstances, usually where the landlord and occupier are related or where the landlord has allowed the occupier into possession rent free, there is neither a tenancy nor a contractual licence (since there cannot be a contractual licence in the absence of a contract). This exception provides an explanation for the outcomes in *Cobb v Lane*,[58] *Marcroft Wagons Ltd v Smith*[59] and (to a certain extent) *Isaac v Hotel de Paris Ltd*,[60] as well as the earlier Court of Appeal decision in *Booker v Palmer*.[61] However, the scope of this exception is limited. Thirdly, the relationship between the parties may have been that of vendor and purchaser rather than that of landlord and tenant. This will be the case where the parties have exchanged contracts for the sale and purchase of the property which is being occupied as well as where the agreement, having been made 'subject to contract', is not itself enforceable.[62] Fourthly, the owner may have had no power to grant a tenancy. This was a particular problem with requisitioning authorities in war-time, and the issue arose once more, some years later than *Street v Mountford*, in the leading decision of *Bruton v London & Quadrant Housing Trust*.[63]

For a Term at a Rent

Returning briefly to Lord Templeman's tripartite mantra, the two criteria of 'term' and 'rent' escaped serious analysis in *Street v Mountford*, for the very good reason that on the facts of the case neither was in issue. On the basis that Mrs Mountford had been granted a tenancy of the flat, it would be a periodic tenancy arising from the payment of a weekly rent, and no problems of certainty of term or rent would therefore arise.[64] But to say

[56] *Street v Mountford* 1985] 1 AC 809, 818 (HL).
[57] See, eg, *Norris v Checksfield* (1991) 63 P & CR 38 (CA).
[58] *Cobb v Lane* [1952] 1 All ER 1199 (CA).
[59] *Marcroft Wagons Ltd v Smith* [1951] 2 KB 496 (CA).
[60] *Isaac v Hotel de Paris Ltd* (above n 42).
[61] *Booker v Palmer* [1942] 2 All ER 674 (CA) (evacuee allowed to live in cottage for the duration of the war).
[62] See *Isaac v Hotel de Paris Ltd*, above (n 42); cp *Bretherton v Paton* (1986) 18 HLR 257 (CA).
[63] *Bruton v London & Quadrant Housing Trust* [2000] 1 AC 406 (HL), discussed below, p 202.
[64] For recent authority on periodic tenancies and certainty of term, see *Mexfield Housing Co-operative Ltd v Berrisford* [2011] UKSC 52; [2012] 1 AC 955.

that in the absence of any rent being reserved there could be no tenancy was not only controversial, it was quite simply wrong: one need look no further than the interpretation section in the Law of Property Act 1925;[65] and this particular heresy was later exposed by the Court of Appeal in *Ashburn Anstalt v Arnold*.[66]

AG SECURITIES *v* VAUGHAN; ANTONIADES *v* VILLIERS IN THE HOUSE OF LORDS

Three-and-a-half-years after *Street v Mountford*, the tenancy/licence issue resurfaced before the House of Lords. *AG Securities v Vaughan* and *Antoniades v Villiers*,[67] two very different cases on the facts, raised the same underlying problem, namely how a court, faced with more than one occupier of residential property, was to answer the vexed question of whether exclusive possession had been granted. The constitution of the House of Lords was different: only Lord Templeman and Lord Bridge remained of those who had decided *Street v Mountford*, the other judges being Lord Ackner, Lord Oliver and Lord Jauncey.

Antoniades v Villiers: The Facts

Mr Villiers and Miss Bridger were occupiers of a one-bedroom flat owned by Mr Antoniades at 6 Whiteley Road, London SE19. Having inspected the property together and been told that the rent was £174 per month, they were each required to sign a separate written agreement, described as a licence, under which each agreed to pay a monthly sum of £87. Under the terms of the agreement Mr Antoniades, described throughout as the licensor, was entitled 'at any time to use the rooms together with the licensee and permit other persons to use all of the rooms together with the licensee'. Each occupier signed an addendum to the agreement, conceding that the licence did not come under the Rent Acts and undertaking to vacate the flat should he or she marry any other occupier. The agreements were very similar to those which had been used in *Somma v Hazelhurst*[68] but which had been deemed to be sham agreements in *Street v Mountford*. At first instance, Mr Antoniades failed in his attempt to recover possession, the County Court judge holding that Mr Villiers and Miss Bridger were Rent Act protected tenants. However, Mr Antoniades appealed successfully to the Court

---

[65] Law of Property Act 1925, s 205(1)(xxvii).
[66] *Ashburn Anstalt v Arnold* [1989] Ch 1.
[67] *AG Securities v Vaughan; Antoniades v Villiers* [1990] 1 AC 417 (HL).
[68] *Somma v Hazelhurst* [1978] 1 WLR 1014 (CA).

of Appeal, Bingham and Mann LJJ holding that the agreements were indeed licences, not tenancies, and that they had been validly terminated.[69]

AG Securities v Vaughan: The Facts

The facts were, as Lord Oliver put it, 'startlingly different'[70] from those in *Antoniades v Villiers.* The appellant company owned a block of flats known as Linden Mansions, Hornsey Lane, London. Flat 25 comprised six rooms as well as a kitchen and a bathroom. Four of the rooms were furnished as bedrooms, the other two as a lounge and a sitting room. The company then entered into separate agreements with four different individuals. Each agreement was expressed to be a licence and conferred on the licensee the right to use the flat 'in common with others who may have or may from time to time be granted the same right'. The four individuals who were the defendants to the possession action had each commenced occupation at different times. The company took steps to fill vacancies as and when they occurred, providing a draft agreement to the intending occupier and a rent being agreed that reflected the market conditions of the time. As a consequence, each of the defendants was paying a different monthly sum. The allocation of the bedrooms was delegated to the current occupiers, the practice being that when a bedroom fell vacant the remaining occupiers would have the opportunity of taking over that bedroom, the least popular bedroom then being offered to the new occupier. When the defendants applied for the registration of a fair rent, the company sought a declaration that they were licensees. The company succeeded in the County Court; but the defendants appealed successfully to the Court of Appeal, Fox and Mustill LJJ holding that they were joint tenants of the flat and protected under the Rent Acts.[71]

Joint Tenancy or Separate Licences?

It was clear, following the overruling of *Somma v Hazelhurst* in *Street v Mountford,* that a landlord who allowed two or more persons to share the occupation of his premises but who sought to argue that those persons did not have exclusive possession would have a formidably difficult task. The likely outcome would be that the court would hold that those who shared occupation did so pursuant to a joint grant of exclusive possession and were therefore to be characterised as joint tenants rather than individual

---

[69] *AG Securities v Vaughan; Antoniades v Villiers* [1990] 1 AC 417, 437.
[70] Ibid, 470.
[71] Ibid, 422.

licensees. Any attempt by the landlord to rely on the terms of the written agreement as evidence that the parties intended to create a licence would be likely to fail on the basis that such terms were sham or artificial devices. In *AG Securities v Vaughan; Antoniades v Villiers* the House of Lords considered further what the court should do in order to ensure that landlords do not circumvent legislation protecting occupiers of residential accommodation through disingenuous drafting. Lord Oliver's speech is clear, concise and to the point:

> The critical question ... in every case is not simply how the arrangement is presented to the outside world in the relevant documentation, but what is the true nature of the arrangement. The decision of this House in *Street v Mountford* established quite clearly that if the true legal effect of the arrangement entered into is that the occupier of residential property has exclusive possession of the property for an ascertainable period in return for periodical money payments a tenancy is created, whatever the label the parties may have chosen to attach to it.[72]

The 'true nature of the arrangement' is to be gleaned from a wide-ranging survey of the background to the documentation, as Lord Templeman states:

> In considering one or more documents for the purpose of deciding whether a tenancy has been created, the court must consider the surrounding circumstances, including any relationship between the prospective occupiers, the course of negotiations and the nature and extent of the accommodation and the intended and actual mode of occupation of the accommodation.[73]

It was the potential breadth of this survey which had caused concern to the Court of Appeal in *Antoniades v Villiers*. It was felt that the County Court judge had overstepped the mark in taking account of the conduct of the parties subsequent to their contract as being an admissible aid to the construction of that agreement. However, as Lord Oliver noted, while 'subsequent conduct is irrelevant as an aid to construction', it is nevertheless 'admissible as evidence on the question whether the documents were or were not genuine documents giving effect to the parties' true intentions'.[74] Applying this approach to the facts of *Antoniades v Villiers*, there could be only one outcome. The occupiers were a couple. There had been no meaningful negotiations, the occupiers simply being required to complete and to sign pre-prepared standard form agreements: it was a case of 'take it or leave it'. The accommodation was 'not suitable for occupation by more than one couple, save on a very temporary basis',[75] there was no discussion between the parties as to how and when the landlord might seek to

---

[72] Ibid, 466.
[73] Ibid, 458.
[74] Ibid, 469.
[75] Ibid, 467.

introduce other occupiers, and, despite having a financial incentive to do so, the landlord had never attempted to obtain increased rental income by such means. It was no surprise that the House of Lords held that the offending clause was nothing more than a pretence, and that once it was disregarded it was clear that the two written agreements were interdependent. Indeed, had either Mr Villiers or Miss Bridger declined to enter into the agreement offered, Mr Antoniades would have refused to allow the other into occupation. The true effect of the agreement between the parties was to confer a joint right to exclusive possession of the flat; and accordingly the defendants were held to be joint tenants.

Turning to the appeal in *AG Securities v Vaughan*, the most significant finding at first instance was that the written agreements were not shams. On the contrary, they reflected the flexible relationship between the landlord company and the occupiers. Construing the written agreements, their Lordships held that there was no joint grant of exclusive possession to the occupiers since—in the event of one leaving—the remaining three could not exclude the new occupier nominated by the landlord. The Court of Appeal had come to a different view, holding that each time an occupier left, there was a surrender and re-grant of the tenancy, but this conclusion was, in the view of Lord Oliver, 'entirely unreal',[76] and it wholly failed to deal with the fact that none of the four unities (possession, interest, title, time) appeared to exist on the facts of the case. It was also significant that it was never contended that any of the occupiers had exclusive possession of their own bedrooms.[77] Had that been the case, then it would have been strongly arguable that they had a tenancy of that part of the property, together with a licence to use the common parts (the lounge, the sitting room, the kitchen and the bathroom). Such tenancies were protected under the Rent Acts, as well as being potentially assured tenancies under the Housing Act 1988.[78]

Shortly after these appeals were decided, the Court of Appeal heard *Mikeover Ltd v Brady*.[79] A clause imposing an obligation on an occupier to share with those 'who have been granted' a like right did not permit the landlord to introduce further occupiers in the future, and so, as a matter of construction, did not itself derogate from a grant of exclusive possession. However, the two agreements, in providing for the occupiers (a couple) to make separate payments, were held to impose several rather than joint liability for the rent. It followed that the occupiers could not be joint tenants as the arrangement lacked unity of interest and that they were licensees. Particularly striking on the facts (although the Court denied that it was determinative of the outcome) was the landlord's refusal to accept

[76] Ibid, 473.
[77] Ibid, 472.
[78] Housing Act 1988, s 3.
[79] *Mikeover Ltd v Brady* [1989] 3 All ER 618 (CA).

the proffered payment of the whole rent by the occupier who remained following the departure of her partner. Nevertheless, *Mikeover Ltd v Brady* must be treated with some care as an authority. It should be noted that in *Antoniades v Villiers* itself the written agreements expressed rental liability to be several rather than joint, but the House of Lords seemed to consider that such provision was a pretence or a sham.

In *AG Securities v Vaughan; Antoniades v Villiers*, both appeals were allowed. The decision of the House of Lords turned ultimately on the extent to which the agreements of the individual occupiers were dependent on one another. In *Antoniades v Villiers* the agreements were clearly inter-dependent, for all the reasons discussed above, whereas in *AG Securities v Vaughan* the agreements were truly independent of one another. In passing, it is submitted that the most lucid speech in the House of Lords in the two appeals, and the one that most repays re-reading, is that of Lord Oliver.

THE AFTERMATH

In the five years or so following *Street v Mountford*, there were, perhaps inevitably, a considerable number of decisions of the Court of Appeal and the High Court which analysed the reasoning and explored the consequences of the decision as it applied in particular to residential property; and, as we have seen, two such cases ultimately found their way to the House of Lords. Since then, litigation on the tenancy/licence issue, at least at appellate level, seems to have become far less common. This trend is perhaps not surprising when one considers the legislative developments during the same period of time. Within three years of *Street v Mountford*, Parliament enacted the Housing Act 1988, a statute which began the process of phasing out the Rent Acts by providing that, save in certain transitional circumstances, tenancies entered into after 14 January 1989 would no longer qualify as Rent Act protected tenancies. Instead, such tenancies, which would previously have been Rent Act protected tenancies, would normally take effect as 'assured tenancies'.[80] While assured tenancies confer a statutory security of tenure similar to that afforded to Rent Act regulated tenancies, they do not subject the landlords to rent control, thereby removing the main disincentive to granting a lease to an occupier of residential property. Further legislative reforms followed, notably the Housing Act 1996, which made the 'assured shorthold' the default form of tenancy in the private sector of residential property.[81] This sub-species of assured tenancy renders the recovery of possession by land-lords following the termination of the lease a relatively routine matter, and there is certainly no meaningful statutory security over and above the rights

---

[80] Housing Act 1988, s 1(1).
[81] Ibid, s 19A, inserted by the Housing Act 1996, s 96(1).

conferred by the contract. The trade-off is that tenants may make claims to reduce the level of the rent from that contractually agreed, but they may do so only on the basis that the rent agreed exceeds the market rent.[82] The rent regulation applicable to assured shorthold tenancies, to say the least, falls some way short of the rent control imposed on Rent Act tenancies and it is unlikely to deter landlords from letting on such terms.

The most interesting, and controversial, decision since *AG Securities v Vaughan* was handed down by the House of Lords at the end of 1999. In *Bruton v London & Quadrant Housing Trust*,[83] a local authority licensed a charitable housing trust to use a block of flats to provide temporary accommodation for homeless persons. The agreement between the authority and the trust did not grant any proprietary interest in the block of flats. The trust then purported to confer a weekly 'licence' of one of the flats to Mr Bruton, retaining for itself certain rights, which it would later contend denied exclusive possession to the occupier. Sometime later, Mr Bruton claimed damages from the trust for breach of the repairing covenant statutorily implied into leases (but not licences) of dwelling-houses granted for a term of less than seven years.[84] The House of Lords held that the agreement, properly construed, conferred exclusive possession on Mr Bruton and that exceptional circumstances did not exist by virtue of the identity of the landlord or its agreement with the council not to grant tenancies. None of this was contentious. However, the House of Lords, led by Lord Hoffmann, held that the fact that the trust had no proprietary interest in the block of flats was immaterial. In other words, although the trust could not grant a legal estate in the land to Mr Bruton, he had somehow obtained a tenancy in the flat. Lord Hoffmann explained this startling proposition as follows:

> A lease may, and usually does, create a proprietary interest called a leasehold estate or, technically, a 'term of years absolute'. This will depend upon whether the landlord had an interest out of which he could grant it. Nemo dat quod non habet. But it is the fact that the agreement is a lease which creates the proprietary interest. It is putting the cart before the horse to say that whether the agreement is a lease depends upon whether it creates a proprietary interest.[85]

Thus the spectre of the non-proprietary lease came into being. It met with immediate criticism, and it was anticipated that it would give rise to a great deal of further litigation. Somewhat surprisingly, that has not been the case. It remains good authority,[86] and so the current law is that although the

---

[82] Ibid, s 22.

[83] *Bruton v London & Quadrant Housing Trust* [2000] 1 AC 406 (HL).

[84] See Landlord and Tenant Act 1985, s 11.

[85] *Bruton v London & Quadrant Housing Trust* [2000] 1 AC 406, 415 (HL).

[86] The concept of the non-proprietary lease has been endorsed by the House of Lords in *Kay v Lambeth LBC* [2006] UKHL 10, [2006] 2 AC 465 and by the Supreme Court in *Berrisford v Mexfield Housing Co-operative Ltd* [2011] UKSC 52, [2012] AC 955.

creation of a tenancy usually involves the granting of a proprietary interest, it will not do so where the landlord had no estate out of which such an interest could be granted.[87] It is important to emphasise that *Bruton* does not challenge the requirement of exclusive possession laid down in *Street v Mountford*. However, it is arguable that it may modify what is meant by exclusive possession: a tenant holding under a non-proprietary lease may be in a weaker position in defending his possession than the tenant who has the protection of a legal estate. The outcome of *Bruton*—casting the net of repairing liability for sub-standard housing wider—is far less controversial than its reasoning, although few concerned with the integrity of our property law would consider that the ends justified the means.

The one area where the tenancy/licence issue has been litigated recently is in relation to agreements affecting commercial property. The rationale for paternalism in this context has tended to be relatively weak as there is usually an arms-length relationship with both parties being independently advised by lawyers during the negotiations for the agreement. Nevertheless, following *Street v Mountford*, there were a number of decisions where courts applied the principles laid down in that case to agreements affecting non-residential property. The security of tenure afforded to occupiers of business premises by Part II of the Landlord and Tenant Act 1954 applies only to tenants, not to licensees, and in determining whether an occupier was or was not a business tenant the courts initially adopted the *Street v Mountford* principles.[88] However, the Court of Appeal now seems to have accepted that where a contract has been negotiated between parties of equal bargaining power, with the benefit of legal advice, provisions which clearly indicate the parties' intentions as to whether the agreement confers a tenancy or a licence should normally be enforced.[89] In this context at least it is now possible to identify some judicial support for Lord Denning MR's argument that the intention to create a tenancy should be of significance. We recall Lord Denning MR's reference to the possibility of contracting out of the business tenancy legislation.[90] As a result of amendments to the legislation, contracting out of the statutory security regime has been facilitated further; and it is no longer necessary for the parties to obtain the prior

---

[87] See C Harpum, S Bridge and M Dixon (eds), *Megarry & Wade, The Law of Real Property*, 8th edn (London, Sweet & Maxwell, 2012) para 17-032.

[88] See, eg, *London & Associated Investment Trust plc v Calow* (1986) 53 P & CR 340, 352 (Ch D); *Vandersteen v Agius* (1992) 65 P & CR 266 (CA); and, for recent judicial dicta, see *Mann Aviation Group (Engineering) Ltd (in administration) v Longmint Aviation Ltd* [2011] EWHC 2238 (Ch), [34] (Sales J).

[89] *National Car Parks Ltd v Trinity Development Co (Banbury) Ltd* [2001] EWCA Civ 1686; [2002] 2 P & CR 18, [29]; *Clear Channel UK Ltd v Manchester CC* [2005] EWCA Civ 1304; [2006] L & TR 7, [29].

[90] *Shell Mex & BP Ltd v Manchester Garages Ltd* [1971] 1 WLR 612, 616 (CA); see esp the quote from Lord Denning on p 191 above.

sanction of the County Court.[91] That being the case, it seems all the more appropriate to accord greater autonomy to the parties in deciding whether their agreement should take effect as a tenancy or as a licence.

The combined impact of the decisions in *Street v Mountford* and *AG Securities v Vaughan; Antoniades v Villiers* was to make avoidance of the Rent Acts and other protective legislation by private landlords exceptionally difficult if not impossible. However, within a very short time of those decisions, the coming into force of the Housing Act 1988 rendered avoidance of the Rent Acts unnecessary; and by the time of the Housing Act 1996 the landlord's incentive to prefer licensees to tenants had largely disappeared. Although the two decisions remain of importance in setting out how tenancies and licences are to be distinguished, and in defining what a tenancy involves, their consequences in terms of the legislation protecting occupiers of residential property are no longer the same and as a result the focus of litigation between landlord and tenant has shifted significantly.

---

[91] Landlord and Tenant Act 1954, s 38A(1), inserted by the Regulatory Reform (Business Tenancies) (England and Wales) Order 2003, SI 2003/3096, art 22.

9

City of London Building Society v Flegg *(1987)*

Homes as Wealth

NICHOLAS HOPKINS

INTRODUCTION

I
T IS A characteristic of land law that practically and socially significant problems are distilled into a paradigm of the acquisition of property rights and the priorities of competing rights. While questions of acquisition and priority are distinct, there is a logical correlation between them insofar as any expansion of the circumstances in which property rights are acquired necessarily puts greater pressure on the priority rules that determine the enforcement of those rights against third party purchasers or creditors. Since the 1925 property legislation priority rules have been largely statute-based and the exact balance drawn between competing rights has therefore become a matter of statutory interpretation (with the notable exception—not applicable to the case under discussion—of the continuing role of the doctrine of notice in unregistered land). Although significant parts of the 1925 legislation have been repealed and replaced, the essential framework of priority rules still mirrors that provided by the earlier legislation. While the formal acquisition of rights is also governed, or restrained, by statutory formalities, informal acquisition through equity's doctrines has become increasingly significant. This is particularly so since the twentieth century witnessed the 'emergence of a property owning, particularly a real-property-mortgaged-to-a-building-society-owning-democracy'.[1] The spread of home ownership was unforeseen at the time of the 1925 legislation.[2]

---

[1] *Pettitt v Pettitt* [1970] AC 777, 824 (Lord Diplock) (HL).

[2] In 1918 home ownership in England and Wales stood at 23%. By 2000 it had reached 70.6%. Source: Department of Communities and Local Government, Live Tables on Household Characteristics, Table 801, 'Household Characteristics: Tenure Trend from 1918', available at: www.communities.gov.uk/documents/housing/xls/141491.xls.

Since then, equity's doctrines of the resulting trust and now, predominantly, the common intention constructive trust, have provided a potent means for non-legal owners to establish beneficial interests in the home.[3] The use of mortgage finance, not merely to purchase the home but also to release equity for other purposes, has placed increasing pressure on priority rules in the specific context of disputes between occupiers with property rights who wish to remain in their home and creditors and mortgage lenders who wish to realise their security interest to discharge a debt. The most difficult cases arise where the home is co-owned and the occupier(s) in dispute with the creditor are not legally responsible for repayment of the debt. Underlying this debate is a policy question of the extent to which (if at all) the home should be treated differently from other property. This question pits the 'use value' of the home—in Rudden's terms, the 'thing as thing' against its 'investment value'—the 'thing as wealth'.[4]

The decision of the House of Lords in *City of London Building Society v Flegg*[5] marks a key stage in how the balance is drawn between occupiers and creditors in priority disputes. The House of Lords held that beneficial interests that have been overreached by payment of capital money to two (or more) trustees cannot be enforced against a creditor as overriding interests, despite the beneficiary's occupation of the home. The seeds of the case were planted in the 1925 legislation in the schema adopted for the regulation of co-ownership of land. The legislation imposed a trust for sale in all cases of co-ownership and expanded the operation of the overreaching mechanism to ensure that on the execution of the trust the beneficial interest 'is not defeated or destroyed by the disposition, but is shifted so as to become a corresponding interest or power in or over the proceeds'.[6] Further, the effect of the equitable doctrine of conversion, applied to trusts for sale as a direct consequence of the existence of a duty to sell, was that from the time the trust was created the interest of the beneficiaries was confined to an interest in the proceeds of sale (and the rents and profits pending sale), rather than an interest in the land. Against this, section 70(1)(g) of the Land Registration Act 1925 (LRA 1925) protected as an overriding interest, binding against purchasers without appearing on the register, the

---

[3] In *City of London Building Society v Flegg* [1988] AC 54 (HL) the Fleggs' beneficial interest was established though a resulting trust. The utility of that trust in the context of the home has since been doubted and the common intention constructive trust is now preferred: *Stack v Dowden* [2007] UKHL 17, [2007] 2 AC 432; *Jones v Kernott* [2011] UKSC 53, [2012] 1 AC 776.

[4] B Rudden, 'Things as Thing and Things as Wealth' in JW Harris (ed), *Property Problems: From Genes to Pension Funds* (London, Kluwer Law International, 1997).

[5] *City of London Building Society v Flegg* [1988] AC 54 (HL).

[6] J Farrand (ed), *Wolstenholme and Cherry's Conveyancing Statutes* Vol 1, 13th edn (London, Oyez, 1972) 51.

property rights of those in actual occupation of the land. Its purpose was described by Lord Denning MR in the following terms:

> Fundamentally its object is to protect a person in actual occupation of land from having his rights lost in the welter of registration. He can stay there and do nothing. Yet he will be protected. No one can buy the land over his head and thereby take away or diminish his rights. It is up to every purchaser before he buys to make inquiry on the premises. If he fails to do so, it is at his own risk. He must take subject to whatever rights the occupier may have.[7]

However, it was not until the decision of the House of Lords in *Williams & Glyn's Bank Ltd v Boland*,[8] some seven years before *Flegg*, that it became apparent that an issue arose as regards the relationship between the overreaching mechanism and overriding interests. In *Boland*, it was held that the beneficial interest of a spouse in occupation of a home was binding as an overriding interest within section 70(1)(g) of the LRA 1925 against a mortgagee who had dealt with a sole trustee. Once that point was decided, not only was it apparent that the relationship between overriding interests and overreaching would need to be resolved, but it was imperative to do so given the practical significance of the issue. In his judgment in *Flegg*, Lord Oliver noted that since the decision in *Boland*

> it has been widely assumed by those called upon to advise banks and building societies that, so long as capital moneys arising from an exercise of their powers by trustees for sale holding on the statutory trusts have been paid in accordance with the statutory provisions to not less than two trustees or a trust corporation pursuant to the provisions of section 27 of the Law of Property Act 1925, a purchaser need not concern himself with the beneficial interest in the property even where one or more of the beneficiaries is or are in actual occupation of the property at the time of the transaction.[9]

In this respect, the facts of *Flegg* raised the right issue at the right time. Given the inevitability and significance of the point it is perhaps a surprise that it took as long as seven years for the matter to reach the House of Lords. However, factual patterns giving rise to equitable co-owners in occupation with two trustees rather than a single trustee are more complex and therefore rarer than the classic case of a matrimonial home in sole legal ownership, which has provided the bedrock of priority disputes between beneficiaries and creditors.

The effect of the decision in *Flegg* was to curtail the practical application of the House of Lords' previous decision in *Boland* and, by doing so, to create a sharp division between one and two trustee trusts: the former remaining governed by *Boland* with the beneficial interests of those in actual occupation

---

[7] *Strand Securities Ltd v Caswell* [1965] Ch 958, 979–80 (CA).
[8] *Williams & Glyn's Bank v Boland Ltd* [1981] AC 487 (HL). See ch 6.
[9] *City of London Building Society v Flegg* [1988] AC 54, 76E–G.

of the land taking priority over the mortgagee; and the latter now governed by *Flegg* with beneficial interests unenforceable against the mortgagee. The creation of this bipartite distinction, which continues to govern priority disputes between mortgagees and beneficiaries, would be sufficient alone to merit the description of the case as a landmark. However, *Flegg* is also a landmark case for at least two further reasons. First, the decision marked a policy choice to favour—or, following *Boland*, to rebalance—the claims of creditors over beneficiaries. The tide had already turned since *Boland* and the impact of the decision had been curbed.[10] Notwithstanding, *Flegg* appears to have marked a turning point in the attitude of the courts and from the time of the decision *Boland* has appeared the high water mark in the protection of beneficiaries. The willingness of the House of Lords in *Boland* to require conveyancers to 'adjust their practice, if it be socially required'[11] seems not to have been echoed until, in a different context, *Barclays Bank plc v O'Brien*[12] reignited the debate as to the extent to which transactional practice should change to protect spouses with property rights in their home. By that stage, attention had shifted away from priority issues affecting equitable co-owners to the position of joint legal owners whose consent to a mortgage is procured by undue influence. Secondly, as the only case on the operation of overreaching to be heard by the highest appellate court, *Flegg* remains the most authoritative judicial consideration of the mechanism. The decision—to give precedence to overreaching above overriding interests—has survived (largely) intact despite the fact that the doctrinal basis on which the decision was based now looks outdated, if it has not been entirely removed, and the treatment afforded to the home by overreaching now appears increasingly outdated in light of other developments.

FACTS AND DECISIONS IN THE LOWER COURTS

By a conveyance dated 18 October 1977, Mr and Mrs Maxwell-Brown became registered proprietors of the property, Bleak House, which was transferred on an express trust for sale for themselves as joint tenants. The purchase price was £34,000, of which £18,000 had been provided by Mr and Mrs Flegg, the parents of Mrs Maxwell-Brown, from the proceeds of sale of the bungalow that had been their home for 28 years and from their savings. Mr and Mrs Flegg expected the remaining £15,000 to be raised by a

---

[10] *Bristol and West Building Society v Henning* [1985] 1 WLR 778 (CA); *Paddington Building Society v Mendelsohn* (1985) 50 P & CR 244 (CA).
[11] *Williams & Glyn's Bank v Boland Ltd* [1981] AC 487, 510 (Lord Scarman).
[12] *Barclays Bank plc v O'Brien* [1994] 1 AC 180 (HL).

legal mortgage over Bleak House granted by Mr and Mrs Maxwell-Brown, though in fact the couple had granted a mortgage for £20,000. Mr and Mrs Flegg had resisted legal advice that Bleak House should be conveyed into the names of all four parties as they did not want to be held legally liable for the mortgage. The effect of the transfer in these circumstances was that the express trust for sale was displaced by a resulting trust under which Mr and Mrs Maxwell-Brown held title to Bleak House on trust for sale for themselves and Mr and Mrs Flegg as tenants in common. Bleak House then became the home of the Maxwell-Browns and the Fleggs and remained the home of the Fleggs at the time of the judgment. In 1979 and 1981, the Maxwell-Browns granted further charges over Bleak House without the knowledge or consent of the Fleggs. By 1981, the Maxwell-Browns were in financial difficulties. Unknown to the Fleggs, the Maxwell-Browns had defaulted on the original mortgage and an order for possession had been made against them. On 8 January 1982, again without the knowledge or consent of the Fleggs, and in an apparent attempt to stave off the order for possession, the Maxwell-Browns executed a further and final charge by way of legal mortgage in favour of the City of London Building Society to secure a loan of £37,500, which was used to discharge the three previous mortgages. Default on this mortgage led to the bankruptcy of the Maxwell-Browns, who took no part in the proceedings. Instead, the proceedings raised an issue of priorities between the security interest held by the City of London Building Society and the Fleggs' beneficial interests. The building society sought a declaration that the mortgage was enforceable against the Fleggs and an order for possession of Bleak House. The basis of its argument was that the payment of the mortgage money to two trustees had operated to overreach the beneficial interests of the Fleggs. The Fleggs argued that by virtue of their actual occupation of the home their beneficial interests took priority over the mortgage as overriding interests. They therefore relied on the previous decision of the House of Lords in *Boland*, which they argued should apply despite the fact there had been only one trustee in that case, and on the statutory provisions governing overriding interests. The Fleggs also relied on section 14 of the LPA 1925.

The building society succeeded in their action at first instance before Judge Thomas, but an appeal against the decision by the Fleggs was allowed by the Court of Appeal. The Court of Appeal found in favour of the Fleggs on two distinct grounds. The first and principal argument concerned the relationship between overreaching and overriding interests. Dillon LJ, with whose judgment Kerr LJ and Sir George Waller agreed, held that the outcome in *Boland* was not dependent on the fact that there had been only one trustee. Hence, in the view of the Court of Appeal, the disposition of the legal title took effect subject to the beneficial interests of the Fleggs, which were protected as overriding interests by virtue of their actual occupation of the land. A subsidiary argument was based on the effect of section 14 of the LPA 1925. That section, which is contained in Part I of the LPA 1925 (the same part in which the overreaching provisions of sections 2 and 27 are contained) provides, '[T]his Part of this Act shall not prejudicially affect the interest of any person in possession or in actual occupation of land to which he may be entitled in right of such possession or occupation'. The Court of Appeal considered, as a separate basis for the decision, that as a result of section 14, the mortgage executed in favour of the City of London Building Society, despite being executed by two trustees, did not overreach the Fleggs' beneficial interests.

DECISION IN THE HOUSE OF LORDS

The House of Lords unanimously reversed the Court of Appeal's decision. Full judgments were given by Lord Oliver and Lord Templeman, who also expressed agreement with Lord Oliver. The remaining members of the panel, Lord Bridge, Lord Mackay and Lord Goff, concurred with the judgments of Lord Oliver and Lord Templeman. Perhaps notably there is no overlap in the composition of the panel in the House of Lords between *Boland* and *Flegg*. However, Templeman J (as he then was) had decided *Boland* at first instance in favour of the Bank and had seen his decision in that case reversed by the Court of Appeal and House of Lords. The decision of the House of Lords is based on two factors: a doctrinal analysis of the statutory provisions combined with an assessment of the legislative policy the provisions are intended to achieve. In both respects there is little, if any, substantive difference in the reasoning adopted by Lord Templeman and Lord Oliver. Lord Oliver's judgment is the leading one, given Lord Templeman's concurrence, and is also broader in its scope. There is, however, a notable difference in the approach taken by their Lordships. Lord Templeman's judgment is focused on the interpretation of the key statutory provisions. With this interpretation in place, Lord Templeman then moves to find his analysis of those provisions consistent with the policy of the 1925 property legislation. In contrast, Lord Oliver begins by setting out the policy implications of the case before moving to consider the statutory provisions. Hence, Lord Oliver approaches the doctrinal analysis of the legislation with a clearly stated view of the policy that the analysis should support. In the House of Lords, the two grounds for decision by the Court of Appeal—the relationship between overreaching and overriding interests and the effect of section 14 of the LPA 1925—are largely conflated, and the effect of section 14 is subsumed within the analysis of the relationship between overreaching and overriding interests. However, it is useful to discuss the section 14 point separately, not least as the House of Lords decision in *Flegg* appears to have marked the quietus of the provision.

The Policy of the Legislation

Lord Oliver and Lord Templeman took the same view of the policy the legislation is intended to achieve. Lord Oliver noted the significance of the issue and the implications of the case in the following terms:

> If it be the case, as the Court of Appeal held, that the payment by the appellants in the instant case to two properly constituted trustees for sale, holding upon the statutory trusts, provides no sensible distinction from the ratio of the decision of this House in *Boland*'s case, the legislative policy of the 1925 legislation of keeping the interests of beneficiaries behind the curtain and confining the investigation of title to the devolution of the legal estate will have been substantially reversed by judicial decision and financial institutions advancing money on the security of land will face hitherto unsuspected hazards, whether they are dealing with registered or unregistered land.[13]

Lord Templeman noted the general aim of the 1925 legislation of drawing a balance between the public interest in the marketability of land on the one hand, and the interests of beneficiaries in preserving their rights on the other.[14] Overreaching is the mechanism used to achieve this balance and, in his view, the statutory provisions on overriding interests or section 14 of the LPA 1925 'cannot have been intended to frustrate this compromise and to subject the purchaser to some beneficial interests but not others depending on the waywardness of actual occupation'.[15]

Overreaching and Overriding Interests

Lord Oliver approached the appeal in four stages.[16] First, by discussing the nature of the interest enjoyed by tenants in common of land prior to the 1925 legislation; secondly, by considering the effect of the 1925 legislation on that position and the policy of the legislation; thirdly, by determining how the case would be decided had the facts arisen in unregistered land; and fourthly, by addressing the impact on that result of the LRA 1925. His analysis is therefore rooted in the history of interests in land and reflects the prevailing classical view that there was no substantive difference between registered and unregistered titles. As a result, there was an expectation, acknowledged by Lord Oliver, that the two systems would dovetail.[17] A significant feature of his judgment is the prominence afforded to the doctrine

---

[13] *City of London Building Society v Flegg* [1988] AC 54, 76–77.
[14] Ibid, 73–74.
[15] Ibid, 74.
[16] Ibid, 77.
[17] Ibid, 84.

of conversion. This is despite the fact that the doctrine had been the subject of criticism by the House of Lords in *Boland*.[18]

In relation to the first two issues, Lord Oliver explained that the 1925 legislation removed the possibility of a legal tenancy in common. Instead, tenancies in common take effect in equity behind a trust for sale of a legal joint tenancy. The purpose of this was to ensure, through the operation of the overreaching mechanism, that on a sale or mortgage of the land the beneficial interests would shift to the proceeds of sale. In the meantime, through the doctrine of conversion, the interests are deemed already to be in the proceeds of sale. However, Lord Oliver noted that 'by judicial construction' the beneficiaries retained some of the incidents of legal ownership that tenants in common would have enjoyed prior to the 1925 legislation. As Lord Oliver acknowledges later in his judgment, the incidents of legal ownership that may still be enjoyed include, on appropriate facts, occupation of the land.[19] Lord Oliver then considered the provision for overreaching in section 2(1)(ii) of the LPA 1925, its application to mortgages and the requirement of a minimum of two trustees in section 27(2). He further noted the power conferred on trustees for sale to mortgage the land[20] and the protection afforded to purchasers dealing with trustees for sale. At the time of the decision, section 26(3) of the LPA 1925 provided that purchasers were not concerned with whether the trustees for sale had complied with their duty to consult the beneficiaries. Further, section 17 of the Trustee Act 1925 exonerates purchasers or mortgagees who deal with trustees from being concerned with ensuring that money is raised and applied in accordance with the trust.

From this review of the legislative provisions, Lord Oliver concluded that the scheme of the legislation is to enable a purchaser or mortgagee who pays money to at least two trustees to accept a conveyance or mortgage without reference to the beneficial interests. Drawing again on the doctrine of conversion, he emphasised that the beneficiaries are 'interested only in the proceeds of sale and rents and profits until sale, which are kept behind the curtain and do not require to be investigated'.[21] Therefore, at least in unregistered land—in response to his third question—Lord Oliver explained that beneficial interests are overreached and the purchaser absolved from enquiry, but only if the statutory requirements in sections 2 and 27 of the LPA 1925 for the payment of capital money are respected. Until that time, the beneficiary can assert the incidents of ownership, including occupation,

---

[18] *Williams & Glyn's Bank v Boland Ltd* [1981] AC 487, 507.
[19] *City of London Building Society v Flegg* [1988] AC 54, 81.
[20] LPA 1925, s 28(1), conferred on trustees for sale the same powers enjoyed by tenants for life under the Settled Land Act 1925.
[21] *City of London Building Society v Flegg* [1988] AC 54, 79.

against the trustees and any purchaser who has not complied with the statutory requirements.[22] However, once overreaching occurs, the purchaser or mortgagee is no longer concerned with the beneficiary's interest in the proceeds of sale.

Having established what the outcome would be in relation to unregistered land, Lord Oliver then addressed, in the final part of his judgment, the position in registered land. After briefly considering the background to the LRA 1925, Lord Oliver set out the statutory definitions of legal estates, minor interests and overriding interests. He noted the provisions of the Act reflect 'the same philosophy as is apparent in the Law of Property Act of keeping behind the curtain those interests which are overreached'.[23] Finally, Lord Oliver set out the key priority provisions contained in sections 20 and 70(1)(g) of the LRA 1925. Section 20 provided that a disposition of a registered estate (including a mortgage) for valuable consideration conferred on the transferee or mortgagee, when registered, the estate expressed to be created subject only to 'incumbrances and other entries, if any, appearing on the register' and 'overriding interests'. Section 70(1)(g) included as an overriding interest, '[T]he rights of every person in actual occupation of the land or in receipt of the rents and profits thereof, save where inquiry is made of such person and the rights are not disclosed'. Against this legislative background, Lord Oliver turned to address the relationship between overreaching and overriding interests in light of the decision in *Boland*. The outcome in *Flegg* turned on the question whether the interest of a tenant in common in occupation of registered land is, by reason of the occupation, incapable of being overreached without the consent of the occupier but is an overriding interest under section 70(1)(g).[24] This in turn depended on the basis of the decision in *Boland*. Was the decision dependent on the fact that there was only one trustee and so overreaching could not occur, or was it based purely on the relationship between the legislative categories of minor interests and overriding interests?

In the view of the Court of Appeal, the decision in *Boland* was founded on the distinction between a minor interest and an overriding interest. The fact there was only one trustee was not crucial to the decision but merely 'part of the narrative of the background of the case'.[25] Dillon LJ referred to Lord Wilberforce's judgment in *Boland* in which he had concluded that in the scheme of the LRA 1925 the fact of occupation converted a minor interest into an overriding interest.[26] On the basis of this interpretation

[22] Ibid, 81.
[23] Ibid, 85.
[24] Ibid, 86–87.
[25] *City of London Building Society v Flegg* [1986] 1 Ch 605, 617 (CA).
[26] Ibid, 616.

of the relationship between the two categories of interest, if the beneficial interest under a trust for sale came within the statutory definition of a minor interest even where there are two trustees, then the beneficiaries' occupation necessarily converted that minor interest into an overriding interest. The definition of minor interests in section 3 of the LRA 1925 included 'in the case of land held on trust for sale, all interests and powers which are under the Law of Property Act 1925 capable of being overridden by the trustees for sale'. Dillon LJ considered that this must refer to a case where there are two or more trustees as only then were the interests capable of being overreached. On Dillon LJ's analysis therefore, beneficial interests under a trust for sale where there are two or more trustees are minor interests. The Fleggs' actual occupation of the land converted their minor interests into overriding interests which were binding on the purchaser or mortgagee under section 20.[27]

On this crucial point of statutory interpretation Lord Oliver disagreed with the judgment of the Court of Appeal. He considered an analysis of the Court of Appeal and House of Lords judgments in *Boland* to reveal that the fact there was only one trustee was 'an essential part of the reasoning upon which the judgments were based'.[28] It was because the interests had not been overreached that their classification as minor or overriding interests arose for consideration. It was against that background that Lord Wilberforce's discussion of the distinction between minor interests and overriding interests on which Dillon LJ had relied had been given. Echoing an argument advanced on behalf of the City of London Building Society,[29] Lord Oliver explained, '[o]nce the beneficiary's rights have been shifted from the land to capital moneys in the hands of the trustees, there is no longer an interest in the land to which the occupation can be referred or which it can protect'.[30] The beneficiary's interest was no longer 'for the time being subsisting' with reference to the land for the purpose of section 70(1)(g) so as to be capable of protection as an overriding interest.

Lord Templeman reached the same conclusion from an analysis of the statutory provisions. He stated that interests 'cannot at one and the same time be overreached and overridden and at the same time be overriding interests'.[31] He distinguished *Boland* on the basis that there the wife's interest had not been overreached as capital money had been paid to a sole trustee.[32]

---

[27] Ibid, 617.
[28] *City of London Building Society v Flegg* [1988] AC 54, 89 (HL).
[29] Ibid, 87–88.
[30] Ibid, 91.
[31] Ibid, 73.
[32] Ibid, 74.

Section 14 of the Law of Property Act 1925

As has been seen, in the Court of Appeal section 14 was considered to provide a separate ground on which the Fleggs could succeed. Dillon LJ relied on the judgment of Denning LJ in *Bull v Bull*,[33] who had considered section 14 to preserve the right of an equitable tenant in common to remain in occupation.[34] On the basis of Denning LJ's judgment, Dillon LJ considered that the interest of an equitable tenant in common in occupation constitutes an interest 'to which he may be entitled in right of such possession or occupation' for the purposes of section 14. As such, that section operated to prevent the interests of the beneficiaries from being overreached in the absence of their consent. On Dillon LJ's view, therefore, the beneficial interest held by a beneficiary in occupation was prevented from being overreached in two distinct ways: through its status as an overriding interest under section 70(1)(g) of the LRA 1925 and, separately, through section 14 of the LPA 1925.

Lord Oliver addressed section 14 in the context of his analysis of provisions of the 1925 legislation. He noted that 'the ambit of section 14 is a matter which has puzzled conveyancers ever since the Law of Property Act was enacted'.[35] However, the section cannot 'enlarge or add to whatever interest it is that the occupant has "in right of his occupation"'.[36] In particular, it cannot preserve as an interest in land a beneficial interest that has been overreached. To do so, Lord Oliver suggested, would enable the section 'to defeat the manifest purpose of the legislature' reflected in the other provisions of the 1925 legislation.[37] Drawing again on the doctrine of conversion, Lord Oliver explained that the beneficiary's occupation is a means of enjoying in specie the rents and profits until sale. The occupation is 'fathered' by the interests under the trust of sale.[38] Once that interest has been overreached by sale, in the terms of section 14, the beneficiary no longer has an 'interest ... to which he may be entitled in right of such ... occupation'. Hence, in Lord Oliver's judgment overreaching simultaneously prevents the beneficiary from having recourse to section 14 or invoking section 70(1)(g). As a result of overreaching, the interest no longer subsists with reference to the land and therefore the beneficiary no longer has an interest which may give rise to a right of occupation. Lord Oliver emphasised that in *Bull v Bull* the dispute was between the beneficiary and trustee

---

[33] *Bull v Bull* [1955] 1 QB 234.
[34] *City of London Building Society v Flegg* [1986] 1 Ch 605, 619 (CA).
[35] *City of London Building Society v Flegg* [1988] AC 54, 80 (HL).
[36] Ibid.
[37] Ibid, 81.
[38] Ibid, 83.

(rather than a purchaser or mortgagee) and concerned the interest of the beneficiary prior to sale.

Adopting a restrictive construction of the section, Lord Templeman explained that the Fleggs were not 'prejudicially affected' within section 14 by the overreaching provisions of the LPA 1925, but by the failure of the Maxwell-Browns as trustees to account to them for the capital money obtained. He considered that the section could not confer on beneficiaries in occupation 'rights which are different from and superior to' the rights of beneficiaries not in occupation at the time overreaching takes place.[39] Lord Templeman therefore interpreted section 14, compatibly with the overreaching mechanism, on the basis that a beneficial interest is not prejudicially affected when it can no longer be enjoyed in specie in the land.

ANALYSIS OF THE DECISION

Lord Oliver and Lord Templeman each provided a doctrinal analysis of the provisions of the 1925 legislation that accorded with their view of the policy that the legislation was intended to achieve. The decision did not come as a surprise to commentators, but that is not to say that it was necessarily welcomed. In respect of both their interpretation of the provisions of the legislation and of its policy the House of Lords had made a clear choice. As regards the doctrinal analysis, Gardner did not doubt that the decision was correct, but acknowledged the practical result—that the ability to stay in the home depends on whether there is one or two trustees—'may well look rather far-fetched'.[40] He noted that the requirement of two trustees for overreaching to take place was directed at minimising the risk of embezzlement of the funds and has 'no sensible role in the resolution of the conflict between the competing interests'.[41] But the analysis adopted by the House of Lords was not inevitable. Smith explained that 'there is no easy right or wrong answer' to the question whether overreaching took precedence over section 14 of the LPA 1925.[42] The House of Lords' view that the legislation required no limits to be placed on overreaching 'is not a necessary deduction from the wording of the legislation'.[43]

As regards the policy of the 1925 legislation, the House of Lords is undoubtedly correct that there was an intention to keep trusts behind the curtain and confine the investigation of title to the legal estate. However, its wholehearted endorsement of this policy in according total precedence

---

[39] Ibid, 72.
[40] S Gardner, '"Bleak House" Latest—Law Lords Dispel Fog?' (1988) 51 *MLR* 365, 369.
[41] Ibid.
[42] R Smith, 'Trusts for Sale and Registered Land—Orthodoxy Returns' (1987) 103 *LQR* 520, 522.
[43] Ibid.

to the overreaching mechanism reflected a choice that was far from obvious in view of *Boland*. Hence, Swadling highlighted 'the complete change in attitude' between the emphasis on security of ownership in *Boland* and the free marketability of land in *Flegg*.[44] He commented, 'one wonders what has happened to the demands of social justice which justified their Lordships decision in 1980 [in *Boland*] over such a brief passage of time'.[45] The House of Lords' analysis of the statutory provisions is rooted in the effects of the 1925 property legislation and in particular in the change in status of a tenancy in common from a legal estate to a beneficial interest under a trust for sale. The House of Lords appears to take at face value the consequences of the imposition of a trust for sale including the doctrine of conversion. In doing so, Gardner suggests that the decision 'epitomised ... the gap between theory and reality'.[46] By adopting an entirely historical approach, there is a failure on the part of the House of Lords to acknowledge that the priority issue it was asked to resolve, or the practical consequences of that issue of which the court was well aware, could not have been anticipated at the time of the legislation. It had arisen as a result of social changes in home ownership that had taken place since that time.

The regulation of co-ownership trusts and the legislative landscape interpreted by the House of Lords have changed since the decision in *Flegg*. Following recommendations of the Law Commission, the Trusts of Land and Appointment of Trustees Act 1996 (TOLATA 1996) replaced the trust for sale with the trust of land. Trustees of co-owned land are no longer under a duty to sell, but have 'all the powers of an absolute owner' (section 6(1) of TOLATA 1996) including therefore a power to sell and a power not to sell.[47] The absence of a duty to sell removes the basis on which the doctrine of conversion applied and the doctrine is abolished by section 3 of TOLATA 1996. Trustees retain the power to mortgage land (by virtue of section 6(1)) and remain under a duty to consult the beneficiaries in the exercise of their functions (section 11). The purchaser protection provision of section 26(3) of the LPA 1925 is replaced by section 16 of TOLATA 1996, which is confined in its operation to unregistered land. In registered land, purchaser protection is left to the general priority rules which at the time of TOLATA 1996 were contained in the LRA 1925 and are now contained in the Land Registration Act 2002 (LRA 2002). Occupation is a right conferred on certain beneficiaries by section 12, rather than stemming from the incidents of ownership enjoyed by legal tenants in common prior to 1925.

The LRA 2002 has removed the terminology of minor interests and overriding interests from the legislation, while the equivalents to sections 20(1)

---

[44] W Swadling, 'The Conveyancer's Revenge' [1987] *Conv* 451, 452.
[45] Ibid.
[46] S Gardner, 'Trusts for Sale—The Age of Consent' (1988) 104 *LQR* 367, 367.
[47] Law Commission Report No 181, *Transfer of Land: Trusts of Land* (1989) para [10.6].

and 70(1)(g) of the LRA 1925 are now found in section 29 and paragraph 2 of schedule 3 to the LRA 2002. Notwithstanding, the basic pattern of protection remains unchanged: completion by registration of a purchase or mortgage of a registered estate confers priority over pre-existing property rights that are not entered on the register or protected (through schedule 3) despite the absence of registration. The terminology of overriding interests has been removed, but the concept remains. Schedule 3, paragraph 2, like its predecessor in section 70(1)(g), protects the property rights of those in actual occupation. To benefit from this protection, the purchaser or mortgagee must comply with any limitations on the owner's powers (including requirements of consent and consultation) that have been entered on the register in the form of a restriction, or are otherwise imposed by the LRA 2002. But the purchaser or mortgagee can otherwise assume the registered proprietors to be free of limitations on their owner's powers.[48]

Importantly, there is nothing in these changes to cast doubt on the basic proposition provided by *Flegg* that a beneficial interest under a trust that has been overreached by payment to two or more trustees is no longer an interest 'relating to land' which is capable of being enforced against a mortgagee by (now) paragraph 2 of schedule 3 to the LRA 2002. Neither TOLATA 1996 nor the LRA 2002 made substantive changes to the overreaching provisions in sections 2 and 27 of the LPA 1925. TOLATA 1996 made consequential amendments to the provisions by replacing references to the trust for sale with trust of land. However, bearing in mind the extent to which the decision was grounded in the nature of the tenancy in common as a beneficial interest under a trust for sale and the effect of the doctrine of conversion, it is not inconceivable that the changes should give cause to question *Flegg*, or at least provided an opportunity to do so. Further, of greater significance than the statutory changes is the shift in ethos brought about by TOLATA 1996. The development of the trust of land specifically sought to address the artificiality of the imposition of a trust *for sale* in the context of the co-owned home in acknowledgement of the social changes that had taken place since the 1925 legislation.[49] As is considered further below, the legislation reflects the significance of the use of property as a home, or the 'thing as thing'. The Law Commission report that led to TOLATA 1996 contains no discussion of the application of overreaching to the trust of land, but simply an assumption that the doctrine will continue to apply.[50] Instead, the operation of overreaching had become the subject

---

[48] LRA 2002, s 26.
[49] Law Commission Report No 181, *Trusts of Land* (1989) above (n 47) para [3.2].
[50] Ibid, paras [3.6] and [6.1].

of a separate Working Paper[51] and a subsequently published Report.[52] That work led to a recommendation, which has never been implemented, that the interest of a beneficiary (of full age and capacity) in occupation should not be overreached without her or his consent.[53]

The merits of the Law Commission's proposals on overreaching are finely balanced. The proposals are consistent with the policy of TOLATA 1996 of providing a scheme of regulation consonant with the imposition of trusts in the context of the co-owned home. Like TOLATA 1996, the recommendations emphasise the significance of the 'thing as thing'. Further, protection from overreaching complements and reinforces the right to occupy conferred on certain beneficiaries by section 12 of TOLATA 1996. In contrast, however, Harpum suggested that in the context of other recommendations of the Law Commission (including those for TOLATA 1996) its proposals on overreaching were 'fundamentally flawed'[54] and would result in 'the end of the curtain principle in conveyancing'.[55] It is now generally accepted, as Harpum advocated, that the basis of overreaching lies in the trustees' powers.[56] In *Flegg*, Lord Oliver offers implicit support for this view as he refers in his judgment to 'interests which are overreached by the exercise of the trustees' powers'.[57] In view of this, Harpum suggested limiting the powers of mortgage conferred on trustees to prevent second mortgages.[58] If the trustees' powers provide the basis of overreaching, then there is an undeniable logic in solving problems with the operation of the mechanism by adjusting those powers. Notwithstanding, Harpum's suggestion goes too far. By limiting the powers conferred on trustees in all trusts (subject to the possibility of additional powers being conferred)[59] Harpum's approach places barriers in the way of legitimate second mortgages. This is particularly significant as the House of Lords has acknowledged (subsequent to the

---

[51] Law Commission Working Paper No 106, *Transfer of Land—Trusts of Land: Overreaching* (1988).

[52] Law Commission Report No 188, *Transfer of Land—Overreaching: Beneficiaries in Occupation* (1989).

[53] Ibid, para [4.3].

[54] C Harpum, 'Overreaching, Trustees' Powers and the Reform of the 1925 Legislation' (1990) 49 *CLJ* 277, 329.

[55] Ibid, 330.

[56] This view on the basis of overreaching is favoured in the seminal academic discussion of the mechanism by Harpum, above (n 54). For further endorsement see, eg, J McGhee (ed), *Snell's Equity*, 32nd edn (London, Sweet & Maxwell, 2010) para [4.013] and B McFarlane, *The Structure of Property Law* (Oxford, Hart Publishing, 2008) 394–404. An opposing view is expressed by P Sparkes, *A New Land Law*, 2nd edn (Oxford, Hart Publishing, 2003) para [13.51] and N Jackson, 'Overreaching in Registered Land Law' (2006) 69 *MLR* 214.

[57] *City of London Building Society v Flegg* [1988] 1 AC 54, 81 (HL).

[58] Harpum above (n 54) 331. He suggested that the mortgaging powers of trustees should be limited to executing a first mortgage to purchase the land and to raise money for improvement or repair.

[59] Ibid.

time that Harpum was writing) a 'public interest' in ensuring that 'wealth currently tied up in the matrimonial home does not become economically sterile'.[60]

Leaving aside the merits of the Law Commission's recommendations on overreaching, it is unfortunate that the issue was carved out of the general work on trusts of land. Work on the two reports was clearly undertaken in close proximity of time—the final report on overreaching was published six months after the recommendations on trusts of land—but there is surprisingly little cross-referencing between them. In particular, the report on overreaching reflects the law as it stood at the time, not the proposed recommendations on trusts of land. There is no discussion of the basis of the decision in *Flegg* or as to whether the changes proposed by the introduction of the trust of land, including the abolition of the doctrine of conversion, would affect the operation of overreaching.

The question whether the decision in *Flegg* survived intact following TOLATA 1996 arose in *Birmingham Midshires Mortgage Services Ltd v Sabherwal*,[61] but was addressed only by the judge at first instance in the County Court (Mr Recorder Isaacs QC). Although the case went on appeal, the Court of Appeal noted that the judge's conclusion on the effect of TOLATA 1996 was not directly challenged.[62] The judge had identified ten reasons for concluding that *Flegg* was unaffected by the subsequent legislation, only three of which are referred to by the Court of Appeal.[63] The first in fact concerned the timing of the transaction in issue in the case. The transaction pre-dated the enactment of TOLATA 1996 and could not therefore be affected by the statute. Secondly, the judge noted that TOLATA 1996 did not exclude the overreaching provisions of the LPA 1925, but had amended them for consistency with the terminology of TOLATA 1996. However, this merely reflects the Law Commission's own assumption that overreaching continued to apply. Thirdly, the judge considered the abolition of conversion to be irrelevant by reference to a statement by Lord Oliver in *Flegg* in which he accepted (following *Boland*) that a beneficial interest under a trust for sale was an interest in the land for the purposes of section 70(1)(g) (until sale) despite the operation of the doctrine.[64] On a full analysis this statement must, however, be set against the extent to which Lord Oliver relied on the doctrine in understanding the nature of the equitable tenancy in common and the weight this carried in his judgment.

Despite the comments in *Sabherwal*, there is one respect in which TOLATA 1996 may, unintentionally, have impacted on the operation of

---

[60] *Barclays Bank plc v O'Brien* [1994] 1 AC 180, 188 (Lord Browne-Wilkinson) (HL).
[61] *Birmingham Midshires Mortgage Services Ltd v Sabherwal* (2000) 80 P & CR 256 (CA).
[62] Ibid, [22].
[63] Ibid.
[64] *City of London Building Society v Flegg* [1988] 1 AC 54, 90 (HL).

overreaching. This relates to the powers conferred on trustees by the Act and the significance of the trustees' powers to the operation of overreaching. As has been seen above, it is now generally accepted that the basis of overreaching lies in the trustees' powers. If this is correct, then a transfer made *ultra* vires cannot have overreaching effect (for example, a mortgage granted by trustees who have no power to mortgage the land).[65] Trustees who act beyond their powers necessarily commit a breach of trust. In *Flegg*, Lord Templeman noted at the outset of his judgment that the grant of the mortgage by the Maxwell-Browns constituted a breach of trust.[66] However, their breach was committed *intra* vires. As trustees, the Maxwell-Browns had power to mortgage the land, but they had done so for their own purposes rather than for the purposes of the trust. There is no further discussion in the House of Lords of the effect of the breach of trust on the operation of overreaching.[67] Indeed, Lord Oliver makes no reference to the fact that the mortgage that attracted the operation of overreaching was made in breach of trust. The case necessarily stands as authority for the proposition that a transfer made *intra vires* but in breach of trust *can* still have overreaching effect.

As has been seen, section 6(1) of TOLATA 1996 confers on trustees 'all the powers of an absolute owner'. This broad statement is qualified by section 6(6) which provides that the powers 'shall not be exercised in contravention of ... any rule of law or equity' and by section 11, which imposes a duty on the trustees to consult the beneficiaries in the exercise of their powers. On one view, the effect of sections 6(6) and 11 is that the grant of a mortgage in breach of trust, or in the absence of consultation with the beneficiaries, is invariably ultra vires.[68] If this view is correct,[69] then trustees who grant mortgages in the same circumstances as those executed by the Maxwell-Browns in *Flegg* would now be acting ultra vires.

---

[65] Harpum above (n 54) 283–85 and 294–96.

[66] *City of London Building Society v Flegg* [1988] 1 AC 54, 70 (HL).

[67] The effect of the fact a transfer has been made in breach of trust on the operation of overreaching is a matter that has attracted a voluminous literature but little comment by the courts. See, G Ferris and G Battersby, 'The Impact of the Trusts of Land and Appointment of Trustees Act 1996 on Purchasers of Registered Land' [1998] *Conv* 168; M Dixon, 'Overreaching and the Trusts of Land and Appointment of Trustees Act 1996' [2000] *Conv* 267; G Ferris and G Battersby, 'Overreaching and the Trusts of Land and Appointment of Trustees Act 1996: A Reply to Mr Dixon' [2001] *Conv* 221; G Ferris and G Battersby, 'General Principles of Overreaching and the Reforms of the 1925 Legislation' (2002) 118 *LQR* 270; G Ferris and G Battersby, 'The General Principles of Overreaching and the Modern Legislative Reforms 1996–2002' (2003) 119 *LQR* 94; G Ferris, 'Making Sense of Section 26 of the Land Registration Act 2002' in E Cooke (ed), *Modern Studies in Property Law Volume 2* (Oxford, Hart Publishing, 2003); S Pascoe, 'Improving Conveyancing by Redrafting Section 16' [2005] *Conv* 140.

[68] Ferris and Battersby, 'General Principles of Overreaching and the Reforms of the 1925 Legislation', above (n 67) 283–94.

[69] See, to the contrary, Pascoe, above (n 67) and Dixon, above (n 67).

The decision is therefore reversed indirectly, but necessarily, through the scope of the trustees' powers provided by TOLATA 1996. This reversal would, further, be confined to registered land as section 16 of TOLATA 1996 protects purchasers (including mortgagees) of unregistered land against any breach by the trustees of section 6(6) (unless the purchaser has actual notice of the contravention) and section 11. This view of TOLATA 1996 appeared to be implicitly adopted in the first instance decision in *HSBC Bank plc v Dyche*.[70] There, on the basis that the transfer in issue was unauthorised, Judge Purle suggested, 'it is difficult to see how that could as a matter of general principle overreach [the beneficiary's] interest'.[71] Judge Purle's statement is made without acknowledgment that it is inconsistent with the House of Lords' decision in *Flegg* (despite the fact the decision is referred to in the judgment). The absence of discussion of *Flegg* in the Law Commission's work leading to TOLATA 1996 makes the suggestion that the legislation may have inadvertently reversed the decision plausible, but no less remarkable. Such a significant change could not be achieved without a full discussion of the issue.

THE LEGACY OF THE DECISION: HOMES AS WEALTH

The legacy of *Flegg* is that, despite legislative and judicial changes in other aspects relating to the legal regulation of the co-owned home, on a sale or mortgage by two or more trustees the 'use' value of the home—the 'thing as thing' is invisible to the law. As Rudden notes, '[a]n interest capable of being over-reached is one that treats its object not as thing but as wealth'.[72] This effect of overreaching is apparent in explanations of why some equitable interests are capable of being overreached while others are not. The Law Commission acknowledged that the interests exempt from overreaching are those that could not be 'properly represented in terms of money'.[73] In *Sabherwal*, Mrs Sabherwal relied on the developing view of the close relationship between trusts and proprietary estoppel to claim an interest in her home, arising by virtue of substantial financial contributions she had made, through estoppel rather than trust. Legal title was held by her two sons, who had defaulted on a mortgage executed over the home. By relying on estoppel, Mrs Sabherwal hoped to avoid the overreaching consequences of the mortgage as nothing in the terms of sections 2 and 27 of the LPA 1925 indicated that an estoppel interest was subject to overreaching. The

---

[70] *HSBC Bank plc v Dyche* [2009] EWHC 2954 (Ch D). On this point, see N Gravells, 'HSBC Bank plc v Dyche: Getting Your Priorities Right' [2010] *Conv* 169.

[71] *HSBC Bank plc v Dyche* [2009] EWHC 2954, [37].

[72] Rudden, above (n 4) 155.

[73] Law Commission Working Paper No 106, *Overreaching* (1988) above (n 51) para [2.12], referring to *Wolstenholme and Cherry's Conveyancing Statutes*, above (n 6) 55.

attempt to avoid the consequences of *Flegg* in this way failed. The Court of Appeal (endorsing an explanation in Megarry and Wade) considered that the 'essential difference' in understanding the scope of overreaching is that between 'family' and 'commercial' interests.[74] Commercial interests, such as equitable easements and rights of entry, fall outside the scope of over-reaching because they 'cannot sensibly shift from the land affected by it to the proceeds of sale'.[75] In the Court of Appeal's view, rather than providing a means of circumventing *Flegg*, the close link between estoppel and trusts demonstrated that overreaching applied equally to both. Robert Walker LJ (as he then was) explained, '[i]n this type of family situation, the concepts of trust and equitable estoppel are almost interchangeable, and both are affected in the same way by the statutory mechanism of overreaching'.[76] The difficulty with the rationales for the scope of overreaching offered by the Law Commission and in *Sabherwal* is the same: they rely on an assumption that 'family' interests can be represented by money *because* of their status as such. By doing so, they focus exclusively on the investment value of the home—the 'thing as wealth'.

From one perspective, the focus on the investment value of the home in *Flegg* provides—or restores after *Boland*—the orthodoxy. Following his discussion of *Bull v Bull*, which had been relied on by the Court of Appeal in *Flegg*, Lord Oliver drew a sharp distinction between the interest of the tenant in common against the other beneficiaries or trustees on the one hand and his rights against purchasers on the other.[77] This distinction looms large in the case law. In relation to priority disputes between beneficiaries and creditors, *Flegg* stands as one of a series of cases through which *Boland* has been sufficiently circumvented as to be confined to its facts (a mortgage granted other than for the acquisition of the property by a sole trustee and without the knowledge or consent of a beneficiary).[78] Similarly, in relation to applications for sale by creditors the case law has become notorious for the emphasis that the courts have almost invariably placed on protecting the quantifiable and financial interests of creditors.[79]

Viewed in the light of other developments, however, the focus on the investment value of the home through the application of overreaching appears an increasingly outdated approach. It stands in contrast to three

---

[74] *Birmingham Midshires Mortgage Services Ltd v Sabherwal* (2000) 80 P & CR 256, [28].
[75] Ibid.
[76] Ibid, [31]. More recently Lord Walker has cast doubt on the relationship between constructive trusts and estoppel: see *Stack v Dowden* [2007] UKHL 17; [2007] 2 AC 432, [37].
[77] *City of London Building Society v Flegg* [1988] 1 AC 54, 81.
[78] In addition to the cases referred to above (n 10) see especially *Abbey National Building Society v Cann* [1991] 1 AC 56 (HL).
[79] See especially L Fox, *Conceptualising Home: Theories, Laws and Policies* (Oxford, Hart Publishing, 2007) and N Hopkins, 'Regulating Trusts of the Home: Private Law and Social Policy' (2009) 125 *LQR* 310.

key developments. The first is the change in ethos towards the regulation of trusts of land brought about by TOLATA 1996. As has been seen, the introduction of TOLATA 1996 was a response to the artificiality of regulating co-ownership through a trust for sale in light of social changes that had resulted in the spread of home ownership and co-ownership. While providing a single scheme for the regulation of all trusts which consist of or include land, in key respects TOLATA 1996 acknowledges the 'use' value of property and recognises that different factors may need to be considered where the property is a home. The 'use' value is reflected most clearly in the express conferral on certain beneficiaries of a right to occupy under section 12 of the Act. More generally, however, the legislation is balanced in favour of 'use' over 'investment'. While, as has been seen, trustees have a power to sell and a power not to sell, the legislation is weighted against sale. Hence, a sale can be prevented by the settlor of an express trust removing the power of sale,[80] but a sale cannot be compelled. Even where (in an express trust) trustees are placed under a duty to sell, a power to postpone is implied and the trustees are exempt from liability for breach of trust by failing to exercise the duty.[81] To this extent, TOLATA 1996 appears as the antithesis of free marketability of land. Specific considerations that arise where a property is a home are found in section 15, which provides a non-exhaustive list of factors for the court to take into account in determining applications brought under section 14, and in section 335A of the Insolvency Act 1986, inserted into that Act by TOLATA 1996, which governs applications for the sale of land made by trustees in bankruptcy. Section 15(1)(c) directs the court to take into account the welfare of minors who occupy, or might reasonably be expected to occupy, the property as their home. Section 335A(2)(b) (as amended) provides specific factors for the court to consider where the property is or has been the home of the bankrupt or their (current or former) spouse or civil partner.

The second development is the recognition by the courts that when determining ownership of property, specific considerations arise when dealing with the home. In *Stack v Dowden*, Baroness Hale explained that '[i]n law "context is everything" and the domestic context is very different from the commercial world'.[82] Subsequent cases suggested a willingness to distinguish the domestic and commercial contexts according to the functional 'use' of property as a home.[83] A broad distinction between domestic and commercial contexts is problematic in practice.[84] The distinction has been

---

[80] TOLATA, s 8(1).

[81] TOLATA, s 4(1).

[82] *Stack v Dowden* [2007] UKHL 17; [2007] 1 AC 432, [69].

[83] *Adekunle v Ritchie*, Leeds County Court, judgment (21 August 2007); *Lasker v Lasker* [2008] EWCA Civ 347; [2008] 2 P & CR 14.

[84] N Hopkins, 'The Relevance of Context in Property Law: A Case for Judicial Restraint?' (2011) 31 *Legal Studies* 175.

carried over by the House of Lords to proprietary estoppel,[85] but is absent from the Supreme Court judgment in *Jones v Kernott*[86] in which the Court had the opportunity to revisit *Stack v Dowden*. However, the Supreme Court confirmed that different treatment will be afforded to ownership of the home by removing the presumption of resulting trust in respect of 'the purchase of a house or flat in joint names for joint occupation by a married or unmarried couple, where both are responsible for any mortgage'.[87] In light of the distinction drawn by Lord Oliver in *Flegg* between the rights of co-owners between themselves and their trustees on the one hand, and third parties on the other, it is notable that the courts' readiness to treat the home differently in determining ownership in *Stack* and *Kernott* arose in actions between the co-owners. The decisions in those cases may necessarily impact on third parties by affecting the share against which a debt for which one co-owner is accountable is secured. However, the courts appear emboldened where the interests of third parties are not directly in issue.

The third development is the impact of the Human Rights Act 1998 (HRA 1998). Leaving aside the contentious argument relating to changes in the trustees' powers discussed above, a challenge based on the European Convention on Human Rights (ECHR) may now present the most likely means of circumventing *Flegg*. The success of such a challenge, however, remains a matter of conjecture. The compatibility of overreaching with the HRA 1998 has been raised in two cases, but the substantive merit of the claim has not been addressed. In the Court of Appeal in *Sabherwal* an attempt to distinguish *Flegg* was made on the basis that section 2 of the LPA 1925 should be interpreted in a manner compatible with Article 8 of the ECHR (right to respect for the home). The claim was rejected on the basis that the HRA 1998 was not yet in force and the mortgagee was not a public authority.[88] Subsequently, in *National Westminster Bank plc v Malhan*,[89] the argument was advanced that the distinction between one and two trustee cases arising from the combined effect of *Boland* and *Flegg* gives rise to discrimination under Article 14 in conjunction with Article 8 and Article 1 of Protocol 1 (A1P1) (right to peaceful enjoyment of possessions). Counsel had conceded that the claim to overreaching could not be challenged under Article 8 or A1P1 alone. On the facts, Mrs Malhan's claim to a beneficial interest failed and so the operation of overreaching did not arise. In an obiter discussion, the Vice-Chancellor noted that the claim would fail on the facts as the charge in question had been granted prior

---

[85] *Yeoman's Row Management Ltd v Cobbe* [2008] UKHL 55; [2008] 1 WLR 1752; *Thorner v Major* [2009] UKHL 18; [2009] 1 WLR 776.

[86] *Jones v Kernott* [2011] UKSC 17; [2012] 1 AC 776.

[87] Ibid, [25] (Lord Walker and Baroness Hale).

[88] *Birmingham Midshires Mortgage Services Ltd v Sabherwal* (2000) 80 P & CR 256, [34].

[89] *National Westminster Bank plc v Malhan* [2004] EWHC 847.

to the HRA 1998 coming into force.[90] In any event, the Vice-Chancellor appeared disposed towards arguments advanced on behalf of the bank which he considered to carry 'much force'.[91] Despite this, it is far from clear that the difference in treatment between one and two trustee trusts arising from *Boland* and *Flegg* can be justified. As has been seen above, Gardner has highlighted that the practical result of the decisions that the ability of the beneficiary to stay in the home is dependent on the number of trustees is 'far-fetched' and was not the purpose of requiring a minimum of two trustees for overreaching to take place.

In light of subsequent developments, the loss of the use value of the home through overreaching may be challenged under either Article 8 or A1P1. The concession of counsel to the contrary in *Malhan* appears premature. Further, even though the action will necessarily involve private parties this is no barrier to a claim as the statutory framework within which overreaching operates (discussed in *Flegg* and since amended) attracts the requirement in section 3 of the HRA 1998 for the courts to interpret legislation in a manner compatible with the ECHR '[s]o far as it is possible to do so'. This appears particularly pertinent in light of Smith's suggestion in response to Flegg that the legislation gives no right or wrong answer to the relationship between overreaching and a claim to an overriding interest.[92] If Article 8 or A1P1 is engaged, the question arises whether the interference can be justified by legitimate qualifications within the State's margin of appreciation. Any interference must be proportionate in both its aim and its impact on the individual.

The use value of the home is the focus of protection under Article 8. 'Home' has an autonomous meaning in the case law of the European Court of Human Rights (ECtHR) as a place of residence with which the individual has 'sufficient and continuing links'.[93] There is thus some resonance between the concept of home in Article 8 and the use of occupation as a trigger for protection in the scheme of land registration. Any affinity between Article 8 of the ECHR and paragraph 2 of schedule 3 to the LRA 2002 is, however, limited. The concept of home under Article 8 is not dependent on, or limited by, property rights,[94] which are the pre-requisite of protection under the LRA 2002. Possession proceedings brought against a beneficiary in occupation by a mortgagee claiming the benefit of overreaching will engage Article 8 as the most extreme interference with the right to respect for the occupier's home. A1P1 has been interpreted by the ECtHR as containing a general

---

[90] Ibid, [51].
[91] Ibid, [53].
[92] See Smith, above (n 42).
[93] *Gillow v United Kingdom* (1986) 11 EHRR 335.
[94] A Buyse, 'Strings Attached: The Concept of Home in the Case Law of the ECHR' [2006] *European Human Rights Law Review* 294.

principle of peaceful enjoyment of property and specific rules concerning the deprivation of 'possessions' and controls on the use of property. As is acknowledged in *Flegg*, the effect of overreaching is to 'shift' the beneficial interests from the land to the proceeds of sale. There is therefore no deprivation of the beneficial interest, but the effect is to deprive the beneficiary of the right to occupy that is now conferred by section 12 of TOLATA 1996. For that to engage A1P1 would require the right to occupy to constitute the relevant 'possessions' within the Article. Notwithstanding, in any event, shifting the beneficial interest into the proceeds of sale affects the peaceful enjoyment of property by controlling the identity of the property in which the beneficial interest vests and against which the beneficiary's rights can be asserted. This suggestion is, however, subject to an argument that the operation of overreaching is an inherent limitation on the beneficiary's interest, the operation of which does not therefore constitute an interference with peaceful enjoyment of the property.[95]

If either (or both) of Article 8 and A1P1 are engaged, justification for the interference may lie in the economic well-being of the country through maintaining a well-balanced property and lending market and/ or the protection of the security rights of mortgagees. Even if accepted as legitimate, the principal difficulty with the operation of overreaching for the purposes of Article 8 and A1P1 is that there is no opportunity for the proportionality of the interference with the justification to be assessed. In a different context, through *Manchester City Council v Pinnock*[96] and *Hounslow LBC v Powell*,[97] the Supreme Court has held that local authority tenants at risk of losing their homes through mandatory procession proceedings, in which the domestic legislation gives no discretion to the court whether to order possession, 'should in principle have the right to raise the question of the proportionality of the measure, and to have it determined by an independent tribunal in the light of Article 8'.[98] Section 3 of the HRA 1998 has been used in these cases to interpret the legislation as requiring compatibility with Article 8. Logically, the same approach should be taken in respect of A1P1 so that the proportionality of an interference with peaceful enjoyment of possessions is tested before an independent tribunal. Possession proceedings against a beneficiary following overreaching are different in their nature than those at issue in *Pinnock* and *Powell*. A claim to possession by the mortgagee is a consequence of (and dependent on) overreaching taking place. The operation of overreaching is the result

---

[95] See, eg, *Aston Cantlow and Wilmcote with Billesley Parochial Church Council v Wallbank* [2004] AC 546 (HL). On this point in relation to overreaching, see A Goymour, 'Proprietary Claims and Human Rights—A "Reservoir of Entitlement"?' (2006) 65 *CLJ* 696, 714–15.

[96] *Manchester City Council v Pinnock* [2011] UKSC 6; [2011] 2 AC 104.

[97] *Hounslow LBC v Powell* [2011] UKSC 8; [2011] 2 AC 186.

[98] *Pinnock* [2011] 2 AC 104, [45] (Lord Neuberger MR).

of the trustees' exercise of the powers conferred on them under TOLATA 1996. However, a comparison may be drawn with arguments based on Article 8 raised in the context of applications for sale of trust land by creditors under TOLATA 1996 and trustees in bankruptcy under the Insolvency Act 1986. In that context, the courts have accepted that where there is discretion whether to order sale, the legislation is compatible with Article 8 as the court is able to consider the proportionality of the application.[99] In contrast, the courts have doubted the compatibility of section 335A of the Insolvency Act 1986 with Article 8 as following a one-year adjustment period that section directs that sale should be ordered unless there are 'exceptional circumstances'.[100] As a result, in the absence of a finding of such circumstances, there is no discretion through which the proportionality of sale with Article 8 can be considered. The courts' response has been to suggest a broadening of the definition of exceptional circumstances as a means of conferring discretion.[101] Against the background of *Pinnock* and *Powell* on the one hand, and case law on applications for sale by creditors and trustees in bankruptcy on the other, there are grounds for considering that the automatic loss of the home by overreaching raises a question of compatibility with Article 8.

CONCLUSION

In *City of London Building Society v Flegg*, the House of Lords was required to consider the relationship between two key concepts contained in the 1925 legislation: the overreaching mechanism and overriding interests. The seeds of the case were planted in the legislation, but germinated by social changes and patterns of co-ownership of the home. Balancing the competing interests of beneficiaries in occupation and mortgage lenders has become a practically and socially important function of land law in which the issues are distilled into a paradigm of questions of acquisition and priority. In *Flegg*, the House of Lords had a choice as to the balance to be drawn between overreaching and overriding interests. The choice made by the House of Lords to give precedence to overreaching provides, or restores to orthodoxy after *Boland*, an approach in favour of claims by mortgagees. The decision sees the home exclusively as wealth, but has survived despite legislative and judicial developments that have emphasised the value of the 'thing as thing' or as the home as a home.

---

[99] *National Westminster Bank plc v Rushmer* [2010] EWHC 554 (Ch), [2010] 2 FLR 362 (in relation to TOLATA 1996) and *Nicholls v Lan* [2006] EWHC 1255 (Ch), [2007] 1 FLR 744 (in relation to the Insolvency Act 1986).
[100] *Barca v Mears* [2004] EWHC 2170 (Ch), [2005] 2 FLR 1.
[101] Ibid.

10

Stack v Dowden *(2007)*; Jones v Kernott *(2011)*

Finding a Home for 'Family Property'

ANDREW HAYWARD

INTRODUCTION

O N 9 NOVEMBER 2011, the Supreme Court handed down their decision in *Jones v Kernott*.[1] The judgment provided a structured methodology to be applied to joint legal title disputes over the family home and built upon the framework established in the earlier House of Lords' decision in *Stack v Dowden* decided in April 2007.[2] Initially, both were heralded as 'landmark' decisions and, as a result, they caught the attention of the general public.[3] Following *Stack v Dowden*, Alex Ralton noted 'hysteria in the popular press' alongside extensive coverage by the media.[4] Indeed, Patricia Jones, one of the litigants in *Jones v Kernott* even appeared on BBC Breakfast alongside Marilyn Stowe, a well-known family law practitioner, to discuss the implications of the Supreme Court's ruling for separating couples.[5]

Within the legal community, the initial reaction to both decisions was slightly more cautious. However, after the dust had settled and the sensationalism in the media had abated, both decisions generated relatively

---

[1] *Jones v Kernott* [2011] UKSC 53, [2012] AC 776.

[2] *Stack v Dowden* [2007] UKHL 17, [2007] 2 AC 432.

[3] *Stack v Dowden* was viewed as 'landmark' by L Brady, 'Cohabitees warned over property rights' *The Guardian* (London, 26 April 2007). Similarly, *Jones v Kernott* was referred to as 'landmark' by L Reed, 'Cohabitees' property rights: still as clear as mud' *The Guardian* (London, 10 November 2011).

[4] A Ralton, 'Establishing a Beneficial Share: *Rosset* Revisited' [2008] 38 *Family Law* 424, 424.

[5] See: www.marilynstowe.co.uk/2011/11/10/kernott-v-jones-on-bbc-breakfast/.

extensive criticism.[6] A common perspective taken by commentators recognised the significance of both decisions but then queried the judicial methodology used and their practical implications. For example, Graham Battersby noted that *Stack v Dowden* was a 'landmark decision', as it was the first case in this area to reach the House of Lords since *Lloyds Bank plc v Rosset* decided in 1991,[7] yet ultimately viewed the reasoning of the majority as creating 'major causes for concern'.[8] This viewpoint was developed by other academics[9] but Martin Dixon went further to lament that there was 'little that can be worse' than what *Stack v Dowden* had created.[10] So, perhaps supporting the viewpoint that fame brings notoriety, the academic reception to both decisions has been generally critical. This reaction was even acknowledged by Lord Walker and Baroness Hale in their joint opinion in *Jones v Kernott*, where they noted that *Stack v Dowden* had been met with academic comment ranging from 'qualified enthusiasm' to 'almost unqualified disapprobation'.[11]

This chapter reflects on whether *Stack v Dowden* and *Jones v Kernott* deserve to be labelled landmarks in the law. After analysing the two decisions, it advances the argument that the key sticking point for land lawyers was the seemingly discretionary nature of the judicial exercise instigated by the recognition of 'context' in *Stack v Dowden* and the sanctioning of 'fairness' in *Jones v Kernott*. Immediately after both decisions were decided, comparisons to family law adjudication (an area often typified by the use of judicial discretion) were plentiful with newspaper headlines ranging from 'Unmarried couples come closer to winning legal divorce rights'[12] to 'Unmarried couples granted new legal protection by courts'.[13] While newspapers are understandably sensationalist, it was telling that similar comparisons were made in the academic commentary. Naturally

---

[6] For positive comment regarding *Stack v Dowden*, see T Etherton, 'Constructive Trusts: A New Model for Equity and Unjust Enrichment' (2008) 67 *CLJ* 265 and M Harding, 'Defending *Stack v Dowden*' [2009] *Conv* 309.

[7] *Lloyds Bank plc v Rosset* [1990] UKHL 14, [1991] 1 AC 107.

[8] G Battersby, 'Ownership of the Family Home: *Stack v Dowden* in the House of Lords' (2008) 20 *Child and Family Law Quarterly* 255, 255.

[9] See, eg, P Sparkes, 'How Beneficial Interests Stack Up' [2011] *Conv* 156 and W Swadling, 'The Common Intention Constructive Trust in the House of Lords: An Opportunity Missed' (2007) 123 *LQR* 511.

[10] M Dixon, 'The Never-Ending Story—Co-ownership after *Stack v Dowden*' [2007] *Conv* 456, 456.

[11] *Jones v Kernott* [2011] UKSC 53, [2012] AC 776, [2].

[12] F Gibb, 'Unmarried couples come closer to winning legal divorce rights' *The Times* (London, 26 April 2007). See also F Gibb, 'Unmarried couples win rights to half of shared properties' *The Times* (London, 25 April 2007).

[13] T Ross, 'Unmarried couples granted new legal protection by courts' *The Telegraph* (London, 9 November 2011).

legal disciplines influence the conceptualisation of family property,[14] but this chapter advances the argument that these comparisons are symptomatic of a broader issue; namely, that family property is still struggling to find a home within the framework of land law in England and Wales.[15] Cumulatively, it is the indeterminate status of family property that results in commentators questioning whether family property actually belongs within land law.[16]

However, after drawing on the theoretical literature on judicial discretion, this chapter argues that land law can accommodate the discretionary judicial methodology used in *Stack v Dowden* and *Jones v Kernott*. While it is indisputable that 'discretionary resolution is par excellence the technique of family law', judicial discretion is not alien to land law.[17] Alongside express grants of discretion to the judiciary by Parliament, discretion is implicitly embedded within any type of judicial analysis that relies on the interpretation of facts and thus there is obvious scope for its application in the often fact-heavy cases in this area. Furthermore, the movement towards a more discretionary, functionalist and pragmatic approach is hardly surprising seeing as 'common intention', which underpins the prevailing approach, provides a problematic foundation for equitable intervention in this area. If these aspects were recognised, both *Stack v Dowden* and *Jones v Kernott* can be viewed as modernising landmark authorities that rightfully deserve a home within land law.

THE LAW BEFORE *STACK v DOWDEN*

Before analysing *Stack v Dowden* and *Jones v Kernott*, a key preliminary observation must be made. Both decisions were disputes between legal co-owners. The well-known methods of acquiring an interest in the home, as delineated by the House of Lords' decision in *Lloyds Bank v Rosset*, were not relevant as the presence of legal co-ownership resulted in the prima facie

---

[14] See, eg, WT Murphy and H Clarke, *The Family Home* (London, Sweet & Maxwell, 1983) v, where the authors note that the family home is 'best understood as a zone of intersection between property law and family law'; R Probert, 'Family Law and Property Law: Competing Spheres in the Regulation of the Family Home' in A Hudson, *New Perspectives on Property Law, Human Rights and the Home* (UK, Routledge Cavendish, 2003); and AJ Cloherty and DM Fox, 'Proving a Trust of a Shared Home' (2007) 66 *CLJ* 517, 517–18, where the authors note that the trust engaged when couples purchase property 'sits uneasily between different legal regimes and their competing rationales'.

[15] See J Dewar, *Law and the Family*, 2nd edn (London, Butterworths, 1992) 183.

[16] See, eg, M Dixon, 'Editor's Notebook: The Still Not Ended, Never-Ending Story' [2012] *Conv* 83, 86, where the author remarks 'call it family law, call it an exercise of the court's inherent equitable jurisdiction, but, maybe, do not call it property law'.

[17] S Gardner, 'The Element of Discretion' in P Birks, *The Frontiers of Liability* (Oxford, OUP, 1994) 186, 199.

sharing of beneficial ownership.[18] Although *Stack v Dowden* and *Jones v Kernott* undoubtedly contributed to the discourse in sole legal title disputes, particularly in relation to whether they update the 'concrete "bright-line" formulae' of *Lloyds Bank v Rosset*,[19] these statements were strictly obiter and this chapter, therefore, will focus solely on joint legal title disputes.[20]

Prior to *Stack v Dowden* the legal framework applicable to the purchase of property in joint names was relatively straightforward. As Lord Upjohn remarked in *Pettitt v Pettitt*, a property dispute between spouses, a conveyance of property into joint names at law 'operates to convey the beneficial interest to the spouses jointly, ie with benefit of survivorship'.[21] However, despite equity following the law, Lord Upjohn noted that the presence of the beneficial joint tenancy was seldom 'determinative' as equal sharing can be easily dislodged in favour of unequal sharing through a tenancy in common.[22] The ease with which a beneficial joint tenancy could be displaced was underlined in *Bernard v Josephs*, where Griffiths LJ stated that it was the default option but applied only in the 'somewhat unlikely event' that no indication as to intention can be found.[23] Within the context of the family home and in the absence of an express contrary declaration of trust, unequal contributions to the purchase of land represent the primary method of displacing a beneficial joint tenancy.[24] It was this relationship between the strength of the starting point and the 'solid tug of money' that provided the context to the House of Lords' decision in *Stack v Dowden*.[25]

STACK *v* DOWDEN

The Factual Background

The parties formed a relationship in 1975 when Miss Dehra Dowden was 17 and Mr Barry Stack was 19. In 1983, a property, previously owned by an acquaintance of Miss Dowden called 'Uncle Sidney', was purchased by Miss Dowden and conveyed into her sole name. For the trial judge, this

---

[18] The 'express' and 'inferred' common intention acquisition routes were developed out of the earlier House of Lords' decision in *Gissing v Gissing* [1971] AC 886.

[19] S Gardner, 'A Woman's Work ...' (1991) 54 *MLR* 126, 128.

[20] On the issue of whether these decisions affect the acquisition of an interest, see N Piska, 'A Common Intention or a Rare Bird? Proprietary Interests, Personal Claims and Services Rendered by Lovers Post-Acquisition' (2009) 21 *Child and Family Law Quarterly* 104.

[21] *Pettitt v Pettitt* [1970] AC 777, 814 (HL).

[22] Ibid. See also *McKenzie v McKenzie* [2003] 2 P & CR D15 (Ch).

[23] *Bernard v Josephs* [1982] Ch 391, 402 (CA).

[24] Other factors that rebut a beneficial joint tenancy include words or conduct indicating severance or acquisition of property for business purposes.

[25] *Hofman v Hofman* (1965) NZLR 795, 800 (Woodhouse J).

point in time indicated the presence of 'a partnership as man and mistress'.[26] This property was acquired using a mortgage loan (amounting to £22,000) taken out in Miss Dowden's name which she repaid alongside assuming sole responsibility for the household bills. In conjunction, a down payment of £8000 was provided from a bank account in Miss Dowden's name. Four children were born and, after each maternity leave, Miss Dowden returned to work as an electrical engineer, subsequently becoming 'the most highly qualified electrical engineer in the London area'.[27]

Following extensive renovations to the property made by both parties, it was subsequently sold at a substantial profit in 1993. A new property was purchased for £190,000 but, unlike the first, it was taken out in joint names, albeit without an express declaration of trust.[28] Their contributions to the acquisition of the jointly owned property were unequal. Miss Dowden contributed approximately £129,000 (using the proceeds of sale of the first property) and alongside Mr Stack, assumed liability under a mortgage amounting to approximately £65,000. Two endowment policies were taken out, one in joint names, the other in Miss Dowden's sole name. The mortgage interest and joint endowment policy premiums were paid by Mr Stack. Ultimately, this mortgage was repaid with Mr Stack contributing £27,000 and Miss Dowden contributing £38,435. Upkeep costs, such as utilities bills were largely met by Miss Dowden. Both made investments, but kept separate banks accounts.

Following the breakdown of their relationship in 2002, Mr Stack provided undertakings to keep away from the property after proceedings under Part IV of the Family Law Act 1996 were issued. In 2004, Mr Stack obtained an order for sale and equal division of the proceeds of the property, coupled with equal division of the joint endowment policy. Miss Dowden appealed and, in 2005, the Court of Appeal ordered that the proceeds of sale be divided in a ratio of 65:35 in her favour.[29] The basis was that this apportionment represented a 'fair' share following the principles laid down by the Court of Appeal in *Oxley v Hiscock*.[30]

---

[26] *Stack v Dowden* [2007] UKHL 17, [2007] 2 AC 432, [73] (Baroness Hale).

[27] Ibid, [74].

[28] It did contain a declaration that the survivor could give good receipt for capital moneys arising from a disposition.

[29] For incisive analysis, see J Mee, 'Joint Ownership, Subjective Intention and the Common Intention Constructive Trust' [2007] *Conv* 14.

[30] *Oxley v Hiscock* [2004] EWCA Civ 546, [2005] Fam 211. Space precludes a detailed analysis of this authority; but see G Battersby, '*Oxley v Hiscock* in the Court of Appeal: The Search for Principle Continues' (2005) 17 *Child and Family Law Quarterly* 259.

The Judgment in the House of Lords

The House of Lords handed down their decision on 25 April 2007.[31] The beneficial ownership was to be divided 65:35 in Miss Dowden's favour. The majority—namely Baroness Hale, Lord Walker, Lord Hope and Lord Hoffman—reached this outcome, first, by creating a strong presumption of beneficial joint tenancy in cases of joint legal ownership and, secondly, by rebutting this presumption in favour of an unequal distribution of the beneficial ownership. Thus, within the 'domestic'[32] or 'consumer' context,[33] 'equity follows the law' and joint legal ownership prima facie generates joint beneficial ownership.[34] Departure from equality is permitted in 'exceptional'[35] or 'unusual'[36] cases and would be achieved after a survey of the whole course of conduct between the parties which would, in turn, assist the court's divination of the parties' 'actual, inferred or imputed' intentions in relation to the property.[37] For the majority, this entire process occurred under the rubric of the common intention constructive trust and, as 'many more factors than financial contributions may be relevant to divining the parties' true intentions', unequal financial contributions alone were not enough to rebut the presumption of beneficial joint tenancy.[38] Indeed, to assist in the divination of the parties' intentions, the Court provided what have now been termed, the 'paragraph 69 factors', which include 'the purpose for which the home was acquired', 'the nature of the parties' relationship' and the parties' 'individual characters and personalities'.[39] When applied to the facts of the dispute, this was not a 'real domestic partnership' which would support maintaining equal sharing.[40] Rather, Miss Dowden 'contributed far more to the acquisition' of the property,[41] there was no pooling of assets, 'even notionally, for the common good'[42] and there were 'strictly separate' savings and investments.[43] As Baroness Hale concluded,

---

[31] *Stack v Dowden* has been comprehensively analysed: see Swadling, above (n 9); N Piska, 'Intention, Fairness and the Presumption of Resulting Trust after *Stack v Dowden*' (2008) 71 *MLR* 114 and R George, '*Stack v Dowden*—Do As We Say, Not as we Do?' (2008) 30 *Journal of Social Welfare and Family Law* 49.

[32] *Stack v Dowden* [2007] UKHL 17, [2007] 2 AC 432, [58], [60] (Baroness Hale).

[33] Ibid, [52], [54], [58].

[34] Ibid, [56].

[35] Ibid, [33] (Lord Walker).

[36] Ibid, [68]–[69], [92] (Baroness Hale).

[37] Ibid, [60].

[38] Ibid, [69].

[39] Ibid.

[40] Ibid, [87].

[41] Ibid.

[42] Ibid, [90].

[43] Ibid.

this was 'strongly indicative that they did not intend their shares, even in the property which was put into both their names, to be equal'.[44]

Lord Neuberger, in the minority, rejected the creation of a presumption of beneficial joint tenancy within the domestic context and believed that 'the same principles should apply to assess the apportionment of the beneficial interest as between legal co-owners, whether in a sexual, platonic, familial, amicable or commercial relationship'.[45] However, he reached exactly the same division of the beneficial ownership, in a somewhat swifter manner, through applying the presumption of resulting trust. Advocating the application of principles of contract, land and equity that had been 'established and applied over hundreds of years',[46] he rejected the new approach of the majority and adopted the 'resulting trust solution'.[47] Thus, for Lord Neuberger, where property is acquired in joint names and the only information available is financial contribution, the property will be held in the same proportions as the contributions to the purchase price. If additional evidence exists enabling the pinpointing or inference of an intention based on party conduct, the resulting trust can be 'rebutted and replaced, or (conceivably) supplemented, by a constructive trust'.[48] When these principles were applied to the dispute, Lord Neuberger stated that there was 'simply no evidence' to justify departing from the 65:35 allocation of the property, as determined by the presumption of resulting trust.[49]

THE SIGNIFICANCE OF *STACK v DOWDEN*: LAND LAW IN CONTEXT?

Stack v Dowden is undoubtedly a significant decision. It was the first case to reach the House of Lords that concerned a cohabiting relationship as earlier authorities like *Pettitt v Pettitt, Gissing v Gissing* and *Lloyds Bank v Rosset* all concerned property disputes between married couples.[50] Moreover, it was the first opportunity for the House of Lords to consider a joint legal title dispute, thereby bypassing the normal discussion of acquisition routes. Yet, as Rebecca Probert has noted, the practical impact of this decision will be slightly limited for a variety of reasons.[51] Statistically, the

---

[44] Ibid, [92].
[45] Ibid, [107] (Lord Neuberger).
[46] Ibid, [101].
[47] Ibid, [110].
[48] Ibid, [124].
[49] Ibid, [137].
[50] While the principles apply irrespective of whether the parties are married or cohabiting, the types of inferences to be drawn from party conduct will vary; see *Bernard v Josephs* [1982] Ch 391, 402 (Griffiths LJ).
[51] R Probert, 'Cohabitants and Joint Ownership: The Implications of *Stack v Dowden*' [2007] *Family Law* 924 and R Probert, 'Equality in the Family Home' (2007) 15 *Feminist Legal Studies* 341.

decision is unlikely to have a direct impact on the majority of cohabiting couples as, in comparison with married couples, cohabitants are less likely to be owner-occupiers. Furthermore, even if cohabitants decide to become owner-occupiers, they are less likely to have joint legal ownership. However, these observations do not diminish the significance of the decision in relation to the conceptualisation of family property, the search for common intention and the trajectory of trusts of the family home development.

As will be further explored below, key issues raised by *Stack v Dowden* included the strength of the presumption of beneficial joint tenancy and its relationship with established principles of co-ownership[52] alongside the sanctioning of what Lord Neuberger, extrajudicially, termed the 'heretical doctrine' of imputed intentions.[53] With the former, it was questioned by academics why a joint name purchase by cohabitants resulted in a strong presumption of beneficial joint tenancy with survivorship. For the latter, there was fear of the courts artificially ascribing to parties' intentions as to beneficial ownership that they did not possess.[54] In light of these issues, it was understandable why land lawyers felt that family property was left in a precarious position following *Stack v Dowden*.

More pertinent for this chapter is the precise location of family property within legal taxonomy in light of *Stack v Dowden*. In one sense, it is arguable that the area continued to be conceptualised as belonging to the realm of land law and this would correlate with conventional classifications of land law that view questions of property ownership without undue weight attached to specific 'contexts'.[55] Even Baroness Hale, who was instrumental in the majority judgment in *Stack v Dowden*, stated that it was for the 'law of property' to refashion a response to property division following relationship breakdown.[56]

However, it could be argued that a different process had commenced. A key feature of *Stack v Dowden* was 'context', so much so that Baroness Hale boldly stated that 'in law, context is everything'.[57] There was already an appreciation of context in family property disputes and, as John Dewar had previously identified, trusts of the family home operated within a specific

---

[52] See, eg, A Briggs, 'Co-ownership and an Equitable Non-sequitur' (2012) 128 *LQR* 183.

[53] Lord Neuberger 'The Conspirators, The Tax Man, The Bill of Rights and a Bit about The Lovers' (Chancery Bar Association Annual Lecture, 10 March 2008) para [19].

[54] For a cautious view on imputation, see *Fowler v Barron* [2008] EWCA Civ 377, [2008] 2 FLR 831, [47] (Arden LJ); and see A Hayward, 'Family Values in the Home: *Fowler v Barron*' (2009) 21 *Child and Family Law Quarterly* 242.

[55] See N Hopkins, 'The Relevance of Context in Property Law: A Case for Judicial Restraint?' (2011) 31 *Legal Studies* 175, 176, noting that the reference to the 'domestic' and 'commercial' context is merely 'a useful explanatory device' which, ultimately, 'encounters difficulties when given legal effect'.

[56] *Stack v Dowden* [2007] UKHL 17, [2007] 2 AC 432, [46] (Baroness Hale).

[57] Ibid, [69].

sub-species of land law.[58] For example, the common intention constructive trust has no application outside the realm of trusts of the family home. Yet this viewpoint was further developed in *Stack v Dowden*, through not just the majority's clear differentiation between the 'domestic' and 'commercial' contexts, but through the fact that entry into the 'domestic context' activated a set of avowedly family-centric legal principles. What the majority's approach in *Stack v Dowden* suggested was a further compartmentalisation of this area premised on the distinctive nature of the home. Despite Baroness Hale's views to the contrary, this may have fuelled the view that family property, as an area, was gradually shifting away from land law.

Ultimately, the context-driven approach of the majority has generated difficulties, particularly in terms of drawing boundaries between contexts. For example, a property used as a home and business naturally causes problems when determining which set of principles to apply.[59] Equally, it could be queried whether the label 'domestic context' was indeed different from 'cohabitation context'. Furthermore, once within the domestic context, there was the potential for further subdivision, often depending on the relationship of the parties concerned which would confuse judicial methodology.[60] After *Stack v Dowden*, there was not only a concern in relation to giving legal effect to different 'contexts', but there was also concern as to the precise judicial methodology deployed within the domestic context. It was this latter issue that provided the primary debate in *Jones v Kernott*.

JONES v KERNOTT

The Factual Background

Miss Patricia Jones, a mobile hairdresser, and Mr Leonard Kernott, a self-employed icecream salesman, met in 1980 and began a relationship. They cohabited in a caravan, purchased in Miss Jones' sole name and, shortly after the birth of their first child in 1984, purchased a family home for £30,000. This property was purchased in joint names. To finance the acquisition Miss Jones used the proceeds of sale from the caravan, amounting to £6000 alongside an endowment mortgage taken out in joint names. Post-acquisition, Miss Jones paid the mortgage and household expenses using her own income and contributions made by Mr Kernott. In 1986, they

---

[58] J Dewar, 'Land, Law, and the Family Home' in S Bright and J Dewar (eds), *Land Law: Themes and Perspectives* (Oxford, OUP, 1998) 327.

[59] See *James v Thomas* [2007] EWCA Civ 1212, involving a sole legal title dispute, and observations in *Stack v Dowden* [2007] UKHL 17, [2007] 2 AC 432, [32] (Lord Walker).

[60] See *Adekunle v Ritchie* [2007] EW Misc 5, [65], where Judge John Behrens noted that a platonic relationship as opposed to an intimate relationship may make it 'easier to find that the facts are unusual'.

decided to improve the property by building an extension and Mr Kernott undertook some of the labouring work. A second child was born in 1986.

Mr Kernott left the property in 1993. From then on, Miss Jones took over the repayment of the mortgage, the endowment policy premiums and the household expenses. She also looked after the two children with limited financial assistance from Mr Kernott despite applying for child support from the Child Support Agency. Although the parties placed the property on the market in 1995, it was not sold owing to poor property prices. In order for Mr Kernott to acquire a property in his sole name elsewhere, both parties instead cashed in a joint life insurance policy. In 1996, Mr Kernott acquired a property and concentrated on that property up until 2006, when he served a notice of severance in relation to the jointly owned property. Miss Jones applied under section 14 of the Trusts of Land and Appointment of Trustees Act 1996 for a declaration as to her entitlement to both the jointly owned property and the property subsequently acquired in Mr Kernott's sole name. However, Miss Jones decided not to pursue an interest in the property solely owned by Mr Kernott and instead focused her attention on the jointly owned property, which by 2008 had a significantly increased value of £245,000.

At trial Judge Peter Dedman held that Miss Jones was entitled to a 90 per cent share of the beneficial interest, thereby leaving Mr Kernott with a 10 per cent share. The basis for this allocation was that the initial intention of the parties to establish a family home had been superseded by a different intention when Mr Kernott left the home and concentrated on his own property. Miss Jones was entitled to a larger share owing to the deposit being paid on acquisition and the greater financial contribution made towards the mortgage and household expenditure, particularly after the departure of Mr Kernott. In the Chancery Division of the High Court, Nicholas Strauss QC explored what would constitute a fair share for both the parties in light of the whole course of conduct between them. Following the permissibility of 'actual, inferred or imputed' intentions in *Stack v Dowden*, Nicholas Strauss QC believed that a common intention could be attributed to the parties if an actual or inferred intention was unavailable. In short, a court can attribute to the parties 'an intention which they did not have, or at least did not express to each other'.[61] His analysis of the majority view in *Stack v Dowden* was that this should be performed in limited circumstances and he stated that 'the court should not *override* the intention of the parties, in so far as that appears from what they have said or from their conduct, in favour of what the court itself considers to be fair'.[62]

[61] *Jones v Kernott* [2009] EWHC 1713, [2010] 1 All ER 947, 959.
[62] Ibid (emphasis added).

On that basis, Nicholas Strauss QC noted that the approach taken by Judge Peter Dedman was permissible as the judge 'did not override any different intention which, from their words or conduct, could reasonably have been attributed to them' and therefore the approach was 'in accordance with the common intention of the parties'.[63]

The majority in the Court of Appeal (Wall and Rimer LJJ, Jacob LJ dissenting) awarded a 50:50 division of the beneficial interest. The majority held that the passage of time, the fact that Miss Jones assumed all responsibilities for the jointly owned property and also the fact that Mr Kernott acquired a property in his sole name were evidentially insufficient to adjust their presumptive beneficial interests in the property. These facts could not be used to infer a 90:10 division and the imputation of an intention the parties did not possess was not permissible. For Wall LJ, if the parties wanted their beneficial interests to alter post-acquisition, they needed to give effect to that intention formally as the Court could not 'spell such an intention out of their actions'.[64] Accordingly, and following severance of the beneficial joint tenancy, Miss Jones and Mr Kernott held the beneficial interest as tenants in common in equal shares.

The Judgment in the Supreme Court

The Supreme Court restored the order of the trial judge, thereby supporting a 90:10 division of the beneficial ownership in favour of Miss Jones.[65] Drawing on the earlier decision in *Stack v Dowden*, the Supreme Court stated that, as equity follows the law, joint tenants at law meant joint tenants in equity. This could be displaced if evidence, 'deduced objectively from conduct', revealed a different common intention at the time of acquisition or subsequently.[66] Once satisfied that the parties intended unequal sharing and that it was not possible to discern by direct evidence or conduct what shares were intended, 'the answer is that each is entitled to that share which the court considers fair having regard to the whole course of dealing between them in relation to the property'.[67]

In particular, the Court emphasised that this survey of the whole course of dealing should have a 'broad meaning' which draws on the paragraph 69 factors used in *Stack v Dowden* and should not be restricted to financial

---

[63] Ibid, 963.

[64] *Jones v Kernott* [2010] EWCA Civ 578, [2010] 3 All ER 423, [62].

[65] The Supreme Court decision has been extensively analysed: see J Mee, '*Jones v Kernott*: Inferring and Imputing in Essex' [2012] *Conv* 167, R George, 'Cohabitants' Property Rights: When is Fair Fair?' [2012] *CLJ* 39; and S Gardner and K Davidson, 'The Supreme Court on Family Homes' (2012) 128 *LQR* 178.

[66] *Jones v Kernott* [2011] UKSC 53, [2012] AC 776, [51] (Lord Walker and Baroness Hale).

[67] Ibid, quoting *Oxley v Hiscock* [2004] EWCA Civ 546; [2005] Fam 211, [69] (Chadwick LJ).

considerations alone.[68] When applied to the case, it was apparent that Miss Jones and Mr Kernott intended to set up a shared family home up until Mr Kernott left in 1993. His departure and subsequent purchase of another property enabled Baroness Hale, Lord Walker and Lord Collins to infer unequal sharing in equity. Lord Kerr and Lord Wilson agreed with the final result but believed that inferring a change of intention from conduct was not possible. Instead, as there was insufficient evidence to infer a change to the parties' original intentions, imputation was 'the only course to follow'.[69]

THE SIGNIFICANCE OF *STACK v DOWDEN* AND *JONES V KERNOTT*: 'CONTEXT' PLUS 'FAIRNESS'

Whereas the leitmotif of *Stack v Dowden* was 'context', it is arguable that the leitmotif of *Jones v Kernott* was 'fairness'. As a result, *Jones v Kernott* represented a significant shift from merely viewing the home in 'context' to instead, in limited circumstances, drawing on a concept that has a close connection to family law. This shift is important when considering the location of family property. In order to interrogate further the shifting classification of family property, it is important to delineate how both decisions correlate with the underlying concerns of land law.

Providing a comprehensive analysis of the foundational motivations of land law is outside the scope of this chapter, but a few key observations can be made that resonate with *Stack v Dowden* and *Jones v Kernott*.[70] First, there is a concern in land law for any legal framework to be expressed with simplicity and clarity which enables parties (including third parties such as creditors) to interact in full knowledge of their obligations and the consequences of their actions.[71] As Carol Rose has noted, land law has a signalling function and is 'heavily laden with hard-edged doctrines that tell everyone where they stand'.[72] Secondly, land law is also concerned with providing legal certainty, particularly in light of the fact that land is a highly prized, finite resource. In essence, it provides 'the rules by which a necessary element of legitimacy is conferred upon the de facto possession of

---

[68] Ibid.

[69] *Jones v Kernott* [2011] UKSC 53, [2012] AC 776, [72] (Lord Kerr).

[70] For a thorough exposition, see S Panesar, *General Principles of Property Law* (London, Longman, 2001).

[71] It is not just the legal framework that needs to be clear but also property itself: 'Property must come in neat, discrete, pre-packaged conceptual compartments, immune from capricious tampering or even well-intentional amplification': K Gray and SF Gray, 'The Idea of Property in Land' in S Bright and J Dewar (eds), *Land Law: Themes and Perspectives* (Oxford, OUP, 1998) 32.

[72] C Rose, 'Crystals and Mud in Property Law' (1987–88) 40 *Stanford Law Review* 577, 577.

scarce goods and resources'.[73] This generally occurs through the insistence on compliance with formalities; land law rules can structure interpersonal dealings with real property and, where clear and precise, they can minimise litigation. Even in instances where land law turns a blind eye to the failure to comply with formalities, for example in the informal acquisition of property interests, the elements for a claim are often relatively precise and identifiable.[74] Ultimately, both of these concerns fall within a larger concern, which Peter Birks has termed the 'primarily facilitative' nature of land law, which is premised on the clear classification and easy transmissibility of interests in land.[75] So, when these concerns are translated into the context of family property, an example where they are clearly accommodated would be the court's rigorous enforcement of express declarations of trust that enable parties to determine in advance the beneficial ownership of the property concerned. As the Law Commission noted, '[i]t is essential, in order to reward those who make proper provision, that courts continue rigorously to enforce express declarations of trust'.[76] Thus, where parties form an express declaration it provides 'virtually irrebuttable evidence'[77] of beneficial entitlement leaving 'no room for the application of the doctrine of resulting, implied or constructive trusts'.[78]

However, both *Stack v Dowden* and *Jones v Kernott* have been widely criticised in the academic commentary for conflicting with these concerns of land law. Putting to one side the concerns regarding the democratic legitimacy of the judiciary pushing forward this area,[79] when surveying the academic discourse there are two points where the decisions are challenged—and both are linked to the use of 'context' in *Stack v Dowden* and 'fairness' in *Jones v Kernott*. The first challenge is doctrinal and involves querying the assumptions underpinning the particular divisions of beneficial ownership in the two decisions and the judicial methodology used. The second challenge is practical and focuses on the unpredictability generated by the judicial exercise involved.

From a doctrinal perspective, the creation of a strong presumption of beneficial joint tenancy within the domestic context has been a much-criticised aspect of both *Stack v Dowden* and *Jones v Kernott*. Writing extrajudicially

---

[73] KJ Gray and PD Symes, *Real Property and Real People: Principles of Land Law* (London, Butterworths, 1981) 4.

[74] See generally N Hopkins, *Informal Acquisition of Rights in Land* (London, Sweet & Maxwell, 2000).

[75] P Birks, 'Before We Begin: Five Keys to Land Law' in S Bright and J Dewar (eds), *Land Law: Themes and Perspectives* (Oxford, OUP, 1998) 457.

[76] Law Commission Report No 278, *Sharing Homes: A Discussion Paper* (2002) para 2.52.

[77] K Gray and S Gray, *Elements of Land Law*, 5th edn (Oxford, OUP, 2009) para 7.1.29.

[78] *Goodman v Gallant* [1986] 1 All ER 311, 314 (Slade LJ).

[79] For criticisms of judicial activism in this area, see J Mee, '*Burns v Burns*: The Villain of the Piece' in S Gilmore, J Herring and R Probert, *Landmark Cases in Family Law* (Oxford, Hart Publishing, 2010) 175, 197; and Lord Neuberger, above (n 53) [9].

shortly after *Stack v Dowden*, Lord Neuberger queried 'the confident and strong assumption that unmarried parties should be taken to have intended a joint tenancy in equity'.[80] The multitude of reasons for the acquisition of property by cohabitants in joint names suggests that the application of the law of survivorship may not always be a desired outcome.[81] Moreover, and in spite the views of Lord Walker and Lady Hale in *Jones v Kernott*, it is likely that Lord Neuberger would believe that the law would be assuming too much by viewing a joint name purchase as 'strong' evidence of 'an emotional and economic commitment to a joint enterprise'.[82] Similarly, these judicial leaps based on assumptions about party intention have generated extensive criticisms because they have also formed the normative basis behind the court's process of inferring (and also imputing) intentions. For example, many were left scratching their heads in relation to the precise significance of separate bank accounts and investments in *Stack v Dowden* as a reason for justifying departure from equal sharing.[83] Empirical research reveals that 'a joint account may not always mean equal sharing in practice, and that individual accounts may not necessarily signify separate financial entities or lack of commitment'.[84] However, the rigid separation of finances proved highly informative for the majority in the House of Lords in *Stack v Dowden* and represented an indicator as to the nature of the parties' relationship.

The same consternation occurred following the interpretation given to Mr Kernott's departure from the family home in 1993, which Lord Walker, Lady Hale and Lord Collins found persuasive when inferring intentions. It is perhaps understandable why the Supreme Court was divided as to whether that fact was sufficient to justify an inference of changed intentions or whether, in the welter of facts, it would have been 'more realistic' simply to impute the intentions independently of conduct as Lord Kerr and Lord Wilson did.[85] While reliance on party intention as a basis for equitable intervention has long been criticised, the explicit discourse regarding the

---

[80] Lord Neuberger, above (n 53) [11].

[81] As Lord Neuberger noted in *Stack v Dowden* [2007] UKHL 17, [2007] 2 AC 432, [113], a joint names purchase may be the 'solicitor's decision or assumption' or 'the lender's preference for the security of two borrowers'.

[82] *Jones v Kernott* [2011] UKSC 53, [2012] AC 776, [19].

[83] See, eg, C Burgoyne and S Sonnenberg, 'Financial Perspectives in Cohabiting Heterosexual Couples: A Perspective from Economic Psychology' in J Miles and R Probert, *Sharing Lives, Dividing Assets: An Interdisciplinary Study* (Oxford, Hart Publishing, 2009) 89, 105, noting that 'the business of gauging people's intentions on the basis of certain financial arrangements is fraught with difficulty'.

[84] Ibid, 103.

[85] *Jones v Kernott* [2011] UKSC 53, [2012] AC 776, [89] (Lord Wilson).

dividing line between inference and 'fair shares' based on imputation has been a key source of academic debate and criticism.[86]

A more practical concern for both academics and practitioners has been the effect that both decisions would have on litigation. Through creating the strong presumption of beneficial joint tenancy, there was a view that it would prevent litigation, as the mere fact of joint registration would lock-in beneficial entitlement and abate unnecessary challenges.[87] Baroness Hale noted in *Stack v Dowden* that this strong presumption was to prevent parties spending 'far more on the legal battle than is warranted by the sums actually at stake'[88] and thus the task of dislodging equal beneficial sharing was not to be 'lightly embarked upon'.[89] This was particularly significant seeing as litigation eats away at the parties' respective shares. Indeed, the media speculated that following Mr Stack's unsuccessful appeal to the House of Lords he would be facing over £100,000 in legal costs.[90]

Yet, as noted above, the practical consequence has been a significant proportion of cases being deemed 'exceptional', thereby rebutting of the presumption of beneficial joint tenancy.[91] Take both *Stack v Dowden* and *Jones v Kernott* that provide worked examples of how to do this, particularly *Jones v Kernott*, which saw not only a rebuttal of the presumption, but also a stark disparity in the size of shares ultimately awarded. Thus, a pattern has emerged in the case law illustrating a trend towards 'exceptional' cases. As a result, the occurrence of this trend generated support for Lord Neuberger's Chancery approach premised on the resulting trust that would appease land lawyers as he viewed it as 'clear simple and cheap to apply'.[92] As the author has argued elsewhere, the reason why there is unpredictability could be the fact that Baroness Hale's approach in *Stack v Dowden* can be seen as 'overly formulaic' as the approach is based on categorisations of types of property and, at the same time, 'overly fluid' owing to the intrusiveness of the judicial analysis rendering cases 'exceptional'. In short,

---

[86] This can also be seen in the case law perhaps suggesting the somewhat 'academic' question of the permissibility of imputation, see, eg, *Bank of Scotland plc v Brogan* [2012] NICh 21, where Deeny J noted that he had 'neither the leisure, nor on the facts of this case, the duty to add my tuppence worth to the debate'.

[87] The ability to invoke the presumption *only* where there has been a transfer into joint names was underlined in the unreported Court of Appeal decision in *Thompson v Hurst* [2011] EWCA Civ 537 (unreported), where parties intended to purchase the property in joint names but were dissuaded following mortgage advice.

[88] *Stack v Dowden* [2007] UKHL 17, [2007] 2 AC 432, [68] (Baroness Hale).

[89] Ibid.

[90] See J Mills, 'Warning to Unmarried Couples over Home Rights' *The Daily Mail* (London, 25 April 2007).

[91] See, eg, *Adekunle v Ritchie* [2007] EW Misc 5; *Kali Ltd v Chawla* [2007] EWHC 1989; and *Laskar v Laskar* [2008] EWCA Civ 347, [2008] All ER (D) 104. Equal division was awarded in *Fowler v Barron* [2008] EWCA Civ 377, [2008] 2 FLR 831 and in *Hameed v Qayyum* [2008] EWHC 2274.

[92] Lord Neuberger, above (n 53) [9].

'the symbolic principle that the home is different invariably yields to the practice of heightened contextual analysis rendering cases exceptional'.[93] This time-consuming exercise of rebutting the beneficial joint tenancy generates uncertainty not only for the parties and practitioners, but also for third parties involved in the dispute.[94] As a direct result, the practitioner community has attempted to recover some degree of legal certainty through further encouraging parties to form express declarations of trust.[95] Yet even the apparent conclusiveness of the express declaration of trust—which has almost achieved dogmatic status—has been queried with fears of implied trusts being able to override a validly created express declaration.[96]

If these two routes for challenge are further analysed, an overriding feature of the decisions is that they are antagonistic to the aforementioned values that land law prioritises because the combined use of 'context' and 'fairness' suggest that this area is family law adjudication masquerading as land law. Although a broad generalisation, family law is arguably informed by values such as flexibility, fairness and viewing interpersonal relationships from a 'functional perspective'.[97] As will be explored below, both decisions display the use of judicial methodology that has at its heart an appreciation of relationship dynamics. Indeed, from a broad perspective it can be viewed as falling within what John Dewar has termed the 'familialization of property law', a process whereby 'both judges and the legislature have modified general principles of land law or trusts to accommodate the specific needs of family members'.[98] Although this process of intertwining considerations usually found in family law has been arguably present within trusts of the family home discourse for a while, the extent to which it has occurred has been limited. The significance of *Stack v Dowden* and *Jones v Kernott* is the greater acknowledgment of its connections to family law which fuels the dialogue suggesting the departure of family property from land law.

---

[93] A Hayward, 'The "Context" of Home: Cohabitation and Ownership Disputes in England and Wales' in M Diamond and T Turnipseed, *Community, Home and Identity* (London, Ashgate, 2012) 179, 206.

[94] For the operation of these principles in the context of bankruptcy, see *Segel v Pasram* [2008] EWHC 3448; *Shah v Baverstock* [2007] BPIR 1191; and see also *C Putnam & Sons v Taylor* [2009] EWHC 317, concerning a creditor.

[95] See E Cooke, 'In the Wake of *Stack v Dowden*: The Tale of TR1' [2011] *Family Law* 1142.

[96] See M Pawlowski, 'Informal Variation of Express Trusts' [2011] *Conv* 245 and K Fretwell, 'The Cautionary Tale of *Jones v Kernott*' [2012] *Family Law* 69, 72.

[97] On the general nature of family law and the values underpinning the discipline see, J Dewar, 'The Normal Chaos of Family Law' (1998) 61 *MLR* 467; A Diduck, 'What is Family Law For' (2011) 64 *CLP* 287 and Notes and 'Looking for a Family Resemblance: The Limits of the Functional Approach to the Legal Definition of Family' (1990–91) 104 *Harvard Law Review* 1640.

[98] Dewar, 'Land, Law, and the Family Home', above (n 58) 328. See also A Hayward, '"Family Property" and the Process of Familialization of Property Law' (2012) 23 *Child and Family Law Quarterly* 284.

To develop this point further, both decisions immediately prompted comparisons with how the property would have been divided had the parties been married and ancillary relief used. According to Jo Miles and Rebecca Probert,[99] the presumption of beneficial joint tenancy 'may seem to resemble' the 'yardstick of equality' created by the House of Lords' decision in *White v White*[100] and further developed in *Miller v Miller; McFarlane v McFarlane*.[101] As they note, a key distinction does exist, namely that a presumption of beneficial joint tenancy is an expression of party intention whereas the approach in ancillary relief is merely the fact that the fruits of the marriage partnership should, in principle, be shared. Similarly, this resemblance was also noted by practitioners with some querying whether *Jones v Kernott* will become the 'the new *White*'.[102] On top of the context-specific presumption of beneficial joint tenancy, Robert George has further cemented the comparisons between trusts of the family home cases with ancillary relief drawing on the explicit fairness dialogue visible in *Jones v Kernott*. He noted that *Jones v Kernott* arguably clarified the position regarding the use of fairness discussed in *Stack v Dowden* and stated that it can only be 'imposed as a "fallback position" if more conventional property law analysis proves fruitless'.[103] Yet, as will be explored below, it is likely that the difficulties of pinpointing express and inferred common intentions may result in a more intensive engagement with the residual concept of fairness and, in turn, the continuation of this more holistic, discretionary method of adjudication. This suggests that in practice there will be a continued visibility of reasoning akin to family law—but does this pose a dilemma for land law?

A 'NEW PRAGMATISM' IN FAMILY PROPERTY

The combined use by the courts of 'context' and 'fairness' in what ostensibly appears a discretionary manner should not be used as reason for land lawyers to jettison family property from land law. Discretion, in its many guises, is deeply embedded within judicial decision-making and present at all stages of the adjudicative process. To develop this further, it should be noted that using a fact-sensitive, discretionary approach is certainly not an

---

[99] J Miles and R Probert, 'Sharing Lives, Dividing Assets: Legal Principles and Real Life' in J Miles and R Probert, *Sharing Lives, Dividing Assets: An Interdisciplinary Study* (Oxford, Hart Publishing, 2009) 12.

[100] *White v White* [2001] 1 AC 596 (HL).

[101] *Miller v Miller; McFarlane v McFarlane* [2006] UKHL 24, [2006] 2 AC 618.

[102] R Bailey-Harris and J Wilson, 'Hang on a Minute! (Or is *Kernott* the New *White*)' *Family Law Week* http:www.familylawweek.co.uk/site.aspx?i=ed79632.

[103] R George, *Ideas and Debates in Family Law* (Oxford, Hart Publishing, 2012) 104, drawing on George, 'Cohabitants' Property Rights', above (n 65).

alien approach to land law or, more broadly, a common law jurisdiction like England and Wales.[104] As noted above, it is true that land law has a traditional commitment to bright-line rules, a desire for legal certainty along with a preference for regimented legal taxonomy. Various observations can be found supporting the desire for courts in this area 'to decide property disputes by the application of legal principle and not by the exercise of untrammelled discretion, in relation to the facts as found'.[105] These observations also align with a prevalent desire to 'concretise' the use of discretion more generally across legal areas.[106] But there are various examples in land law where discretion, in its many forms, is both present and, more importantly, vibrant.[107]

A closer examination of the historical development of family property, particularly owing to its relationship to equity, reveals a long engagement with judicial discretion which was explicitly discussed in both *Stack v Dowden* and *Jones v Kernott*. Section 17 of the Married Women's Property Act 1882, which provided that a judge could decide 'as he sees fit' any question as to title or possession of property between husband and wife, generated a continual engagement with judicial discretion from the 1950s onwards.[108] The broadest formulations of this provision arguably represented, in a Dworkinian sense, a 'strong discretion', namely an ability whereby the decision-maker is 'simply not bound by standards set by the authority in question'.[109] Thus, as Evershed MR noted in *Rimmer v Rimmer*,[110] it was truly 'palm tree justice'.

Observations regarding discretion were also prominent in trusts of the family home cases even after the introduction of comprehensive ancillary relief for married couples in 1970. This latter system provided a more classical understanding of an express conferral of judicial discretion, namely 'as an area left open by a surrounding belt of restriction'[111] but, unlike section 17, this conferral included statutory factors that could guide the use of discretion. Interestingly, comparison was often made in trusts of

---

[104] CE Schneider, 'Discretion and Rules: A Lawyer's View' in K Hawkins, *The Uses of Discretion* (Oxford, OUP, 1991) 47.

[105] R Walker, 'Which Side "Ought to Win": Discretion and Certainty in Property Law' (2008) 6 *Trust Quarterly Review* 5, 6.

[106] See N Lacey, 'The Jurisprudence of Discretion: Escaping the Legal Paradigm' in K Hawkins, *The Uses of Discretion* (Oxford, OUP, 1991) 361, 362, noting the search for 'legal methods of confining, structuring, and controlling discretion' which was advocated earlier in KC Davis, *Discretionary Justice: A Preliminary Inquiry* (Baton Rouge, LA, Louisiana State University Press, 1969).

[107] See S Juss, *Judicial Discretion and the Right to Property* (London, Pinter, 1998).

[108] See O Stone, 'Matrimonial Property—The Scope of Section 17' (1957) 20 *MLR* 281 and L Rosen, 'Palm Tree Justice' (1966) 110 *Solicitors' Journal* 239.

[109] R Dworkin, *Taking Rights Seriously* (London, Butterworths, 1977) 32.

[110] *Rimmer v Rimmer* [1952] 2 All ER 863, 865 (CA), quoting from *Newgrosh v Newgrosh* (1950) 100 LT Jo 525.

[111] Dworkin, above (n 109) 31.

the family home cases between ancillary relief applicable to married couples and the trust principles relied on by cohabitants, and a shift in emphasis in this particular comparison over time reveals a deepening connection with discretion.[112] For example, after the introduction of ancillary relief the comparison between the remedies available to married couples and cohabitants was often illustrative of the courts simply stating that a distinction existed. Thus, in *Bernard v Josephs,* a dispute between an unmarried couple, Lord Denning MR drew attention to the fact that 'there is no such legislation for couples like these'.[113] Likewise, in *Burns v Burns* May LJ compared the result in that case with that which would have arisen under the Matrimonial Causes Act 1973 and lamented that Mrs Burns 'can justifiably say that fate has not been kind to her'.[114] Yet more recent decisions express strong concerns that the courts in trusts of the family home cases have been engaging with a de facto judicial discretion akin to that of the Matrimonial Causes Act 1973, prompting Waite LJ to state firmly that 'this is an area of the law in which there is no scope for discretion'.[115] Similarly, in the Court of Appeal decision in *Jones v Kernott* Wall LJ stated categorically that 'this is not a case under the Matrimonial Causes Act 1973'.[116]

In contrast to statutory express grants of judicial discretion, these judicial observations show that discretion can operate in a more implicit manner—which is arguably the approach visible in *Stack v Dowden* and *Jones v Kernott*. Robert Goodin has noted that it can take the form of 'informal discretion' where it is implicit or assumed.[117] In this context the judiciary assume or infer judicial discretion in the absence of an express mandate. Likewise, as Carol Harlow and Richard Rawlings note, this process can occur after 'constant allusion to standards: "necessary", "essential", "exceptional", or "reasonable" and the presence of these standards provide "significant freedom of manoeuvre"'.[118] When transposed on to *Stack v Dowden* and *Jones v Kernott*, it can be argued that the framework created in relation to retaining or rebutting the beneficial joint tenancy, specific only to joint legal title disputes, can be viewed as a developing form of 'assumed' discretion. Similarly, 'fairness' used in *Jones v Kernott* is now embedded within the trust framework and will invariably provide further decision-making latitude to the judiciary and, ultimately, freedom to manoeuvre at the quantification stage.

---

[112] It should be noted that trust principles remain applicable to married couples where the marriage is subsisting or where a third party is involved.

[113] *Bernard v Josephs* [1982] Ch 391, 397 (CA).

[114] *Burns v Burns* [1984] Ch 317, 345 (CA).

[115] *Midland Bank v Cooke* [1995] 4 All ER 562, 574 (CA).

[116] *Jones v Kernott* [2010] EWCA Civ 578, [2010] 3 All ER 423, [55].

[117] RE Goodin, 'Welfare, Rights and Discretion' (1986) 6 *OJLS* 232, 234.

[118] C Harlow and R Rawlings, *Law and Administration* (London, Weidenfeld and Nicolson, 1984) 617.

When faced with a legal dispute, discretion is also a factor or, indeed, an option for adjudication considered by a judge.[119] Maurice Rosenberg has suggested that 'whatever the court, wherever it sits, the judge soon finds himself talking, wondering and, at times, thinking about discretion and its implications'.[120] This judicial impulse was developed further by Simon Gardner noting that 'even the apparently routine application of settled rules depends on the finding of particular facts, and fact-finding will reflect the individual approach of the fact-finder'.[121] In short, 'deciding the facts' can be viewed as the gateway for discretion or, as Aharon Barak has noted, the 'first area of judicial discretion'.[122] For the author, once the multifaceted nature of judicial discretion is recognised this polarisation between the foundational values and adjudication techniques of land law and family law breaks down. As a consequence, recourse by the courts to discretionary resolution through the medium of the trust, like that demonstrated in *Stack v Dowden* and *Jones v Kernott*, should be analysed further and not unnecessarily criticised.

Alongside recognising the pervasiveness of discretion, the gradual shift towards a more discretionary judicial approach can also be viewed as an inevitable process in light of both the unique context of family home disputes and the perpetuation of common intention analysis. This suggests that the deployment of 'context' in *Stack v Dowden* and the use of 'fairness' in *Jones v Kernott* were certainly not bolts out of the blue. Put simply, the significance of both *Stack v Dowden* and *Jones v Kernott* is that the shift in approach arguably reveals judicial pragmatism.[123] The work of Patrick Atiyah further underlines this trend towards a more pragmatic approach to the resolution of disputes. He noted that in the first half of the twentieth century courts resolved conflict through adherence to principles, meaning that 'they were less concerned with doing justice in a particular case and more concerned with the impact of their decision in the future'.[124] By contrast, he noted that by 1980 judicial decision-making had become 'highly pragmatic' and a 'great deal less principled'.[125] This trend has continued into the twenty-first century; and both *Stack v Dowden* and *Jones v Kernott*

---

[119] Lord Bingham, 'The Discretion of the Judge' (1990) 5 *Denning Law Journal* 27, 28.

[120] M Rosenberg, 'Judicial Discretion of the Trial Court, Viewed from Above' (1970–71) 22 *Syracuse Law Review* 635, 635.

[121] Gardner, 'The Element of Discretion' above (n 17) 193.

[122] A Barak, *Discretionary Justice* (New Haven and London, Yale University Press, 1989) 13.

[123] See M Pawlowski, 'Imputed Intention and Joint Ownership—A Return to Common Sense: Jones v Kernott' [2012] *Conv* 148, 156, terming the residual use of fairness both 'eminently sensible and practical'.

[124] PS Atiyah, 'From Principles to Pragmatism: Changes in the Function of the Judicial Process and the Law' [1980] *Iowa Law Review* 1249, 1251.

[125] Ibid.

vividly embody the drive towards pragmatic solutions in areas where courts are required to divine intentions using 'small evidential nuggets'.[126]

Discretionary resolution is appropriate in the unique context of trusts of the family home disputes. While the need to pinpoint relevant facts is often a concern for any form of litigation, the modern conceptualisation of trust principles predicated on common intention generates additional difficulties. There are 'always vexed questions' when courts are using often highly contested facts to determine party intentions.[127] Both *Stack v Dowden* and *Jones v Kernott* clearly evince this as both cases involved the acquisition of property that occurred 20 years prior to the date of the dispute thereby generating for the court a complex pattern of interaction to decipher. This pattern produced a wealth of conflicting and contradictory evidence of party intentions and this is the first area where discretion comes into play.

Faced by the welter of facts, two consequences then arise. First, the courts are required to harness this analysis within the bounds of common intention analysis and, secondly, they are repeatedly told that they must find a result and not 'shirk more difficult computations'.[128] An inclination towards discretionary resolution therefore seems irresistible, particularly when it is noted that this type of scenario is one where discretion often arises, namely where there is 'some absence or indeterminacy of the legal materials'.[129] In relation to the first consequence, it is trite to say that common intention provides a problematic basis for intervention in this area.[130] It is widely thought of as 'grotesque' to expect parties to hammer out agreements as to beneficial ownership or engage in unromantic discussions.[131] Indeed, even where intentions have been found, there has been notable variation as to the size of shares awarded. As Judge John Behrens noted in *Aspden v Elvey*: '[t]he figure is somewhat arbitrary but it is the best I can do with the available material'.[132]

The initiatives evident in *Stack v Dowden* and *Jones v Kernott* are arguably attempts to preserve the use of common intention while fully engaging with the actual nature of property disputes. By sanctioning the residual

---

[126] *Midland Bank v Cooke* [1995] 4 All ER 562, 567 (Waite LJ).

[127] *Young v Laurentani* [2007] 2 FLR 1211, [1] (Lindsay J).

[128] *Rimmer v Rimmer* [1952] 2 All ER 863, 867. This point is further emphasised in *Pettitt v Pettitt* [1970] AC 777, 799 (Lord Morris), who noted that '[t]he search must still be to find an answer to the question as to where ownership lies. The court has to reach decision in very difficult circumstances but the task, the duty and the objective of the court does not change. The court is not suddenly absolved from its duty'.

[129] J Bell, 'Discretionary Decision Making' in K Hawkins, *The Uses of Discretion* (Oxford, OUP, 1991) 88, 97.

[130] For criticism, see N Glover and PN Todd, 'The Myth of Common Intention' (1996) 16 *Legal Studies* 325 and U Riniker, 'The Fiction of Common Intention and Detriment' [1998] *Conv* 202.

[131] *Pettitt v Pettitt* [1970] AC 777, 810 (Lord Hodson).

[132] *Aspden v Elvey* [2012] EWHC 1387, [128] (Judge John Behrens).

use of fairness when quantifying shares, the Supreme Court in *Jones v Kernott* was able to overcome the difficulty seen in *Midland Bank v Cooke* where the parties formally stated that they did not have an intention as to shares.[133] Here, a pragmatic fix can be seen that endeavours to maintain allegiance to common intention while simultaneously ensuring that the court reaches a result.

While discretionary resolution has been present within the area for decades, *Stack v Dowden* and *Jones v Kernott* intensify its use. The close factual analysis of the 'partnership' between the parties concerned and the marginalisation of financial contributions will continue to generate comparisons to family law adjudication. Similarly, the distinction between the consumer context and the commercial context will further provoke remarks concerning the actual intentions of the judiciary in redeveloping this area of law. But the fact is that until statutory intervention occurs, this area remains land law, albeit a land law that is being recalibrated better to accommodate family property disputes. While many land lawyers will feel uncomfortable regarding this shift, it should be noted 'land law has ... become an instrument of social engineering'[134] and it frequently 'embodies a broad range of value judgments'.[135] Gray and Symes were undeniably correct when they noted that land law 'exerts a fundamental influence upon the lifestyles of ordinary people'.[136]

As previously noted, the processes used in both *Stack v Dowden* and *Jones v Kernott* have been extensively criticised, especially where the creation of a family-centric framework produces outcomes that could have been achieved under a resulting trust. However, for the author the use of close factual analysis of contributions to the property is arguably beneficial for changing the judicial dialogue in this area and providing expression to the myriad of contributions to the home. By exploring relationship dynamics, this may represent a departure from the language of orthodox land law, but at the same time it is an important process of modernisation that bridges the gap between the formal legal framework and the factual circumstances it seeks to regulate. Further cases are needed to refine and recalibrate the principles laid down in *Stack v Dowden* and *Jones v Kernott*. Through clarifying the process of imputation and the precise applicability of the presumption of beneficial joint tenancy, the courts may help to generate the legal certainty that land law, traditionally conceived, so often craves. Invariably, this will be assisted if judges 'place on record the circumstances

---

[133] *Midland Bank v Cooke* [1995] 4 All ER 562, 567–69 (Waite LJ).

[134] Gray and Symes, above (n 73) 4.

[135] Ibid, 5.

[136] Ibid, 4. This more dynamic vision of land law, that recognizes other foundational values than mere 'efficiency', is presented by H Dagan, *Property: Values and Institutions* (Oxford, OUP, 2011).

and factors that were crucial to [their] determination'.[137] For the author, rather than falling into the trap of criticising an area for novelty or difference, there is potential to view these developments as an opportunity for modernisation and dynamism.

CONCLUSIONS: FINDING A HOME FOR 'FAMILY PROPERTY'

Stack v Dowden and *Jones v Kernott* challenge the 'purity and logic of the law of property'.[138] A problematic reaction to the functionalist and discretionary judicial exercise deployed when the courts are divining the parties' common intentions is to see both decisions as resembling discretionary family law which requires, at best, compartmentalisation and, at worst, removal from land law. The unpredictability and uncertainty generated by these decisions strike at the core of land law and this triggers academic responses that advocate extricating this body of principles from land law itself. An alternative reaction has been to support statutory cohabitation reform providing rights and remedies to cohabitants on relationship breakdown.[139] As Elizabeth Cooke has stated, this would ensure that 'the soft stuff we describe as "family law"' can resolve the messiness and normal chaos of interpersonal relationships'.[140] However, if we recognise that statutory reform is not on the horizon and that—even if it were introduced—it would not resolve all questions of property ownership, there is urgency behind recognising the potential of land law in this area. Fragmenting family property from land law would represent a missed opportunity and potentially stymie development in this area.[141]

Both *Stack v Dowden* and *Jones v Kernott* represent landmark cases in land law. This chapter has advanced the argument that, while they have been criticised within the academic community for their engagement with 'context' and 'fairness', the more discretionary approach introduced may more sensitively engage with relationship dynamics. Equally, a beneficial by-product of this redevelopment is that it forces land lawyers to confront and reconsider the foundational tenets of their discipline. For the author, this pushing at the boundaries of land law should be welcomed, particularly if the modern application of land law is to reconcile its treatment of home

---

[137] Rosenberg, above (n 120) 665.

[138] R Probert, 'Cohabitation: Current Legal Solutions' (2009) 62 *CLP* 316, 332.

[139] See, eg, Law Commission Report No 278, *Sharing Homes* (2002), above (n 76) and, more recently, Law Commission Consultation Paper No 179, *Cohabitation: The Financial Consequences of Relationship Breakdown* (2006) and Law Commission Report No 307, *Cohabitation: The Financial Consequences of Relationship Breakdown* (2007).

[140] E Cooke, 'Cohabitants, Common Intention and Contributions (Again)' [2005] *Conv* 555.

[141] Sadly, this viewpoint is not altogether unprecedented. See Schneider, above (n 104) 48, noting that 'where an area of law—like my own field of family law—seems poor in rules and rich in discretion, they [the academic community] begin to wonder whether it is really law'.

ownership, possession and purchase with the realities of people's lived experiences. Thus, the change in direction ushered in by *Stack v Dowden* and *Jones v Kernott* provides a timely opportunity for a critical reappraisal of the trusts of the family home framework and, more importantly, this process needs to take place within land law itself.

In *Cowcher v Cowcher* Bagnall J famously stated that, in determining property rights, 'the only justice that can be attained by mortals, who are fallible and are not omniscient, is justice according to law; the justice which flows from the application of sure and settled principles to proved or admitted facts'.[142] However, as this chapter has suggested, the inherent terrain of family property disputes means that the facts themselves, let alone whether or not they are 'proved or admitted', are often simply not available. What happens as a result of their conspicuous absence is the pragmatic invocation of presumptions, assumptions and imputations which may, over time, develop to become the new 'sure and settled principles'. For the author, the legacy of *Stack v Dowden* and *Jones v Kernott* is that, although imperfect decisions made by 'fallible' judges, they have generated a paradigm shift in the field of family property which may trigger a new dynamism in this area. This is beneficial not only to land law in general, but also to litigants who may benefit from the application of a more family-centric type of judicial analysis. Let us not forget, as Lord Collins reminded us in *Jones v Kernott*, that 'the courts are courts of law, but they are also courts of justice'.[143]

---

[142] *Cowcher v Cowcher* [1972] 1 All ER 943, 948.
[143] *Jones v Kernott* [2011] UKSC 53, [2012] 1 AC 776, [66].

11

Manchester City Council v Pinnock (2010)[1]

Shifting Ideas of Ownership of Land

SUSAN BRIGHT

INTRODUCTION

IT MAY LOOK strange to suggest that such a recent Supreme Court decision merits the appellation of being a landmark case, particularly given that its importance relates to the application of a modern statute. Indeed, the judgment in *Pinnock* came very shortly after the tenth anniversary of the implementation of the Human Rights Act 1998. During that decade, however, the scope of the Article 8 right to respect for the home generated an unusual amount of judicial activity seeking to tease out how it impacted on the right to recover possession of residential property, including three cases before the House of Lords. Yet whereas the English judiciary resisted the idea that Article 8 could disturb the established order of property rights, the European Court of Human Rights in Strasbourg showed no such hesitancy, repeatedly asserting that any person at risk of interference with his home should be able to have the proportionality of the measure determined by an independent tribunal.[2] In the face of the 'unambiguous and consistent approach of the European Court of Human Rights' the Supreme Court in *Pinnock* departed from the earlier decisions of the House of Lords and agreed that, at least where a local authority is

[1] *Manchester CC v Pinnock* [2010] UKSC 45, [2011] 2 AC 104. Acknowledgements: I am extremely grateful to many people who have advised on the drafting, have helped with materials and been willing to chat about the ideas in this chapter. In alphabetical order they include: Anne Davies, Simon Gardner, Amy Goymour, Andre van der Walt, Lisa Whitehouse, Alison Young and Paul Yowell. As will appear, I have been inspired particularly by reading Andre van der Walt's book, *Property in the Margins* (Oxford, Hart Publishing, 2009).
[2] *McCann v United Kingdom* App no 19009/04 (2008) 47 EHRR 40, [50].

seeking possession of a person's home, 'the court must have the power to assess the proportionality of making the order and, in making that assessment, to resolve any relevant dispute of fact'.[3]

Although the practical import of the decision has only just begun to be worked out in County Courts, it will seldom make much difference to the outcome.[4] In terms of the rhetoric of ownership and our doctrinal thinking about property rights, however, it heralds a much more contextualised understanding of what it means to assert ownership of land and of how claims for the recovery of land should be resolved. It is these dimensions that are explored in this chapter. The first section sets out ideas about ownership with an emphasis on the importance of the trespassory rules that protect it and the 'self-seekingness' of ownership. These dimensions come together in the right to possess, a core ingredient of an owner's powers. In the following section, the jurisprudence of Article 8 is explained, along with the decision in *Pinnock*. The final section evaluates how *Pinnock* causes us to revise our understanding of land ownership. It is no longer the case that where an owner seeks recovery of land from an occupier with no right to remain there as against the owner, an order for possession will be a 'foregone conclusion' as Lord Millett had asserted in *Harrow LBC v Qazi*.[5] When Article 8 is engaged, the judicial enquiry will need to extend beyond the simple facts of 'property rights' to encompass a broader range of considerations that include examining the justification for seeking possession as well as the impact that an order will have on the occupier and his family. An owner's right to possess will no longer automatically trump all other considerations.

OWNERSHIP

The Ownership Idea: Pre-*Pinnock*

Ownership is a complex idea. Although we all intuitively have a fair grasp of what it means to own something and of the variety of things that owners can do, it has proven surprisingly difficult to capture the essence of ownership through a theoretical model that embraces all possible forms. The most useful analysis for present purposes is that presented by the various writings of Harris. He provides a framework for understanding what it means to state

---

[3] *Manchester CC v Pinnock* [2010] UKSC 45, [2011] 2 AC 104, [46], [50].
[4] D Cowan and C Hunter, '"Yeah But, No But"—Pinnock and Powell in the Supreme Court' (2012) 75 *MLR* 78, 90–91.
[5] *Harrow LBC v Qazi* [2003] UKHL 43, [2004] 1 AC 983, [103].

that X is the owner of land within the common law.[6] There are three kinds
of assertions that are implied by this claim.[7] The first is that X will have the
protection of trespassory rules. These are the rules that impose obligations
on non-owners not to make use of the land without the owner's consent.[8]
As Harris points out, it is not *necessary* to the concept of ownership that
trespassory rules give in specie protection, but in English law a landowner
has traditionally (at least, pre-*Pinnock*) had a right of specific civil recovery
against dispossessors.[9] The protection rule means that it would be wrongful for anyone else to meddle with the land without X's consent (or specific
legislative authorization).[10] The second implication from the claim of X's
ownership of land is that X is able to do what he likes with the land, subject to what Harris refers to as property-limitation rules (that is, rules that
curtail ownership privileges and powers, such as planning rules or nuisance
laws).[11] This gives the claim 'jural content'.[12] Whereas many property theo-
rists set about trying to capture the essence of ownership by articulating,
perhaps in list form, the various rights that owners have, for Harris it is the
very open-endedness of the owner's use privileges and powers to control
the use made by others of the land that captures the essence of ownership.
The open-endedness of these relationships he describes as 'the ownership
spectrum'.[13] Harris points out a further dimension of ownership: the fact
that it allows owners to act in a self-interested manner. Although Harris
does not himself treat this as part of the jural content, it does seem to be
intimately linked with it, as it is the (open-ended) use privileges and powers
to control that can be exercised by X without regard to others and in order
to promote his own interests and desires. A similar thought is expressed by
Katz who argues that the central concern of the structure of ownership in
property law is the preservation of the owner's position as the 'exclusive

---

[6] For convenience, but also because it has rhetorical significance, X is referred to in this
chapter as 'owner' of land, even though some commentators deny that ownership is a relevant
concept in English land law. X may be either a freeholder or a leaseholder: the common law
has examples of judges freely referring to both freeholders and leaseholders as 'owners', eg, in
McPhail v Persons Unknown [1973] Ch 447, 455 (CA) a leaseholder is referred to as owner.
In *Hunter v Canary Wharf Ltd* [1997] 1 AC 655 (HL), as Harris points out, Lord Hoffmann
implicitly falls into the category of those who deny a law of ownership in England (at 703) while
happily referring to 'landowners' (at 709): JW Harris, 'Reason or Mumbo Jumbo: The Common
Law's Approach to Property' (2002) 117 *Proceedings of the British Academy* 445, 464.

[7] Harris, 'Reason or Mumbo Jumbo', above (n 6) 461.

[8] JW Harris, *Property and Justice* (Oxford, Clarendon Press, 1996) 5.

[9] If this were to change, it would not mean that X is no longer the owner of the land.

[10] Harris, 'Reason or Mumbo Jumbo', above (n 6) 461–62.

[11] Harris also exempts 'property-independent prohibitions': Harris, *Property and Justice*,
above (n 8) 32–33. An example would be a law that prohibits stabbing with a knife—where
the rule here applies independently of ownership of the property (the knife). If the property is
land, an example might be a prohibition on 'fly-tipping', which prevents all persons (not only
owners) from dumping rubbish.

[12] Harris, 'Reason or Mumbo Jumbo', above (n 6) 461.

[13] Harris, *Property and Justice*, above (n 8) 5.

agenda setter' for the owned thing.[14] This is not a claim that can be made by *all* owners, for some are under obligations to have regard to others (and this is something that will be considered below), but it is the case that all *private* landowners can pursue 'self-seekingness'. The third implication from an ownership claim, which need not detain us, is that of title. To say that X is owner of land implies that he has acquired a good title to it.

It is the first two assertions—the protection rule and the jural content—that *Pinnock* impacts on. These two dimensions converge in the right to possess, which Honoré describes as 'the foundation on which the whole superstructure of ownership rests'.[15] Further, according to Harris, it

> may be divided into two aspects, the right (claim) to be put in exclusive control of a thing and the right to remain in control, *viz.* the claim that others should not without permission, interfere. Unless a legal system provides some rules and procedure for attaining these ends it cannot be said to protect ownership.[16]

The protective dimension nowadays works though the possession claim under CPR 55 which is used for recovery of the land both from those whose occupation is (or was) consensual (tenants, licensees) and from trespassers (where the occupier entered or remained on the land without the consent of a person entitled to possession of the land) (CPR 55.1(b)). Prior to *Pinnock* the right to recover possession of land was available automatically to an owner of land, unless a specific right to occupy had been granted to the occupier,[17] and irrespective of the owner's reasons for recovering possession.

The common law contains many illustrations of both the self-seekingness of ownership privileges and powers, and of the absoluteness of the right to recovery of possession; and of instances where these two attributes of ownership coalesce. A well known illustration of self-seekingness can be seen in the actions of Mr Pickles, who was allowed to divert water percolating through his land even though the effect was to deny this water supply to the inhabitants of Bradford, even if 'churlish, selfish and grasping' and even if his 'conduct may seem shocking to a moral philosopher'.[18] Less well known are two cases from around the same period in which railway station owners were able to deny access to commercial rivals (as omnibus

---

[14] L Katz, 'Exclusion and Exclusivity in Property Law' (2008) 58 *University of Toronto Law Journal* 275.

[15] AM Honoré, 'Ownership' in AG Guest (ed), *Oxford Essays in Jurisprudence* (Oxford, OUP, 1961) 113. Harris states that this right characterises 'the combined effect of ownership interests and trespassory rules': Harris, *Property and Justice*, above (n 8) 126.

[16] Harris, *Property and Justice*, above (n 8) 113.

[17] Statute may extend rights to possess that began as consensual grants of occupation, as with security of tenure rights under the housing legislation, and requiring certain minimal periods of notice to be given in the interest of social justice (as with the Protection from Eviction Act 1977).

[18] *Bradford Corporation v Pickles* [1895] AC 587, 601 (HL).

operators and hotel operators) in order to protect the station owners' commercial interests.[19]

The absoluteness of the right to recovery of possession underpins the approach to Article 8 that was taken by the majority in the first of the House of Lords decisions, *Qazi*.[20] Mr Qazi and his then wife had been granted a secure joint tenancy by Hounslow London Borough Council. Some years later his wife left and served a notice to quit on Hounslow LBC, thereby terminating the joint tenancy. Although Mr Qazi applied for a tenancy in his sole name, his application was turned down and Hounslow LBC began possession proceedings. By the time the possession proceedings were heard in the county court, Mr Qazi was living in the house with his new wife and two children. His defence, based on Article 8, was rejected. The answer was a 'foregone conclusion':[21] Mr Qazi had no contractual or proprietary right to occupation and therefore the owner could recover possession. As Lord Scott put it: 'The fate of every possession application will be determined by the respective contractual and proprietary rights of the parties'.[22] Article 8 cannot be 'allowed to diminish or detract from the landlord's contractual and proprietary rights'.[23] The personal circumstances of Mr Qazi and the other occupiers were not relevant.

There is nothing surprising about the outcome in *Qazi* if we approach it through the lens of traditional property doctrine. In *Property in the Margins*, van der Walt refers to this as the 'rights paradigm', a set of doctrinal, rhetorical and logical assumptions and beliefs about the relative value and power of discrete property interests in the law and society.[24] Within this there is a structured hierarchy of rights; and strong property rights (in English law terms, estates in land) will always trump weaker rights or 'no-rights'.[25] The rhetoric surrounding property concepts reinforces the trumping power of ownership. As Singer notes, by identifying a particular person as owner we commonly presume that that person wins disputes about property.[26]

Examples abound. In *Qazi*, Hounslow LBC, as the owner of the land, was able to trump Mr Qazi as he had 'no-rights' and his personal circumstances

---

[19] *Barker v Midland Railway Company (1856)* 18 CB 46; *Perth General Station Committee v Ross* [1897] AC 479 (HL).

[20] *Harrow LBC v Qazi* [2003] UKHL 43, [2004] 1 AC 983.

[21] Ibid, [103] (Lord Millett).

[22] Ibid, [144].

[23] Ibid, [146].

[24] Van der Walt, above (n 1) 27.

[25] Van der Walt draws on the language of 'no-rights' from Hohfeld's work as meaning the opposite of claim rights and the correlative of duties: W Hohfeld, 'Some Fundamental Legal Conceptions as Applied in Judicial Reasoning' (1913) 23 *Yale Law Journal* 16, 30. In this chapter, I use 'no-rights' more specifically to mean 'no lawful right, as against the owner, to occupy'. It is discussed more fully below, at the text accompanying n 97.

[26] JW Singer, *Entitlement* (New Haven, CT, Yale University Press, 2000) 83.

were simply not relevant. Likewise, in *McPhail v Person Unknown*, the Court of Appeal emphasised the inevitability of possession being granted to the owner once ownership rights are played against 'no-rights': 'when the owner of a house comes to the court and asks for an order to recover possession against squatters, the court must give him the order he asks. It has no discretion to suspend the order'.[27]

The doctrinal logic of this system will determine the outcome of property disputes 'in terms of an abstract, syllogistic logic, in which contextual issues such as the general historical, social, economic or political context of the dispute and the personal circumstances of the parties have no relevance or effect'.[28] No matter that those evicted have nowhere else to go, and the evicters seek (only) to make profit.[29] Personal circumstances carry no legal weight, even if a young family is involved which has had to walk the streets and will again be made homeless: 'however great their despair', they must leave if they have 'no-rights' in the face of the local authority's right to summary possession.[30]

A Qualification to Self-seekingness: Pre-*Pinnock*?

As was hinted at earlier, although the idea of self-seekingness underpins ownership by *private* persons, it is not a feature of ownership by other legal persons whose functions and powers are qualified. Perhaps the most obvious example for property lawyers is the trustee, who must exercise all its powers as owner of legal title in a fiduciary manner that protects the interests of the beneficiaries.

Harris recognises that these types of cases lack the 'crucial feature of legitimate, self-seeking exploitation' associated with the 'ownership spectrum',[31] preferring to call them 'quasi-ownership interests' which involve a 'mix of powers modelled on those of ownership interests proper and those connected with the particular function being discharged'.[32] The point is illustrated by the Court of Appeal decision in *R v Somerset County Council, ex parte Fewings*[33] (although the powers of local authorities have changed significantly recently and it is likely that this case would now be decided differently).[34] In *Fewings*,

---

[27] *McPhail v Persons Unknown* [1973] Ch 447, 460 (Lord Denning MR).
[28] Van der Walt, above (n 1) 27.
[29] *McPhail v Persons Unknown* [1973] Ch 447, 461 (CA).
[30] *Southwark LBC v Williams* [1971] Ch 734, 744 (CA).
[31] Harris, *Property and Justice*, above (n 8) 105. Waldron similarly talks about the importance of being free to disregard the interests of others in deciding how to act: J Waldron, *The Right to Private Property* (Oxford, OUP, 1998) 295, 302.
[32] Harris, *Property and Justice*, above (n 8) 267.
[33] *R v Somerset County Council, ex parte Fewings* [1995] 1 WLR 1037, 1042 (CA).
[34] By the Localism Act 2011, discussed below.

the Council had passed a resolution to ban stag hunting on Over Stowey Customs Common on the basis that it 'involved unacceptable and unnecessary cruelty to the red deer who were the victims of the chase'. It justified its right to do so by reference to the 'full-blooded model of ownership', asserting that it is for the landowner to decide what activities to allow on its land. But, as Sir Thomas Bingham MR remarked, local authorities are not free to act entirely as they wish:

> To the famous question asked by the owner of the vineyard: 'Is it not lawful for me to do what I will with mine own?' (St Matthew xx 15) the modern answer would be clear: 'Yes, subject to such regulatory and other constraints as the law imposes'. But if the same question were posed by a local authority the answer would be different. It would be: 'No, it is not lawful for you to do anything save what the law expressly or impliedly authorises. You enjoy no unfettered discretions. There are legal limits to every power you have'.[35]

A private landowner can do all that it is not prohibited, which means that it can seek possession for any reason, good or ill—development opportunity, dislike of the occupier, breach of occupancy terms, simply because he wants to. But non-private owners may have to take account of other considerations. When deciding whether to evict occupiers the trustees of an alms-house charity must, for example, take account of their fiduciary responsibilities and the terms of the trust deed as well as general laws.

The majority of Article 8 cases to date concerning actions for the recovery of land have involved local authority landowners, whom Harris would describe as having 'quasi-ownership' interests. As a quasi-owner, is a local authority prevented from recovering possession for self-seeking reasons? There are some constraints on local authorities, but the major constraint—that they can only do what is impliedly or expressly authorised, demonstrated in *Fewings*—has now gone. The Localism Act 2011 gives local authorities the power to do anything that individuals generally may do (s 1(1)), even if it is not 'for the benefit of the authority, its area or persons resident or present in its area (s 1(4)(c)).[36] It is not yet clear how far this change reaches into the values that underpin the exercise of local authority powers, but it must now be doubtful whether local authorities remain (legally) constrained by what Oliver has referred to as principles

---

[35] To that principle must be added the further one that the powers conferred on a local authority may be exercised for the public purpose for which the powers were conferred and not otherwise: Lord Bingham in *Magill v Weeks and another* [2001] UKHL 67, [2002] 2 AC 357, [19]. Statutory limits on powers explain why, in contrast to the earlier railway company cases, the airport authority in *Cinnamond v British Airports Authority* could not turn back a passenger who comes to the airport 'at its own discretion without rhyme or reason, as a private landowner can' but rather could exercise its power to exclude only if 'the circumstances fairly and reasonably warrant that step being taken': [1980] 1 WLR 582, 588 (Lord Denning MR).

[36] s 1 was brought into force on 18 February 2012.

of considerate altruism.[37] There are, of course, other kinds of constraints on their powers, such as political expediency, and although this may now be a somewhat dated perspective, there may still be a sense that they can be 'trusted ... to exercise their powers in a public-spirited and fair way in the general public interest'.[38]

Judicial review has now become a useful tool that acts as a check on the actions of public authorities, enabling an occupier to challenge the decision to bring possession proceedings on the grounds that it is procedurally unfair, irrational (or *Wednesbury* unreasonable), or that doing so breaches a legitimate expectation held by the tenant.[39] Following *Kay v Lambeth LBC*,[40] this became known as the 'gateway (b)' defence. By the time of the later House of Lords decision in *Doherty*, gateway (b) had evolved so that it was not confined to judicial review in the traditional and very narrow *Wednesbury* sense.[41] Quite how much this differed from *Wednesbury* was not clear; it was clearly driven by a desire to address Article 8 concerns without having to admit a stand alone Article 8 defence.[42] Lord Hope said that the court should consider whether the decision to evict was reasonable 'having regard to the aim which [the local authority] ... was pursuing and to the length of time that the appellant and his family have resided on the site'.[43] Lord Mance suggested that deciding whether the decision to evict was unreasonable could be considered 'either in the *Wednesbury* sense or in a more relaxed sense which takes full account of the basic interest which any occupant has in his or her home'.[44] Even if it could be said that there was a consensus that personal circumstances may be a relevant consideration (which was doubtful) it was only within the context of a public law challenge.

In practice, there is little to suggest that a local authority is not legally free to act in a self-seeking way, particularly since the Localism Act 2011, provided that there is no procedural impropriety. Further, even prior to the

---

[37] Writing in 1999, Dawn Oliver argued that 'public bodies do not have interests of their own or residual, unreviewable freedoms. They must justify their actions in terms of the public interest, not their own interests. They are under duties of altruism and public service, and they are not entitled to protection of their dignity, autonomy, respect, status or security in their own right: in effect they are subject to principles of considerate altruism': D Oliver, *Common Values and the Public–Private Divide* (London, Butterworths, 1999) 114.

[38] *Shelley v London CC* at the CA stage [1948] 1 KB 274, 283 (Lord Greene MR).

[39] See Lord Hope in *Kay v Lambeth LBC* [2006] UKHL 10, [2006] 2 AC 465, [110].

[40] *Kay v Lambeth LBC* [2006] UKHL 10, [2006] 2 AC 465.

[41] *Doherty v Birmingham CC* [2008] UKHL 57, [2009] 1 AC 367.

[42] This also raises the issue of whether, post-*Pinnock*, the courts will revert to a narrower approach. Early indications are that county courts appear to conflate—and sometimes confuse—whether a defence is based on gateway (a) (that law itself is incompatible with Art 8), gateway (b) or Art 8: *Chesterfield Borough Council v Bailey* (unreported) 22 December 2011; *London Borough of Southwark LBC v Hyacienth* (unreported) 22 December 2011.

[43] *Doherty v Birmingham CC* [2008] UKHL 57, [2009] 1 AC 367, [55].

[44] Ibid, [136].

recent expansion in local authority competency, the rights paradigm has in any event always underpinned judicial responses to possession claims by local authorities. As has been seen from cases such as *Southwark v Williams*[45] and, indeed, *Qazi*,[46] the court would not deny summary possession to a local authority if the occupier had no proprietary, statutory or contractual right to occupation, even if the occupier had good reasons to want to stay. The ownership rights of the local authority would still prevail against the 'no-rights' of the occupier.

A Brief Summary of the State of Play Pre-*Pinnock*

To recap on the discussion so far, the position before *Pinnock* was that the rights paradigm in English property law meant that the fact of ownership was always a sufficient reason for granting an order for possession against an occupier who had no proprietary, contractual or statutory right to be in occupation. It did not matter if the owner had no good reason for recovering the land and was doing so only for self-seeking purposes. Nor did it matter if the occupier had very strong attachment to the particular property or a forced move would cause major personal difficulties. Even if the landowner was a public authority, it could recover possession provided that this was a proper exercise of its statutory functions, although there was a long-step check on procedural abuse through the possibility of a judicial review challenge.

ARTICLE 8

Article 8: The Reasoning Process

The rights paradigm described by van der Walt operates as a logical, almost scientific, system in which, once the hierarchy of rights is known, we can work out who should win a property dispute. Human rights law is much less clear-cut. Further, it is far from obvious from the wording of Article 8 alone just how a court should approach a possession question. It states:

1. Everyone has the right to respect for his private and family life, his home and his correspondence.
2. There shall be no interference by a public authority with the exercise of this right except such as is in accordance with the law and is necessary in a democratic society in the interests of national security, public

---

[45] *Southwark LBC v Williams* [1971] Ch 734 (CA).
[46] *Harrow LBC v Qazi* [2003] UKHL 43, [2004] 1 AC 983.

safety or the economic well-being of the country, for the prevention of disorder or crime, for the protection of health or morals, or for the protection of the rights and freedoms of others.

Certain things are clear from the jurisprudence. 'Home' has an autonomous meaning in the European Court of Human Rights jurisprudence,[47] and is not limited to premises which are lawfully occupied or which have been lawfully established. In order to be a 'home' the occupier must have 'sufficient and continuous links'.[48] It is also now clear, after some early ambivalence in English law,[49] that losing one's home will involve an interference—indeed, a particularly extreme form of interference.[50]

It follows from this that, if a public authority evicts someone, this will violate Article 8 unless that interference is 'justified' within the terms of Article 8(2). (The less certain application to private owners is discussed below.) There are three steps to justification.[51] First, the interference must pursue one of the legitimate aims.[52] This does not appear to be difficult to establish. The tendency is to accept readily that laws implementing domestic housing policy pursue one of the legitimate aims. Sometimes this acceptance is very unquestioning, as in two Croatian cases where the European Court of Human Rights refers to the fact that eviction is in accordance with domestic law and 'therefore pursued the legitimate aim of the economic well-being of the country'.[53] This is so even if the state itself has not clearly articulated the purposes behind a measure. In *Zehentner v Austria*, judicial sale and eviction was found to serve the legitimate aim of protecting the rights and freedoms of others, serving the interests of creditors in obtaining payment of their claims.[54] In *McCann v United Kingdom*, the legitimate aim of protecting the rights and freedoms of others was served by eviction as it protected the landlord's right to regain possession against someone

---

[47] *Buckley v United Kingdom* App no 20348/92 (1996) 23 EHRR 101, [63]; *Harrow LBC v Qazi* [2003] UKHL 43, [2004] 1 AC 983, [9], [23], [61] and [95].

[48] *Buckley v United Kingdom* App no 20348/92 (1996) 23 EHRR 101, [52]–[54]; *Harrow LBC v Qazi* [2003] UKHL 43, [2004] 1 AC 983, [9], [64] and [68].

[49] In *Harrow LBC v Qazi* [2003] UKHL 43, [2004] 1 AC 983, two members of the majority (Lords Scott and Millett) took the view that if eviction was clearly justified then it did not matter whether you said that Art 8(1) was not 'engaged' or that it was 'engaged' but the Art 8(2) justification was automatically satisfied: [103], [107], [137], [149].

[50] *McCann v United Kingdom* App no 19009/04 (2008) 47 EHRR 40, [50].

[51] *Kryvitska v Ukraine* App no 30856/03 (unreported), [42].

[52] These are the interests of national security, public safety or the economic well-being of the country, for the prevention of disorder or crime, for the protection of health or morals, or for the protection of the rights and freedoms of others.

[53] *Orlic v Croatia* App no 48833/07 (unreported), [62]; *Paulic v Croatia* App no 3572/06 (unreported), [39]. In *Kryvitska v Ukraine* App no 30856/03 (unreported) it was sufficient that the authorities sought vacation of the flat 'in order to gain profit' [46] (thus benefiting the economic well-being of the country).

[54] *Zehentner v Austria* App no 20082/02 (2011) 52 EHRR 22, [55].

with no right to be there (ownership); and protected others, that is, those seeking housing.[55]

The second step to justification is that the interference must be 'in accordance with the law', a question that 'does not merely require that the impugned measure should have a basis in domestic law but also refers to the quality of the law in question'.[56]

Finally, the interference must be 'necessary in a democratic society'. It is this dimension that introduces the notion of proportionality: in order to be 'necessary, it must answer a "pressing social need" and, in particular, be proportionate to the legitimate aim pursued'.[57] There appear to be two aspects to this question of proportionality, although the jurisprudence is by no means clear on this.[58] The first (and 'especially material')[59] is not specific to the individual, but emphasises the need for the law to enable proportionality issues to be aired. The European Court of Human Rights has repeatedly asserted that *any* person

> at risk of an interference with his right to a home should in principle be able to have the proportionality and reasonableness of the measure determined by an independent tribunal in the light of the relevant principles under Article 8 of the Convention, notwithstanding that, under domestic law, he or she has no right to occupy a flat.[60]

There are several instances of the Court finding a violation because the investigation under the domestic law is limited to simply exploring whether the occupier has a right to occupy or 'no-rights', and giving no opportunity for proportionality to be examined.[61] But proportionality also involves a much more personal dimension: whether the measure as applied to *this* occupier *in these circumstances* and in *this manner* is proportionate. The Court will pay particular attention to vulnerability[62] and to attachment

---

[55] *McCann v United Kingdom* App no 19009/04 (2008) 47 EHRR 40.

[56] Ie, sufficiently clear and with a measure of legal protection against arbitrary application: *Kryvitska v Ukraine* App no 30856/03 (unreported), [43].

[57] *Zehentner v Austria* App no 20082/02 (2011) 52 EHRR 22.

[58] There may be a further dimension to proportionality, which is concerned with whether the measure involves using a 'sledgehammer to crack a nut'. Barak claims that proportionate means requires '(a) a rational connection between the appropriate goal and the means utilized by the law to attain it; (b) the goal cannot be achieved by means that are less restrictive of the constitutional right; (c) there must be a proportionate balance between the social benefit of realizing the appropriate goal, and the harm caused to the right': A Barak, 'Proportionality and Principled Balancing' (2010) 4 *Law and Ethics of Human Rights* 1, 6. The jurisprudence on Art 8 does not focus on this.

[59] *Zehentner v Austria* App no 20082/02 (2011) 52 EHRR 22, [58].

[60] *McCann v United Kingdom* App no 19009/04 (2008) 47 EHRR 40, [50].

[61] *Paulic v Croatia* App no 3572/06 (unreported), [42]–[45]; *Zehentner v Austria* App no 20082/02 (2011) 52 EHRR 22, [65]; *McCann v United Kingdom* App no 19009/04 (2008) 47 EHRR 40, [55].

[62] *Zehentner v Austria* App no 20082/02 (2011) 52 EHRR 22, [61], [63]; *Manchester CC v Pinnock* [2010] UKSC 45, [2011] 2 AC 104, [64].

to the particular dwelling.[63] Where a whole community which has a long history of undisturbed presence and an established community life faces eviction, proportionality may require that due consideration 'be given to the consequences of their removal and the risk of their becoming homeless'.[64] Failure to give adequate judicial reasons can be taken into account as part of the necessary balancing: in, *Kryvitska*, for example, a violation of Article 8 was found because the judicial authorities had not demonstrated in their reasoning that they had weighed up the legitimate aim of economic well-being (the state sale, for profit, of the flat) against the argument that the long-term resident family with two minor children would be rendered homeless.[65]

The *Pinnock* Case

Mr Pinnock had been a secure tenant of Manchester City Council (the 'Council') since 1978 but in 2007 Recorder Scott Donovan granted a demotion order in the Manchester County Court following a six-day hearing. The basis for the demotion was the antisocial behaviour of Mr Pinnock's five children and of his partner. One day before the order would have lapsed (which would have meant Mr Pinnock becoming a secure tenant again) the Council served a notice under section 143E of the Housing Act 1996 indicating that it would seek possession, justified by further antisocial behaviour of two of his sons. Mr Pinnock asked for a review of the decision to seek possession (in accordance with section 143F), but the review panel upheld the notice. The Council sought possession and an outright order for possession was granted by Judge Holman at the end of 2008. On appeal one of the arguments made for Mr Pinnock was that the order for possession would violate his Article 8 rights.

Whereas an order for possession can be made against a secure tenant only if both a ground for possession under schedule 2 to the Housing Act 1985 is proven and it is reasonable to order possession, section 143D(2) of the Housing Act 1996 states that the court 'must make an order for possession unless it thinks that the procedure under sections 143E and 143F has not been followed'. This was understood by Stanley Burton LJ in the Court of Appeal to restrict the role of the County Court to one of considering whether the correct procedure had been followed. It did not enable the Court to review 'the substance or rationality of the landlord's decision, or whether or not it is consistent with the tenant's or other occupiers'

---

[63] *Gladysheva v Russia* App no 7097/10, [95].
[64] *Yordanova v Bulgaria* App no 25446/06, [126].
[65] *Kryvitska v Ukraine* App no 30856/03 (unreported), [50]–[51].

Convention rights'.[66] The appeal therefore raised the issue of whether Article 8 enabled Mr Pinnock to ask for the proportionality of the eviction to be considered notwithstanding the seemingly narrow wording of the Housing Act 1996.

Article 8 in *Pinnock*

Prior to *Pinnock*, the English courts had refused to accept that Article 8 demanded that the opportunity for a proportionality assessment should be available in every case involving the loss of one's home at the hands of a local authority or other public body. The rather convoluted gateways (a) and (b) that developed following Lord Hope's judgment in *Kay* were an attempt to accommodate Article 8 into the possession process, but they do not permit of a full proportionality review. Gateway (a) is limited to a challenge to the law itself, that is, that the measure or rule is itself incompatible with Article 8 (as was found by the House of Lords in *Doherty*).[67] Gateway (b) is case specific but it is a public law challenge focused on the decision-making process, albeit that the standard of review has been influenced over time 'by Convention ways of thinking'.[68] It does not permit an examination of the specific factual circumstances of the claim as is required by a proportionality inquiry under Article 8.

    Pinnock is, therefore, a landmark case as the Supreme Court made clear that gateways (a) and (b) are not sufficient to satisfy the demands of Article 8. At paragraph [45] in *Pinnock* Lord Neuberger MR laid out a number of key propositions drawing on the established jurisprudence of the European Court of Human Rights:

i.   Any person at risk of being dispossessed of his home at the suit of a local authority should in principle have the right to raise the question of the proportionality of the measure, and to have it determined by an independent tribunal in the light of Article 8, even if his right of occupation under domestic law has come to an end;

ii. Traditional judicial review (that does not permit the court to make its own assessment of the facts) is inadequate for this purpose as it is not appropriate for resolving sensitive factual issues;

---

[66] *Manchester CC v Pinnock* [2009] EWCA Civ 852, [2010] 1 WLR 713, [50].

[67] *Doherty v Birmingham CC* [2008] UKHL 57, [2009] 1 AC 367. Although the law contained in the Caravan Sites Act 1968 was found to be incompatible with the Human Rights Act 1998 because the statute excluded the Gypsy community from its procedural safeguards, the House of Lords declined to make a declaration of incompatibility as Parliament had already made changes to the relevant regime (although they were not in force at the time).

[68] *Doran v Liverpool CC* [2009] EWCA Civ 146, [2009] 1 WLR 2365, [52] (Toulson LJ, drawing on Lord Walker's remarks in *Doherty v Birmingham CC* [2008] UKHL 57, [2009] 1 AC 367, [109]).

iii. Where the measure includes proceedings involving more than one stage it is the proceedings as a whole which must be considered to see if Article 8 has been complied with;

iv. If it would be disproportionate to evict a person, then it will be unlawful to evict him so long as the conclusion obtains.

In relation to the demoted tenancy regime, Lord Neuberger MR took the view that in requiring the court to consider if the correct procedure has been followed for ending a demoted tenancy the wording of section 143D(2) of the Housing Act 1996 requires the court to consider whether the procedure has been *lawfully* followed and that this meant that it was open to a court to have regard to the defendant's Article 8 rights.[69] On the particular facts, however, the Supreme Court considered that even though Mr Pinnock had lived at this property for more than 30 years, it was proportionate to make a possession order given the seriousness of the incidents of antisocial behaviour of his children in the vicinity of the property, including resisting arrest, burglary and causing death by dangerous driving.[70]

More broadly, the effect of *Pinnock* is that in every case involving a claim for possession of a home brought by a public body it must be possible for the occupier to raise the issue of proportionality. The practical outworking of this in the busy schedules of County Court judges will be challenging, and Lord Neuberger MR, while acknowledging that this may require certain statutory and procedural provisions to be revised, noted that the 'wide implications' of the obligation to consider proportionality are 'best left to the good sense and experience of judges sitting in the County Court'.[71] The majority of possession claims are dealt with summarily, in a hearing that lasts at most a few minutes. It will be for the occupier to flag up the desire to raise an Article 8 defence;[72] and, unless the issue 'crosses the high threshold of being seriously arguable',[73] the County Court judge will simply deal with the possession claim according to the traditional rights paradigm. But, if the threshold is crossed, the question must then be addressed 'whether making an order for the occupier's eviction is a proportionate means of achieving a legitimate aim'.[74]

The Supreme Court in *Powell* (decided shortly after *Pinnock*) makes clear that, 'in the overwhelming majority of cases', there will be no need for a local authority to 'explain or justify its reasons for seeking a possession order'.[75] What Lord Hope describes as the 'twin aims' will, taken together,

---

[69] *Manchester CC v Pinnock* [2010] UKSC 45, [2011] 2 AC 104, [77].

[70] Ibid, [127] and [132].

[71] Ibid, [63] and [57] respectively.

[72] Although it is unrealistic to expect occupiers—unless they have taken legal advice—to do so.

[73] *Hounslow LBC v Powell* [2011] UKSC 8, [2011] 2 AC 186, [33] (Lord Hope).

[74] Ibid.

[75] Ibid, [37] (Lord Hope).

satisfy the legitimate aim requirement. Lord Hope summarises them as (a) vindication of the authority's ownership rights and (b) enabling the local authority to comply with its public duties in relation to the allocation and management of its housing stock.[76] In effect, the legitimate aim can be taken as read, and the question becomes whether an order for possession will be proportionate in the light of the 'occupier's personal circumstances and any factual objections she may raise'.[77] It is evident from the Supreme Court judgments that their expectation is that a finding that possession is disproportionate will be unusual; but how this plays out in County Courts will be difficult to track as very few cases are reported. There have, however, already been a few cases in which possession was held to be disproportionate, including *Chesterfield BC v Bailey*.[78] That case involved a *Monk* issue:[79] a secure joint tenancy of a three-bedroom house was ended by the husband's notice to quit. The council sought possession and offered Mrs Bailey a two-bedroom flat; under the allocations policy that they operated Mrs Bailey would not qualify for a three-bedroom house as only she and one adult son lived there (although another adult son was periodically resident). Asking whether possession was a 'proportionate means of achieving a legitimate aim', the judge took account of the fact that possession would be a vindication of the council's property rights, its needs to prioritise and allocate housing in a manner that was fair, the waiting list for properties of this size and the offer of a two-bedroom flat to Mrs Bailey. Against these factors were the considerations that Mrs Bailey lost her secure tenancy through no fault of her own, and with no notice, that a home with security of tenure is 'something of immense value',[80] that the opportunity to recover the property was a 'windfall' to the council,[81] that she had been a council tenant for 17 years (and tenant of this particular property for nine years) and that she had spent money on the property.[82] The judge concluded that the decision to seek possession was neither necessary in a democratic society nor proportionate in the circumstances of this case.

---

[76] Ibid, [36] (Lord Hope), drawing on Lord Neuberger MR's discussion of these aims in *Manchester CC v Pinnock* [2010] UKSC 45, [2011] 2 AC 104, [55]–[54].

[77] *Hounslow LBC v Powell* [2011] UKSC 8, [2011] 2 AC 186, [37] (Lord Hope).

[78] *Chesterfield Borough Council v Bailey* (unreported) 22 December 2011. See also *Southwark LBC v Hyacienth* (CC, unreported) 22 December 2011; *Southend-on-Sea v Armour* (QBD, unreported) 18 October 2012.

[79] *Hammersmith and Fulham LBC v Monk* [1992] 1 AC 478 (HL), where it was held that with a joint tenancy an effective notice to quite can be served by only one of the joint tenants. The rule in *Monk* has since been held by the Court of Appeal in *Sims v Dacorum BC* [2013] EWCA Civ 12 to be compatible with Article 8, but *Chesterfield* did not concern compatibility of the general rule but rather whether the particular possession proceedings against Mrs Bailey were justified and proportionate.

[80] Something which none of the occupiers had enjoyed in *Powell* or *Pinnock*.

[81] Because the husband left and served notice to quit: there would not otherwise have been any grounds for recovering possession.

[82] *Chesterfield Borough Council v Bailey* (unreported) 22 December 2011 [60]–[65].

OWNERSHIP POST-*PINNOCK*

Public and Private Ownership Post-*Pinnock*

At several points in this chapter, a distinction has been referred to between X as a public body and X as a private owner. There are two reasons for drawing such a distinction. The first relates to the scope or applicability of the Human Rights Act 1998. The second is concerned with how a possession claim can be justified with reference to the legitimate aims.

Ever since the enactment of the Human Rights Act 1998 there has been uncertainty as to its application between private persons. Section 6 of the Human Rights Act 1998 makes it 'unlawful for a public authority to act in a way which is incompatible with a Convention right'. Thus, a local authority seeking possession must clearly comply with Article 8. In the majority of cases, housing associations[83] will also need to do so. By section 6(3)(b) the definition of a public authority is extended to include 'any person certain of whose functions are functions of a public nature'. The majority of housing associations will carry out some public functions, depending on factors such as whether they are in receipt of public funding and the extent to which they are exercising governmental functions.[84] If so, then unless the particular act complained of is a private act (section 6(5))—which possession proceedings are unlikely to be[85]—a housing association must also comply with Article 8. Yet, whether Article 8 can be raised as a defence against a private landowner is unclear. In *Pinnock*, Lord Neuberger MR touched on the issues that would be relevant to this question but firmly stated that what the Supreme Court said in that case was intended to have no bearing on cases involving a private landowner seeking to recover possession of land.[86]

The fact that a possession order must be granted by a court, which is a public authority, suggests that Article 8 should apply irrespective of the public–private owner distinction, and Lord Hope's speech in *Kay v Lambeth* strongly suggests that this means that a court must safeguard Article 8 rights whether or not the party seeking possession is a public authority.[87] It is also probably sufficient to engage the Human Rights Act

---

[83] Or 'registered providers of social housing' as they are known since the Housing and Regeneration Act 2008.

[84] See *R (Weaver) v London Quadrant Housing Trust* [2009] EWCA Civ 587, [2010] 1 WLR 363.

[85] Generally if the provision of social housing is found to be a public function, then so too will the termination of a right to occupy social housing: *R (Weaver) v London Quadrant Housing Trust* [2009] EWCA Civ 587, [2010] 1 WLR 363, [76]–[80].

[86] *Manchester CC v Pinnock* [2010] UKSC 45, [2011] 2 AC 104, [50].

[87] *Kay v Lambeth* [2006] UKHL 10, [2006] 2 AC 465, [64], [104]. A trickle of county court decisions shows district judges applying the proportionality test to private landowners: see, eg, *Malik v Persons Unknown* CLCC, unreported, discussed on the blog nearlylegal.co.uk.

1998 that a statutory basis for possession is involved (such as a ground for possession under the housing legislation) rather than a common law rule, even when private parties are involved.[88]

Of course, it is terribly unsatisfactory that it cannot be said for certain whether or not Article 8 can be used as a defence to a possession claim issued by a private landowner, but it is likely that at least in some cases the occupier can rely on it (those involving, perhaps, termination of a tenancy on the mandatory rent arrears heading (Ground 8)). If this proves to be the case, and Article 8 can sometimes be engaged even when a private landowner is seeking possession, there will remain the issue as to whether the approach to what constitutes a legitimate aim that justifies the interference will be different from when possession is sought by a public authority.

Self-seekingness and Possession Post-*Pinnock*

It was mentioned earlier that although land held by public authorities represents a form of 'quasi-ownership', a public authority landowner is nonetheless entitled—putting to one side Convention rights—to recover possession from an occupier with 'no-rights', subject only to the public law controls. Convention rights aside, a private landowner is not even subject to this constraint and can recover land for self-interested reasons simply because he is the owner. Assuming that Article 8 is engaged, does the principle of self-seekingness still apply post-*Pinnock*? It may be helpful to think of Article 8 as having two limbs: the justification limb, requiring an owner seeking possession to prove that possession is in accordance with the law and is in pursuit of a legitimate aim; and the impact limb, which, given that a legitimate aim exists, considers whether the eviction is proportionate, taking account of the impact that it will have on the occupier. Although these two limbs are not to be applied separately and sequentially, but feed into one another, the self-seekingness question is primarily to do with justification as it looks at whether the reasons or motives for seeking possession matter.

In the context of a public authority, the 'twin aims' can generally be taken to justify its reasons for seeking for possession, without further explanation. The European Court of Human Rights suggests in *Kryvistak v Ukraine* that vindication of the owner's rights will not suffice where the owner is the

---

[88] As examples of Convention rights being engaged in actions with private parties, seemingly because statutory provisions were involved, see *Pennycook v Shaws (EAL) Ltd* [2004] EWCA Civ 100, [2004] Ch 296; *Ghaidan v Godin-Medoza* [2004] UKHL 30, [2004] 2 AC 557. In *Webber v Network Rail* [2003] EWCA Civ 1167, [2004] 1 WLR 320, the Court of Appeal treated Art 1 Protocol 1 (right to peaceful enjoyment of possessions) as engaged when the Landlord and Tenant Act 1954 was involved, even though private parties were involved (but found that there was no disproportionality).

state itself,[89] although elsewhere the Court has stated that it is 'legitimate for authorities to seek to regain possession of land from persons who did not have a right to occupy it'.[90] Lord Hope emphasises in *Powell* that it is the two aims taken together that satisfy the legitimate aim requirement.[91] It will, presumably, be open to an occupier to challenge this in any particular case in which they claim that the public authority has not sought possession for reasons connected to its housing obligations.[92] But generally the legitimate aim requirement is unlikely to affect the justification of a local authority's decision to seek possession.

The more intriguing question is how *Pinnock* might affect the justification necessary for a private landowner to seek possession assuming that Article 8 is engaged. Will vindication of the owner's right suffice for a legitimate aim? Lord Neuberger mentions that 'unencumbered property rights ... are of real weight when it comes to proportionality'.[93] The (very brief) remarks in *Kryvistak* also suggest that for private owners the fact of ownership is sufficient to justify seeking possession. Further, as Lord Neuberger MR hints at in *Pinnock*, Article 1 of the First Protocol to the Convention may also have a role to play.[94] This guarantees, in substance, the right to property.[95] In *Property and Justice*, Harris argues that ownership operates as a 'principle' so that an appeal to the values underlying ownership is used to help solve a dispute. The examples he gives from the common law, such as Mr Pickles, illustrate how owners are allowed to do as they wish, for whatever reason, provided the act is not prohibited. As Harris observes, this 'freedom to act, self-seekingly, in relation to that which is one's own has served as a powerful normative lodestone'.[96] There also appears to be recognition in the recent 'occupy and protest' cases that the fact that land is privately owned will be a relevant consideration in applications to recover land from protestors, as if the values of private ownership support stronger exclusionary powers.[97]

---

[89] On the grounds that this would protect the 'interests of the State and cannot be covered by the Art 8.2 exception concerning the protection of rights and freedoms of others': *Kryvitska v Ukraine* App no 30856/03 (unreported), [46].

[90] *Yordanova v Bulgaria* App no 25446/06, [111].

[91] *Hounslow LBC v Powell* [2011] UKSC 8, [2011] 2 AC 186, [36].

[92] This ought to be the case, but Lord Hope's speech in *Powell* makes this difficult. The twin aims are 'assumed' and the 'court need be concerned only with the occupier's personal circumstances and any factual objections she may raise': *Hounslow LBC v Powell* [2011] UKSC 8, [2011] 2 AC 186, [37]. Latham reads this is an irrebuttable presumption and argues that this reflects a 'managerial approach' rather than an approach recognising the occupier as 'rights-bearer': A Latham, 'Talking Without Speaking, Hearing Without Listening? Evictions, the Law Lords and the European Court of Human Rights' [2011] *PL* 703.

[93] *Manchester CC v Pinnock* [2010] UKSC 45, [2011] 2 AC 104, [54].

[94] Ibid, [50].

[95] *Marckx v Belgium* (1979) 2 EHRR 330, [63].

[96] Harris, *Property and Justice*, above (n 8) 90–93.

[97] *The Mayor of London v Samede* [2012] EWCA Civ 160 [45] (Lord Neuberger MR).

However, although the value of the owner's autonomous choice is to be taken seriously, it does not follow that it will necessarily be a paramount consideration. If Article 8 is engaged in a claim for possession by a private owner, it is likely that vindication of the owner's rights, supporting autonomous choice, will justify the seeking of possession, but it does not follow that it will necessarily be sufficient to lead to a finding of proportionality. While there must be justification for the action, it must also be proportionate, taking account of the impact it has on the occupier's right to respect for the home. In a given case, if there is no reason as to why the owner wants possession apart from the fact of ownership, while there are particularly strong reasons as to why the occupier should stay in the home, perhaps the length of time for which this has been home, vulnerability and the absence of alternative suitable accommodation, then it may be that the court would find it disproportionate to order possession.

The Ownership Idea Post-*Pinnock*

It may turn out to be the case that there are not many situations in which possession is denied on the basis of a successful Article 8 defence, but even if that is so, *Pinnock* forces us to re-evaluate what it means to assert that 'X owns land'.

As has been seen in the discussion of ownership pre-*Pinnock*, a number of ideas coalesce around the right to possess which in English law is protected by an order for the recovery of the land. This reflects the 'rights paradigm', in which the strong rights of estate holders will automatically trump the claims of occupiers with 'no-rights', even if they are self-seeking. Post-*Pinnock*, the right to possess is no longer absolute. It cannot be said that it will automatically trump the claims of those with 'no-rights'. This appears to be a significant, landmark, shift in the way that ownership operates in English land law, but before that conclusion is reached, there are two further dimensions to discuss.

The first relates to the use of the phrase 'no-rights' that has been used in this chapter. When van der Walt introduces this idea, he is writing in a civilian law context and states that property interests are primarily valued according to the their status as 'either property rights, personal rights or no-rights'.[98] In this chapter, the phrase 'no-rights' is used specifically to refer to 'no lawful right, as against the owner, to occupy'. In English law, a right to occupy may be a property right (such as a tenancy) or a personal right (such as a contractual licence) or a right conferred by statute (such as rights under the Rent Act 1977) but each may be protected in specie. It is

---

[98] Van der Walt, above (n 1) 27.

the occupier with 'no-right to occupy land' that according to the rights paradigm will always be trumped by an owner. Defining it in this manner avoids the challenge: 'but what about the Article 8 *right* itself: if this Convention *right* is engaged then it is not correct to say that the occupier has "no-rights"'. The challenge does, however, draw attention to what the Article 8 *right* is or, more usefully for our purposes, what it is not. The Article 8 right to respect for the home is not a right that carries specific jural content that is matched by a correlative duty. Certainly the 'right-holder' cannot claim that Article 8 gives a right to occupy; if he has no other proprietary, contractual or statutory right to occupy, Article 8 at best gives her the chance to say that the owner should not be granted possession if this would be disproportionate in the circumstances. Although the Convention uses the language of rights, and this is important because of the strong rhetorical force of rights-language, the Convention articles behave, as Green has argued, like principles and carry a dimension of weight but do not dictate any particular course of action.[99]

The second aspect to discuss in assessing the significance of *Pinnock* relates to whether the rights paradigm really was as dominant, even before *Pinnock*, as suggested in the earlier part of the chapter. In his study, van der Walt concludes that ownership is 'not nearly as strong as the rhetoric of the rights paradigm suggests. Ownership is regularly and routinely subjected to surprisingly many marginal, weak or other non-property interests for a number of policy reasons'.[100] There are, of course, examples within English law of the rights paradigm being restricted; the primary examples perhaps being the rights given to tenants through the housing legislation, and the acquisition of rights through adverse possession.[101] But these operate quite differently from Article 8. Given the way in which relativity of title works in English law, the adverse possessor has rights from day one; but these rights will not be effective as against an owner who has a better right to possession. Once the limitation period elapses, the (original) owner is then prevented from recovering the land. The (original) owner can recover possession within the limitation period or he is barred from doing so because of the expiration of time. His ability to recover possession does not depend on the personal situation of the occupier, or on the owner's justification for seeking possession.

The strongest challenge to the rights paradigm is found in tenancy law. In both the public and private sectors, protection (often called security of tenure) is given to certain tenants through the discretionary grounds for

---

[99] A Green, 'A Philosophical Taxonomy of European Human Rights Law' (2012) 1 *European Human Rights Law Review* 71.

[100] Van der Walt, above (n 1) 26.

[101] Rights of public access to land are a further limitation, as van der Walt notes. But this restriction is of a quite different nature as the right-holder here is merely seeking an access right against the owner, not a possession right.

possession.[102] In both sectors a tenancy cannot come to an end without a court order.[103] With the discretionary grounds for possession the owner will have to satisfy the court that a statutory ground for possession exists—such as rent arrears, nuisance behaviour (akin to a justification requirement) and the court must consider it reasonable to order possession (akin to an 'impact limb'). Thus, if the tenant has this statutory protection, then vindication of the ownership rights is *not* sufficient to recover possession: some additional 'justification' is needed. Further, when considering reasonableness, the court is to take into account all relevant circumstances,[104] which can include 'genuine emotional attachment' to the property 'as part of the family', the fact that 'decades of family memories which they hold dear' were located in this home and that the property provided a 'profound sense of security—connected as it is with their family memories—which sustains them'.[105] As when an Article 8 defence is raised, the housing legislation requires judges to look at both justification and impact. Article 8 is, therefore, not the first inroad into the rights paradigm. However, the housing legislation works differently. First, the housing legislation applies only when occupation began consensually, whereas Article 8 can be relied on by those who took occupation without the consent of the owner—as, for example, in *Leeds v Price*, where gypsies moved onto the council's recreation ground.[106] Secondly, it is possible to define the situations in which a tenant may be protected under the housing legislation so that an owner purchasing land subject to a pre-existing tenancy, or deciding to rent out land, is able to take an informed decision about the investment impact of the occupation. The owner takes on a 'known risk'. An Article 8 defence, on the other hand, can be raised by anyone in occupation of a home and it is not possible to predict when it might bite. Thirdly, and importantly, if possession is refused in a tenancy case, the consequence is that occupation continues on the same basis as before—with the parties' rights regulated by their contractual relationship. This will also be so with tenancy cases in which an occupier succeeds with an Article 8 defence; but it is unclear what the basis of continuing occupation will be in other contexts.[107] The landlord

---

[102] Local authority sector protected tenants are known as secure tenants; private sector protected tenants as assured tenants.

[103] Housing Act 1988, s 5; Housing Act 1985, s 82.

[104] *Cumming v Danson* [1942] 2 All ER 653, 655 (Lord Greene MR).

[105] *Bracknell Forest BC v Green*, [2009] EWCA Civ 238, [15–17]. See also *Battlespring v Gates* (1984) 11 HLR 6 (CA).

[106] *Leeds CC v Price* [2005] EWCA Civ 289; [2005] 1 WLR 1825.

[107] Where the occupier remains following a successful Art 8 defence, what is their legal status? The occupier will not usually have a 'property right' in the traditionally recognised sense (unless, for example, the defence prevented a landlord from terminating a lease). Gray discusses the idea of 'equitable property' deriving from conscientious obligations to deal with an asset or resource in a certain way: K Gray, 'Equitable Property' (1994) 47 *CLP* 157. Although his vision of equitable property has a community dimension, promoting access to 'common wealth', perhaps the status of an occupier who cannot be removed can also be regarded as involving a kind of equitable property?

of a protected tenant has no right to possess without a court order; the landowner seeking to evict an occupier with 'no-rights' does have a right to possess, albeit that he may be prevented from enforcing this if this would be disproportionate. Finally, there is perhaps a question as to the legitimacy of the change to property doctrine and values. Housing legislation is the result of parliamentary process in which the impact on owners, housing supply and the occupiers has been carefully balanced. This cannot be said of Article 8.

PINNOCK AS A LANDMARK CASE

Pinnock clearly has landmark status in the sense of having settled the short, but intense, battle between the European Court of Human Rights and English domestic courts, and acknowledging that everyone at risk of eviction at the hands of a local authority has the right to raise a proportionality defence on the basis of Article 8. It does, however, also have a wider significance in terms of the idea of ownership and the right to possess. It is not that there have been no earlier examples of the owner's right to recover possession being restricted—sometimes severely and even for successive generations as with some tenancy laws—but Article 8 introduces restrictions of a different order. The right to recover possession of land that is occupied as a home by someone with no lawful right to occupy can no longer be seen as automatic, no longer a foregone conclusion that flows from a simple application of a traditional understanding of the hierarchy of rights in land. However strong the desire of the judiciary not to disturb the way in which possession cases are listed for summary hearing day-in, day-out, in County Courts, Article 8 requires a new way of thinking about the right to recover possession. When Article 8 is engaged, and raised as a defence,[108] the owner will not be entitled to an order for possession merely by showing that the occupier has no lawful right to occupy; it will be necessary to show that the recovery of possession is justified by the pursuit of a legitimate aim. This may not be difficult if it turns out that vindication of his ownership rights will generally suffice for private owners; and the twin aims of ownership rights and housing management concerns will be sufficient for local authorities. But the proportionality question does require a shift towards a contextualised, non-hierarchical way of thinking, in which factors extraneous to property doctrine come into play, such as the personal or social circumstances of the occupier and the effect that eviction will have on his and his family or community. This is a different way of thinking about ownership. To adapt Dworkin's phrase, post-*Pinnock*, courts must not only 'take ownership seriously' but also 'take home seriously'.

* * * * * * *

[108] But only, if Lord Hope's view prevails, if it is a 'seriously arguable' defence.

POSTSCRIPT

The issue of whether Article 8 can be relied on as a defence to possession proceedings brought by a private owner is due to be considered by the UK Supreme Court in 2016 in an appeal from *McDonald v McDonald* [2014] EWCA Civ 1049. Arden LJ stated (at [45]) that 'there is no clear and constant line of decisions that the proportionality test applies in disputes between tenants and private landlords where the tenant relies on Article 8'.

Index